Transpersonal Knowing

SUNY series in Transpersonal and Humanistic Psychology
Richard D. Mann, editor

TRANSPERSONAL KNOWING

Exploring the Horizon
of Consciousness

EDITED BY
Tobin Hart,
Peter L. Nelson,
and Kaisa Puhakka

STATE UNIVERSITY OF NEW YORK PRESS

Published by
State University of New York Press, Albany

For information, address State University of New York Press,
State University Plaza, Albany, N.Y., 12246

Production by Cathleen Collins
Marketing by Fran Keneston

Library of Congress Cataloging in Publication Data

Transpersonal knowing : exploring the horizon of consciousness / edited by
Tobin Hart, Peter L. Nelson, and Kaisa Puhakka.
          p. cm.—(SUNY series in transpersonal and humanistic psychology)
     Includes bibliographical references and index.
     ISBN 0–7914–4615–8 (alk. paper)—ISBN 0–7914–4616–6 (pb : alk. paper)
     1. Transpersonal psychology.   I. Hart, Tobin.   II. Nelson, Peter L.
     III. Puhakka, Kaisa.   IV. Series.
     BF204.7 .T72 2000
     150.19'8—dc21   99-049022

10 9 8 7 6 5 4 3 2 1

For
Mahalia and Maia

Contents

Acknowledgments

Special appreciation goes to Debbie Dickenson, Shannon Smith, and Denise Oglesby for assistance in preparation of this collection. Thanks go to Don Rice and members of the Department of Psychology as well as the College of Arts and Sciences at the State University of West Georgia for providing support for this project.

Chapter 3, "Inspiration as Transpersonal Knowing" by Tobin Hart. Excerpts are used by permission of Sage Publications from: Hart, T. (1998). Inspiration: Exploring the Experience and its Meaning. *Journal of Humanistic Psychology, 38*(3), 7–35.

Chapter 5, "Reflection and Presence: The Dialectic of Awakening" by John Welwood. An earlier version of this chapter appeared in 1996 in *The Journal of Transpersonal Psychology, 28*(2), pp. 107–128. It is used here by permission of the Institute of Transpersonal Psychology.

Chapter 8, "Spiritual Inquiry" by Donald Rothberg. This chapter is reprinted with permission from: Rothberg, D. (1994). Spiritual Inquiry. *ReVision, 17*(2), pp. 2–12. ReVision is published by Heldref Publications.

Chapter 11, "Deep Empathy" by Tobin Hart. Sections are excerpted with permission of Sage Publications from: Hart, T. (1999). The Refinement of Empathy. *Journal of Humanistic Psychology, 39*(4), pp. 111–125. Sections are excerpted by permission of the publisher from Hart, T. (1997). Transcendental Empathy in the Therapeutic Relationship. *The Humanistic Psychologist, 25*(3), pp. 245–270.

Chapter 12, "The Love that Dares Not Speak its Name" by Jenny Wade. Excerpts from the *Epic of Gilgamesh,* Translated, with an Introduction and Notes, by Maureen Gallery Kovacs are with the permission of Stanford University Press. Copyright 1985, 1988. A poem from the Mirabai is originally from Schelling, A. (Trans.) 1998. *For the Love of the Dark One: Songs of the Mirabai.* Prescott, AZ: Hohm Press, p. 41. Used with permission.

Chapter 13, "Service as a Way of Knowing" by Arthur J. Deikman. The writing of an earlier version of this chapter was supported by the Fetzer Institute. Extract entitled "wisdom" is reprinted with permission from *The Way of the Sufi* by Indries Shah (Octagon Press Ltd. London) published in 1980.

1

Introduction

These are times of transition in culture and consciousness. Changes are taking place in the most fundamental of human activities that we will call "knowing." Not just what counts as "knowledge" but the ways in which something comes to be "known" are called into question. The truths of modern science and, for many, religion as well, are no longer seen as absolute but rather as relative to their context of language, culture, and epistemic assumptions. The methodologies of the sciences and the humanities are under constant scrutiny and revision. In postmodernity, knowing has been greatly humbled by its self-acknowledged limits.

Sensitivity to the plurality of perspectives on all truths is the postmodern legacy that has been embraced by a significant number of scientists, most intellectuals, and, increasingly, the general population. Whether expressed in crass relativism ("any opinion is as good as another") or in sophisticated deconstructionist arguments, the influence of cultural and linguistic context is widely recognized. Indeed, it appears that much of human consciousness is transitioning through a significant epistemic shift: our "knowing" is becoming increasingly aware of its own processes.

The hazards of this epistemic shift are very much in evidence today. Psychological disturbances that suggest premature opening to modes of experience that fall outside the more familiar rational orientation appear to be on the rise. There is widespread uncertainty and confusion about what counts as "knowing." The extremes of cynicism ("nothing counts") and naive susceptibility to anything that is impactful ("everything counts equally") run rampant. So does self-absorption in the form of psychological preoccupation with self-esteem and intellectual discourse that turns upon itself in futile, self-reflexive closed-loop "talk about talk." In such "talk" the forms of knowing do not change and the activity of thinking holds onto them tightly.

The self-reflexive, snake biting its own tail discourse is, however, not the only alternative for knowing to become self-aware. Instead of trying to grab hold of itself, knowing can hold its forms lightly and perhaps let go of them altogether, thus allowing the self-awareness of knowing to transform its own process. Glimpses of this occur frequently in everyday life. Many people have had the experience of a sudden insight, often preceded by an impasse in their thinking. Just before the "aha!" moment, the structures of thinking dissolve, out of which "knowing" then emerges afresh. Moments of insight illustrate the peculiar nature of knowing, namely that its self-awareness catalyzes change in its own process. This "self-awareness" should not be mistaken for "self-consciousness" (e.g., when a person's spontaneity is arrested by self-consciousness that reifies a "self"). Nor should it be mistaken for a conceptual analysis. Rather, the activity of knowing, such as a flash of intuition, knows itself in this very activity. This transparency or self-knowing is at the same time a self-transcending process whereby knowing liberates itself from its own ground, eventually (often almost immediately) to create new grounds. In this way, knowing that knows itself is a constantly changing activity.

Many transpersonal theorists believe that an accelerated change is currently taking place. For these theorists, the monolithic rationality of modern science is breaking down, and there is a growing recognition of alternative modes of human knowing. The direction of this process, or whether it even has a particular direction, is not clear. Some see it as being evolutionary and as manifesting distinct transitional stages in a progressive integration of knowing through self-awareness. But among those who take the evolutionary view, there is considerable disagreement about how the stages should be conceived. Others question the usefulness of linear developmental schemes of any kind. Whatever their position on the evolutionary hypothesis, however, most transpersonalists seem to agree that we are witnessing a genuine opening in the horizons of knowing. We are increasingly sensitized to the differences in perspective that reflect the varieties of ethnic groups and subcultures within the larger cultural matrix, even as we move toward globalized culture. And it appears that in some cases the awareness of multiple perspectives has the effect of loosening the hold of any particular perspective (though in other cases it has the opposite effect—witness the raise of ethnic and religious fundamentalism). "Perspective" itself then becomes more tenuous, more fluid, less binding on the knowing that operates within its confines. The consequent undermining of perspectival truth has no doubt contributed to the general loss of faith in the traditional ways of rational knowing—those of science and religion. At the same time, it appears to have allowed more expression of alternative, nonrational modes of knowing. Thus we not only have multiple perspectives on knowing, but apparently multiple modes of knowing. Some of these modes may involve simultaneous awareness of several perspectives, others perhaps do not involve perspectives at all.

But what is this knowing that reveals itself in the process of knowing becoming aware of itself? What are the varieties of modes through which it manifests? Current transpersonal literature contains broad characterizations of "postconventional" or "transrational" consciousness (e.g., Walsh, Washburn, Wilber), largely drawn from mystical literature. Some detailed empirical studies are also available on the developmental shifts toward the "postconventional" (e.g., Kegan, Loevinger, Cook-Greuter). What is lacking, however, are first-hand investigations of the phenomena of this type of knowing. Given that all descriptions are, by necessity, conventional, first-hand familiarity with what is taken to be "postconventional" seems crucial. Such familiarity, and the opening up of conventional perspectives that comes with it, provides a better chance of negotiating the inevitable marriage of the conventional and postconventional in a descriptive endeavor. The challenge of this marriage is that, on one hand, all descriptions depend on conventional understanding and are bound to the forms of language and culture in which such understanding occurs. On the other hand, postconventional knowing is not—at least not completely—bound to such forms. Descriptions inspired by first-hand familiarity tend to have a dialectical transparency (of knowing knowing itself) that facilitates the emergence of postconventional knowing. On the other hand, descriptions obtained from secondary sources are more likely to encourage the reduction of this knowing to the conventional forms through which it is understood.

The secret of a successful marriage is the mutual recognition of the irreducibility of either party to the other. That is, neither has the "truth" for both, but the truth evolves in their relationship. The descriptions and maps of postconventional knowing, then, can never have the final word. They are, of necessity, unfinished and partial. It is important to appreciate the difference between unfinished and partial and to recognize that conventional maps and descriptions are limited in both of these ways. Because they are unfinished, they are best kept maximally inclusive, open and evolving. Wilber's evolutionary theory is a good example of this. But because they are necessarily partial and offer a particular angle or perspective, they need to be complemented by alternative perspectives. Thus we are suggesting that the approach best suited for the descriptive endeavor and mapmaking for postconventional knowing may indeed be multiperspectival.

In the domains of conventional knowing, such as is typical of the natural and social sciences, the existence of multiple perspectives signifies an unstable, "revolutionary" phase, as Kuhn named it, that is a way station to an integration of these perspectives by a new, more accommodating perspective.

However, with the shift from conventional to postconventional, the integration is not conceptual, thus does not call for a more accommodating perspective but for a mode of knowing that is not perspectival, or at least to some degree not bound to particular perspectives. Thus in postconventional knowing, the capacity to simultaneously hold multiple perspectives may be a way station to an "aperspectival" mode of knowing that increasingly depends on an awareness that accommodates all perspectives without affirming or taking up a position in any of them. The project of this book takes place in this way station, and we believe that the nature of this project is such that the existence of multiple perspectives may be more appropriate for it than a single perspective, however open and accommodating it might be. The lesson from multiple perspectives is not that truth is ultimately relative or unknowable but rather that any perspectives we take on should be held onto lightly, with no more attachment to them than one has to a used pair of disposable contact lenses.

But if the criteria for postconventional knowing cannot be found in conventional descriptions and maps, how then is this knowing "known"? In conceiving the project of this book, we were acutely aware of the difficulty inherent in trying to address the kind of knowing that is not "known" through conventional forms and methods and that may not even be available to all people at all times. Frankly, we do not know (in conventional terms) what this knowing actually is, or who knows and who does not know about it. With this topic, there is a great danger of talking about what one does not know, and of not even knowing that one does not know. External, consensually validated standards may offer some guidelines and criteria, but not the knowing itself. For its revelation, we have nothing else to fall back on but the interior view of this knowing. A dialogue among those who access the interior view is essential for the ongoing revisioning of the external standards that the changing manifestations of knowing call for. Such a dialogue can also facilitate access to, and encourage people to trust and give voice to, their own knowing. We hope that this book will contribute to these aims.

The authors of the following chapters have come as much as possible from their own authentic knowing, whether through personal narrative or through analysis and conceptualization informed by such knowing. We did not wish to impose a preconceived framework of interpretation. Rather, we challenged the authors to stay as close, and as faithful, to their own knowing as possible and make connections to existing theories and interpretive frameworks, not so much to "find fit" as to clarify or enhance the understanding of the knowing they were exploring. The interpretive perspectives in which the authors embed their knowing are rather divergent. However, we believe that the lack of uniformity is not simply a matter of the newness of the territory being explored but is intrinsic to the territory itself. Even so, certain basic themes across the chapters seem to emerge such as authenticity—that this is one's own knowing; immediacy—there is little or no conceptual mediation; connectedness—the boundaries that separate and create the sense of an isolated self seem to dissolve; and transformative capacity—the knower is changed by the knowing and at the same time, openness to change in one's sense of identity opens one to the knowing.

The chapters roughly fall into three groups. There is much overlap among the groups, and their boundaries are not sharply defined, but they provide our rationale for ordering the sequence of the chapters that follow. The first six chapters (Puhakka, Hart, Nelson, Welwood, Hanna, Khan) approach transpersonal knowing directly by exploring its essential features and the transformational processes involved in shifting to such knowing. The next three chapters (Rothberg, Washburn, Ferrer) examine developmental conditions and epistemological issues relevant to transpersonal knowing. The last group of chapters explore specific contexts that provide openings to transpersonal knowing, such as in empathic encounters between persons (Hart), sexual experiences (Wade), and service (Deikman).

An Invitation to Authentic Knowing begins this collection. Kaisa Puhakka defines "authentic knowing" as "knowing by and for oneself." Such knowing makes direct contact with the known and nourishes a sense of well-being. Depending on the depth of contact and clarity of discernment in a moment of knowing, the usual self-experience and intentional (subject-object) structure of consciousness become more transparent and fluid or may dissolve altogether. Puhakka inquires into the nature of authentic knowing as well as some cultural and psychological defenses against it. She then explores the shift from intentionally structured consciousness to direct knowing or awareness and offers a brief experiential journey through this shift. Finally, she suggests that bliss, perfection, and love are not the exclusive qualities of mystical experience but are, in more or less subtle ways, present in any moment of knowing.

Inspiration as Transpersonal Knowing by Tobin Hart describes inspiration as an epistemic event that provides psychological and spiritual sustenance, not only to great artists and mystics, but that is available to nearly everyone. Inspiration occurs as a particular shift in awareness and is characterized by contact and connection, opening, clarity, and energy. The constellation of these characteristics define inspiration and suggest a means for cultivating and inviting this shift. This epistemic event offers a powerful complement to the narrow rationality of the empirical sciences and to normal waking consciousness. In addition, most contemporary mental health complaints are characterized by a constricted epistemic style that is described as the opposite of inspiration. Inspiration may provide a direct antidote to many of these difficulties.

Mystical Experience and Radical Deconstruction: Through the Ontological Looking Glass by Peter L. Nelson addresses the nature of transpersonal knowing as engendered through mystical experience. Starting with the kinds of claims made by mystics throughout the centuries, the author brings a phenomenological lens to the examination of these assertions by means of an exploration of his own mystical experience. Although mystical experience is often considered to be the *sine qua non* of spiritual experiencing and is believed to lead to a unique epistemic frame from which ultimate reality is known, Nelson raises some important questions about the epistemics of this process. To accomplish this task he examines the psychophenomenological mechanism through which spiritual knowing arises and then reframes this process with the aid of William James's radical empiricism and the critical process known as deconstruction. In concluding, the suggestion is that spiritual knowing and the ongoing process of deconstructing our epistemic frames are one and the same.

In *Reflection and Presence: The Dialectic of Awakening* John Welwood reminds us that conceptual reflection allows cognitive analysis and understanding of what is going on and why. But he suggests that a further step on the path of self-knowledge involves learning to *be with* our experience in an even more direct and penetrating way, which he calls *unconditional presence.* Here the focus is not so much on what we are experiencing as on how we are with it. Welwood asks: What kind of preliminary practices or inner work are most relevant and useful for modern people as a groundwork for nondual realization? What special conditions may be necessary to nurture and sustain nondual presence outside of retreat situations? And how can this spacious, relaxed quality of presence be integrated into everyday functioning? He explores the uses and limitations of psychological reflection in spiritual practice, suggesting that it can serve as a stepping-stone both toward and "back" from nondual presence—as a bridge, in other words, that can begin to unlock deeper qualities of being and help to integrate them more fully into everyday life.

Dissolving the Center: Streamlining the Mind and Dismantling the Self by Fred J. Hanna presents the author's experiences and observations in the course of over thirty years of his exploration of consciousness. Hanna describes progressive changes at the center of consciousness brought about or facilitated by his meditative practices and transcendent experiences. At the focus of his description are three major stages and several substages of psychospiritual development that he calls "precentered," "centered," and "decentered." His first-hand reports shed light on various insights that occur as a result of dismantling the mind and self. One aspect of his description concerns the removal of mental phenomena that hinder and obstruct the natural occurrence of transcendence.

Illuminative Presence by Zia Inayat Khan highlights the epistemology of the illuminative philosophy (founded by Shihab al-Din Suhrawardi, d. 1191) as a compelling discursive reconstruction of mystical experience. The illuminative philosophy identifies reality with apparency, a perspective that affirms both sensory and suprasensory perceptions. The most important contribution of illuminative epistemology is the theory of knowledge by presence, which distinguishes between representational, predicative knowledge and presential, intuitive knowledge. Presential knowing is nothing more or less than an immediate, essential encounter between subject and object. This epistemic mode, which constitutes the self and underlies all knowledge, is intensified and expanded in mystical awareness.

Spiritual Inquiry by Donald Rothberg explores the contemporary importance of the idea that there are forms of systematic and disciplined inquiry leading to the resolution of spiritual questions. Based on an examination of practices and texts drawn from many cultural and historical periods, he offers a typology of five interrelated modes of spiritual inquiry: systematic contemplation, radical questioning, metaphysical thinking, critical deconstruction, the cultivation of visions and dreams. There seem to be methods with qualities similar to those usually taken to be at the heart of Western concepts of science and inquiry, systematic observation, questioning of core assumptions, and critical analysis. He then, however, questions the premature assimilation of these methods through contemporary Western concepts, considering the complexities of relating these mainly premodern approaches to the contemporary natural and human sciences. He asks whether new modes of inquiry, new institutions, and new practices are needed for contemporary spiritual inquiry.

Transpersonal Cognition in Developmental Perspective by Michael Washburn begins by distinguishing three basic types of cognition: agentic (ego-initiated, sequential) cognition and two types of intuitive (spontaneous, holistic) cognition: imaginal intuition and mental intuition. Pursuing a developmental perspective, he traces the prepersonal, personal, and transpersonal forms of these three types of cognition. According to Washburn, the transition from prepersonal to personal stages is marked by a disappearance of imaginal intuition (based on concrete symbols), and the transition from personal to transpersonal stages is marked by a reemergence of imaginal intuition on a higher level. He proposes that the development of transpersonal cognition can be understood as a progressive integration of reawakened imaginal intuition with the agentic cognition (especially formal operational thinking) and mental-intuitive cognition (understanding of conceptual meanings and postoperational intuition of higher holistic patterns) of personal stages. Washburn also proposes that the development of transpersonal cognition should be understood as but one dimension of a more complex process, a process that culminates in a higher union of the ego with the nonegoic potentials of the deep psyche.

Transpersonal Knowledge: A Participatory Approach to Transpersonal Phenomena by Jorge Ferrer introduces an epistemic approach to transpersonal and spiritual phenomena alternative to the contemporary experiential understanding of these events. First, the main conceptual and practical shortcomings of the *experiential approach* that guides contemporary transpersonal studies are identified. Then an outline of his participatory approach is offered, showing how it not only averts these pitfalls but also situates transpersonal theory in greater alignment with spiritual values and ways of life. Central to this epistemic turn is a shift in the understanding of transpersonal phenomena from individual inner experiences to epistemic events in which individual consciousness can participate but that can also occur in relationships, communities, and places.

Deep Empathy by Tobin Hart focuses on the specific process of deep empathic knowing, particularly useful in the therapeutic context. A map of the refinement or development of empathy is presented and identifies nine forms of empathic knowing. While empathy is typically understood to emerge from cognitive perspective taking as well as one's feeling capacity, the activity of deep empathy involves a more direct knowing. This involves a loosening of conventional self-other boundaries and subtle shifts in awareness. This chapter explicates such concepts as therapeutic resonance, deep countertransference, alignment, attunement, and intersubjectivity.

The Love That Dares Not Speak Its Name by Jenny Wade suggests that sexual experiences can involve transpersonal knowing, often when the partner becomes a focus point of contemplation in an altered state. In such altered states, identification may occur outside normal ego boundaries. Moreover, expansion of ego boundaries characterizes not only the psychologically advanced transpersonal knowing but the more primitive prepersonal as well. Wade describes the intricacies of three broad types knowing. In some love relationships, self-boundaries blur with those of the other, reopening prepersonal bonding (regression) and absorption by the partner. A more advanced state consists of absorption into the beloved, in which the two seem to achieve union. Self is subservient to the we-ness of the experience, but the knower is never entirely gone in this instance, which is usually felt in the ecstatic appreciation of the other and of the union between the two. At the Unity level the objects and relationships and voidness involve the events going forward, but the physical events serve merely as an occasion for the experience and not a particularly important one at that. The lovers are no more important than the spaces in between them and are no different from the other entities surrounding them.

Although service is usually discussed as a moral issue, in *Service as a Way of Knowing*, Arthur Deikman introduces a view of service based on the idea that it enables us to experience the connected aspects of reality—that which we call the spiritual. He draws upon both developmental psychology and the spiritual traditions to clarify the relationship between intention, self, and mode of consciousness. By showing that consciousness serves our basic intention, he clarifies the function of traditional spiritual activities and points to service as a way of knowing aspects of reality closed to ordinary consciousness.

We welcome you to this volume and hope that this material provides not only an opportunity for reflection, but also an invitation to explore first-hand the knowing that is described.

2

An Invitation to Authentic Knowing

KAISA PUHAKKA

A Taste of Knowing

Like many children, I often dreamed of God, and Heaven seemed near—perhaps just on the other side of the sunlit crowns of the tall pine trees that towered over the playground. I longed to know God directly and without intermediaries. Faith did not satisfy me; I wanted to know authentically, by myself, for myself. At age 11 while saying my evening prayers, such knowing opened up to me—or rather I opened up to it. In this knowing, all that could be said in a prayer had already been said and heard, and the One to whom I would have directed my prayer was already where my prayer originated. I stopped in my tracks, was thrown off all tracks, into an openness to what was always, already everywhere present. The sense of knowing that came with it was nothing like what I had learned in Sunday school. I might have asked my elders for explanations, so I could go on praying as before. But I did not do so, for this knowing was somehow more enlivening than any explanation they could have given me and more satisfying than the praying I had done in the past.

Later, I delved deeply into the spiritual and religious traditions, both Eastern and Western, and found ways of knowing there. Though the ways as well as objectives varied vastly among the traditions, the knowing itself was always the same, a direct contact between knower and known that obliterates their distinction altogether, if only for a split second. The discovery of this was itself an act of knowing. Through meditative practice, I learned to enter into altered states that were sometimes quite sublime and similar to those described by mystics. Needless to say, these experiences were the major mileposts on my spiritual journey.

11

Knowing and States of Consciousness

Eventually, I made a discovery that had an even greater impact on my life and work than did the mystical experiences. I came to see that this direct knowing is not the same as an altered state. Certain states of consciousness facilitate knowing (just as others hinder it), but the coming together of knower and known is not itself a state of consciousness. Rather, it is an act that can occur in various states, altered or ordinary.

Some altered states are extraordinary and have an intense emotional impact, yet little knowing occurs in them. For example, certain states of yogic absorption described in Hindu and Buddhist literature (Aranya, 1983; Rahula, 1974) are associated with heavenly, blissful vistas quite unlike anything found in this world. Yet afterward one may be left with just a vague longing for a paradise lost without any gain in knowing or connectedness to the world in which one lives. Some altered states, on the other hand, are associated with moments of knowing profound enough to change the person's life.

From the descriptions of such states, provided by religious saints, mystics, and ordinary people, it is impossible to tell whether the experience did or did not have a transformative effect on the person. Consider, for example, the experience of a 17-year-old youth in which he, without any physical reason, suddenly found himself in a most palpable and terrifying encounter with death, only to realize within the inert silence of his body that he was Spirit transcending the body, a deathless "I." The description continues in his own words as follows:

> All this was not dull thought; it flashed through me vividly as living truth which I perceived directly, almost without thought-process. "I" was something very real, the only real thing about my present state, and all the conscious activity connected with my body was centered on that "I."(Osborne, 1971, p. 10)

As far as mystical experiences go, there is nothing extraordinary about this description. What is extraordinary is that the knowing accessed in this experience stayed with the youth for the rest of his life. "Absorption in the Self continued unbroken from that time on," he reports (Osborne, 1971, p. 10). The youth was Ramana Maharshi, who, after that experience, became one of the greatest spiritual teachers of the past century.

Often enough, however, the experience fades away in a matter of hours or days, and with it the insights and illuminations, however vivid and profound at the time, fade as well. What we remember afterward may depend on the state of consciousness. For example, information learned while intoxicated is often forgotten in a subsequent state of sobriety, only to be remembered the next time the person gets intoxicated. Some researchers (e.g., Tart, 1975; Fischer, 1980) theorize that everything about mental and psychic functioning may be state-dependent, so that one moves

> from one waking state to another waking state; from one dream to the next; one amobarbital narcoanalysis session to the next; from LSD to LSD; from epileptic aura to aura; from one creative, artistic, religious, or psychotic inspiration or possession to another creative, artistic, religious, or psychotic experience; from trance to trance; and from reverie to reverie. (Fischer, 1980, p. 300)

True, everything that can be known or represented as a content of experience appears to be subject to the influence of states. Yet I had come to see that knowing itself is not essentially state-dependent. More than that, I had come to see that knowing is not a "state" at all but rather an "activity." This activity provides connectedness across states and affects transformations more substantial and lasting than fluctuations in states of consciousness (Aranya, 1983; Puhakka, 1995). For most people, authentic knowing, by which I mean knowing by direct contact, is fleeting and sporadic, if it happens at all. But for some, such knowing is a way of being. Ram Dass's guru, Baba Neem Karolie, is a rare example of the latter. When Ram Dass gave him some LSD, it apparently had no effect on him. The amount of LSD Ram Dass reports witnessing his guru ingest was thrice the usual dose (Dass, 1971). In this volume, Hanna describes moving out of a mescaline-induced state of consciousness into awareness unaffected by the drug. A less spectacular feat that many people are able to perform is to pay mindful attention to their state, for example, while drinking alcohol, thereby increasing the degree of continuity between the intoxicated and sober states. An unexpected calamity or accident sometimes forces a person to suddenly become very attentive and "sober up." All of these examples suggest that knowing is not a state of consciousness but an activity of awareness that can bring about shifts and integrate states of consciousness.

Openness and Discernment

Recognizing the difference between knowing and states of consciousness helped demystify the subject for me and opened up possibilities of knowing in contexts other than those in which altered states are deliberately induced, such as ingestion of drugs or certain kinds of formal meditative practice. Later on, as a psychotherapist and supervisor, I witnessed and participated in the coming together of knower and known in the precious moments of insight that sometimes shifted the lives of clients and students. These moments varied greatly in profundity and transformative capacity, but they all involved, however fleetingly, a melting away of a barrier either within one person's psyche or within the interpersonal ambiance between the two persons.

In psychotherapy and other interpersonal contexts, it became obvious that knowing has much to do with empathy. Empathy is the capacity to understand another person's experience (or one's own) with such intimacy as to be able to touch the interiority of this person's psyche and, from the viewpoint of that interiority, "feel with" him or her. Empathy thus understood is very different from narcissistic identification in which the other's viewpoint is assimilated into one's own and also different from projection in which one imposes one's own viewpoint upon the other. There are conditions that facilitate empathy, such as emotional responsiveness to the other and resonance with his or her cultural and idiosyncratic meanings. What is essential to empathy, however, is a direct contact that is nonverbal and mutually recognized, even if not always verbally acknowledged.

Thinking of knowing as empathy and contact helps highlight something that is very important about it; namely, it does not seize or possess its object. Like a bird in flight that leaves no trace, the touch of knowing does not grab but leaves things as they are. Contact is openness, or an opening. This point bears emphasizing, as the more common understanding of contact is that it closes upon and seizes its object, as when a fist closes upon a coin to hold it. Holding, however, arrests and controls. Whether done lovingly or harshly, holding is not the same as making contact. Holding arrests by creating a barrier, whereas contact occurs to the degree that there is openness or freedom from barriers. For the less than fully enlightened beings that most of us are, the openness is a matter of degree. We could envision regions[1] of openness that come into existence when contact occurs and disappear when contact is not there. The regions vary in size depending on the depth of contact. Within such a region, freedom from barriers of all kind, internal as well as external, creates an unbounded opening; something that appears close to, if not identical with, Heidegger's (1962) notion of "clearing." Contact is a clearing for awareness to discern what is there.

Discernment is essential to knowing, just as contact is. Let me clarify what I mean by discernment and how discernment differs from discrimination. Discrimination presupposes distinctions already operative in thinking and perception, whereas discernment is intrinsic to awareness. We could say that discernment is the "light" of awareness that "shows" or "reveals." For example, in the context of a mystical experience, one could conceivably "discern" the Ground of Being that is intrinsic to All, but one could not "discriminate" it since there is nothing with which it contrasts. Discernment is an activity of awareness that may be present not just in extraordinary and mystical experiences but in perfectly "ordinary," everyday experiences as well.

The presence of discernment is evident whenever fresh insights occur, when one notices what goes unnoticed by others in one's field of expertise, perhaps in one's entire culture, or within one's own or another person's psyche. William James's (1890/1983) description of the stream of consciousness exemplifies such freshness of insight, of seeing what others had missed. Other psychologists of the time who took themselves to be empirical scientists (e.g., Wundt; Titchener) had described the data of the senses and their associations—these were the basic "elements" from which complex experiences were built. James was able to turn his attention to what had been assumed to be empty space between the elements and saw the "fringes" and "transitory parts" (p. 236) between the elements. He saw that whatever one focused on, even the fringes themselves, had further fringes. Thus he came to reject the atomistic paradigm of his colleagues that viewed consciousness as an empty container of discontinuous bits and pieces of sensation in favor of a holistic paradigm in which consciousness is a continuous stream.

What enabled James to turn his attention to what others had not noticed? Where others had settled for assumptions about elements and empty space, James (1967), true to his radical empiricism, was willing to make contact afresh, to hold himself out to an openness where novelty could be discerned. Contact, which we now understand to be openness, and discernment, are inseparable as the two sides of the coin that is knowing.

"Knowing" and "Having Knowledge"

I have talked about "knowing" as an act or activity. Others who have appreciated the active mode in knowing, most notably Brentano, Husserl, and later phenomenologists, have taken intentionality to be essential to this act. Knowing (or "consciousness"), for these thinkers, is "of" something. The trouble with taking intentionality to be essential is that it shifts the focus to the intended object or content, no matter how much one wishes to stay with the intentional act itself. It appears to me that the moment of knowing is already gone by the time one becomes aware of an object as *object*, as something that presents itself to a subject and is capable of being described and reflected upon. The "knowing" investigated in this chapter happens prior to its forming into an intention, prior to there being anything of which one could "have knowledge."

"Knowing" and "having knowledge" may be distinguished as follows. "Knowing" is a moment of awareness in which contact occurs between the knower and the known. This contact is nonconceptual, nonimaginal, nondiscursive, and often extremely brief. "Having knowledge," on the other hand consists of descriptive or interpretive claims to the effect that "such-and-such is the case." The distinction between knowing and knowledge is not merely conceptual or logical; it is empirical and temporal. That is, the moment of contact is an actual event, however brief in duration, that precedes making knowledge claims. This moment may be accompanied by mental images, impressions, or thoughts. Such mental images, impressions, and thoughts may in many cases be indeed necessary for understanding what the knowing is "about." But the knowing itself is not an image or a thought. Rather, it is an act of contact. What is contacted by this act are, to borrow Husserl's terms, "things themselves." The act of contact breaks out of our solipsistic representational world of images and meanings, and also out of the collective solipsism of socially determined meanings, into genuine, empathic interconnectedness.[2]

It is a valuable contribution of postmodern thought to emphasize that "knowledge" is necessarily contextual. The knower is immersed within the context that separates him or her from the content. The context can never be completely turned into content, and so it remains the unknowable horizon that leaves knowledge necessarily incomplete and fragmentary. A state of consciousness, including beliefs and feelings that one is aware of as well as others buried in the subconscious, forms such a context. "Context" is simply an extension of "state of consciousness." Knowledge is always "had" in some state of consciousness or other, and its content is bound by the context formed by that state and its psychological, social, cultural, and the like contingencies. The boundaries between states form the limits of what is known at any given time. Shifts from one state (and context) to another introduce discontinuities and fragmentation of experience. These discontinuities are subtle enough to pass unnoticed when one is immersed in the content of experience, but they become evident when one pays close attention to the moment to moment flow of experience through the shifting contexts.

Knowing, on the other hand, provides connectedness and integration of experience across contexts. Even though it occurs in a context, being devoid of content, it is free of contextual influence. But because it has no content, knowing is extremely subtle and so tends to pass unnoticed. What is typically noticed are the content of mental images and thoughts that accompany or follow it. When the entire experience during the moment of contact is taken to be "about" this content, a shift from knowing to having knowledge occurs. A handshake provides a palpable illustration. The actual contact between the hands may be missed under a deluge of images and thoughts propelled by desires or fears and various personal agendas the participants may have concerning their meeting. Yet something in the moment of contact between the hands may inform these thoughts and images as well, even when the actual contact was barely noticed. For discernment naturally and spontaneously operates in the openness of contact, however fleeting it may be.

Dimensions of Contact and Discernment

The quality of contact and of discernment varies along three dimensions. First, there are degrees of *contactfulness* or *depth*. These are associated with a shift from discernment of the exteriors or surfaces of things to an awareness that reaches increasingly to the interior of things. Second, the *permeability* of the participants in the contact varies from "solid" or impermeable to increasingly "porous" or permeable. The quality of discernment likewise changes from "opaque" to increasingly "transparent" and "spacious." Third, there are varying degrees of aliveness, wakefulness, or *presence*, associated with contact. Presence, depth, and permeability in turn are associated with a subtle but increasingly discernible sense of well-being or even bliss that seems intrinsic to awareness itself.

These three dimensions of contact and discernment are mutually dependent. For example, the greater the depth of contactfulness, the more permeable and less solid are the things that come into contact. Also, the more presence, aliveness, and wakefulness the greater the experienced contactfulness. The handshake, though a relatively crude example of knowing, again serves to illustrate the interplay of these features. Thus the depth or contactfulness of a handshake can vary from a perfunctory act that barely touches the surfaces of flesh to an electrified comingling of the interiors of living bodies and minds. The perfunctory shake tends to be experienced as a contact between the surfaces of two solid objects, whereas a firm, inviting handshake that mutually engages the participants tends to be experienced as a much more permeable contact, perhaps even as a momentary entry into a shared space. The latter type of handshake is also likely to be accompanied by an awakening that enlivens the participants' minds and bodies for minutes or perhaps hours afterward (and, of course, may also stir up mental images and fantasies—not to be mistaken for knowing).

Let me pause for a moment here to clarify the meanings of some words used above. The words "permeable," "solid," "surface," and "interior" are meant to be taken in as precise and nonmetaphorical sense as language allows. We are accustomed to reserving these words for physical things. But they are just as applicable to what we usually take to be mental phenomena (Tulku, 1977, 1987). Thus, there is a kind of "solidity" that mental images and thoughts possess that is similar to the solidity of physical objects. Like physical objects, mental images are in varying degrees permeable. When they are solid, they tend to clash with other images and thoughts, and deflect attempts to make contact. The more permeable they are, the more they reveal their interiors and interconnections. Generally speaking, immersion in the content of mental images and thoughts lends them solidity. For these contents only manifest surface meanings while their interiors remain occluded, hidden within the contextual (cultural, linguistic, intrapsychic, etc.) underpinnings that give rise to them. On the other hand, a detached observation of mental activity, such as is cultivated in certain meditative practices (see e.g., Thera, 1988; Young, 1993), reveals the contours of the objects as changing and more permeable, and as continuous with their interiors and contextual bases.

Appreciating the qualities of relative permeability in both physical and psychical phenomena helps soften the dualism of body and psyche. It becomes easy to see that a handshake is not just a physical analogy but an actual instance of knowing. Body is capable of knowing, and so is psyche. The domains of knowing may differ, but the knowing in both cases involves direct contact. An empathic touch that involves no physical contact can be subtler and deeper and involve greater permeability of the participants. In some instances, their boundaries may altogether dissolve into a moment of radical openness of a shared space of awareness.

Another dualism that begins to loosen is that of "subjective" vs. "objective." The coming together of the subject and object, or the knower and the known, in the act of knowing obliterates their distinction in the moment of contact. To be sure, the coming together may not be complete but rather a matter of degree, depending on the depth of the contact or the permeability of the participants in the contact. To the degree that contact occurs, it involves an *ontological shift*—it is not a matter of the subject "viewing" the object but rather the subject is now "being" the object. But note: the subject is not being the object "in" his or her subjective experience or viewpoint. By "ontological shift" I mean a shift not just from one viewpoint to another (by the "same" subject) but a shift in the constitution of the viewing subject. In other words, a transformation of the subject takes place. As contact deepens and permeability increases, the isolated "subject" is transformed into a connected "intersubject." Knowing is not merely a subjective experience of assimilating the object. In interpersonal contexts, the mutuality of the contact in empathic knowing attests to the fact that the knowing transcends the boundaries of subjectivity and is genuinely intersubjective. But even to call this way of being "intersubjective" is a bit misleading for it is not something that happens between distinct "subjects." Thich Nhat Hanh's (1995) term "interbeing" captures the ontological shift better. It refers to the mutual connectedness of all things, human and nonhuman, living and nonliving. Knowing, then, is awareness of interbeing even as one *is* interbeing.

The Taboo Against Knowing

Anyone who has tried to be aware is likely to have discovered that this is quite tricky—now awareness is there, now it's gone, and when it is gone, we don't know that it's gone, until it's there again. The attempt to take hold of awareness launches a strange hide-and-seek game—thinking tries to capture awareness, and awareness, being devoid of qualities or form through which it could be identified, eludes capture. When thinking has its way, the unthinkability of awareness suffices as proof of the latter's nonexistence, and the game ends right there. But awareness can sometimes tempt the curiosity of thinking, and another round of the game then ensues—thinking now attempts to hold onto awareness but, unable to grab hold of any form or quality that would sustain it in this activity, thinking begins to disappear. It may, for a moment, fizzle out of existence altogether. To see how this happens, just try to think of awareness—*not* thoughts, images, or memories of awareness, but awareness itself! Much like a snake swallowing its own tail, thinking now becomes an utterly self-defeating project. So in an act of self-preservation, thinking quickly recoils from awareness. The familiar preoccupations of thinking return, and the open horizon that for a moment had surrounded, pervaded (and undermined) its usually solid basis is soon closed off. But perhaps not before it glimpsed what is most alarming of all—the insubstantiality of the self, the very thinker who undertook this project in the first place (Loy, 1992).

Thinking, understood as a mental-cognitive activity in the broadest sense, affirms the existence of the subjective self in an act of reflection. But more than affirm, thinking and reflecting create and recreate the sense of self in endless mental activity. The self has no existence apart from such activity, and this activity in turn is traceable to the workings of language, culture, and social environment. The existence of the subjective self is thus precariously dependent on the constructive activity of thinking. But the reverse also seems to be the case—the sense of self, or of subject, appears to be essential to thinking. Without a center of subjectivity, thinking would seem impossible; at the very least, the lack of center raises the frightening specter of being lost in a schizophrenic-like confusion and disorganization.

Not surprisingly, thinking is deeply disdainful of the prospect of awareness operating free of its control. For in such a prospect thinking contemplates its own demise. And insofar as our self-identity is vitally dependent on thinking, we contemplate the annihilation of our selves. So we, as thinking selves, regard awareness with unease and suspicion, perhaps contempt and derision, that belie a fear of madness worse than death—a fear that the self already is and always has been nonexistent (Loy, 1992), and that we are capable of knowing it, perhaps already know, if only we let ourselves. For every act of knowing, however fleeting and mundane, dissolves the self in the moment of contact.

Knowing, then, is extremely dangerous from the point of view of the self we think we are. Foucault (1980) has called attention to the danger authentic knowing poses to the power elite in the dynamics of social oppression.

The danger we are exploring here intrudes into the intimacy of our psyche, threatening not only the power role of the self as the owner of our being but exposing its very existence as ephemeral and hollow to the core. Only when the threat that knowing poses to the self's very existence is fully appreciated can we understand why the moments of knowing are so rare and when they do occur, why they tend to be instantly forgotten. There is a taboo against knowing buried deep within the human psyche that is more powerful, more profound than the taboo against sex or even against death.[3] All good parents want their children to grow into responsible adults, well informed and capable of love and work, capable of taking responsibility for their lives, making decisions for themselves. But do parents want their children to be capable of knowing for themselves? Probably it does not even occur to them that they *could* want such a thing, or that their children (or themselves) *could* have the capacity for knowing. This is how a taboo works—what is forbidden is not even known to be forbidden (Laing, 1972).

Perversions of Knowing

Rather than knowing, many children grow up coping. Coping perverts knowing by aborting the aspiration for contact inherent in a genuine desire to know. Coping refers to the ways in which people seek to reduce anxiety and satisfy their needs. Astute observers of human nature (e.g., Horney, 1950; Laing, 1970, 1972; Miller, 1981) have noted the mixed blessing that our mechanisms of coping bring to our lives—the gifts of security and satisfaction are bought at the price of one's own authentic experience and truth. This being so, coping can never deliver full satisfaction, and the anxiety never goes away completely. In its subtler manifestations, coping refers to our very personality and "styles" of knowing and being. Usually we think of "personality style" as something that makes a person who he or she is and accounts for the unique flavor and patterns of creativity as well as of stagnation in his or her life. A personality style is, indeed, all of these. It provides form and containment to creative expression. The more flexible the style, the more accommodating of creativity it is. However, the agenda of minimizing anxiety or warding off threat that is inherent in a "style" aborts knowing even as the person reaches out in the attempt to know. The project of knowing then remains incomplete, unfinished, to be continued in a repetition of the same pattern that titillates yet frustrates the need to know. In this way, a style is a self-feeding pattern that, with self-identification and growing attachment, tends to solidify into "who I am" or "personality."

All styles are designed to abort contact. Some do it by pulling back from openness, others from discernment. Most people manifest some capacity for openness and discernment, but rarely to an equal degree for both. Some seem very open, always willing to be surprised, awed, astonished by what is happening around them. Yet these same people often are impressionistic and forgetful and tend not to pay attention to detail or be concerned about clarity. On the other hand, others seem to have a remarkable capacity for discernment; they have excellent concentration and their attention catches the subtlest of detail with great clarity. Yet these people often do not seem very open and do not like to be surprised by the unexpected. I have sketched here the familiar "hysterical" and "obsessive-compulsive" styles described by Shapiro (1965). In their more flexible manifestations, these styles represent normal, healthy functioning. These two styles do not exhaust all possibilities, but they are common enough that most people will recognize features of one or the other or both in their own habitual ways of thinking and behaving. Let us take a closer look at how these styles pervert authentic knowing.

People who manifest the hysterical style are drawn to things in wonder and excitement. Yet, they do not "see" what is around them very clearly, they are forgetful and prone to excessive fantasy. They can be lively and engaging, yet at the same time, emotionally shallow. "The hysterical person does not feel like a very substantial being with a real and factual history," observes Shapiro (1965, p. 120). People who manifest the obsessive-compulsive style, on the other hand, tend to be realistic in a down to earth and rather unimaginative manner. They can be remarkably effective working with rules and organizational schemes. With a narrow focus of concentration, they are ready to grasp the object that is already intended before it is perceived. "These people not only concentrate; they seem always to be concentrating" (Shapiro, 1965, p. 27).

Both styles are defenses against contact even as they masquerade as ways of knowing. The obsessive-compulsive "already knows" and thus closes off openness to contact before it occurs. This provides a sense of security and control. But it also prevents discernment from operating freely in the clearing of awareness. Instead, discernment is co-opted into the service of rigid thought constructions. This is how discernment becomes perverted in the obsessive-compulsive style. The hysterical style copes with contact by retreating into sentimental wonder and fantasy. Imagination and fantasy take the place of discerning awareness, and, being ever present, they muddy the clarity of the hysteric's openness; and herein lies the perversion manifested in this style.

When the levels of anxiety or deprivation are intolerable, these and other styles usually (in the "normal" or "well-adjusted" case) work. The hysteric is rescued from the nastiness and dangers of the world by fantasy and in real life often by another person more willing to deal with the world. The obsessive-compulsive is protected against the surprises of an unpredictable, chaotic world by well-organized strategies of thinking and action. Yet at a subtle level, the hysteric will remain anxious, scared of a world never squarely met, hungry for the satisfactions that excitement and wonder promise but never quite deliver. Similarly, anxiety remains the constant companion for the obsessive-compulsive, propelling him or her to devise more and more strategies to hold at bay the source of anxiety that never allows itself to be fully controlled by such strategies.

Thus at levels that we are used to tolerating and perhaps no longer notice, coping styles perpetuate the very anxiety and lack of satisfaction they are designed to alleviate. In this way there is always more "work" for them to do, and the staying power of our coping styles is ensured—so long as we cooperate by remaining unaware of what is happening.

Knowing Is Natural

But few people exist in a constant, unmitigated state of unawareness. Indeed, only in extreme cases (the so-called "personality disorders") is the person's being so fully and exhaustively controlled by automatic coping mechanisms that there is no free awareness. For most people, moments of awakening and connecting occur spontaneously now and then, playfully rattling coping mechanisms and loosening up personality styles. Knowing is natural, and those who have tasted it like it, in spite of the dread it may arouse. They reach for it even while retreating behind their coping and yearn for it even when it has been virtually snuffed out of existence by a taboo.

How do we access the knowing that is our birthright? An obvious and tempting answer is, by getting rid of the gatekeeper that prevents access. The gatekeeper is, of course, the self that our coping mechanisms are designed to protect. Through the ages, spiritually engaged people have found the narrowly focused, egoic self a burden on their quest. Nowadays, increasing numbers find the self and its sufferings a burden in daily life. So for various reasons, both psychological and spiritual, many people are drawn to spiritual practices that encourage them to "let go" of the self, sometimes with disastrous consequences (Engler, 1984). Even in the best of cases, the intent to let go of the self can lead to endless and unproductive self-torment, for obviously there is nothing to let go of, and no one to do the letting go (Epstein, 1988; Beck, 1993). The project of letting go of the self is conceived and pursued by the very mind that creates and maintains the self by its thinking activity. So the project is doomed to fail—until *it* is let go. And how does one do this? The answer is, one doesn't. For once again, there is no one to do and nothing to be done. This is another way of saying that knowing is natural—it cannot be manufactured, much less forced. But perhaps it can be cultivated.

Shifting to Awareness

There are numerous well-tried methods and practices that facilitate the shift from thinking to awareness. Stilling the mind and bringing the incessant thinking process to rest is a preliminary practice for making the shift, and methods for such a practice have been developed in contemplative traditions both Eastern and Western. There is a growing recognition that psychotherapy, geared toward insight into and release of subconscious emotionally charged sources of psychological turbulence, confusion, and tension, can be valuable and in some cases indispensable as an adjunct to a contemplative practice (e.g., Epstein, 1995; Grof, 1985; Grof & Grof, 1990; Vaughan, 1986). The methods of Buddhism (Goldstein, 1976; Khantipalo, 1987; Sayadaw, 1984; Young, 1993) and also of the Yoga-Sutras (Aranya, 1983; Coster, 1972; Taimni, 1981) are particularly well suited for cultivating contact and discernment. In these traditions the importance of removing psychological obstacles to awareness that are often deeply buried within the subconscious is well recognized (see Hanna, 1994, also in this volume; Puhakka, 1995). With the help of all these methods one can develop one's capacity and tolerance for prolonged moments of awareness and also increase their frequency. However, no method or procedure is guaranteed to take one from thinking to awareness; the shift happens spontaneously when it does. And on occasion, it happens to people who have not taken up any formal awareness practice.

Few people, however, are accustomed to dwelling in bare, naked awareness for any length of time without much practice. As soon as one awakens to bare awareness, there is a tendency to quickly wrap oneself in thinking again and tightly clutch the familiar fabric of mental noises and pictures for comfort and a sense of identity. Thus, contact with awareness tends to be limited, sporadic, and full of gaps. Thinking fills the gaps and creates a sense of continuity and purpose that accompanies everyday consciousness. Intentionality is at the basis of this sense—even if the objects change, the directedness toward an object is almost always there. This characteristic of consciousness was known to Husserl (1929/1967) as well as to the Buddha (Hanh, 1996). In Tibetan Buddhist literature, one finds descriptions of subtle states that occur in advanced meditation practice. In such states the activity of the senses that produces objects for consciousness ceases, and with this, consciousness itself as we ordinarily know it ceases (Thondup, 1989; Nyima, 1994). Intentional consciousness, then, is clearly not the same as awareness. Unlike consciousness, awareness has no direction, no center of subjectivity, and no intentionality or purpose. It has no form and no qualities through which it could be defined, and it is presupposed by any epistemological category that would attempt to define it.

So how does one discourse about awareness, let alone describe the shift from thinking to awareness? Just as the question was raised a moment ago for one who would make the shift from thinking to awareness, it must now be raised for the writer presuming to describe it. No doubt such a project is doomed to a fate similar to that of thinking when it tries to capture awareness. Nevertheless, I will attempt to trace the disappearing contours of the shift as far as they are still discernible.

Several writers have recognized that the shift from thinking to awareness involves a subtle but radical change in the structure of consciousness. Heidegger (1966) hints at this change when he talks about a kind of meditative thinking that is simply *waiting* without *waiting for* anything. Transpersonal psychologists (Walsh & Vaughan, 1993; Wilber, 1990) talk about a move from a mental-reflective mode to contemplative modes of knowing and being. The contemplative modes of knowing have been associated with a freedom from egoic self-identification that seems to imply a change in the structure of subjectivity. Let us examine this change more closely.

With the shift from thinking (intentional consciousness) to awareness, the sense of self as the center of subjectivity and owner of experiences gives way to a subjectivity that spreads throughout awareness, as in three-dimensional space. In this space wherever there is objectivity, or "something to see," there is simultaneously and coextensively the "seeing" as well. Wilber (1997) describes simple awareness in similar terms: "When I rest in simple, clear, everpresent awareness, every object is its own subject. Every event 'sees itself,' as it were, because I am now that event seeing itself" (p. 294). Subject and object coincide fully and their distinction collapses altogether. But note, this is not reductionism into either a subjective or an objective "Oneness." It is not that subject collapses into object, or object into subject. Only their distinction disappears, and with it their confinement to separate domains.

To intentional consciousness, things (whether mental images or physical objects) appear "in front," as it were, so that only one side is directly seen. Subject and object remain polarized. To awareness in which subjectivity is distributed throughout, everything that appears is seen from all directions at once; there is no "backside" of things hidden from view. Phenomenologists such as Husserl and Merleau-Ponty also maintain that the "backside" is not hidden from view but is given directly in perception. However, for these phenomenologists it is given "as backside," which means that the perception to which it is given is still perspectival, still involves a subject viewing from a particular location and direction. When subjectivity spreads out in three dimensions, it becomes capable of simultaneously accommodating all possible perspectives within the region of its spread. There is then no "front" as opposed to "back" side at all; this kind of seeing is truly aperspectival. It could also be characterized as "three-dimensional," in contrast to the "two-dimensional" seeing of intentional consciousness.

Experiential Inquiry into Awareness

The meanings of words like "two-dimensional," "three-dimensional," and "distributed subjectivity" may seem stretched beyond intelligibility here. At the very least, they run the risk of remaining abstract and elusive unless they can be grounded in experiential observation. But how is such an observation to be carried out? Awareness, being as much subject as it is object, cannot observe itself simply as object. It somehow must also observe itself as subject. When thought through logically, subject observing subject seems an impossibility. However, when carried out experientially, such a self-reflexive act of observation brings about profound changes in its own structure in the very process of the act. Varela, Thompson, & Rosch (1991) have described the positive feedback and open-endedness that is inescapable in any inquiry that takes the inquirer (mind, consciousness, or awareness) as its object. An inquiry into awareness feeds back into itself to alter the most fundamental structures of the observing consciousness, eventually to reveal awareness as it is, divested of all structures.

How does one carry out such an inquiry? As with any fresh inquiry into what is hitherto unknown and undefined, we must begin by asking not "what is it?" but rather, with the resolution to put ourselves into an encounter with awareness that is prior to any question, or answer, as to its "whatness." As Merleau-Ponty (1968) noted, such an encounter is "indubitable since without it we would ask no question" (p. 159). So we must begin by situating ourselves in an encounter with awareness. And "where" does this encounter take place? Of course, it takes place wherever we happen to be at the present moment—that is, right "here." Let us then begin the inquiry. Is this "here" an extensionless point or an extended space? Most of us would be inclined to consider the "here" to be an area vaguely extending around ourselves in all three dimensions. But how far does the "here" extend out before it becomes "there"? We might extend our arms to draw an imaginary line in front and say, "Here! This is how far it extends." The lamp on my desk falls on this side, the flower vase on the bookshelf on that side. Yet this imaginary line is arbitrary; the "here" could be extended indefinitely to include the flower vase and beyond. How, then, does the "there" become "here"? And how does the "here" become "there"? The answer, (again confirmable by direct experiential inquiry) is that when continuity of awareness is broken, then objects appear across a gap "over there" and are presented to the subject "in here." Our experiential inquiry into the location of awareness reveals only "here," extending out indefinitely in unbroken continuity, spreading and embracing the lamp, the flower vase, and other things in all directions—until we stop the process of inquiry, perhaps because of being distracted, feeling exhausted, or simply because we are not used to being so fully present for prolonged periods of time. Suddenly, I am "back here" in a smaller, denser, more familiar space. Glancing "over there," I see the lamp, and "over there," the flower vase. There is now a gap between myself and those objects.

Resuming our inquiry, we bring attention back to awareness "here." But this time, let us ask, how far does the "here" of our present situation extend "inward" toward the subject I take to be my self? The answer, ascertained again by actual experimentation, is that the "here" extends all the way in, all the way through, so long as I let myself be truly present. There is then nothing left of myself outside of what's here to have a perspective on it. This is the amazing, perhaps a bit disorienting, revelation that comes with carrying out the inquiry: there is no subjective center located somewhere "in" here, and no distance that would hint at the subject or the self as being at one end of the distance and the world at the other. There is just continuous awareness pervading all, softening and making transparent the distinctions between inner and outer, here and there, self and no self.

Proceeding with the inquiry further, we let awareness freely expand in all directions, unhindered by any distinction between "here" and "there," "inner" and "outer." This last phase of the inquiry is extremely subtle and easily eludes attempts to sustain it long enough to note what happens. But if we are able to do it, we may find that the lamp, the flower vase, and other things are embraced by awareness not only from all sides simultaneously but pervaded from within as well. Things that are bathed in such boundless awareness become vibrant and in a way ephemeral. Yet the materiality and form of the lamp or flower vase do not disappear. Rather, they become transparent, revealing themselves as patterns of energy and a dynamic interplay of activities and mutual dependencies that constitute their manifestation at this moment as this particular lamp and that flower vase. These patterns of energy and dynamic interplays may include qualities of the artistry, craft, or manufacturing process, or of the chemical composition of the materials. Thus everything remains just as it is, only now seen with astonishing richness and perspicuity.

Perfection, Bliss, and Love

The foregoing investigation of awareness, carried out experientially, is likely to yield its conclusions gently and inoffensively, perhaps even with a subtle taste of bliss. The moment of boundlessness in which there is no distinct self may be experienced as relaxing and revitalizing, indeed as liberating. There is none of the horror and dread with which reflective thinking contemplates the absence of the self.

When distributed throughout the "space" of awareness in which objects appear, subjectivity contacts not only the exterior surfaces of the objects but pervades their interiors as well. They become transparent, luminous, and, because they are seen so fully and completely, perfect in being just the way they are. Ephemeral visions of luminosity and perfection are described in the mystical literature of various spiritual traditions. These visions are not about a reality beyond the one in which we live or about a Heaven that is not found here on earth. As our experiential inquiry into awareness may have intimated, they are about the ten thousand things of this very earth, of the coming together of Heaven and earth when thinking gives way to simple, naked awareness. As the Third Zen Patriarch put it, "If the mind makes no discriminations, the ten thousand things are as they are, of single essence" (Sengstan, 1976). Meister Eckhart, the thirteenth-century Christian mystic said it thus:

> For the person who has learned letting go and letting be / no creature can any longer hinder. / Rather / each creature points you toward God / and toward new birth / and toward seeing the world as God sees it: / transparently. (Fox, 1983, p. 55)

And here is my favorite from the Tibetan Vajrayana tradition:

> Since everything is but an apparition, perfect in being what it is, having nothing to do with good or bad, acceptance or rejection, one may well burst into laughter.[4]

Everything is up for laughter? Indeed, it is. The transparency with which everything reveals itself to awareness lights up both mind and heart. The mystics of ancient India knew that bliss (*ananda*) is an essential quality of awareness in which object (*sat*) and subject (*chit*) come together.

The coming together of object and subject is an act of love that involves an ontological shift from isolated being to expanded interbeing. Though the intimate connection between knowing and love has on occasion been noted (e.g., Laing, 1970), the effortless, relaxed, blissful quality of this act is virtually unrecognized by Western philosophers and psychologists (William James, 1948, is a rare exception). Yet everyday experience manifests this subtle bliss from time to time, for example, in the unselfconscious smile that spontaneously spreads on a person's face in a moment of awakening and contact, perhaps while watching a bird in flight, lifting a fallen child, or just sitting. In such a moment the self's boundaries melt away, and just for an instant, the person is in Heaven with all things of this earth.

Conclusion

Authentic knowing is not a privilege of the elect but is within the reach of every human being. It is not something extraordinary that requires special setting or circumstances. Rather, it is natural and could be active any time, anywhere, once the barriers to it are removed. This is a point I have emphasized throughout this chapter. The other point is that authentic knowing nevertheless occurs very rarely. The precious moments of such knowing are forgotten with a thoroughness reminiscent of altered states. Our coping mechanisms isolate these moments and build fences around them and indeed turn them into veritable altered states. Fear is responsible for this, and I have explored the vicissitudes of fear also in this chapter.

Every person short of enlightenment stands poised between love and fear, being pulled at each moment toward one or the other depending on his or her unique dynamics and life predicament. However, no one freely and naturally aspires to the isolation and compressed subjectivity that are associated with fear. On the other hand, who would not savor the taste of freedom and fulfillment of a moment of knowing when subjectivity spreads out boundlessly and connects seamlessly in a perfect act of love? My own experience suggests that there is a tilt in the delicate balance between love and fear, and that once one gives in to this tilt, the various methods of psychotherapy and meditative practices available today can greatly accelerate the removal of obstacles to authentic knowing, interbeing, and love.

Notes

1. Heidegger's (1966) notion of "region" or "regioning" as a nonrepresentational, nondual "expanse" that is at the same time an "abiding" (p. 65–67) appears very close to the meaning of "region" used here.
2. For Husserl (1929/1967) also, the way out of solipsism is through "transcendental intersubjectivity" and what he calls "transcendental empathy" (p. 34). (See Hart in this volume.)
3. Michael Washburn's (1995) notion of "primal repression," which is completed around age five, elucidates the intra-psychic underpinnings of the anthropological notion of "taboo." According to Washburn, primal repression is necessary for the protection of the ego and the development of rationality. Such a repression, he argues, closes direct access to the source of our libidinal energies as well as spiritual aspirations.
4. This quote is attributed to Longchenpa.

References

Aranya, H. (1983). *Yoga philosophy of Patanjali*. Albany: State University of New York Press.
Beck, C. (1993). *Nothing special: Living Zen*. San Francisco: HarperSanFrancisco.

Coster, G. (1972). *Yoga and western psychology.* New York: Harper Colophon.

Dass, R. (1971). *Be here now.* New York: Crown Publishing.

Engler, J. (1984). Therapeutic aims in psychotherapy and meditation: Developmental stages in the representation of self. *Journal of Transpersonal Psychology, 16*(1), 25–61.

Epstein, M. (1988). The deconstruction of the self: Ego and "egolessness" in Buddhist insight meditation. *Journal of Transpersonal Psychology, 20*(1), 61–69.

Epstein, M. (1995). *Thoughts without a thinker.* New York: Basic Books.

Fischer, R. (1980). State-bound knowledge: "I can't remember what I said last night, but it must have been good." In R. Woods (Ed.), *Understanding mysticism* (pp. 286–305). Garden City, NY: Doubleday Image Books.

Foucault, M. (1980). *Power/knowledge: Selected interviews and other writings, 1972–1977* (C. Gordon, Ed.). New York: Pantheon.

Fox, M. (1983). *Meditations with Meister Eckhart.* Santa Fe, NM: Bear & Company.

Goldstein, J. (1976). *The experience of insight: A natural unfolding.* Santa Cruz, CA: Unity Press.

Grof, S. (1985). *Beyond the brain.* Albany: State University of New York Press.

Grof, S., & Grof, C. (1990). *The stormy search for the self.* Los Angeles: Tarcher.

Hanh, T. N. (1995). *The heart of understanding: Commentaries on the Prajnaparamita Heart Sutra.* Berkeley, CA: Parallax Press.

Hanh, T. N. (1996). *Breathe! You are alive.* Berkeley, CA: Parallax Press.

Hanna, F. (1994). The confines of the mind: Patanjali and the psychology of liberation. *Journal of the Psychology of Religion, 2–3,* 101–126.

Heidegger, M. (1962). *Being and time.* New York: Harper & Row.

Heidegger, M. (1966). *Discourse on thinking.* New York: Harper & Row.

Horney, K. (1950). *Neurosis and human growth: The struggle toward self-realization.* New York: W.W. Norton.

Husserl, E. (1967). *The Paris lectures* (P. Koesternbaum, Trans.). The Hague: Martinus Nijhoff. (Lectures originally given 1929)

James, W. (1948). *Essays in pragmatism.* New York: Macmillan.

James, W. (1967). *Essays in radical empiricism and a pluralistic universe* (R. Barton Perry, Ed.). Glouchester, MA: Peter Smith.

James, W. (1983). *The principles of psychology.* Cambridge, MA: Harvard University Press. (Original work published 1890)

Khantipalo, B. (1987). *Calm and insight: A Buddhist manual for meditators.* London: Kurzon Press.

Laing, R. (1970). *The divided self.* Middlesex, England: Penguin Books.

Laing, R. (1972). *The politics of the family.* New York: Vintage Books.

Loy, D. (1992). Avoiding the void: The lack of self in psychotherapy and Buddhism. *The Journal of Transpersonal Psychology, 24*(2), 151–178.

Merleau-Ponty, M. (1968). *The visible and the invisible.* Evanston, IL: Northwestern University Press.

Miller, A. (1981). *The drama of the gifted child.* New York: Basic Books.

Nyima, C. R. (1994). *The union of Mahamudra and Dzogchen.* Arhus, Denmark: Rangjung Yeshe Publications.

Osborne, A. (1971). *The teachings of Ramana Maharshi.* New York: Samuel Weiser.

Puhakka, K. (1995). Religious Experience: Hinduism. In R. Hood (Ed.), *Handbook of religious experience* (pp. 122–143). Birmingham, AL: Religious Education Press.

Rahula, W. (1974). *What the Buddha taught.* New York: Grove Press.

Sayadaw, M. (1984). *Practical insight meditation.* Kandy, Sri Lanka: Buddhist Publication Society.

Sengstan (1976). *Verses on the faith mind* (R. B. Clarke, Trans.). Virginia Beach, VA: Universal Publications.

Shapiro, D. (1965). *Neurotic Styles.* New York: Basic Books.

Taimni, I. (1981). *The science of yoga.* Wheaton, IL: Quest Books.

Thondup, T. (1989). *The practice of Dzogchen, by Longchen Rabjam.* Ithaca, NY: Snow Lion.

Tart, C. (1975). *States of consciousness.* New York: E.P. Dutton.

Thera, N. (1988). *The heart of Buddhist meditation.* York Beach, ME: Samuel Weiser.

Tulku, T. (1977). *Time, space and knowledge.* Berkeley, CA: Dharma Publishing.

Tulku, T. (1987). *Love of knowledge.* Berkeley, CA: Dharma Publishing.

Varela, F., Thompson, E., & Rosch, E. (1991). *The embodied mind: Cognitive science and human experience.* Cambridge, MA: MIT Press.

Vaughan, F. (1986). *The inward arc.* Boston: Shambhala.

Walsh, R., & Vaughan, F. (1993). *Paths beyond ego.* Los Angeles: Jeremy P. Tarcher.

Washburn, M. (1995). *The ego and the dynamic ground.* Albany: State University of New York Press.

Wilber, K. (1990). *Eye to eye: The quest for the new paradigm.* Boston: Shambhala.

Wilber, K. (1997). *The eye of spirit: An integral vision for a world gone slightly mad.* Boston: Shambhala.

Young, S. (1993). The purpose and method of vipassana meditation. *The Humanistic Psychologist, 22*(1), 53–61.

3

Inspiration as Transpersonal Knowing

TOBIN HART

I suspect that we have all had moments that we would call inspiring. We might recall the power evoked in listening to Martin Luther King Jr.'s "I have a dream" speech, the invigoration that a particular piece of music engenders, the spreading of love and compassion as we witness the purity of a young child's heart, and the sense of being uplifted by a selfless act of courage or a heroic accomplishment. These moments fill us and move us, providing a kind of psychological or spiritual sustenance. And we stand in good company; Hebrew prophets, medieval poets, ancient Greek philosophers, and contemporary artists all describe something similar that they refer to as inspiration. While typically associated with the great artist or mystic, inspiration is a term that is regularly used to refer to highly significant moments in the lives of nearly all of us.

This chapter considers inspiration as a specific epistemic event, an activity of knowing. It has a distinct difference from the kind of knowing characteristic of the typical normal waking state, which a constant internal dialogue dominates. In the normal waking state awareness is subservient to analysis, the possibility of full participation in the event is often thwarted by the expectation of evaluation of it, and deep contact is prohibited by chronic categorizing of the other. This style of knowing is skewed by the acceptance of subject-object dichotomies and the objectivism that rationalizes this into place. These norms are described as more or less rational, linguistic, distant, and empirical (in a narrow sense of the word, emphasizing measurement rather than experience). We begin to notice the destruction that emerges out of such an "I-It" style of knowing. When we treat the other as some "thing" disconnected from us, it becomes much easier to propagate violence upon it, whether the other is the natural world, a fellow human, or even some disowned part of ourselves. At the same time that this may define our cultural norms with respect to knowing, we see evidence of (as well as the longing for) alternatives. Renewed interest in the long tradition of mystical knowing (evinced in the growing popularity of transpersonal psychology, meditation, and everything from the urban shamans to angels) may signal cultural recognition of the need for epistemic correction. This chapter uncovers inspiration as one way of shifting the center of our knowing.

The understanding of inspiration as a specific nonrational process of knowing is common across cultures and time. The word itself, stemming from the Latin "inspirare" implies being breathed into, filled, or inflamed. In ancient inspired creativity the Muses are described as whispering, breathing, or singing into the recipient, providing the source for music, poetry, and so forth. Related to inspirare and perhaps its Greek origin (Heschel, 1962) is "enthusiasm," which implies possession (by a god) or having a god in oneself. The myth of Dionysus provides a model of inspiration via ecstasy, that is, a contact with or possession by some transcendent knowledge through losing oneself in passionate abandon. Of this path Nietzsche wrote: "[The] triumphant cry of Dionysus breaks the spell of individuation, opening the way to the Mothers of all Being, to the innermost heart of things" (cited in Vogt, 1987, p. 34). Nietzsche saw the path of Dionysus as an opportunity for wholeness and unity precisely because it "prescribes" an alternative form of knowing, one that "tears down the barriers that have been erected by excessive rationality and individuation" (p. 34). Williams (1982) suggests that inspiration exists as a specific mental process; "[it] describes the poet in the process of learning . . . [it is] a means of gaining knowledge . . . of achieving wisdom" (p. 1).

In accounts of contemporary creativity, we seem either to be waiting for inspiration to get us started or for that moment of discovery that will constitute a breakthrough or illumination in the way we have been thinking about a problem.

We also use the word inspiration to address issues relating to religion and meaning. We may speak of a revelation (e.g., Heschel, 1962) or an inspiring prayer that provides hope and perspective. Underhill (1911/1961) describes inspiration as "the opening of the sluices, so that those waters of truth in which all life is bathed may rise to the level of consciousness" (p. 63). Laski (1968) considers inspiration as a "special immediate action or influence of the Spirit of God (or of some divinity or supernatural being) upon the mind or soul" or "a breathing in or infusion of some idea, purpose, etc. into the mind" (pp. 280–281). Assagioli (1965, 1973) suggests that inspiration occurs when the ego or personality contacts a higher or transpersonal self. Emerson understood the divine self—the "oversoul"—as the recipient of inspiration from God; Milton conceived of inspiration as knowledge of

God (Williams, 1982). In general, transpersonal experiences are regularly described as including transformative nonrational learning (e.g., Bucke, 1901/1969; James, 1902/1990; Laski, 1968; Maslow, 1971, 1983; May, 1982; Underhill, 1911/1961; Wilber, 1995).

What is common among all of these descriptions is the understanding of inspiration as a specific and nonrational process of knowing. Inspiration is the poet in the process of learning, the prophet beholding the voice of God, the artist hearing the Muse, and the "ordinary" person becoming, if only for a moment, extraordinary.

The Event Itself

Inspiration emerged as a birdsong for Milton, like a dream for van Gogh, a song for Goethe, a flash of light for Tchaikovsky, a beneficent power for Dickens, as a golden chain linking earth and heaven for Homer, and as love for Dante, who wrote: "I am one who, when love breathes in me, takes note, and in that manner in which he dictates within me, go setting it down" (cited in Williams, 1982, p. 11). These descriptions hint that inspiration is often ephemeral or fleeting, making it difficult to articulate directly. But as the experience is revealed further, three general phenomenological characteristics emerge that help to identify and define inspiration: *contact* and *connection*; *openness* and *receiving*; *vibrancy* and *clarity*. Along with these dimensions, the event becomes embodied into *form* and/or *being*.

Contact and Connection

A kind of direct contact and connection occurs in the moment of inspiration. This phenomenon is accompanied or perhaps accomplished by a shift in the sense of self-separateness. While the degree of expansion or alteration of personal boundaries vary, connection and contact are described as distinct from "normal" subject-object dicotomization. Wilber (1996) describes such contact in witnessing great art:

> [It] grabs you, against your will, and then suspends your will. You are ushered into a quiet clearing, free of desire, free of grasping, free of ego, free of the self contraction. And through that opening or clearing in your own awareness may come flashes of higher truths, subtler revelations, profound connections. (p. 90)

Note the epistemic shift at the center of this description and the content (truths, revelations, connections) that is the result of an inspiration. Heschel (1962) describes this as "a moment of being overwhelmed" (p. 445). I remember some years ago teaching an undergraduate college class. I was a graduate student at the time and this was my first teaching responsibility. I was speaking about some idea mentioned in our text and then I began to say things that did not seem to come from my "normal self." The words seemed riveting, wise, and profound beyond my conscious understanding of the material. They seemed to move all of us very deeply. I was not even sure exactly what I had said, but the enraptured students and comments of appreciation afterward seemed to confirm that this was a potent event. The class, myself included, seemed to be transported into a space that felt more fine-tuned, more loving, and more connected with the best of us and with each other. I suddenly and truly loved them and could feel the tissue that connected us. I have to say that it did not feel like "me" that was speaking, but maybe the best part of me and this part felt like it had assistance in some way, or rather, like I was assisting the event. As Heschel (above) notes, there was a sense of being overwhelmed.

The distance between self and other inherent in the observation and analysis of normal waking consciousness becomes replaced with the intimacy of contact. One person I spoke with described the following sense of connection: "I wasn't just a mind thinking thoughts or just a body working hard, I was a totality. My person had expanded to include the friend I was with and the birds and the sunset and even the dock."[1] The most expansive experiences spoke of a connection with everything—an experience and awareness of the unity of all existence. These are the numinous experiences often described in mysticism and represented by the following description from another person I spoke with:

> I remember my first realization of everything being connected. I was fifteen or sixteen, sitting in silence in my special spot outside and sort of tuning in to nature, the little birds and insects here and there. Then suddenly I had this realization of everything being connected. Both in the sense of [everything being] just part of the same but then what was most amazing to me was there was also a sense of everything being equal—the majestic mountain, the blade of grass, and me.

In addition to turning "outward" and "upward" for inspiration, other moments of inspiration involve "inward" and "downward" connection. For example, we might embrace some aspect of ourselves, our "earthy soul" rather than some "external other" and in so doing our identity—who we think we are—is affected. One woman described overcoming her own shyness to have a successful experience selling shoes in a shoe store. She did not have a numinous experience but claimed new self-efficacy and personal power as she reconciled with some previously alienated part of herself. She says: "I learned that I could trust and accept myself. I came to see that who

I am is different from who I thought I was." Another woman describes a moment of inspiration while vacuuming:

> It was a shift from my usual feeling of vacuuming which was just something to get through—a necessary burden to be done as quickly as possible. But then it just shifted, I appreciated the convenience of the vacuum, was in wonder about its technology, I was fully enjoying what it and I were doing. I was really there in the room and with this tool; I went from drudgery to real enjoyment. It seems trivial that this was an inspiration but that is what it feels like.

I should note that this same woman also described profoundly mystical experiences of inspiration. At the root of these moments was a shift in the way she knew the world—her epistemic style—moving her from a thinking observer to a connected, present, aware participant. Inspiration involves not only a kind of ascendant experience in which we seem to move near some heavenly realm, but it also emerges from deep decent into form and flesh. It is not the direction but the depth of the connection and contact that welcomes inspiration. We will return to this idea again.

Where conventional thinking and perception is often maintained by a belief in objectivism and manifest in the perceived separation between objects, inspiration breaks through those distinctions. Rather than remaining apart from or in distant observation of an "other," our boundaries are altered as we experience a connection that we may express as empathy (see Hart, this volume) and compassion. We move from categorizing to contact and in so doing practice "accommodation" (see Hart, 1997) as we meet the other openly. Love, acceptance, trust, and appreciation are often the outcome of inspiration and appear to have ties to this degree of connectedness. As one person describes: "I saw how much my loving is what is most meaningful and that it hurts when I feel hardened toward my husband or curt, disconnected from my children."

Openness and Receiving

Inspiration is experienced as an opening that occurs quite unexpectedly and spontaneously for some. I remember a drive I took along one of the Great Lakes a few summers ago. I had just left my wife and children for a few days, I was enjoying the freedom of a summer drive without anyone asking me to turn the radio down or put the window up. I suddenly took notice of the huge cumulus clouds set against a brilliant blue sky; in that moment, I was transported and transfigured—full and free like the clouds, vibrant like the sky; joy, power, and peace all at once . . . chest bursting . . . no words, just being and knowing. I felt like my awareness opened into a directness and immediacy, without linguistic preconception or the need for immediate interpretation. This way of being is easily overwhelmed by the rhythms of a busy, responsible, adult day. In this case, a break from typical responsibilities and the trigger of a beautiful vista seemed to set the stage for this unexpected opening. Along with such opening, a sense of awe, relief, freedom, and gratitude emerge.

In the words of one person: "Everything in my body just opened up." And when such opening does occur, it often comes with a simultaneous sense of being filled or flowed through. One man described an inspiration while helping others: "It felt like I was being raised into a waterfall that gushes over and through me, and the drops that linger awaken a dormant part of me that is not separate from the waterfall or from those I am helping." Ancient Athenian philosopher Philo offered a similar sense of the event: "I have approached my work empty and suddenly become full, the ideas falling from a shower from above and being sown invisibly" (cited in Heschel, 1962, p. 333). A writer reported to me: "When my writing is inspired it's like automatic writing; it's almost like taking dictation." Likewise, Puccini wrote: "The music in this opera was dictated to me from God: I was merely instrumental in putting it on paper and communicating it to the public" (Abell, 1964, pp. 156–157). Again, the root meaning of the word *inspire* (to be filled or infused) expresses this dimension precisely. When the connection is intense enough, the container or the self seems to disappear and "being filled" or "flowed through" is then experienced as a fullness or awakening without a sense of being a separate container.

This raises the question of the source of inspiration. What or whom are we opening to, and receiving from? Do we open to the unconscious, a divinity, or something else? It has been interesting to watch the proliferation of writings and interest in channeling during the 1980s and angels in the 1990s. While these areas make fertile ground for charlatans on one side and wishful thinkers on the other, these cultural phenomena hint at important issues regarding inspiration. The concept of knowing or gaining information from some disembodied source and through some nonrational mode represents the precise opposite of the objectivist, empirical rationality that has provided the modernist's highest knowing. Therefore, the widespread popularity of the idea of nonrational knowing and of knowing as a contact with some "other" may hint at the need and longing for a culture-wide epistemic correction. The ancient Greek poets invoked the mythic Muses and Socrates wrote of a divine voice (daimonion) that names a transcendent power, however, the idea of a guardian spirit or of divine intercession had gradually become internalized. Frieden (1985) writes: "Following Greek sources, Roman religion posits that every man has a genius, a familiar spirit;

eighteenth century aesthetics maintains that a great poet has genius; and to-day an extraordinarily creative person is a genius" (p. 15). "The classical conception of a guardian spirit is gradually supplanted by modern ideas of an individual extraordinary mind" (p. 8). We have become epistemically self-sufficient in a style centered in rationality. Self-reliance, hyper-individualism, and the like appear as social values emerging from these beliefs; narcissism, disconnectedness, and arrogance grow as social epidemics from these assumptions. However, it appears that we have passed the apex of hyper-individualism; hints of this shift come through relational theorists like Gilligan (1982), the rise of the importance of social context in the understanding of human behavior, ecological awareness that recognizes our interconnection with nature, and transpersonal and spiritual studies that may seek to understand the unity of consciousness. While the idea of a divinity providing guidance and direction is an ancient one, its reemergence in popular culture and scholarship (e.g., Hillman, 1996) helps to adjust contemporary myths about the boundaries and centrality of the self, correcting the overly individualistic, independent, rational knower that is the hero of modernist mythology.

I should caution that the inside-outside dichotomy elaborated here is a false one, that is, a relative one. It may have value in that it suggests the need for opening and making contact beyond our narrowly defined self. However, while the source of an inspiration is often reported to come from beyond us, when our base of consciousness is altered we may experience this differently. If our openness and connection go deep enough, our "inside" (i.e., consciousness, body, etc.) no longer exists distinct from the "outside." That is, the experiencer does not perceive the source as being "outside" or apart from his or herself. Said another way, when our consciousness expands we do not experience the other (in this case the source of our inspiration) as separate from us, the experience arises without a localized origin.

Once again, what is common is that the inspiration arises as a result of an opening in our knowing that is distinctly different from normal waking consciousness, whether one names the source God, the subconscious, or it remains mysterious. There is a sense that it is opening to an awareness, a state of knowing and being that existed all along—we may think of it as a veil being lifted or a crack in our consciousness that allows us to receive a shaft of illumination.

Using a simplified overview of the tantric yogic concept of chakras, the type and quality of inspiration may be linked to the opening of these centers. For example, the emergence of compassion may be especially associated with the opening of the heart center, creative inspiration has been associated with the opening of the throat chakra, inspiration as dreams and

psychic phenomena through the sixth chakra, and spiritual or mystical revelation with the opening of the crown (see e.g., Nelson, 1994). While this
description is very simplified, through the use of this type of map, we could
begin to differentiate subtleties of certain inspirations (e.g., hearing a voice,
feeling love, feeling like a channel for creativity).

Clarity and Vibrancy

The inspirational moment is described as having the "juices flowing," "an
inner push," "a flowering." As one woman mentions: "It is like streams; like
bubbling, an up-rising or swelling that travels up. . . . I felt every cell of my
skin." And its outcome, regardless of the previous state of health or mind,
is a riveting and immediate lift described as being renewed, uplifted, purified, or cleansed. Such vibrancy is often matched with sensory clarity: "My
hearing, my sight became so clear;" "everything felt so alive." Rollo May
(1975) describes his own experience: "Everything around me became suddenly vivid. . . . There was a special translucence that enveloped the world,
and my vision was given special clarity" (p. 62). Some degree of a transient
synesthetic or merged sensory experience frequently accompanies such
clarity as indicated in the following description of hearing a piece of music:
"It was as if I could see the different shapes, movement and the color and
density of the music." While neuroscience reports that synesthetic perception occurs extremely rarely, the evidence that this sensory merging happens frequently in the state of inspiration challenges these assumptions. It
also suggests that rather than existing as an evolutionary artifact (Cytowic,
1995), synesthetic perception may serve as a marker of alternative or expanded knowing. Merleau-Ponty (1945/1962) maintained that synesthetic
perception is the rule and that "we are unaware of it only because scientific
knowledge shifts the center of gravity of experience, so that we have un-
learned how to see, hear, and generally speaking feel, in order to deduce .
. . [what we sense]" (p. 229). Synesthetic perception does not, in and of itself, constitute inspiration. It manifests as an experience that results from
an expansion of perceptual norms that can accompany or spring out of inspiration. As Blake (circa 1790–93/1966) wrote: "If the doors of perception
were cleansed everything would appear to man as it is, infinite. For man
has closed himself up, till he sees all things thro' narrow chinks of his cavern" (p. 154). Inspiration provides an opening from the cavern.

Inspiration often includes a distinct expansion of awareness and understanding. As one person said: "It didn't come analytically, although it
made perfect sense, but as a flash of clarity." May (1975) reported, "The insight broke into my mind against what I had been trying to think about rationally" (p. 61). Rather than a decision or the answer to a question

emerging directly, the shift is regularly reported as gaining an expanded perspective: "There is a grasping of unexpected connections or seeing a kind of hidden layer of order of reality;" "Sometimes I see little things, sometimes things I should have seen all along, sometimes I understand the big picture;" "A veil was lifted, I saw it all so clearly, I remembered what was most important, I knew what was right to do because it was as if it all fell together perfectly from this view."

The insight or clarity comes out of a shift from linear, rational thinking to an intuitive mode. Intuition and inspiration both represent nonanalytic knowing; however, in and of itself, intuition does not equal inspiration. For example, we may have a flash of intellectual clarity in solving a problem and experience relief or excitement over it without an alteration of boundaries and connection. Instead, our experience may remain quite intellectually contained. Intuition may involve the completion of some gestalt, the coming together of ideas, a "sense" of something; but intuition does not consistently enliven us nor necessarily shift our self-other boundaries as is the case in inspiration (see Hart, 1998b; Washburn, this volume, for elaboration of the analytic-intuitive dialectic).

Traditionally, the scientific community has generally assumed an arrangement of hierarchy and dominance in the functional and neurologic relationship between emotion and cognition. That is, emotion and cognition are typically conceived of as separate phenomena, with intellect being the dominant of the two. However, recent evidence and argument suggests that this interplay may be quite different. Neurological evidence suggests that the flow of information may actually be dominated by emotion (Cytowic, 1995). A nonlinear, nonhierarchical model of brain functioning may prove more reasonable and allows for the possibility of a more complex relationship between emotion and cognition. Consistent with this likely complexity and interdependence, the phenomenological evidence from the experience of inspiration shows a simultaneity and qualitative equivalence in emotion and cognition. That is, there is no suggestion that an intellectual insight leads to an emotion or vise versa; rather, they come as part of the same experience. This might be called emotional-cognition, full-body knowing, or something similar. It may be most accurate to describe this knowing as the by-product of (or intermediary step in) the expansion of awareness and the transcendence of self-other boundaries that lies at the heart of inspiration.

It is important to note that this expanded style characterized by synesthetic perception and emotional-cognitive understanding exists between the moment of inspiration and its embodiment. It serves as a benchmark on the exploration of inspiration, but it would be a distraction if we saw synesthesia as some perceptual and cognitive end state. We could simply cultivate synesthetic perception and never experience the fuller contact and openness of inspiration.

Form and Being

Inspiration was occasionally translated into immediate action; at other times, it was used as an impetus or an affirmation to steer one's energies in a particular direction; for others the impact did not incite action but a shift in their sense of Being. It may be useful to distinguish two ways that inspiration manifests: into form and into being.

The scientist searching for the solution to a question, the artist creating a composition, the student looking for just the right topic for her paper, all represent the focus on a problem waiting to be solved; in these and similar realms, inspiration manifests in form and often out of seeking form. This sounds familiar to us and it has been described it as a "light bulb" of an idea popping in, or a fleeting image for the potter of "what feet to put on the pot."

Often inspiration does not manifest into form (e.g., solution, art, invention), but it does consistently affect what we might call Being, without concern for any tangible product. Inspiration affecting Being does not reserve itself for the dramatic mystic revelation or the awakening of deep compassion, for example, but may also manifest in the "small moments" and become captured by the little stories (Lyotard, 1984) effecting our day-to-day experience. As one parent describes: "My sixteen month old learned how to kiss me the other day, she did this so tenderly that I was inspired; it reminded me of the loving tenderness, of the pure love that I want to express to others." Another person recalled the depths of joy: "It was the first time I cried out of joy; I was surprised as I thought that people only cried when they were sad." These moments involve neither a solution to a problem nor a momentous spiritual awakening. They provide a potent, dramatic, uplifting emotional-perceptual shift. They result in a sense of hope, meaning, value, and clarity for life. These events may lift us out of a numbing depression or a mechanical routine in which we take our lives and the world for granted. They may energize and animate our actions, expand our perceptions, and fill us with vitality and love. These small moments do not necessarily seem as momentous as the dramatic spiritual epiphany, the unitive experience that has provided the ground (and sky) of transpersonal study, but they do serve as the smaller reminders of that connection. They seem to bring Being or consciousness into alignment with what we recognize as most important, regardless of the stage or level of development. They are often described as a remembrance: "It was a remembrance of what I know most deeply;" "It was a recognition of truth that was always there." Plato's anamnesis—the soul's remembrance of truth—is entirely consistent with the descriptions I have heard in the course of my research. In this sense, inspiration provides spiritual sustenance through deep remembrance.

Mental Illness and Inspiration

The opposite of something may give us clues as to its meaning and significance. The opposite of inspiration is consistently described as: flat, boring, lifeless, ordinary, plodding, stagnant, stuck, and empty. When we examine this antithesis we begin to get a sense of the relevance and importance of inspiration to daily living: empty or filled, lifeless or vital, hopeless or hopeful, stagnant or moved, uninspired or inspired. In considering questions of psychological well-being, inspiration seems monumentally important.

If we consider inspiration as one end of a continuum, toward the other end lies a constellation of experiences that have depression as their emotional center. When I have asked others to describe the opposite or the lack of inspiration the responses are consistent: "The opposite of inspiration is depression." "A hopelessness and meaninglessness creep in. Life seems like a great burden." "I feel sick, numb, just going through the motions." "The opposite is dead . . . dull, low, gray, numb, isolated."

Their answers describe the phenomenological opposite of connection, openness, and clarity described earlier. A sense of self-separateness heightens and with it alienation and isolation emerge; "I close off from the world;" "I feel isolated, alone and [I] don't want to deal with other people;" "I experience a lack of connection, I'm isolated." Instead of being energized and peaceful, we hear descriptions of numbness, flatness, and/or agitation and anxiety; "There is worry which breeds anxiety;" "I just muscle through life." Where inspiration bred openness to experience its opposite gets captured in being shut down or closed off; "There is a lack of expansion, a tightness;" "It feels crushing." Clarity is replaced by worry and doubt: "[I feel] self-doubt." "[There is] a decrease in physical activity" and a "lack of trust and faith."

The epistemic style involves constant thinking rather than open awareness. Worry or mind chatter, often obsessive and circular, characterize this state; "The opposite of inspiration is [getting] lost in analytical thought, like when I try to force a decision;" "Worry and inspiration can't exist at the same time. If there is worry or fear or confusion there may be a pulling back from life. Inspiration provides the energy to go forward." Regrets, self-doubts, and focusing on memories of the past or worries about the future typically occur in the absence or opposite of inspiration. With inspiration, the horizon of one's concerns clears, focus expands but remains rooted in the awareness of the present moment. With its opposite, focus seems to darken and contract and people often characterize it as dull or plodding resignation, "forcing" of an outcome or a decision, agitation, or a droning hardness.

, When considered in the context of contemporary mental health concerns these difficulties—depression, anxiety, alienation, confusion, obsession—seem to describe most of the current complaints. What would psychological treatment look like if we saw clients' difficulties as centered, in part, in a lack of inspiration? As inspiration emerges as a way of knowing and being, to what extent does our style of knowing effect our psychological well-being? What role does the constricted epistemic style in our contemporary culture have on our mental and spiritual health?

Related Phenomena

Briefly comparing inspiration to allied phenomena may give some clearer sense of what it is and is not. The term *inspiration* has been used synonymously with motivation. Motivation at times manifests as the pragmatic, active, operational consequence of inspiration, but the energetic spark and the flow or "filling up" of inspiration is described as a more ephemeral and powerful event, an experience of knowing and being. Where motivation involves applying our will toward accomplishing a goal, the inspiration comes as a moment of galvanizing energy and insight that may then be consciously distilled into work on some task. Where inspiration provides the illuminating vision and surge of energy, motivation may emerge naturally or willfully as a next pragmatic step in order to get a "job" done. Where motivation is an act of intent that may be catalyzed by inspiration, the inspiration itself is perceived as emerging from a willingness or allowing. Motivation also may be needed for maintaining the focus that leads toward inspiration. This is often described as the perseverance to stay with the frustration or difficulty. As one scientist I spoke with describes, "[In problem solving] you reach points of frustration. It wasn't going to happen in the first ten minutes. It really took a long time to gel. It required preparation and frustration."

Inspiration as a way of knowing does not constitute a cognitive developmental level such as Piaget's formal operational thought or even a postformal operation such as Wilber's (1995) descriptions of vision-logic or the fifth-order consciousness of Flier's (1995) constructive-developmentalism in which mysticism is not other than reason but a developmental perspective on reason. Rather than a cognitive-developmental stage, inspiration represents a style or form of knowing characterized by the phenomena mentioned above. Inspiration is not confined to a particular stage or order of the broader development of consciousness, it can also occur at any developmental level. For example, an inspiration may emerge as a strong transcendent connection with nature, or an experience of nonduality, or as an event that fosters a holistic sense of self-efficacy and self-esteem. Each of these may reflect different developmental stages (in these examples Wilber's [1995] Psychic, Nondual, and Ego/Centauric levels respectively). These maps may help to locate a stage or order of development in which inspiration manifests, but inspiration is not limited to those who have achieved higher development. While ontological ground is often shifted in a transpersonal experience, inspiration requires only a particular shift in epistemic style.

Flier (1995) reminds us that mysticism constitutes a way of knowing, not something to be known. But we may be absorbed or seduced by the content of such knowing, focusing on some tangible product (e.g., idea, insight) rather than the process itself. However, it is not the product that is the most valuable aspect of inspiration, it is the immediacy and vitality of the activity of knowing—the experience itself, not the outcome. The value of the insight or creative product lies in its ability to move us and remind us into this state of knowing.

What is the relationship between inspiration and peak experiences? "Moments of highest happiness and fulfillment" was an acceptable definition of peak experiences for Maslow (1962, p. 69). Obviously, this very broad definition captures a wide range of experiences. Maslow compiled a list of nineteen phenomenological characteristics, later refined into clusters, which formed a prototypical or perfect peak experience. However, he reported that no one reported all of these characteristics. Some later work (Panzarella, 1980) has attempted to bring more specificity to the phenomenological make-up of peak experience while transpersonal psychology has attempted to understand the "higher end" experiences. This work on inspiration also attempts to look inside subjective experiences, but rather than considering the very broadly defined "peak" experiences as a whole, inspiration considers a more specific process of knowing that may form part of many peak, plateau, or other experiences. Maslow recognized that peak experiences did not always have a noetic or cognitive element and in some later work, suggested that peak experiences are transformative only when they contain a cognitive component (Krippner, 1972, p. 115). This hints at the centrality of the knowing that I have tried to uncover here.

Like inspiration, the shamanic journey involves an altered state or an epistemic shift as a means of obtaining knowledge. Shamanism has enjoyed renewed interest through the work of Eliade (1964), Goodman (1988, 1990), Harner (1980), Larson (1976), Perry (1974), Walsh (1990), and many others. Traditional shamanic experience typically includes an alleged vacating of the body and the soul traveling to other spirit domains. By contrast, in classic descriptions of inspiration the Muses, divinity, an idea, and so forth visits us. We remain embodied, a radio receiver that may tune in one direction or another, or may spontaneously receive a welcome signal, while the shaman is more like a probe traveling to other domains. Using Walsh's (1995) phenomenological mapping we can further, if briefly, differentiate inspiration from shamanic journeying. The ability of the experienced shaman to leave and enter shamanic states at will is not as typical for the inspired individual, although there can be some proficiency developed in welcoming inspiration, but not in willing it. I have found that the use of brief shamanic-like ritual (e.g., drumming, chanting) can open one's availability to inspiration as well as to shamanic journeying. Perhaps some experiences of the shamanic workshop participant are actually experiences of inspiration. They should be differentiated from one another as the following brief comparison identifies. Walsh suggests the shaman maintains partial control of the content. The only sense of control of content with inspiration comes occasionally in the initial direction of focus (i.e., toward a particular issue, question, or form), but there is no sense of shaping the material itself. Awareness of the environment decreases in shamanic journeying but typically heightens in inspiration. Unlike shamanism, during inspiration both arousal and calm increase, and one has no ecstasis or out-of-the body experience; we remain embodied, however, the sense of self becomes expanded, sometimes tremendously.

In addition to the dimensions above, there is no cultural barrier in inspiration, which has sometimes been a complaint of the use of shamanic experience out of its cultural context. While it may be possible to invoke a core shamanic experience that does not require shared culture legacy, there remains some reasonable doubt about this. Inspiration also appears available to a wider range of individuals. Even in cultures where shamanism constitutes part of the mainstream, it is usually undertaken by an elite group who may have special skills, lineage, or status. Inspiration appears egalitarian in that it takes some form in nearly everyone.

Welcoming Inspiration

As an event of knowing, inspiration cannot be willed but it may be wooed or welcomed. Inspiration comes to us through a temporary "atmosphere" composed of three elements: the setting, the "mindset" of the person,[2] and the influence of the "invisibles" or, we could say, mystery.

Setting

Inspiration emerges in a wide range of contexts including: helping others (see Deikman, this volume), acts of creativity, enjoying nature, moving beyond some personal challenge or limitation, perceiving beauty, meditation, and so forth. Specific events, objects, or places, while not exactly causing inspiration directly, may serve as triggers. A particular event or a sacred place, for example, sometimes creates a special atmosphere that swallows our attention and nudges an opening in our awareness. Even a singular object, such as a work of art, that was brought forth through a process of inspiration can become the catalyst itself. If we remain open, the object seems to resonate through us the particular qualities from which it was formed (see Hart, 1998c). Assagioli (1965) tells us that with some pieces of art, "there is much more than mere aesthetic value; they constitute living forces, almost living entities" (p. 283). Such things awaken an "echo in our body" (Merleau-Ponty, 1964, p. 164), or, according to Gurdjieff, evoke corresponding frequencies within us (Brook, 1996). It is not merely the form that provides the power behind these objects, as Canadian painter Emily Carr tries to unravel in her journal, "there is something additional, a breath that draws your breath into its breathing, a heartbeat that pounds on yours, a recognition of the oneness of all things" (cited in Davis, 1992, p. 16).

One woman reports: "When I listen to Puccini I get inspired; it happens almost every time if I pay attention." Does everyone get inspired by Puccini? Probably not. Our individual meaning structures and past experience make certain events more salient to one person than another. However, while the longing, love, and beauty in much of Puccini's work, for example, may be particularly inspiring to one person, it may, given the right internal conditions, inspire a great many.

Inspiration is consuming and contagious, cultivated by our mere association with something or someone. Plato (1962) characterizes the Muse as "a divine power, which moves you like . . . a magnet . . . the Muse inspires man herself, and then by means of these inspired persons the inspiration spreads to others, and holds them in a connected chain" (lines 533, D–E). When inspiration occurs in the presence of others, there is frequently a propagation and sometimes an amplification of the experience, whether hearing a Martin Luther King Jr. speech or during a papal visit (see Biela & Tobacyk, 1987). However, the mere wild or Dionysian-like frenzy of a group does not equal inspiration. We can have enthusiasm, passionate abandon, or a sense of a "group mind" without the expanded sense of knowing that characterizes inspiration.

We often seemed pulled to the level of those around us. We may find that with a good tennis opponent, the quality of our game gets raised. The same kind of shift can occur when we are around someone who is particularly "healthy" or "holy." We may unintentionally be dragged down or raised up depending on the diet of company we keep. Parents of teenagers often become poignantly aware of this. We may also discover that our own inspiration may catalyze another person's experience and their inspiration may move us. The inspired teacher effects the student; the therapist who engages in this altered way of knowing seems to speed up his or her client's understanding.

Set

Even in the midst of the greatest beauty or courage, we may remain unmoved and distant; our awareness may be clouded by some worry or concern. At other times, in the middle of the mundane, inspiration may visit.

Five characteristics describe an internal "mind-set" for wooing inspiration: focus, trust, letting go, listening, and embodiment. These often blur together, but we will tease these apart for the sake of clarity. Assessing our ability on each of these aspects may suggest a means for growing in graciousness toward welcoming inspiration, or, said differently, for honing our skills of knowing.

For inspiration, there is a shift in focus that involves unhitching from the train of normal waking consciousness. *Focus* often emerges out of conscious and deliberate intent, sometimes initially as an invocation of sorts. This takes the form of prayer, meditation, a mantra, or formulating and asking a specific question—directing one's attention in a particular direction. For example, while beginning to sit in meditation I may silently say: "Let me be of service to the highest and best," and often, almost instantly, I notice a kind of jerk in my spine that straightens me up and is then immediately followed by a kind of softening and tingling through my head that signals a shift in my knowing.

The power of ritual, personal or collective, is common to many styles of focusing. The ancient Greek poet asks the Muse for insight; the devout or desperate pray; the religious service attempts to funnel us into a partially common experience through liturgy, communion, common words and actions; the scientist reviews the data and frames the question that is most appropriate to answer; the artist prepares his or her physical and psychological space and directs her energies toward a project.

This is a delicate act in that too much willful focus may enamor us with the apparent control or power of our act of directing, preventing us from opening further. Too narrow a focus may frame the question too tightly, not allowing room for what may come. Without adequate presence or focus we may spin from one thing to another keeping inspiration at bay. In an interview with me an experienced meditator hints at the role of sustaining attention in facing some uncomfortable area of his own existence:

> Sometimes I deliberately try to stay focused on the painful area. There is a natural tendency to want to shove it aside and attend to

something else. But I know when I immerse myself in it, stay focused on it, there can be a kind of softening, loosening it up. I can't make it happen. You have to hang in there. It does it's thing.

This focus involves commitment; as Rollo May (1975) suggests, "the deeper aspects of awareness are activated to the extent that the person is committed to the encounter" (p. 46).

Reaching out provides another way to name this focusing. Husserl describes an "emotive and cognitive reaching out to the other in a self-transcending empathic understanding" (Kohak, 1984, p. 206). This implies an intentionality, a direction, or a desire to make contact with some "other" (e.g., a part of self, an idea, a person). I may focus my attention in contemplation on Mother Mary, for example, and if I am paying attention and do not try to grasp this too tightly, in time I notice a difference, a swelling in my chest, and an awareness that had not been there in the previous moment. This, too, is a delicate move because our reaching out may become compulsive and our attention obsessive, degenerating to an addictive grasping or attachment that "must have" the outcome. Dossey (1993), in reviewing research on prayer and healing, summarizes an interesting observation that healing may be most likely to occur not when a particular outcome is prayed for but when the focus is in the spirit of "thy will be done." While presence or focused attention is critical, the "need" to have a particular outcome may get in the way.

While our intent often sets the stage, at times our focus is narrowed for us. A riveting event such as a death may suddenly catapult us into a clearing to which inspiration visits. While a loving, secure, or beautiful setting may at times be conducive to inspiration, moments of difficulty, frustration, or struggle can also create an atmosphere that nudges our typical state of knowing.

Beyond focus lies *trust*. At its most basic, this seems to involve faith in a nonrational, postreflective way of knowing, although it is sometimes personified (e.g., faith in God) or otherwise explained (e.g., the benevolence of nature, knowing my deepest self). Our normal waking consciousness and our allegiance to rational empiricism accustom us to seeing before believing; however, at times it appears necessary to believe before we can see. This means letting go of preconceived assumptions and suspending disbelief. Trust builds a bridge between the known and the unknown and then allows us to temporarily cross into this other world where inspiration exists within its own economy and logic. This world may not be revealed or reached without our faith or trust.

Experiences of inspiration strengthen trust; "this [inspiration] reminds me that ultimately the world is trustworthy and that I can trust myself and the natural order of things;" "I remembered to trust myself;" "I recognized the inherent wisdom . . . that I knew was there all along;" "I think it is an affirmation of something I already know, but that I usually forget." In this way, faith or trust constitutes not a theoretical belief but . . . "begins as an experiment and ends as an experience" (Inge, 1929/1968, p. xi). The interviews I conducted ended by asking participants what advice they had for themselves in relation to inspiration. Consistently, the majority of responses looked like this: "trust myself;" "trust the benevolence and wisdom of the spirit;" "[let] myself be vulnerable . . . [trust] that an answer will come."

As an example of working with focus and trust, I will confess one of my unintended mantras; it emerged spontaneously—one of those phrases that popped up one day and stuck around for several months. I found that when I was in a particularly difficult period of self-doubt, needing clarity and direction especially around my work, and asked myself (at some subtle level) for a way out, a phrase popped up in my mind: "Sing the song that sings in you." For me this mantra served as an antidote and a catalyst to the density of worry, doubt, confusion, and of trying to "figure out" my way through a problem or through my world. It almost instantly set in motion a settling in, a listening, and trusting. This created an atmosphere or clearing in which inspiration was more likely to visit.

Letting go or allowing follows naturally from trust; but while trust or willingness implies an attitude, letting go more closely resembles an action, one that deepens the encounter. Letting go seems paradoxical in the sense that we must be intentional (willful) as we move toward it, but we let go in the moment of surrender. This has been referred to as "releasement" (Heidegger, 1966), "detachment" (Eckhart, 1981), "wuwei" in Taoism. It occurs subtly, unexpectedly, often with a "give" and requires an attitude of nonattachment or no-grasping. Gerald May (1982) uses the term "willingness" and suggests that our overly willful, in-control cultural norms often exclude the possibility of constructive surrender. I argue that this style of control is held in place by our narrow epistemic norms.

This letting go and openness is not only toward some ascendant revelation but also to the shadow of our unconscious; as Jean Cocteau described, "I do not believe that inspiration falls from heaven . . . the poet is at the disposal of his night" (cited in Ghiselin, 1952, p. 81). It is this willingness to explore the "night," the hidden recesses of self and shadow that can serve this knowing. We could also describe letting go of those habits of thinking and being that maintain our self-separateness and anchor us in our ego. Shifting this can create a general openness or "soft mind" (Suzuki, 1970). As M. C. Richards (1962/1989) says, "What looks like inspiration is really the organic principle trying to find a soft spot to sprout in" (p. 63). Our "soft," flexible, open mind—a mind that can let go—may provide just such fertile ground.

Along with the allowing or letting go we must pay attention or listen. Rollo May (1975) says it is necessary to "hold . . . [oneself] alive to hear what being may speak. [This] requires a nimbleness, a fine-honed sensitivity in order to let one's self be the vehicle of whatever vision may emerge" (p. 91). *Listening* enables us to be meaningfully affected, allowing the inspiration its flowering. It involves expanding and opening one's normal awareness. "When Michelangelo did the Sistine Chapel he painted both the major and the minor prophets. They can be told apart because, though there are cherubim at the ears of all, only the major prophets are *listening*" (Gowan, 1977, p. 250).

We often have insights and inspirations that go unused or seem wasted. That is, our recognition is fleeting, a glint that is easily clouded by the haze of hurried everyday obligations and events. As such there may be no translation into a creative product or no sustained shift in our perspective or our self. How many good ideas or expansive views slip away before we are filled by them? While inspirations are somewhat harder to ignore than intellectual insights, they are delicate experiences that require this "fine-honed" listening in order to come to full bloom.

An inspiration comes to fruition when it is *embodied*. In creativity this is usually thought to be some product such as a painting, poem, or invention. In this sense, the ability to translate the vision into form becomes critical and may require technique that lives up to the promise of the new perspective. This may provide a source of frustration as one's abilities groan and strain under the push of the vision. But even techniques, while often requiring hard work and intentional effort to develop, seem to be elevated by the inspiration, if it is not forced. One seems to paint better or write better than he or she thought possible. And in finding the right form through which to express the vision, the velocity of the inspiration may increase or may pull on us like a child that demands our attention.

As mentioned earlier, a creative product is not the only way that inspiration becomes embodied. An act, an attitude, an insight, a spoken word may express an inspiration and reflect a shift in our being. A change in heart, or perspective, or the way that I treat my children provides just as legitimate (maybe more so) an expression of inspiration as a work of art. This reminds us that inspiration especially serves the living canvas of our lives and does not relegate itself to a few with specialized talent or interest.

Focus, trust, letting go, listening, and embodiment—the extent that these are present in all our activities is reflective of the degree to which we feel the benefits of inspiration in our lives: uplifted, clear, connected, peaceful, and loving. Development in each of these dimensions relates to the regularity of inspiration in our lives. And such regularity may alter the experience a bit. For example, the intensity that was often associated with the first remembered events of inspiration mellowed a bit for those in whom this experience became more common. "My early experiences were more like rapture, ecstasy. Now it is more like an incredible sense of well-being, of clarity and lightness."

Someone suffering from psychological difficulties may not only lack the direct benefits of inspiration but also the prelude to it, the set or techniques that welcome it. This suggests that both the experience itself and the understanding of the mechanism or process that invites inspiration may be usefully facilitated in helping others. Assessing one on each of these dimensions may provide some direction for therapy or other growth work. For example, we might find our inability to focus and be present, to still our minds and listen, or to have faith and trust in the viability of this process may keep inspiration at bay. Thus, developing ability and awareness in the needed area may also help to invite inspiration.

Despite our best efforts and intention, inspiration often comes unexpectedly and out of our direct control. It remains partially *mysterious*. I am reminded of how quantum physicists describe the action of subatomic particles. While probability may suggest where and when the next "sighting" may occur, it cannot predict or make it happen, and so is the case with inspiration. Using other language, it is often experienced as grace, as free giving of a gift that implies the direct control is not fully ours.

Conclusion

Inspiration involves being filled and being moved. Inspiration provides psychological and spiritual sustenance and often provides an education in values by reminding us of what is most important. The event does not take us away from the mundane but brings us most fully into the heart of it, begs for our full presence, and transforms it before our eyes.

I still get chills when I hear Martin Luther King Jr.'s "I have a dream speech." Perhaps you do too. This indicates that in that moment we have begun to shift and open to an aspect of our consciousness that resonates with King's words of justice. Of course such things as beauty, compassion, courage, and so forth may also move us. And simply that momentary recognition and contact can be sufficient to take our breath away, forcing the next breath to be a deep awakening. While inspiration has most often been thought of as infrequent and reserved for the gifted few, it is revealed here as an event that all of us may have a taste of and be able to invite.

The evidence of inspiration as frequent and significant helps to shift the center of gravity away from the exclusivity of the normal waking state and with it a narrow form of rational empiricism as the only viable source of knowing and being. As we remember our ways of knowing, we may reclaim the significance of inspiration in our own lives, recognizing that the way we deal with our family, our work, or even our next meal brings as much an opportunity for inspiration as our sacred practices of art or religion.

Notes

1. All quotations that are not otherwise indicated come from interviews that were conducted in the course of my research. See Hart (1998a) for a methodological description.
2. Nelson's (1990) research confirms the significance of set and setting in relation to a whole range of altered state experiences in which inspiration may belong.

References

Abell, A. M. (1964). *Talks with great composers.* Garmisch, Germany: Schroeder.

Assagioli, R. (1965). *Psychosynthesis: A manual of principles and techniques.* New York: Viking Press.

Assagioli, R. (1973). *The act of will.* New York: Penguin Press.

Blake, W. (1966). The marriage of heaven and hell. In G. Keynes (Ed.), *Blake: Complete Writings* (pp. 148–159). London: Oxford University Press. (Original work etched circa 1790–93)

Biela, A., & Tobacyk, J. (1987). Self-transcendence in the agoral gathering: A case of Pope John Paul II's visit to Poland. *Journal of Humanistic Psychology, 27*(4), 390–405.

Brook, P. (1996). The Secret Dimension. *Parabola, 11*(2), 30–33.

Bucke, R. M. (1969). *Cosmic consciousness: A study in the evolution of the human mind.* New York: E. P. Dutton. (Original work published 1901)

Cytowic, R. E. (1995). Synesthesia: Phenomenology and neuropsychology: A review of current knowledge. *Psyche: An Interdisciplinary Journal of Research on Consciousness, 2*(10).

Davis, A. (1992). *The logic of ecstasy: Canadian mystical painting.* Toronto: University of Toronto Press.

Dossey, L. (1993). *Healing words: The power of prayer and the practice of medicine.* New York: HarperCollins.

Eckhart, M. (1981). *Meister Eckhart: The essential sermons, commentaries, treatises, and defense* (E. Colledge, & B. McGinn, Trans.). New York: Paulist Press.

Eliade, M. (1964). *Shamanism: Archaic techniques of ecstasy.* Princeton, NJ: Princeton University Press.

Flier, L. (1995). Demystifying mysticism: Finding a developmental relationship between different ways of knowing. *The Journal of Transpersonal Psychology, 27*(2), 131–152.

Frieden, K. (1985). *Genius and monologue*. Ithaca, NY: Cornell University Press.

Ghiselin, B. (Ed.). (1952). *The creative process*. New York: Mentor Books.

Gilligan, C. (1982). *In a different voice: Psychological theory and women's development*. Cambridge, MA: Harvard University Press.

Goodman, F. D. (1988). *Ecstasy, ritual, and alternate reality: Religion in a pluralistic world*. Bloomington: Indiana University Press.

Goodman, F. D. (1990). *Where the spirits ride the wind: Trance journeys and other ecstatic experiences*. Bloomington: Indiana University Press.

Gowan, J. C. (1977). Creative inspiration in composers. *Journal of Creative Behavior, 11*(4), 249–255.

Harner, M. (1980). *The way of the shaman*. New York: Harper & Row.

Hart, T. (1997). From category to contact: Epistemology and the enlivening and deadening of experience in education. *Journal of Humanistic Education and Development, 36*(1), 23–34.

Hart, T. (1998a). Inspiration: An exploration of the experience and its meaning. *Journal of Humanistic Psychology, 38*(3), 7–35.

Hart, T. (1998b). A dialectic of knowing: Integrating the intuitive and the analytic. *Encounter: Education for Meaning and Social Justice, 11*(3), 5–16.

Hart, T. (1998c). Spiritual art: Evocation and expression of transpersonal knowing. Manuscript submitted for publication.

Heidegger, M. (1966). *Discourse on thinking* (J. M. Anderson & E. H. Freund, Trans.). New York: Harper & Row. (Original work published 1959)

Heschel, A. J. (1962). *The prophets*. New York: Harper & Row.

Hillman, J. (1996). *The soul's code: In search of character and calling*. New York: Warner Books.

Inge, W. R. (1968). *The philosophy of Plotinus: Vol. 2*. Westport, CT: Greenwood. (Original work published 1929)

James, W. (1990). *Varieties of religious experience*. New York: Vintage Books. (Original work published 1902)

Kohak, E. (1984). *The embers and the stars: A philosophical inquiry into the moral sense of nature*. Chicago: University of Chicago Press.

Krippner, S. (1972). The plateau experience: A. H. Maslow and others. *The Journal of Transpersonal Psychology, 4*(2), 107–120.

Larson, S. (1976). *The shaman's doorway*. New York: Station Hill Press.

Laski, M. (1968). *Ecstasy: A study of some secular and religious experiences*. London: Cresset Press.

Lyotard, J. F. (1984). *The post-modern condition: A report on knowledge*. (G. Bennington & B. Massumi, Trans.). Minneapolis: University of Minnesota Press.

Maslow, A. (1962). *Toward a psychology of being*. New York: Van Nostrand Reinhold.

Maslow, A. (1971). *The farther reaches of human nature.* New York: Penguin.

Maslow, A. (1983). *Religion, values and peak experience.* New York: Penguin.

May, G. (1982). *Will and spirit: A contemplative psychology.* New York: Harper & Row.

May, R. (1975). *The courage to create.* New York: Bantam Books.

Merleau-Ponty, M. (1962). *The phenomenology of perception* (C. Smith, Trans.). New York: Humanities Press. (Original work published 1945)

Merleau-Ponty, M. (1964). Eye and mind. In J. Edie (Ed.), *The primacy of perception* (pp. 159–169). Evanston, IL: Northwestern University Press.

Nelson, J. E. (1994). *Healing the split: Integrating our understanding of the mentally ill.* (Rev. ed.). Albany: State University of New York Press.

Nelson, P. L. (1990). The technology of the praeternatural: An empirically based model of transpersonal experiences. *The Journal of Transpersonal Psychology, 22*(1), 35–50.

Panzarella, R. (1980). The phenomenology of aesthetic peak experiences. *Journal of Humanistic Psychology, 2*(1), 69–85.

Perry, J. W. (1974). *The far side of madness.* Berkeley: University of California Press.

Plato (1962). *Ion.* (W. R. M. Lamb, Trans.). Cambridge, MA: Harvard University Press.

Richards, M. C. (1989). *Centering in pottery, poetry, and the person.* Hanover, NH: Wesleyan University Press. (Original work published 1962)

Suzuki, S. (1970). *Zen mind, beginner's mind: Informal talks on Zen meditation and practice.* New York: Weatherhill.

Underhill, E. (1961). *Mysticism: A study in the nature and development of man's spiritual consciousness.* New York: E. P. Dutton. (Original work published 1911)

Vogt, K. D. (1987). *Vision and revision: The concept of inspiration in Thomas Mann's fiction.* New York: Peter Lang.

Walsh, R. (1990). *The spirit of shamanism.* New York: J. P. Putnam.

Walsh, R. (1995). Phenomenological mapping: A method for describing and comparing states of consciousness. *The Journal of Transpersonal Psychology, 27*(1), 25–56.

Wilber, K. (1995). *Sex, ecology, spirituality: The spirit of evolution.* Boston: Shambhala.

Wilber, K. (1996). Transpersonal art and literary theory. *The Journal of Transpersonal Psychology, 28*(1), 63–91.

Williams, M. E. (1982). *Inspiration in Milton and Keats.* Totowa, NJ: Barnes & Noble Books.

4

Mystical Experience and
Radical Deconstruction

Through the Ontological Looking Glass

PETER L. NELSON

Knowing is that moment to moment reflexive, retrospective activity of awareness that we engage as we navigate the waters of consciousness. It is both the act of immediate experiencing as well as the experience of that experiencing. In its immediacy it appears to be our way of "touching" reality—of directly accessing the who, what, where, and when of our existential worlds. For most of us, most of the time, knowing has a consistency and constancy that allows us to feel and believe that there is an ontologically solid and unchanging world "out there" that we access through our senses. However, on some occasions the regularity and certainty of this daily style of knowing undergoes a radical transformation—such as when one has a mystical experience. To those of us who have had such encounters, mystical experiences appear to be a radically altered way of knowing where reality is experienced afresh, illusions are penetrated, and self and other seem to lose their rigid boundedness. The world appears to become both imminent and transparent. Thus, mystical knowing appears to be both broader and deeper—encompassing a more complete contact with reality.

So, it is often claimed by those mystics and spiritual seekers, who are willing to speak of such things, that once one has encountered the "ultimate ground of being" (a direct encounter with God, Goddess, the "Mysterium Tremendum," the Void, or whatever name is given to the ultimate source of our being), then one has gained a profound spiritual knowledge that subsumes all other knowing thereby bestowing on the knower a unique epistemic position and certainty.[1] This position is one in which it is claimed that the "truth" behind all appearances is revealed and the ultimate ontological source of our knowing, indeed of who we are, is now directly accessed. Those who make these sorts of claims argue with great sincerity and force that this new knowledge is *sui generis* and final—it cannot be questioned because it is not a matter of intellectual debate, but rather the result of a unique and direct awareness. It arises from a unique *spiritual knowing*. The argument usually given is that, if one fails to accept these assertions, then it is because one has not yet had such an experience and without the shared experiential base all attempts at explanation are futile (viz., to know color, one must not be color-blind).

In 1971, while a graduate student at the Psychological Institute of the University of Copenhagen, I had what I believe was a mystical experience—a radical transformation of knowing where time and space collapsed, self and other disappeared, but the totality of my consciousness was permeated by an awareness of a supernal light filling an infinite voidness. At the time, my immediate reaction and understanding after the event was not unlike the claim-making described earlier. I felt and believed with every fiber of my being that my mystical experience had given rise to a unique kind of knowing that had carried me through the looking glass of phenomenal appearances and that I had encountered the ultimate, core "emptiness" of being—the ontological source. At the time I believed that I understood the very nature of the ontological bottom line and my entire world was reinterpreted from this view that I then believed was given as a result of my new and apparently elevated epistemic position. Although I accepted, absolutely, the truth of my new vision at the time, I have come to understand this episode somewhat differently with the passage of time. I accept that the experience was a move into a new epistemic frame—a uniquely different way of knowing—but I no longer accept that way of knowing as above all others—nor do I see it as leading to the attainment of the ultimate and final position at which one can arrive in order to make sense of the phenomenal world. In fact, I now doubt that there is such a final position at all.

My claim is that it is but one of many possible epistemic frames deriving from different ways of knowing. It is not that I believe that there is no truth revealed through such encounters—I certainly do. However, I no longer believe that there is one *final* position from which all truth is knowable in any ultimate sense. Although this encounter at first set me in the philosophical and religious mold of an ontological absolutist—there is one and only one final reality and truth—that position, itself, eventually opened my eyes to other possibilities. Once one other possibility was admitted, I then had to entertain the likelihood of still others. As I followed this process of intellectual and spiritual exploration I was inexorably led to a clearing in the forest, which I now identify as part of that collocation of intellectual perspectives known as Postmodernism. I later realized that the primary compass guiding me was a postanalytic critical method that has emerged in recent years as the primary technique of the postmodern school and usually goes under the rubric of Deconstructionism.[2]

Some would immediately accuse me of having lost my spiritual direction—a loss of faith and belief in what I had directly encountered. Rudolph Otto (1958), the nineteenth-century Christian theologian, might have charged me with having lost contact with the "creature feeling" experienced at the time of my encounter with the "tremendum" (p. 8) and, similarly, some of my Buddhist friends certainly believe that I had redescended back into the samsaric depths from which I had temporarily emerged. This remains to be seen.

However, while I await final judgment regarding my spiritual health, I will give, first, a brief description of my encounter with mystical knowing and, second, using perspectives drawn from consciousness studies and postmodernism, make an attempt to demonstrate that, as I have come to understand it, mystical knowing is part of a progression into spiritual knowing—a progression that has no definite terminus or final structure. This "path," if I can use this term, led me to a recognition that epistemic frameworks are operationally (functionally) created, and I now call this viewpoint Ontological Neutralism—an attempt to maintain no privileged ontological position while simultaneously understanding that any such attempt, *ipso facto*, creates such a position (Nelson & Howell, 1993–94). Thus, I will finally argue that spiritual knowing is to live consciously, with as full an awareness as possible in an unresolvable paradox while still acting and taking responsibility for one's life in a manner that assumes that there is no paradox. This process of maintaining ontological neutrality is the development of a dialectical and witnessing consciousness for which the relativity of epistemic frames is liberating rather than threatening. It is, metaphorically speaking, like surfing the existential waves as we move in and out of different ways of knowing.[3]

A Personal Encounter

My mystical experience began as a rather ordinary evening of listening to music at a friend's apartment in the Christianhavn's district of Copenhagen, Denmark. The apartment in which he lived was condemned, but, as was common in Europe of the early 1970s, squatters, mainly students, often reclaimed these buildings because of the severe housing shortage existent at the time.

His dwelling was on the top story of a five-floor walk-up, and I arrived at about 8 p.m. one weekday evening, somewhat out of breath from lugging my guitar up all those flights of stairs. I was a graduate student in psychology and he in biology, and every Friday night we played music together in a local club to supplement our meager student grants. This evening was supposed to be our rehearsal night, but as I entered, I found him preparing to leave. An emergency meeting of the squatters committee had been called and he had to attend. Jorgen explained how to use his tape recorder and gave me a tape of blues music to listen to as he rushed out the door. His idea for our rehearsal evening was to take some tunes from the tape to add to our usual repertoire.

After he left I spooled the tape onto the machine and sat down to listen, but for some reason I was unable to focus my full attention on the music. Each time I attempted to "get into" the song and "map out" the guitar lines I found myself staring, in my mind's eye, at a very vivid and stylized eidetic image of myself. This image was an exaggerated caricature of a role that had long been part of my self-image—Peter, "the brilliant graduate student." In my mind's eye I could see me talking and gesturing with the exaggerated self-importance and conceit that I usually managed to disguise from myself in those days. However, seen in such direct bold-relief and painful clarity, this internal "picture" made me mentally flinch. In my mind I scrambled to find something else on which to focus my attention and thus to rid myself of this unwanted, absurd specter. Yet, each time I tried to focus my attention back to the task at hand, I seemed unable to sustain any real concentration with my focus continually drawn back, as if by a magnetic force, to my inner caricature.

I cycled through this round of confrontation and avoidance several times, and as I struggled with it for the third or fourth time I was startled by a "voice" talking to me—apparently from my left side. It seemed to come from "outside" like any other aural veridical perception, but no one was there and the quality of the voice was definitely unlike my own internal discursive commentator. It was, in a sense, both "inside" and "outside" of my head at the same time. I paused, looked around and thought, "an hallucinatory projection." Again I attempted to return to "normal" thoughts and to the music, but as I did, I heard the voice again, very clearly this time, and it said, "You are what you are and no matter what you think you are, you will remain what you are. It's all you've got, so you might as well look at it." I was startled by the suddenness and clarity of this second intrusion and my heart began to pound, but, like a man whistling in the dark, I nervously attempted once again to return to what I believed should have been my "normal" world. However, as I endeavored to reconnect to the music, which now seemed to be playing somewhere on the distant periphery of my awareness, the caricatured "self-picture" again returned. This time, for no apparent reason other than a feeling of "why not," I decided to heed the advice of the "voice" and look more closely at this image I was struggling to reject.

I now turned my full attention to that inner picture. My examination of my persona's behavior and qualities proved to be an exceedingly uncomfortable task, and my continuous impulse was to drop the whole process and escape into some other, less confronting activity. However, as I persisted the fear abated and my interest grew in who this person actually was. A sense of detached curiosity now took over. I found that as I persisted in staying with the image, my fear and revulsion lessened and, as that happened, the demand that I look at it diminished. This led to an abatement of my avoidance behavior, which eventually was followed by the caricatured self-representation fading from consciousness. In other words, the less I fought it, the less insistent it became. As it finally disappeared, I thought that I had been released and at last was done with the whole business—not for long, however.

After this first image finally vanished, it quickly was replaced by another—Peter, "the world traveler." Yet again I was confronted by the same feelings of discomfort and an impulse to reject, but this time I decided not to resist from the start, so instead of struggling against it, I continued the process of inner observation I had started with the first appearance. If not very pleasant, it was at least edifying in that it seemed to be a view of myself through a mirror not usually available to me.

During this process I made an important discovery—the negative power of these self-representations seemed to be directly proportional to the harshness of my judgment of them. The more I suspended the judgmental process and became an impartial observer, the more I could see and accept them with the subsequent diminishment of their power to offend. Again, as in the first instance, the new image eventually faded but soon was replaced by yet another—Peter, "the lover." This "self" representation was more fraught with difficulty for me, and I found myself back in the previous, nervous struggle as I harshly judged what I "saw." However, as I gradually relinquished my stance as judge and reentered my newly discovered attitude of impartial witness, the voice spoke again. It asked, "Who is doing all this judging?" My mind raced as I attempted to find the "person" who had been evaluating all these personae.

I can only describe my next response in metaphorical terms. In an attempt to discover the "knower" who was observing the scenes I had been witnessing, it was as if I somehow rotated my eyes 180 degrees around to look inward to the "place" "he" was felt to reside inside of my head. However, this total redeployment of my attention inward had an immediate and dramatic effect of its own. First, the room disappeared from my view;

next, I heard a very loud rushing sound like a waterfall that was accompanied by intense waves, somewhat like convulsing shivers, that ascended repeatedly upward through my body. It was like being cold, but yet I was not chilled.

Second, as the experience rapidly increased in intensity it culminated with the sound roaring in my ears and the discovery that I was now apparently standing in a great cathedral-like marble hall—much like a Byzantine mosque or church but without any evident religious symbolism or icons observable. Many years later I found a painting by Salvador Dali (in one of those very large coffee table collections of his work), which contained a reproduction that has many key aspects of the scene in which I found myself at that moment. When I say found myself, I mean that there was some kind of discontinuity in my awareness such that one moment I was sitting on a makeshift couch in a semiderelict apartment and the next I was in a great stone hall without having instigated any physical change of which I was aware. The experience was fully veridical in the sense that, to my awareness at the time, it had all the apparent properties of my actually being physically in that place. It certainly was nothing like any locale I had ever been or seen previously, which added to its strangeness and the overpowering awe I was experiencing.

As I stood staring in amazement at this utterly strange and impossible scene around me, I noticed that the ceiling above me was comprised of a enormous translucent glass dome with a large hole at its apex through which a luminous blue-white light was streaming. The light was almost like a spotlight, which shone down on me where I stood. There I stood, bathed in this supernal luminosity, mystified, dumbstruck. Looking down, I was shocked to discover that I was fastened to the floor in my upright position by a series of leather straps circumscribing where I stood—like spokes—that were connected to a heavy leather belt around my waist by brass fittings at one end and to the floor by similar brass hooks at the other end. As I looked at my bonds they had a "presence" that seemed to "speak" to me as a symbol in a painting might convey meaning beyond form.

In this state of knowing I understood that these straps were the images or "ego-trips" that I had been inspecting in the theater of my mind only minutes before. At the very moment that I understood their symbolic import, the straps spontaneously unhooked from my belt one after another in rapid succession—the action circumscribing my waist like a wave of activity. As I watched them unhook I had another thought: "It's me who always holds me down by living in my false selves." Now, no longer fastened to the floor, as it were, I seemed to become weightless and I began to float upward. My ascent was rapid and I was soon passing through the hole at the top of the dome and into the supernal light.

As I advanced through the opening in the dome, the sound of rushing water, which had continued throughout the episode, abruptly stopped and, "looking" down (more as an act of attention than physical movement), I discovered that my body also had vanished. All that remained of "me" was an undifferentiated awareness and a total conscious absorption of that awareness into the light that seemed to bath me in total peace. I felt free—freer and lighter of being than I had ever felt in my life before or could have ever imagined feeling. My overall state was one of total and unqualified bliss and peace. There was no longer a "me," but somehow total awareness was still there, but it was not really clear exactly who was having this awareness. I was conscious but did not exist in the usual sense that I had always understood as being in the world. I and everything were one.

I do not know how long I remained in this state—it might only have been minutes, but it could have been hours. There was no reference point for time, so, effectively, it did not exist. However long I remained in that blissful light does not matter. Having arrived there and being there was all that mattered, but that was not a thought at the time. Later, when first attempting a *post hoc* interpretation of this episode, I came to identify my experience as a direct merger with the void—the "ultimate ground of being." No matter how one interprets this encounter of my merger into the light, what remains with me to this day is a wordless and core knowing of who I am beyond role or form—a transcendent *sense* of "identity."

There were no thoughts while there, so it came as a shock when the voice abruptly returned and asked, "What are you going to hold onto now?" The impact of hearing this question intruding into my bliss caused me to become abruptly self-conscious. With that question came the thought that, indeed, I had given up everything I usually held onto and suddenly I felt very vulnerable—like a cripple without his crutches—and I started to feel that I might go into a free-fall or possibly even die if I did not grab hold of something solid and stable immediately. In retrospect, it was at that moment that I existentially understood Otto's (1958) "creature feeling" when confronted with the *Mysterium Tremendum*. At the core of my fear was an intense dread of not being able to return to my life as I had known it. This entire thought process generated a powerful anxiety, and with the emergence of all this emotional agitation the sound of rushing water returned with an increasing intensity that was rapidly followed by a feeling that I was plunging physically downward and out of the light. I was like Icarus falling away from the sun. The descent was short, very intense, and felt like free-falling in space accompanied by a "whooshing" sound that grew in volume with the accelerating speed of my fall and ended with a very loud, jarring but muffled thud as I reentered my previous reality frame. Once again, I found myself sitting on the couch in my friend's Christianhavn apartment.

The sound of rushing water was still quite loud and the waves of convulsive-like shivers continued as before my "exit" from the couch. I felt confused and torn. I desperately wanted to go back to that blissful place/state, but the requirement to let go of everything and feel like I was in a free-fall with nothing to hold onto for safety kept me back. I sat and struggled between the two impulses for over an hour and gradually the sound subsided, and I knew that the window of opportunity for reentry had past. I tried to speak to an American friend who had come there with me that night, but for once in my life words failed me.

Spiritual Emergence?

At the time I had no way of clearly labeling what had happened to me. All I knew at that moment was intense awe, ecstasy, fear, and excitement as I made an entry into a vastly different experiential world. Immediately after this encounter I found myself trying to label, categorize, and explain the experience, but without any success. Many months were spent engaging this process that included intensively reading, researching, and talking to people who seemed to be "in the know." However, this left me no wiser or conceptually better off. Of my first twenty-eight years on earth this had certainly been the most intense, all-encompassing experience I had ever had. My understanding, or what I thought I understood at the time, of myself and the world around me had been radically altered in a matter of minutes. I would spend the next five years obsessed with my attempts to understand how and why this happened to me while at the same time employing various techniques I believed would help me to find my way back to that dazzling state of blissful knowing.[4]

During this period I read a great deal about apparently similar experiences of others, but all these reported encounters came with an attached worldview. These explanations and justifications of why some of us have these encounters, and others not, all seemed to rest on arbitrary moral judgments and a supposedly externally bestowed grace. Having already rejected Western religious traditions, I turned to practitioners of Eastern disciplines who offered explanations ranging from their guru's "mystic power" having been focused on Copenhagen at that moment to, simply, it was my Karma.[5] In the conceptual hands of these Hindu/Buddhist-flavored Westerners, Karma meant nemesis and gurus were quasi-supernatural beings who made or broke you in the spiritual marketplace. In my current understanding much of this kind of westernized Eastern thought can be traced back to two primary sources—the teachings and practices of Blavatsky, Besant, Leadbeater as part of the Theosophical movement in the second half of the nineteenth century[6] and to Vivakananda's introduction of Hindu thought and practices into the West at the beginning of the twentieth century (Bharati, 1976; Gupta, 1973).[7]

Having been well indoctrinated in the empiricist/reductionist philosophical perspective of the West, I felt ill at ease with most of the wide variety of religious and spiritualist theories that were offered by way of explanation for my encounter. Most of these explanations seemed to be justifications for a closely held faith now collectively referred to as New Age thought. For example, a typical explanation of the good or bad events of our lives is that we are being carried along by a "spiritual evolution," which is taking all of us eventually to Cosmic Consciousness. Although I instinctually felt and believed that I had experienced the bottom line of what was real, I made the decision to put the experience on the shelf for awhile, as it were, thus delaying any final epistemological interpretations or ontological ascriptions until such a time that I could piece together the puzzle of what had happened to me and what, if anything, it meant.

From the start of this new chapter in my life I began to understand James (1936) listing ineffability as a primary characteristic of mystical experience. However, from my own encounter I felt that it was not so much that one could not express what had happened, but that the use of language, when trying to describe the experience, so often led to self-contradiction or involved a signifier pointing at the signified that was not available to the knowing we usually depend on (transsubjectivity) hence, it is nonconsensual. Also, there was no way to convey the true quality and impact of affect, atmosphere, and cognition I experienced through mere phenomenological descriptions of mental content and emotional state. I was often left groping for words while the eyes of my listener signaled noncomprehension.

This confusion led to endless frustration for me with each attempt at communication with my fellow, but uninitiated, beings. Although I knew that my rational description was well understood, I was aware that it was not conveying the quintessential quality that marked the mystical state as phenomenologically unique.[8] There seems to be a quality to the reality of these experiences that is *sui generis* and to which we cannot find any clearly related linguistic sign. Instead, we are left with an indirect and metaphorical use of words because our language does not deal well with concepts and experiences that are not spatial-metaphoric and objective-like (Carroll, 1956). At the time, for me, it was like the qualitative difference between the experiential reality of dreams as opposed to waking states, where entering the mystical state appears to be like waking from a dream and it is difficult, if not impossible, to relate the difference to any person who has not yet "awakened."

I now believe that, mistakenly, this initiation is often taken by those "in the know" as indicating a profound spiritual emergence because of the way it upsets the ontological applecart. But in time I came to realize that the mystical state does not necessarily imply greater spiritual attainment or know-how for experients, but more accurately underscores the difference between existential and conceptual knowledge. I now believe that these experiences are more about the reality perceived and known in various states of consciousness and the making and remaking of experiential reality frames with their particular styles of knowing. I eventually came to conclude that spirituality seems to be more a style of how one is in the world rather than the result of a massive shift in consciousness. Certainly the shift may be the beginning of the spiritual emergence, but great self-discipline and ethical remaking are required over some considerable time. As Bharati (1976) has asserted, one who was a "stinker" before having a mystical experience will remain so unless a great deal of moral effort and ethical transformation occur.

So, if mystical experience is not an automatic spiritualizing of the experient what is it? I believe that question only can be answered if we radically revise our notions of awareness, consciousness, and reality and understand mystical encounters as the remaking of one's epistemic frame of reference and, hence, style of knowing.

Reality and Existence

Science, and our derivative commonsensical understanding of the universe, with their absolute Democritian ontologies are, in the words of the philosopher C. D. Broad (1914), "naively real." However, if science is naively real in its epistemological processes, then religio-mystical systems such as Buddhism and Vedantism are naively phenomenological—particularly in the conceptual hands of most Westerners.

What we must recognize is that we are human beings living in a uniquely human existence and awareness—a human epistemic frame. This may seem to be a trivial assertion, but I believe that it is the key to understanding the difficulty we get into when attempting to unpack the world of mystical and hence spiritual knowing. Spiritual knowing attempts to address ultimacy not only in values and meaning, but in terms of the very ontological ground from which everything springs. We must ask the question: "What is ultimately real?" but simultaneously remain cautious in order to avoid naive assumptions about the existence or not of things(or essences)-in-themselves.

Ninian Smart (1973), one of the founders of modern religious studies, clearly makes this distinction when discussing the objects of belief of the religious mind. He states that nonexistent objects can be phenomenologically indistinguishable from existent ones.

I shall distinguish between objects which are real and objects which exist. In this usage, God is real for Christians whether or not he exists. The methodological agnosticism here being used is, then, agnosticism about the existence or otherwise of the main foci of the belief system in question. It is worth noting a complication. I am not denying that existent things can be treated as unreal, just as real things can be non-existent. (p. 54)

He is suggesting that the "reading" of the "real" for any given sociocultural group is in fact the direct "writing" of a consensually experiential "text" (or world) whose meaning derives from the acceptance of the cultural projection as an absolutely existent entity. As Taylor (1983), expounding on Deconstructionism, argues the reading of the text is the writing of the text. In a sense the construal of the world is a constant interactive process in which the map and the territory are interactively involved in an act of mutual cross-creation. True, the map is not the territory—but the map and the territory are inextricably bound to each other in an act of continual and mutual becoming.

Semiotics, or the study of "signs" suggests that the signs of our world continually add up and *point*—as powerful and compelling inference generators—to Reality. Umberto Eco (1984), a semiotician, brings this idea out with power and clarity when the protagonist of his novel, *The Name of the Rose*, attempts to solve a mystery without remembering the power of the relationship of signs. Here, the protagonist, William of Baskerville, confides in his assistant, Adso of Melk, at the end of their long investigation into a series of deaths at a monastery.

I have never doubted the truth of signs, Adso; they are the only things man has with which to orient himself in the world. What I did not understand was the relation among signs. I arrived at Jorge [as the perpetrator] through an apocalyptic pattern that seemed to underlie all the crimes, and yet it was accidental. I arrived at Jorge seeking one criminal for all the crimes and we discovered that each crime was committed by a different person, or by no one. I arrived at Jorge pursuing the plan of a perverse and rational mind, and there was no plan, or, rather, Jorge himself was overcome by his own initial design and there began a sequence of causes, and concauses, and of causes contradicting one another, which proceeded on their own, creating relations that did not stem from any plan. Where is all my wisdom, then? I behaved stubbornly, pursuing a semblance of order, when I should have known well that there is no order in the universe. (p. 492)

The deconstructive act is thus the separation of signs from one another and their context, which allows for a reconstruction into a new or revised reality—an endless process which Sartre (1972) has labeled sorcery.

> We are thus surrounded by magical objects which retain, as it were, a memory of the spontaneity of consciousness, yet continue to be objects of the world. This is why man is always a sorcerer for man. Indeed, this poetic connection of two passivities in which one creates the other spontaneously is the very foundation of sorcery, the profound meaning of "participation." This is why we are sorcerers for ourselves each time we view our me. (p. 82)

What I am suggesting is, that for mystics and scientists alike, reality is experiential—the difference between their conceptions appears to arise more as the result of the assignment of ontological value than through the existence of absolute differences. It should be noted that within both the scientific and mystical worldviews there is no clear-cut agreement as to how ontological status should be assigned. In general, however, the scientific position is that the ultimate ground is an objective, existent material reality with an ontological status separate from that of the observer, and for the mystic it is an inner, revealed truth or ontological principle grounded in a transcendental entity and/or consciousness. In the case of the former, consciousness is merely the place where the real world is reflected in order to be known by the observer, but for the latter it is often taken as the ground of being or ultimate reality itself.

Radical Consciousness

Perhaps James's (1936, 1967) most important contribution to this discussion of mystical experience is not his very general definition of the mystical state, but rather his later attempt to move us away from object or subject as ontological ground and into a radical empiricism. In his final published thinking on consciousness before his death, James explicitly denied the existence or thingness of consciousness as container or place but not its reality as a functional property intrinsically connected to our here-now experience. This notion of consciousness can be understood as being like the "backward cast shadow" as posited by Sartre (1972) in his critique of the transcendental "I" in Husserl's (1962) phenomenology.

This "shadow" we call consciousness, which stalks our every waking moment, is a collective emergent property arising from our awareness of the contiguity of previous present moments as they become the ever-receding past while yet remaining connected to the immediate "now" through our present awareness. Thus, the experience of the immediate present, together with the knowledge of the chain of past presents, implies for most of us the existence of an ongoing experiential entity or being we identify as the "place" or "container" we usually identify as consciousness. In contrast, in his functional approach to this chain of awarenesses James wishes us to take "pure experience" as the singular *operational* "stuff" of which the human world is made. From this stance he argues for a radical empiricism that places subjective events on an equal ontological footing with objective ones, which, in his system, appear to vary more in degree than in any absolute kind from each other.

Here is how James (1967) describes this primal "stuff"—the human universe.

> My thesis is that if we start with the supposition that there is only one primal stuff or material in the world, a stuff of which everything is composed, and if we call that stuff "pure experience," then knowing can easily be explained as a particular sort of relation towards one another into which portions of pure experience may enter. (p. 4)

James accounts for the apparent dichotomy that we all intuitively sense between inner and outer, subject and object, as being the result of the relationship between these qualities becoming part of this pure experience in which one of its "terms" becomes the subject or knower, and the other the object or the known. He describes the paradox of how, in his system, an experiential event can be both internal and external by reference to an analogy of two lines sharing the same point at an intersection. It is the intersection of two processes of pure experience that have two different sets of associations and can be counted as belonging to different groups—the inner or the outer. One such group is the context of our inner biography and the other is the context of an experience we take to be the outer perceptual world. James adds that the central feature of the experiential reference in the creation of the "me" of our biographies is the ongoing experience of our own breathing. This apparent duality of contexts, biography and perceptual world, gives the impression of both subjective and objective worlds simultaneously and separately existing but operating interactively in parallel.

However strange his mechanism for explaining the creation of the subject-object dichotomy might appear on first inspection, by placing James's (1967) "pure experience" at center stage, ontologically speaking, he is, in effect, hinting at a functionally useful way of conceptualizing human reality. Starting with James's "pure experience" we can imagine reality as being operationally defined by the type and style of the attentional and awareness processes used in the act of knowing. Thus, scientific observation and method, which is a cognitive and behavioral approach employing a particular set of experiential operations, is the *style* of scientific knowing that generates scientific knowledge. Likewise, religio-mystical practices (experiences) are styles of knowing that lead to spiritual knowledge.

Thus, without having to make any decisions concerning ontological primacy or requiring a demarcation between knower and known, James's approach suggests that the disjunctions across subject and object as well as different frames of knowing are a product of the operations of awareness and not perceptions of some thing-in-itself. In other words, James's radical empiricism is ontologically neutral—in that it does not require us to decide what ultimately *exists* (as understood in Smart, 1973) outside of our awareness. Also, it is nonepistemic in that epistemology arises only when there are two distinct ontologic categories—subject and object or knower and known. At its core it is simply the knowing occurring before "maps" are constructed. In this book Kaisa Puhakka's notion of the experiential contact before the thought or object is grasped comes closest to what is being suggested here and the grasping she refers to is the "particular sort of relation towards one another into which portions of pure experience may enter" (James, 1967, p. 4).

How can this be the case in any realistic sense you might ask? If we accept the objective world as a given Kantian thing-in-itself, then crossing the boundary of the inner person to reach the object in order to create an inner knowing is impossible. Between the two lies an infinite epistemic chasm separating two completely different ontic categories. However, if, as James suggests, we look to the "stuff" of the world as being pure experience, then we can imagine a field of experience in which knowing across the borders of what are only objectified inferences is not at all illogical or impossible.

In effect, this solves the problem posed by Jorge Ferrer in this volume. He suggests that we must move away from defining transpersonal events as experiences but, instead, frame them as the imposition of "multilocal participatory events"—given as knowledge—into the experiential worlds of individuals. He, like Sartre, seems to want to place our engagement with "the real" on the side of the object in the epistemological equation. What is being suggested here, in contrast, is that we do away with the equation entirely by recognizing that no objective event, no knowledge supposedly borne of such an event—hence no knower and nothing known—can be understood to have ontological or symbolic status apart from the experience through which it is reflexively given to awareness (see Nelson, 1997–98).[9]

Ontic Shift

Much of what is being suggested about the malleable quality of the real (again, in the sense indicated by Smart, 1973) has been reflected partially in the social constructionist movement in psychology and sociology. Gergen (1985), a leading exponent of this view, summarizes the position.

> Social constructionism . . . begins with radical doubt in the taken-for-granted world—whether in the sciences or daily life—and in a specialized way acts as a form of social criticism. Constructionism asks one to suspend belief that commonly accepted categories or understandings receive their warrant through observation. Thus, it invites one to challenge the objective basis of conventional knowledge. (p. 267)

This leads to a notion that

> the terms in which the world is understood are social artifacts, products of historically situated interchanges among people. From the constructionist position the process of understanding is not automatically driven by the forces of nature, but is the result of an active, cooperative enterprise of persons in relationship. In this light, inquiry is invited into the historical and cultural bases of various forms of world construction. (p. 267)

Of course, the "person" and his/her subjective world at the knowing center of this picture is no more absolute than any other construction of any final description regarding what actually exists.

According to Berger and Luckmann (1971), the experiential world of everyday life is taken for granted as being *the* reality (the natural attitude), and it is a world that originates in thought and action and that is maintained by these same processes. It is more likely that we live in a world of multiple realities not unlike what has been suggested by the physicist Wheeler when he posited the notion of multiple universes as a way of understanding the diversity of outcomes that can arise from a single set of causes in the quantum world (Davies, 1990). From this we might conclude that the world is constituted from multiple realities and as one moves from one reality to another one experiences a kind of "shock." Berger and Luckmann attribute this shock to the shift in attentiveness caused by the transition across a kind of consciousness boundary—an example being awakening from a dream. In a sense, when knowing hits a pothole in the existential road, it experiences a jolt in the vehicle of consciousness.

They argue, that of the multiple realities possible, the one that presents itself most convincingly is the reality of everyday life. It is impossible to ignore, it imposes itself with the greatest force, thereby dominating consciousness to the greatest degree. Although human experiential reality tends toward the everyday stratum, it is most often induced into transition by aesthetic and religious experience. For Berger and Luckmann (1971) "leaping" to new provinces of meaning is a metaphor for entering the sacred domain and that all these nonordinary "finite provinces of meaning" (p. 39) are characterized by a turning away of attention from the reality of everyday life.

While there are, of course, shifts of attention *within* the frame of everyday life, the shift to a new finite province of meaning is of a much more radical kind. A fundamental change takes place in the tension of conscious awareness. However, it is important to stress that the reality of everyday life retains its paramount status even as such leaps take place. If nothing else, we return to the interaction and discourse of the everyday and in this frame of reference language keeps the everyday process on track. Although the reality of everyday life may remain paramount, this does not necessarily give it a sense of ultimacy. It is, rather, our writing of the *life text* in a repetitive and continuous way that declares the events of normal, everyday consciousness to be paramount. It is, in effect, an existential (living) *operational definition of reality.*

It thus seems to me, looking at the issue as both mystical experient and scholar, that the conviction held by mystics, vis-à-vis the ultimateness of mystical reality, is due primarily to the complete suddenness, newness, and the radical experiential differences engendered in a "leap" across a worldview boundary—especially when the new (mystical) state appears to subsume the old. It is here that the old now emerges as a mere fragment of the new, larger experiential domain arising from the reshuffling of signs. Thus, this entire process of deconstruction and reconstruction engendered in the mystical encounter would be experienced as a sense of *ontic shift*, which is unconsciously molded and then, in retrospect, consciously given a revised ontological ascription with both processes still being linguistically and culturally contextualized.[10]

This leap into the sacred can be thought of as a quantum-like event. In fact it also may be that the leap itself is a retrospective inference arising as a linguistic filler that is used to conceptualize the "empty" moment during the shift from one experiential world to another. The quantum-like cloud of uncertainty, vis-à-vis knowledge, is "collapsed" into a determined knowing by linguistic filtering and categorical assignment through the act of observation (perception) in a manner similar to that proposed in some interpretations of quantum physics.[11]

Ultimately, I do not differentiate between mystical and other kinds of knowing other than that they are different apparent epistemic frames that tend to highlight different aspects or perspectives of reality as well as providing a different view of the relationship of signs one to the other. The mystical epistemic frame carries with it an inclusiveness regarding the self-other dichotomy whereas our ordinary frame gives rise to a knowing in which self and other are exclusive. The subsumption of "self" into "other" in the mystical form of knowing is certainly a release from a sense of separateness and alienation and thus tends to add to our feeling of having arrived at the "bottom line" as a result of a mystical encounter.

Ordinary experiential reality is not experienced as a leap or as coming with a shock because it is the base "text" or operational definition of reality in which we normally live—our awareness process tends toward that frame. However, for the mystic, the return to the "normal" state after leaving it is also experienced as a shock, and it is the result of this exit and reentry that impels the mystical experient to engage in a subsequent ontological realignment. Thus, it would appear that religious experience is, in some sense, ordinary experience (text), but one in which the shock of transition is great enough to cause a linguistic-ontological reconceptualizing and reordering. Hence, in James's (1967) view, the experiential connectivities are being reordered such that the meaning and linkages of the chaining of "percepts" and "concepts" are redefined—giving rise to a new sense of what is real.

In the operational notion of mystical experience being posited here, reality is conscious experience, which is the "doing" involved with knowing, which then is taken in a retrospective sense to be an overarching structure we label consciousness, which in turn appears to be reality itself (Nelson, 1997–98). I further would argue that the ontological certainty generated in these shifts to mystical consciousness happens only when there is a total subsumption of our usual experiential "self" into the experiential operations that define the new reality. Or, to put it another way, the reading of the "text" of the mystical reality becomes the rewriting of epistemological "text" of self and everyday life in the sense that James's intersecting lines of object and subject appear to become one in conscious awareness.

As I have suggested, in the mystical frame of reference conscious experience often appears to be reality itself. So, experience known across states—such that the experiential world of one state seems ephemeral or less impactfully real when compared to that of another state—will not be taken as having ontological status and therefore not be considered as ultimately real. However, when an experiential state engenders a sense of absolute onticity, because it is able to subsume self and world at its onset with a sudden, all-pervasiveness, it then will be regarded as the position representing ontological bedrock, or ultimate reality. Thus, this state will be taken as the pointer to the absolute ground and everything that is known through it will automatically be taken as arising from that ontological bottom line. We can now revision mystical knowing as being that way of experientially engaging the existential horizon such that self and not-self, perceptions and constructs appear as unified in a new window on reality as given through a revised epistemic frame that is clearly differentiated (experientially) from the frame of daily life. One cannot know otherness without simultaneously knowing one's self and vice versa. There is no subject and no object, but only aware knowingness, which is given as a flashing of awareness into the vast phenomenal void. But is this the totality of spiritual knowing? I will return to this issue later on.

In my own research into mystical and paranormal experiences I have been able to map a general "technology" of the preternatural, which accounts for both the attentional resource issues raised by James (1967) as well as social constructionist notions as they participate in the maintaining or reframing of ontology (Nelson, 1990). In my investigations I found that state of consciousness and hence one's epistemic frame are defined by the "set" and "setting" of the experiential process—including sociocultural context, place, personality style, content of experience at the outset and deployment of attentional resources immediately prior to the shift. The redeployment of attention is an energetic shift in which the hold of perceptual top-down systems is relinquished allowing for a moment of "free" running before a new perceptual "molding" is constituted. As understood here, one's attentional resources are the "direction" of focus and the quality of the "filter" that allows a "picture" to be generated and thus brought into the realm of knowledge.

It also was revealed in a later study that, phenomenologically, many mystical experiences are quite similar to paranormal ones (Nelson, 1991–92). The crucial differences that lead to different interpretations for experients are to be found in personality style, culture, and whether the leap of the transition is intense enough to engender a sense of ontic shift. The most important personality attribute associated with those who can make these state shifts appears to be Trait Absorption (Tellegen & Atkinson, 1974). In addition, some of my recent preliminary experimental work indicates that an individual's ability to consciously redeploy attentional resources in unique ways represents the key operational basis for these state shifts. Thus, an unusual redeployment of attention taken in the context of an absorptive personality sets the stage, so to speak, for the restructuring of frames of meaning and possibly the entire ontological horizon as well.

While in this altered attentional state, it is also possible to actively deconstruct meaning structures that are taken as "givens" in our more usual states. As it happens there already are a number of traditional self-dialectic techniques for accomplishing this sort of shift that come to us from the East. These are practices such as "neti, neti," as advocated by Sri Ramana Maharshi in a yogic tradition of southern India, and the method described in *The Wheel of Analytic Meditation* from the Tibetan Vajrayana Buddhist tradition (Maharshi, 1982; Mi-Pham, 1970). Next, I have reproduced a few illustrative examples taken from a modern translation of the latter nineteenth-century Tibetan text by Lama Mi-Pham where this process can be seen in action quite clearly.

It should be remembered, however, that when reading these excerpts, it most likely will not automatically engender the kind of shift I have been describing. What is required is the personality "set" and the functional "setting" as described previously. However, done against the necessary operational background (such as intensive meditation practice) the dialectical process can produce the epistemic deconstruction and ontic shift I have been outlining.

The text, like most of Buddhist writing, starts with a description of the nature of suffering, which is believed to arise from the transient quality of reality. In effect, it defines the meaning frame from which the deconstruction will take place by stating the cause of the problem as well as its possible solution.

> The cause of confusion and frustration in life
> Is the virulent passion of the mind.
> Distortion and dispersion, the causes of passion,
> Must be replaced by incisive attentiveness.
>
> (Mi-Pham, 1970, p. 43)

This is followed by an explanatory commentary.

> The cause of our frustrations, failings, misfortunes and anxieties is not external. It is to be found within. The confusion of emotional conflict dependent upon distorting vagaries of the mind is the primary obstacle to an understanding of Samsara as Nirvana. Discipline of the mind, concentrating it upon each moment of perception, leads to insight into its nature and its function. Thus, emotional confusion is eliminated. (p. 55)

Notice the emphasis on the "moment of perception" in the previous segment. This should be understood as the moment of knowing. The text now describes the first dialectical procedure to be followed.

> Imagining an image before one
> of whatever is desired most
> And distinguishing the five groupings of elements
> Begin to analyze the imaginary body.
> Flesh, blood, bones, marrow, fat and limbs,
> Sense organs, internal organs and cavities,
> Faeces, urine, worms, hair and nails—
> Distinguish the foul parts of the body.

Categorize and classify these parts
By composition and sensory field.
Then divide and analyze them
To irreducible particles.
Looking for arising desire for any part,
See this "body" as nothing but foul fragments.
Remember it as a dirty machine or frothing scum,
Or a heap of sticks, stones and pus.

(p. 43)

These directions are further explained in a commentary.

The search for the nature of reality begins with the visualization of
the most fascinating object of sexual desire. Men should take a
woman as the object of meditation, women should take a man, and
homosexuals one of their own gender. . . . The mental object is
fixed by the faculty of mind which tends to lock into a perceptual
situation while the discursive faculty of mind thoroughly examines
it. The search is for both the external base of desire for the sex object and for something substantial or self-existent in the world of
created things, the elements of which are collected together under
one of the groups of body-mind constituents. (pp. 58–59)

Thus, the dialectic between the concept of the body as usually held in
awareness and the body reconceived into unappealing reductions leads, in
the context of the meditative redeployment of attention, to a reframing of
meaning both cognitively and affectively.

The other variant of this analytic technique just mentioned is part of
the Hindu tradition and is best illustrated by the teachings of Ramana Maharshi (1982) in his now classic text, *Who Am I?* The phrase, "neti, neti," at
the heart of this method simply means "not this, not this." In this technique
any aspect of our world of objects is examined and the surface appearance
is denied as being the "real." Continuing to dissect inward we will eventually
find that nothing remains and that nothingness, too, is finally dissected
away in an attempt to deconstruct the very ontological core of our perceived reality. Of course, this dialectical investigation also takes place in the
context of a developed meditative practice, which is the "setting" requirement for a redeployed attention.

A Postmodern Interpretation

When the deconstructive process, as conceived earlier here, is fully engaged
over a period of time, eventually there is an epistemic reframing that then,

as in the mystical experience, may be followed by a revision of ontological ascription. Umberto Eco's (1984) character, William of Baskerville, reflects on the process of knowledge building.

> The order that our mind imagines is like a net, or like a ladder, built to attain something. But afterward you must throw the ladder away, because you discover that, even if it was useful, it was meaningless. (p. 492)

However, what William does not tell us is that there is an immediate rebuilding of a new net and/or ladder, whether consciously or unconsciously accomplished. In fact, the late philosopher of science, Sir Karl Popper (1982), describes scientific theories as being like nets as well. In our construction of the empirical picture of the world through science, we are actually only "catching" what the shape and character of our nets will allow. However, whether the deconstruction of the net is accomplished through the use of the scientific analytic method or through spiritual practices, there remains the belief for most that there is a final position or net that is capable of at least catching a glimpse of bottom-line existence.

What I am suggesting is that the very belief in the ultimately real, however engendered, is also subject to possible deconstruction and, through the continual application of that process, we have the possibility of eventually arriving at the realization that there may be no final bottom line. In fact, that realization itself is not merely a new bottom line that there are no bottom lines, but is an entry into a profound unknowing that must be lived as an abiding existential ontological uncertainty—and this, in the sense of spiritual knowing, is what is meant by ontological neutralism. Thus, one arrives at a postmodern revisioning in which one becomes conscious that every choice of word or each deed is an epistemic positioning implying an ontology, but at the same instant we know that this "truth" or "reality" is in some sense temporary. Every position is a reconstruction and we only stop when the new epistemic frame is successful in deafening us to the next knock at the door of our unknowing, which is asking us, yet again, to wake up and know anew.

McCance (1986), in his review of physics, Buddhism, and postmodern thought, asserts that the crisis of understanding for the twentieth century has been precipitated by the collapse of naive realism—or our belief that we can have our ontological cake and eat it, too.

> In the decentering of the Cartesian subject, then, we confront the de-realizing not only of the reified objects of mechanistic science but also of their counterparts, the abstract entities of atomistic individualism. The "I," who created the illusion of objectivity "out there" simultaneously with the creation of itself, is now in crisis. (p. 289)

McCance asserts that the way out of the dilemma today is the same as that suggested by the Buddha in his time—to shatter the illusions of independent objects and the detached neutrality of the observer. But, of course, that includes the illusion of the illusion of objects and observers. And this will cause us to eternally reenter the crisis of unknowing with its panicked inner call to remake meaning. McCance's solution is that we embrace the whole and he concludes by insisting that scholars (and I would argue everyone else as well) must pay closer attention to the "wholism" of the recent interpretations of postmodern physics as argued by a number of physicists such as David Bohm (1980). The attention we pay is not one of epistemic reframing, but rather a recognition of the interdependence of self and other, true and false, and so on. In other words, to keep our attention on the moment of knowing before it is solidified into knowledge. This is the moment of unfettered knowing as described by Puhakka and the source of inspiration as suggested by Hart in this volume.

This is also the view of reality that was so eloquetly expressed in the words of one of Christendom's greatest mystics, Meister Eckhart (Blakney, 1957): "The eye with which I see God is the same eye with which God sees me . . . one vision or seeing, and one knowing and loving" (p. 288).

This affirmation of spiritual connectedness does not condemn us to a reductive ontological ground and thus allows us to frame the position of the knower on either side of the subject/object or human/divine divide. We only make a bifurcation and take a side because to embrace the whole without a clear definition of where we stand within it can appear to make dealing in the realm of the day-to-day seemingly impossible. However, I would argue that the rejection of this wholism—the totality of experience, knowledge, and reality—as well as the plurality this whole implies, simplifies decision making for most of us in our day-to-day frame, but at a considerable cost to the quality of our spiritual lives.

This kind of postmodernist deconstruction of our absolutes suggests a need for a reinterpretation of the polarity of the sacred and the profane as well. Traditional scholars of religion, such as Mircea Eliade (1959), argue that the sacred and profane are two distinct modes of being in the world or "two existential situations assumed by man in the course of his history" (p. 15). They are in the final analysis, modes of being dependent on "the different positions that man has conquered in the cosmos" (p. 15). Eliade asks us to look back to some halcyon time when a person of a traditional society was the true, uncorrupted *homo religiousus* who occupied a "sacred space" characterized by a hierophany that ontologically founds the world, "an absolute fixed point, a center" (p. 21) existing in the homogeneity and infinite expanse of the totality of "profane space." According to Eliade, life's moment-to-moment experience, by being centered in this hierophany, is made sacred.

If the world is to be lived in, it must be founded—and no world can come to birth in the chaos of the homogeneity and relativity of profane space. The discovery or projection of a fixed point—the center—is equivalent to the creation of the world. (p. 22)

I believe that Eliade's description of the connection to the sacred is correct as far as it goes. It is an operational description of how we make the relationship between the sacred and profane, but he seems unaware that it is the *creation* of the sacred and profane as well. It is being argued here that the sacred appears to arise as a result of existentially "writing" the ultimate fixed point from which all meaning is suspended. For Eco (1989), that fixed point is death, as symbolized by the creation of a new point of suspension for Foucault's Pendulum, which is created by his character Belbo when he is executed by being hung in the pendulum's wire.

Eliade is suggesting that the sacred, and hence the experience of the world from a spiritual epistemic, arises as an act of creation or, in the terms of my thesis, as an intentional "reading" and/or "writing" of the life "text." In this context the enactment of religious ritual and initiation appears to be an attempt to create sacred time and space and hence to sanctify experiential reality through a participation that takes us through the ontological looking glass. Eliade claims that this is not merely a reenacting of the sacred time, but it is a reconnecting to the sacred time and hence the foundations of reality itself. The ritual not only defines the occurrence of this rebirth, but its style and quality as well. It is, in essence, the "writing" of the "text" of reality through enactment.

However, from a postmodern perspective it appears that we are not so much contacting an absolute sacred center as we are sensing and coming to know an ontic otherness through our rewriting of the possible and hence the real in ways that radically separate us from the epistemology of everyday life. The fixed center is not so much found as it is made and re-made. This is also evidenced in a historical context. What constitutes a sacred act and/or experience in some past time can, and often does, become today's ordinary and hence profane activity. This process, of course, also works in reverse. The text and signs of the sacred and profane are, therefore, continually in transition as they are read, written, reread, rewritten, read, and written yet again.[12]

Further, I would assert that our fragmented state, the profane life, leads to a relationship to the world in which we deny the sacred, even when it irrupts into awareness, because it does not fit the pictures given by the Newtonian and Judeo-Christian worlds that most of us inhabit. What I am suggesting is that our way of knowing prevents us from recognizing that we are taking every "text," or life scenario, and unconsciously giving them all the same rewrite—thus always finding the sacred and profane to be what we expect.

There are, of course, dangers inherent in this deconstructive/reconstructive process. In a culture such as ours, which does not have any clearly defined roadmaps or guides for this process, there is the possibility that the deconstuctive process will spin out of control into an infinite regress of self unmaking, fear, panic, and further unmaking. It has been an observation of mine that a significant percentage of those who have been diagnosed as paranoid schizophrenics are, in fact, *failed mystics*. They have entered the tunnel of transition and never fully reemerged in a stable epistemic frame. They are permanently in the transitional phase of multiple "readings" and "writings" against which they fight a losing struggle to return to the predeconstructed state. They want to forget, but every attempt at doing so reengages the deconstructive process leaving them as blissless ghost mystics.

Of course, there are ways to fail the mystical encounter without becoming a paranoid schizophrenic. An equally serious but nonpsychotic negative outcome is a narcissistic collapse. In this case the special knowing of the mystical encounter's deconstruction is successfully exited, but the reconstruction is grandiose—"I am now a perfected being. I have transcended the human condition." The *narcissistically wounded mystic* now adopts a stance much like Nietsche's grand romantic character Zarathustra just down from the mount with a message for all of us. This character may rapidly collect a group of followers whose narcissistic wounds are resonated by the charismatic outpourings of such a pseudo-spiritual leader and the followers will serve to reinforce the rigid outcome of this particular style of mystical failure.

Less damaging, but in some ways equally sad, is the *denied mystic*. This person is cast into radical doubt by his or her encounter with mystical knowing and can never trust that other forms of knowing are valid doors to different aspects of the totality of reality. They are stuck in an interpretive ambivalence. Each time the power and certainty of their encounter with mystical knowing confronts them, they rationalize it away. Perhaps they feel as though they are on an existential tightrope and if they look down they will fall into the deconstructive abyss of the failed mystic.

Finally, the successful mystic is one whose epistemic process deconstructs thereby launching them into mystical knowing but who successfully reconstruct a livable reality frame. Nevertheless, these mystics are able to walk the rope, look in different directions, and accept the two worlds of ordinary and nonordinary reality that they integrate and use to facilitate a more fulfilling and creative life.

Conclusion

I would assert that behind the activity of most of our lives there lies a profoundly spiritual impulse—a passion to know the ontological bottom line and align ourselves with it. This search appears to be, like Ricoeur's (1970) description of the discipline of religious studies, hermeneutics engaged in the restoration (or creation) of meaning. In summarizing the postmodern position of this chapter in its attempt to reframe both the mystical and sacred, I would alter that definition to read: hermeneutics in search of a hermeneutical position. Inevitably, this restorative action will require the breakdown of old structures and a reframing of the relationship of signs to each other in ways that can profoundly disturb our ontological certainty. However, if we persist in our spiritual inquiries we must each participate in a creative process where creator and created speak to one another in a dialogue of mutual construction, deconstruction, and reconstruction. It is from this process of *engaged knowing* that inspiration and new meanings arise that are valorized and eventually reified into spiritual knowledge.

Thus, spiritual knowledge—and hence the sacred as known through mystical experience or any other type experiential move through the ontological looking glass—seems to give rise to a sense of awe that we experience during the process of our participation in connecting to what we sense as the ultimate. Whether or not this contact, such as Otto's *Mysterium Tremendum,* refers to an encounter with an actual existent ontological otherness is of no account. What is important from my point of view is the sense of ontic shift that arises as the result of the intensity of feeling engendered as we leap across an epistemic boundary. The *post hoc* ascriptions of source and cause, whether they be Karma, spirit guides, higher intelligence, divine grace, or ultimate emptiness, are of little consequence. From my perspective life, in its constructive and deconstructive cycling, becomes the sacred, which again becomes the profane as we ebb and flow between the various readings and writings of the existential life-text. In this scenario spiritual knowing is that immediacy of connected awareness that occurs at the border between that "reading" and "writing."

So, the question still remains, how does this interpretation of spiritual knowing and the sacred connect to and illumine my mystical experience? My experience certainly subsumed what I understood at that time to be my self-structure and radically altered my relation to otherness—sacred or profane. At the time the revolutionary nature of the experience automatically called to me to reframe my knowledge of self and world. That I certainly attempted to do. However, as the years went by and I reflected back on the event, I thought more and more about the voice that had called my attention, first, to the guises I had used as personae and, second, to the guise of my supposed liberated state.

That first call made me aware that I was clothing myself in a series of constructed selves. As I entered into the experience I discovered that I could deconstruct these selves through an act of discriminating but dispassionate awareness—a kind of disidentification. The second call, however, provided the clue that eventually led to my postmodern reevaluation of mystical experience and spiritual knowing. At the moment that my bliss and sense of liberation were at their pinnacle, the voice returned to make me aware that my new existential position was being created by way of contrast—freedom and liberation versus ego and attachment versus freedom and liberation versus. . . . The shock of crossing the boundary from the ordinary to the mystical was an ontological wake-up call, as was the shock of moving back across the boundary.

What I finally understood is that it is the discovery of the relativity of epistemic frames that liberates us from being stuck in spiritual unknowing, *not the reifications that are built from the remains of one crossing.* Thus, the subtle contact of spiritual knowing emerges only when we let go of whatever ontological anchor that secures us and realize that reality is but one face of one looking glass and spiritual freedom is to consciously leap through it as an act of intentional, creative play.

Notes

1. Upanishadic wisdom has it that "He who knows does not speak, and he who speaks does not know." However, the not-speaking of many sages is often louder than words in proclaiming their supposed direct access to "higher" knowing. Yet many do speak and make claims about reality and truth. Examples of the latter can be seen in the various accounts given in Happold's (1963) well-known anthology.

2. The Western notion of deconstructionism has its origins in the work of the French philosopher, Jacques Derrida (1978). Derrida's deconstructions of Western thought from Plato to Heidegger attack what he identified as "logocentrism," or the human habit of assigning ultimate truth to language and the voice of reason—in essence, making them the word of God. Taylor (1983) explicates Derrida's overall position by making us aware that there is a broad context that saturates all texts, including the internal maps of knowing. This is summarized by Taylor in his assertion that the reading of the text is the writing of the text.

    In the East one finds prototypical forms of deconstructionism given as spiritual practice. In the Tamil-speaking world of India, a classic method of attaining the enlightened state was known as the practice of *neti, neti* (not this, not this), which was expounded by the nineteenth-century Yogi and mystic, Sri Ramana Maharshi (1982). In Tibetan literature, the classic work of the Lama Mi-Pham (1970) attempts to explicate the same process through a detached examination of the body.

3. Thanks to my colleagues Kaisa Puhakka and Tobin Hart for their very helpful suggestions here.

4. I attended yoga classes, learned various meditation techniques, fasted and ingested psychotropic substances. I finally settled on Vajrayana Buddhist practice under the tutelage of Tarthang Tulku Rinpoche. This, however, eventually proved not to be very useful in terms of my original purpose.

5. I remember asking a fellow American living in Copenhagen at that time who followed an Indian guru called Muktananda. He explained that his guru had recently been focusing his attention on Copenhagen, which had "raised" the "spiritual consciousness" of everyone in the city and this is what had affected me.

6. The history of the Theosophical movement is well observed in the critical analysis offered by Peter Washington (1995). Many of the concepts currently used to define and explain spiritual life were first introduced to the West through the teachings of Theosophy, and these ideas were themselves distortions of Hindu and Buddhist thought or *ex nihilis* creations from the fertile imagination of Helena Blavatsky.

7. Although Vivakananda was an Indian Hindu, his Anglicized education in India, his participation in the Brahmo Samaj, and his less than clear interpretation of the teachings of his guru, Ramakrishna, taken in the context of his Indian middle-class upbringing in a British-dominated culture, generated a system of beliefs that was far removed from the traditional Hindu worldview existent before the British Raj. Thus, in this cultural crossover world many then current Indian beliefs were in fact an admixture of traditional Eastern thought coated with a thinly disguised Calvinist Protestantism. Although Ramakrishna was supposedly an authentic master of ecstatic states, which he experienced frequently and with great drama while a priest of Kali, at the temple dedicated to the Goddess at Dakshineswar near Calcutta, Vivakananda never was able to enter into this experiential side of his Master's life. So, according to scholars like Bharati (1976), Vivakananda is to be considered as being a very westernized revisionist who only partially understood and incorporated his master's teaching.

8. For example, Charles Tart (1972) would argue that knowledge is state-specific and it is difficult, if not impossible, to understand state-specific phenomena across states of consciousness.

9. However, I agree with Ferrer's analysis regarding the pitfalls that often accompany the overvaluation of spiritual experiences "collected" as symbols of personal power and accomplishment. In my mind there seems to be very little difference between spiritual experience collecting and body-building when viewed as narcissistic pursuits.

10. Peter Moore (1978) argues that mystical experience is subject to three levels of interpretation by the experient. Part of that interpretive process results from a top-down instantaneous cognitive filtering, which he refers to as "reflexive interpretation." Another, *post hoc,* aspect of the interpretive process he calls "retrospective interpretation." The third forms he refers to as "incorporated interpretation," which includes the cultural belief systems the experient uses as a bottom-line perspective and is therefore also partly reflexive and largely unconscious.

11. In the quantum physical world subatomic "particles," such as electrons, appear to have both wave-like and particle-like characteristics. What determines whether such an "object" is known as either a particle or a wave is, according to standard interpretations, the act of observation. This problem was framed by Heisenberg (1958) as the Uncertainty Principle. The indeterminate nature of subatomic particles is terminated only by the act of observation. One way that this cloud of uncertainty is described uses the mathematics of wave mechanics as developed by Erwin Schrödinger (1959). In this wave description the determination of the position of a subatomic particle, or the termination of its uncertainty, occurs with the collapse of the Schrödinger Wave, which always results from observation (measurement) of the event (Jeans, 1958).

12. For example, whales have changed status a number of times throughout history. First, as sea monsters and guardians of the depths, they had a direct connection to the sacred. Later, in the nineteenth century, they fell from those heights to be seen as a source of lamp oil and lady's girdle stiffeners. Today, taken in the context of the environmental movement, they are again sacred in their symbolic role as the holy eco-other.

References

Berger, P. L. & Luckmann, T. (1971). The social construction of reality: A treatise in the sociology of knowledge. Middlesex, UK: Penguin Books.

Bharati, A. (1976). *The light at the center: Context and pretext of modern mysticism.* London: East-West Publications.

Blakney, R. B. (Ed. & Trans.). (1957). *Meister Eckhart: A modern translation.* New York: Harper Torch Books.

Bohm, D. (1980). *Wholeness and the implicate order.* London: Routledge & Kegan Paul.

Broad, C. D. (1914). *Perception, physics, and reality.* Cambridge: Cambridge University Press.

Carroll, J. B. (Ed.). (1956). *Language, thought and reality: Selected writings of Benjamin Lee Whorf.* Cambridge, MA: MIT Press.

Davies, P. (1990, October 20–21). Waves of paradox. *The Weekend Australian,* 22.

Derrida, J. (1978). *Writing and difference* (A. Bass, Trans.). Chicago: University of Chicago Press.

Eco, U. (1984). *The name of the rose* (W. Weaver, Trans.). London: Picador.

Eco, U. (1989). *Foucault's pendulum* (W. Weaver, Trans.). New York: Harcourt Brace Jovanovich.

Eliade, M. (1959). *The sacred and the profane: The nature of religion* (W. R. Trask, Trans.). New York: Harcourt Brace Jovanovich.

Gergen, K. J. (1985). The social constructionist movement in modern psychology. *American Psychologist, 40,* 266–275.

Gupta, M. (1973). *The gospel of Sri Ramakrishna* (Swami Nikhilananda, Trans.). New York: Ramakrishna-Vivekananda Center.

Happold, F. (1963). *Mysticism: A study and an anthology.* Middlesex: Penguin Books.

Heisenberg, W. (1958). *Physics and philosophy.* New York: Harper Torch Books.

Husserl, E. (1962). *Ideas: General introduction to phenomenology* (W. R. Boyce-Gibson, Trans.). New York: Collier-Macmillan.

James, W. (1936). *The varieties of religious experience.* New York: The Modern Library.

James, W. (1967). *Essays in radical empiricism and a pluralistic universe* (R. Barton Perry, Ed.). Gloucester, MA: Peter Smith.

Jeans, J. (1958). *Physics and philosophy.* Ann Arbor: University of Michigan Press.

Maharshi, R. (1982). *Who am I?* Tiruvannamalai, S. India: Sri Ramanasramam.

McCance, D. C. (1986). Physics, Buddhism, and postmodern interpretation. *Zygon, 21,* 287–296.

Mi-Pham, Lama (1970). The wheel of analytic meditation. In Tarthang Tulku (Trans. & Commentary), *Calm and clear* (pp. 29–92). Emeryville, CA: Dharma Publishing.

Moore, P. G. (1978). Mystical experience, mystical doctrine, mystical technique. In S. T. Katz (Ed.), *Mysticism and philosophical analysis* (pp. 101–131). London: Sheldon Press.

Nelson, P. L. (1990). The technology of the preternatural: An empirically based model of transpersonal experiences. *The Journal of Transpersonal Psychology, 22,* 35–50.

Nelson, P. L. (1991–92). Personality attributes as discriminating factors in distinguishing religio-mystical from paranormal experients. *Imagination, Cognition and Personality, 11(4),* 389–405.

Nelson, P. L. (1997–98). Consciousness as reflexive shadow: An operational psychophenomenological model. *Imagination, Cognition and Personality, 17(3),* 215–228.

Nelson, P. L. & Howell, J. D. (1993–94). A psycho-social phenomenological methodology for conducting operational, ontologically neutral research into religious and altered state experiences. *Journal for the Psychology of Religion, 2–3,* 1–48.

Otto, R. (1958). *The idea of the holy.* Oxford: Oxford University Press.

Popper, K. R. (1982, July 29). On theories as nets. *New Scientist,* 319–320.

Ricoeur, P. (1970). *Freud and philosophy: An essay on interpretation.* New Haven, CT: Yale University Press.

Sartre, J. P. (1972). *The transcendence of the ego: An existentialist theory of consciousness* (F. Williams & R. Kirkpatrick, Trans.). New York: Octagon Books.

Schrödinger, E. (1959). *Mind and matter.* London: Cambridge University Press.

Smart, N. (1973). *The science of religion and the sociology of knowledge.* Princeton, NJ: Princeton University Press.

Tart, C. T. (1972). States of consciousness and state-specific sciences. *Science, 176,* 1203–1210.

Taylor, M. C. (1983). Deconstruction: What's the difference? *Soundings, LXVI,* 387–403.

Tellegen, A. & Atkinson, G. (1974). Openness to absorbing and self-altering experiences ("Absorption"), a trait related to hypnotic susceptibility. *Journal of Abnormal Psychology, 83,* 268–277.

Washington, P. (1995). *Madame Blavatsky's baboon: A history of the mystics, mediums, and misfits who brought Spiritualism to America.* New York: Schocken Books.

Reflection and Presence

The Dialectic of Awakening

JOHN WELWOOD

As a student of clinical psychology in the 1960s, I found myself intrigued by the question: "What allows for real personality changes in people, and how does that change come about?" At that time, I was involved with my teacher Eugene Gendlin at the University of Chicago in his early attempts at developing the Focusing method. The term that Gendlin (1981, 1996) used to describe therapeutic movement was *felt shift*—that moment when a change in feeling resonated concretely in the body, revealing a new sense of meaning and direction. In this critical moment of experiential unfolding—which is correlated with various physiological and cognitive changes—an old fixation gives way, like a flower opening, providing a person with a new experience of themselves and their situation. When I first learned about this, and experienced it myself, it seemed quite mysterious and profound, almost like a mini-mystical experience.

At the same time, I was delving into Zen, and had become interested in the relationship between the felt shift and satori, the sudden awakening that was at the heart of Zen. I was particularly intrigued by the Zen stories where just by hearing the cry of a bird, sweeping the floor, or being slapped by one's teacher, the disciple suddenly woke up and saw reality in an entirely new way. Satori seemed like an immense, cosmic felt shift, where one's whole life suddenly changed, and one walked away a new being. I wondered how the felt shift and satori were related. Were they relatives of each other, two versions of the same thing or something different altogether?

As a budding student of both Buddhism and psychotherapy, this was not an academic question for me, but one that had important personal and professional implications. If the felt shift was a kind of mini-satori, or even a step in that direction, then perhaps Western psychological work could provide a new way to approach the kind of realizations that had previously been the sole province of mystics and monastics.

Psychological Reflection

Later, when I began to practice as a psychotherapist, this question took a new turn. By then I had done a fair degree of both psychological and meditative work, and had experienced powerful impacts from each. Although both types of work required inner attention and awareness, I was also struck by how different they were in their ways of approaching the flow of experience.

On the one hand, the therapeutic process involved stepping back from one's felt experience in order to inquire into it in a dialogical manner. In the course of the therapeutic dialogue—with the therapist and with one's own feelings—felt experience would open up, hidden felt meanings would unfold, and feelings would shift, leading to important cognitive, affective, and behavioral changes (Gendlin, 1964; Welwood, 1982).

At the same time, I was also studying the Mahamudra/Dzogchen meditative tradition of Tibetan Buddhism, which presented a very different approach. The method here involved a more radical opening to whatever experience was at hand, instead of stepping back from it, unfolding felt meanings from it, or engaging in dialogical inquiry. Working with experience in this way could lead to more sudden, on-the-spot kinds of revelation, described variously in terms of *transmutation, self-liberation,* or *spontaneous presence* (Trungpa, 1973; Welwood, 1979; Norbu, 1982, 1986).

In this approach, one directly recognizes and meets one's experience as it is, without concern for what it means, where it comes from, or where it leads. There is no reinforcement of an observing self trying to grasp, understand, or come to terms with some observed content of consciousness. The early stages of Dzogchen/Mahamudra meditation teach the student to let go of fixation on whatever arises in the mind, and this eventually develops the capacity to relax and abide wakefully in the midst of whatever experience is arising. When there is no identification either with the observer or what is observed, awareness remains undisturbed by any divisions, and a new freedom, freshness, clarity, and compassion become available. This nondual awareness, in the words of the Indian teacher, H. L. Poonja (1993, p. 33), "is your very own awareness, and it is called *freedom from everything.*"

While psychotherapy and meditation both led to a freeing of mental and emotional fixations, the meditative approach struck me as the more profound and compelling of the two, because it was more direct, more radical, more faithful to the essential nature of awareness as an open presence intrinsically free of grasping, strategizing, and the subject-object split altogether. At the same time, the reflective dialogical process of psychotherapy provided a more effective and accessible way to work on the issues, concerns, and problems of personal and worldly life—which meditators often tend to avoid dealing with. Yet I had doubts about the ultimate merits of an approach that did not address, and was not designed to overcome, the subject-object struggle that lay at the root of most human alienation and suffering.

Two therapeutic devices I found useful in my early years as a therapist were a particular focus of these doubts. Long before "inner child" work became popularized by John Bradshaw, I discovered that many people who could not relate to their feelings of hurt, fear, helplessness, anger, or sorrow in a helpful, compassionate way *could* do so when they imagined these feelings as belonging to the child still alive within them. Since I had stumbled on this device on my own, rather than adopting it from a preconceived theoretical framework, it seemed all the more impressive to me. Yet I also remained aware of its shortcoming: It left a person inwardly split between an observing "adult" and an observed "child," with most of the feeling-energy seeming to belong to the child.

"Finding the right distance from a feeling" was another useful device, and a central feature of the Focusing method I taught for many years. Many clients who get too close to threatening feelings either become overwhelmed by them or else reject them in order to defend themselves from their intensity. So establishing a certain reflective distance from strong feelings makes it easier to relate to them, just as stepping back from someone who is speaking loudly makes it more possible to hear what they are saying. Finding the right distance involves situating one's attention "next to" the feeling, on the edge of it, close enough to be in contact with it, yet far enough away to feel comfortable. This stepped-back position is a useful therapeutic device that allows an interactive dialogue with feelings that might not otherwise be possible. However, if this is the only way one relates to one's experiences, it can also maintain and reinforce an inner separation—between observing ego and the observed flow of experience—that can eventually become a limitation in its own right.

The further I went with meditation, the less satisfied I was only drawing on reflective methods that maintained this inner division. From the perspective of contemplative practice, the root source of human suffering is this very split between "me" and "my experience." Suffering is nothing more than the observer judging, resisting, struggling with, and attempting to control experiences that seem painful, scary, or threatening to it. Without that struggle, difficult feelings can be experienced more simply and directly, instead of as dire threats to the survival and integrity of "me."

Conventional psychotherapy teaches clients to understand, manage, and reduce the suffering that arises out of identification with a separate ego-self,
but rarely questions the fundamental inner setup that gives rise to it.

Divided and Undivided Consciousness

Although reflective methods are certainly essential for therapeutic work, my
experience with Dzogchen/Mahamudra meditation let me see how they
were still an expression, in Eastern terms, of divided consciousness. The
Sanskrit term for the ordinary, mundane state of consciousness is *vijnana*.
Vi could be translated as *divided* and *jnana* as *knowing*. *Divided* here refers to
the subject/object split, in which the divide between observer and observed, perceiver and perceived is a primary determinant of how and what
we perceive. All conventional knowledge, including what we discover in psychotherapy, happens within the framework of divided consciousness, as
phenomenologist Peter Koestenbaum (1978) observes:

> All knowledge is of this dual sort, and psychotherapeutic inter-
> vention is no exception. . . . Psychotherapy, like all other forms of
> knowledge, is reflection on self; it is self-knowledge and self-
> consciousness. (pp. 35, 70)

When we reflect on self, self becomes divided—into an object of reflection and an observing subject. This is *vijnana* at work. Dividing the field
of experience into two poles is a useful device for most purposes and yields
relative self-knowledge. We learn about our conditioning, our character
structure, our particular ways of thinking, feeling, acting, and perceiving.
While these discoveries can be relatively liberating, *who we are* can never be
identical with the mind/body patterns we discover through reflective discernment. Nor are we identical with the perceiver that stands back from
those patterns and reflects on them. Both these poles are creations of the
conceptual mind, which operates by dividing the experiential field in two
and interpreting reality through concepts based on this division.

Precise attention to the nature of experiencing reveals that most of
our perception and cognition is conditioned by this conceptual divide.
For example, we generally do not see a tree in its unique and vivid immediacy—in its suchness. Instead, our experience of the tree is shaped by
ideas and beliefs about a category of objects called "tree." Krishnamurti
(1976), by contrast, describes what it is like to see a tree in a more direct,
unalienated way:

> You look at this magnificent tree and you wonder who is watch-
> ing whom and presently there is no watcher at all. Everything is

so intensely alive and there is only life, and the watcher is as dead as that leaf. . . . Utterly still . . . listening without a moment of re-action, without recording, without experiencing, only seeing and listening. . . . Really the outside is the inside and the inside is the outside, and it is difficult, almost impossible to separate them. (p. 214)

Just as "the news" pretends to be an accurate and neutral presentation of world events, while concealing its hidden biases, so we imagine that con-ventional divided consciousness gives us an accurate portrayal of what lies before us, while failing to see how our conceptual assumptions usually pro-duce a distorted picture of reality. In this way, we do not experience "things as they are"—in their rich and vivid experiential immediacy. As the great Dzogchen yogi Mipham put it: "Whatever one imagines, it is never exactly like that" (Kunsang, 1993, p. 114).

This habitually distorted perception—where we unconsciously mis-take our cognitive schema for reality—is, in Buddhist terms, *samsara,* "delu-sive appearance." The basis of samsara is the ongoing habit of dividing the field of experience in two and imagining that the observing self is some-thing set apart from the rest of the field. Meditative experience reveals a different kind of knowing, a direct recognition of "thatness" or "such-ness"—the vivid, ineffable nowness of reality, as disclosed in the clarity of pure awareness, free from the constraints of conceptual or dualistic fixa-tion. When this kind of knowing is directed inwardly, it becomes what is called in Zen "directly seeing into one's own nature." In this case, "one's own nature" is not an object of thought, observation, or reflection. Mind in its objectifying mode cannot grasp the immediate beingness of anything, least of all its own nature.

We can only perceive the suchness of things through an awareness that opens to them nonconceptually and unconditionally, allowing them to re-veal themselves in their as-it-is-ness. As the poet Basho suggests:

From the pine tree
learn of the pine tree.
And from the bamboo
of the bamboo.

Commenting on these lines, the Japanese philosopher Nishitani (1982) ex-plains that Basho does not mean

that we should 'observe the pine tree carefully.' Still less does he mean for us to 'study the pine tree scientifically.' He means for us to enter the mode of being where the pine tree is the pine tree it-self, and the bamboo is the bamboo itself, and from there to look

at the pine tree and the bamboo. He calls on us to betake ourselves to the dimension where things become manifest in their
suchness. (p. 128)

In the same vein, Zen Master Dogen advises: "You should not restrict yourselves to learning to see water from the viewpoints of human beings alone.
Know that you must see water in the way water sees water" (Izutsu, 1972,
p. 140). "Seeing water in the way water sees water" means recognizing water in its suchness, free of all concepts that spring from an observing mind
standing back from experience.

Extending these lines from Basho and Dogen into the arena of self-
realization, we might say, "If you want to find out who you are, open directly
to yourself right now, enter into the mode of being where you are what you
are, and settle into your own nature. Just as a snapshot of the bamboo is not
the bamboo itself, how can the mental snapshots you have of yourself—the
ideas and conclusions about yourself you have come to through reflective
observation—be an accurate rendering of who you really are?" Divided consciousness—*vi-jnana*—can never yield *jnana*—direct, unmediated knowing,
undivided consciousness, self-illuminating awareness, self-existing wisdom.
Jnana is a different type of self-knowing, primarily discovered through contemplative discipline, where freedom from the subject-object setup allows
direct "seeing into one's own nature."

Stretched between the disciplines of psychotherapy and meditation, I
found myself continually revisiting these questions: How might psychological reflection serve as a stepping-stone on the path of awakening? Or since
psychological reflection by its very nature was a form of divided consciousness, could it subtly perpetuate a permanent state of inner division in the
name of healing? I knew certain spiritual teachers and practitioners who advanced a critique of therapy to this effect. They argued that psychotherapy
was just a palliative, a way of making the prison of ego more comfortable,
because it did not address, but instead reinforced, the error at the root of
all suffering: identification with a separate self that was always trying to control or alter its experience. At the other extreme, many therapists I knew regarded spiritual practice as an avoidance of dealing with the personal and
interpersonal knots that interfered with living a full, rich, engaged life.

While psychological and spiritual work can certainly have these pitfalls,
I could not side with either of these extreme views. I respected psychotherapy as a domain in its own right, using methods and perspectives that were
valid in their own context, without necessarily having to conform to the
highest standards of nondual realization. And I also felt that it was possible
to build a bridge between psychological reflection, which yields valid relative self-knowledge, even though mediated by divided consciousness, and

the deeper, undivided awareness and wordless knowing discovered in meditation. I wanted to see how these two kinds of self-knowing might work together as part of a larger dialectic of awakening that could include and bring together the two poles of human experience—conditioned and unconditioned, relative and absolute, psychological and spiritual, personal and universal.

It was through pursuing these questions that my own therapeutic approach evolved in the direction of what I now call "psychological work in a spiritual context" or "presence-centered psychotherapy." By providing an intermediate step between conventional psychological reflection and the deeper process of meditation, this way of working has proved to be more congruent with my meditative experience than the way I first practiced therapy. In the remainder of this chapter, I will situate this intermediate step within a larger dialectic of awakening as it unfolds through psychological reflection and spiritual presence.

The Basic Problem: Prereflective Identification

What makes our ordinary state of consciousness problematic, according to both psychological and spiritual traditions, is unconscious identification. As young children, our awareness is essentially open and receptive, yet the capacity to reflect on our own experience does not fully develop until the early teenage years, during the stage that Piaget termed "formal operations." Until then, our self-structure is under the sway of a more primitive capacity—identification.

Because we lack self-reflective awareness in childhood, we are mostly dependent on others to help us see and know ourselves—to do our reflecting for us. So we inevitably start to internalize their reflections—how they see and respond to us—coming to regard ourselves in terms of how we appear to others. In this way we develop an ego identity, a stable self-image composed of self-representations, which are part of larger object relations— self/other schemas formed in our early transactions with our parents. To form an identity means *taking ourselves to be something,* based on how others relate to us.

Identification is like a glue by which consciousness attaches itself to contents of consciousness—thoughts, feelings, images, beliefs, memories— and assumes with each of them, "That's me," or "That represents me." Forming an identity is a way in which consciousness objectifies itself, makes itself an object. It is like looking in a mirror and taking ourselves to be the visual image reflected back to us, while ignoring our more immediate, lived experience of embodied being. Identification is a primitive form of self-

knowledge—the best we could do as a child, given our limited cognitive capacities.

By the time our capacity for reflective self-knowledge develops, our identities are fully formed. Our knowledge of ourselves is indirect, mediated by
memories, self-images, and beliefs about ourselves formed out of these memories and images. Knowing ourselves through self-images, we have become an
object in our own eyes, never seeing the way in which we are a larger field of
being and presence in which these thought-forms arise. We have become pris-
oners of our own mind and the ways it has construed reality.

Reflection: Stepping Back From Identification

The first step in freeing ourselves from the prison of unconscious identification is to make it conscious, that is, to reflect on it. We cannot move from
prereflective identification directly into nondual awareness. But we *can* use
divided consciousness to reflect on divided consciousness. The Buddha
likened this to using a thorn to remove a thorn from one's flesh. All reflection involves stepping back from one's experience in order to examine and
explore its patterns, its feeling textures, its meanings, its *logos*, including the
basic assumptions, beliefs, and ways of conceiving reality that shape our experience. By comparison with identification, this kind of self-reflection represents a giant step forward in the direction of greater self-understanding
and freedom. As Gabriel Marcel (1950) put it, "reflection . . . is one of life's
ways of rising from one level to another (p. 101)."

There are different ways of reflecting on one's experience. Some are
cruder, others subtler, depending on the rigidity of the dualism and the size
of gap they maintain between observer and observed. I would like to distinguish three levels of reflective method: conceptual reflection, phenomenological reflection, and mindful witnessing.

Conceptual Reflection: Cognitive and Behavioral Analysis

The way most of us begin to reflect on our experience is by thinking about
it—using theories and concepts to explain or analyze what is happening.
Concepts allow us to step out of prereflective immersion in experience, so
that we can see it in a new light or from a new angle. Most psychological and
spiritual traditions draw on conceptual reflection at first, introducing certain ideas that help people take a new look at their experience. Buddha's
four noble truths, for example, are a way of helping people step back from
their unconscious suffering in order to consider its nature and cause, as well
as antidotes for it. In Western psychology, developmental theories, maps of
consciousness, and character typologies serve a similar purpose, providing

frameworks that help people analyze, organize, and understand their experience in more coherent ways.

Some kinds of therapy are based primarily on conceptual reflection. They seek to explain or change the problematic *contents* of a client's experience, rather than working with the client's overall *process* of experiencing. This is a relatively crude approach, in that there is no direct encounter with immediate, lived experiencing. Instead, the relation to experience is always *mediated* by theoretical constructs. The therapist draws on some theory of human development or behavior to interpret the client's experience, while the client's main activity is *thinking* and *talking* about his or her experience, at one remove from the experience itself. The therapist might also draw on preformulated techniques to operate on the client's behavior, applying certain cognitive (e.g., reframing, positive affirmations) or behavioral (e.g., desensitization, emotional catharsis) strategies to alter the undesirable contents of experience. This type of approach is often most useful with clients who lack the ego strength or the motivation to encounter their experience in a more direct, immediate way.

Spiritual traditions often formulate the contemplative realizations of great teachers of the past into a "view" that is transmitted to new students in order to help them discover the essence of spiritual realization for themselves. In the Mahamudra tradition, for example, the view of awareness as intrinsically vast and boundless helps point students in that direction, so that they can discover this for themselves. In the words of Lodro Thaye, a great Mahamudra master of the eighteenth century:

> When one meditates with this view
> It is like a garuda soaring through space
> Untroubled by fear or doubt.
> One who meditates without this view
> Is like a blind man wandering the plains.
>
> (Nalanda, 1980, p. 84)

Yet such a view can have no transformative effect if it remains only conceptual. Therefore Lodro Thaye adds:

> One who holds this view but does not meditate
> Is like a rich man tethered by stinginess
> Who cannot bring fruition to himself or others.
> Joining the view and meditation is the holy tradition.
>
> (p. 84)

The danger of any view is that we could start to substitute theory for the reality it points to. Therefore, in the Mahamudra/Dzogchen tradition, the master presents the view along with "pointing-out instructions"—which transmit or experientially reveal to the student the actual state that the view describes. Then the view becomes the ground of a contemplative path whose goal is to realize the view in a full experiential way.

Phenomenological Reflection: Meeting Experience Directly

Conceptual reflection that provides a map of where we are or a strategy for how to proceed gives a general orientation, but has limited value in helping us relate to where we are right now, more immediately. Conceptual mapping and analysis—thinking and talking about experience—must eventually give way to an approach that helps us work directly with experience.

Phenomenological reflection is the putting aside of habitual conceptual assumptions in order to explore experience in a fresher, looser way. Because it does not impose preconceived concepts or strategies on experience, it is a more refined approach. The concepts it uses are "experience-near": they grow out of, describe, and point back to what is directly felt and perceived. In this way phenomenology narrows the gap between observer and observed.

Phenomenological approaches to psychotherapy regard experiencing as a complex, living process that cannot be neatly controlled or predicted. Here the observing consciousness stays close to felt experience, inquiring into it gently, and waiting patiently for responses and insights to come directly from there, rather than from some cognitive schema. Experiencing itself is the guide, revealing directions for change that unfold in the course of exploring it.

For example, a tension in the chest might first reveal itself as anxiety, then upon further reflection, as a sense of helplessness, then as an uncertainty that you are worthy of love. Perhaps you started out feeling judgmental toward the anxiety, or threatened by it, but as it reveals itself as an uncertainty about being lovable, a softer tenderness might arise. And this new way of relating to what you are going through allows it to unfold further, as the anxiety relaxes and you feel more compassionate toward yourself. In this kind of reflection, observer and observed become reciprocal poles of a mutual dance. This stepping-back from habitual reactions and assumptions in order to come into a fresher relationship with lived experience is the essence of what is called, in philosophical terms, "the phenomenological reduction."

Reflective Witnessing: Bare, Mindful Attention

An even subtler kind of reflection happens in the early stages of mindfulness meditation, where one is simply attentive to the ongoing flow of the mindstream, without concern about particular contents of experience that arise. In this approach the gap between observer and observed narrows further, in that there is no interest in operating on the mindstream in any way—through understanding, unfolding, articulation, or moving toward any release or resolution. In the context of meditation, any of these aims would indicate the operation of some mental set or attitude, and thus an interference with the process of freeing oneself from identification with all mind-states. While phenomenological reflection is an attempt to find new meaning, new understanding, new directions, meditation is a more radical path of *undoing*—which involves relaxing any tendency to become caught up in feelings, thoughts, and identifications. Yet mindfulness practice is not yet the totally relaxed nondoing of Dzogchen, for it still requires some effort of stepping back (from identification) and witnessing.

Mindfulness practice provides a transitional step between reflection and nondual presence, incorporating elements of both. Directing mindful attention toward thinking allows us to notice a crucial difference—between thought and awareness, between the contents of consciousness, which are like clouds passing through the sky, and pure consciousness, which is like the wide open sky itself. Letting go of habitual identifications allows us to enter pure awareness, which is intrinsically free of the compulsions of thought and emotion. This is an important step in starting to free ourselves from the prison of dualistic fixation. In the Dzogchen tradition, this is spoken of as distinguishing the mind caught in dualism (Tibetan: *sems*) from pure nondual awareness (*rigpa*). As the Tibetan teacher Chökyi Nyima (1991) describes this distinction:

> Basically there are two states of mind. *Sems* refers to the state of conceptual thinking, involving fixation on some "thing." . . . *Rigpa* means free from fixation. It refers to a state of natural wakefulness that is without dualistic clinging. It is extremely important to be clear about the difference between these two states of mind. (p. 129)

Pure Presence: Awakening Within Experience

Before becoming self-reflective, we remain identified with thoughts, beliefs, feelings, and memories arising in consciousness, and this keeps us imprisoned in conditioned mind. With reflection, we can start to free ourselves from these unconscious identifications by stepping back and observing them. Yet as long as we are stepping back, we remain in a state of divided consciousness. A further step would be to go beyond reflection and, without falling back into prereflective identification, become at-one with our experiencing—through overcoming all struggle with it, through discovering and abiding in the deep, silent source from which all experience arises. This third level of the dialectic, which takes us beyond conventional psychological models and philosophical frameworks, is postreflective—in that it usually follows from a groundwork of reflective work—and *trans-reflective*—in that it discloses a way of being that lies beyond divided consciousness.

Even phenomenology, which, in emphasizing subject-object interrelatedness, is one of the most refined, least dualistic Western ways of exploring human experience, usually fails to go this further step. Peter Koestenbaum (1978), for example, whose work *The New Image of the Person* is a worthy attempt to develop a phenomenological clinical philosophy, and who is generally sympathetic to meditation and transpersonal experience, describes meditation only in terms of stepping back. He considers meditative presence—what he calls the Eternal Now—to be the ultimate phenomenological reduction:

> There is no end to the regressive process of reflection because the field of consciousness is experienced to be infinite. Specifically, *there is infinity in stepping back.* . . . The Eternal Now is an experience in which we are no longer inside space and inside time but *have become an observer* of space and time. . . . In meditation, *the individual takes a spectatorial attitude towards all experiences.* . . . The meditator follows the flow of the body, of a feeling, or of the environment. . . . In this way *individuals can train themselves to become observers rather than participants in life.* (pp. 73, 82, 100, 101, my italics)

Koestenbaum's words are accurate up through the early stages of reflective witnessing in mindfulness practice. However, meditation that only goes this far does not lead beyond divided consciousness. The ultimate purpose of meditation goes far beyond training us to be "observers, rather than participants," as Koestenbaum claims. Its aim is full participation in life, but *conscious* participation, rather than the unconscious participation of prereflective identification. What finally replaces divided consciousness is pure presence.

Of all the phenomenologists, Heidegger and Merleau-Ponty have perhaps gone the farthest in acknowledging a mode of awareness beyond subject and object, as well as its sacred import. Borrowing a term from Meister Eckhart, Heidegger (1977) speaks of *Gelassenheit*, letting-be, using language reminiscent of Buddhist references to suchness:

> To *let be*—that is, to let beings be as the beings which they are—means to engage oneself with the open region and its openness into which every being comes to stand, bringing that openness, as it were, along with itself. (p. 127)

Merleau-Ponty (1968) suggests the need to develop what he calls *sur-réflection*—which might be translated as "higher reflection"—

> that would take itself and the changes it introduces into the spectacle into account. . . . It must plunge into the world instead of surveying it, it must descend toward it such as it is . . . so that the seer and the visible reciprocate one another and we no longer know which sees and which is seen. (pp. 38–39, 139)

These attempts by two great philosophers to point the way beyond traditional Western dualistic thought are admirable. Yet even at its best, phenomenology can point to, but does not provide a true *upaya*, or path, for fully realizing nondual presence.

In the practice of Mahamudra/Dzogchen, meditators discover nondual awareness, at first in glimpses, as the focus on objects of consciousness gradually drops away and they learn to rest in open presence, in what Franklin Merrill-Wolff (1994) called "consciousness-without-an-object." This nondual presence could be described in terms of qualities such as depth, luminosity, or spaciousness, yet in its immediacy there is no self-conscious reflection on any such attributes. Instead, one simply rests in the clarity of wide open, wakeful awareness, without any attempt to alter or fabricate one's experience.

Here there is direct self-knowing, direct recognition of one's own nature as pure being, without self-reflection. When attention is turned outward, perception is clear and sharp, since it is not clothed in concepts. The world is not seen as something separate from awareness, nor is it any less vivid and immediate than awareness itself. Nor is awareness seen as something subjective, "in here," separate from appearances. Awareness and what appears in awareness mutually coemerge in one unified field of presence.

In this unified field of presence, neither perceptions nor awareness can be objectified as anything for the mind to grasp. This ungraspable quality of experience is the basic meaning of the Buddhist term *emptiness*. The Mahamudra tradition speaks of the inseparability of emptiness and awareness, emptiness and clarity, emptiness and appearance, emptiness and energy. We could also speak of the inseparability of emptiness and being. Pure presence is the realization of being-as-emptiness: being without being some-*thing*. Being is empty, not because it lacks anything, but because it cannot be comprehended in terms of any reference point outside itself. Being is precisely that which can never be grasped or contained in any physical boundary or conceptual designation. In Nishitani's (1982) words, "being is only being if it is one with emptiness. . . . In that sense, emptiness might be called the field of 'be-ification' " (p. 124).

Emptiness in this sense is not some "attribute" belonging to awareness, appearance, or being, but their utter transparency when apprehended in pure presence, beyond the subject-object division. This
realization is called by many different names, such as self-illuminating
awareness, *jnana*, buddha-nature, wisdom mind, great bliss, great perfection. As self-illuminating awareness that simultaneously illumines the
whole field of experience, pure presence is intimate engagement, rather
than stepped-back detachment. In contrast to reflection, it does not involve any "doing" at all, as the great Dzogchen master Longchenpa indicates when he says: "Instead of seeking mind by mind, let be" (Guenther,
1977, p. 244).

Once awareness extricates itself from the fetters of conceptual mind,
through reflection and mindfulness, it can self-realize its intrinsic nature as
pure freedom, relaxation, openness, luminosity, and presence. This happens, in Mahamudra terms, through "settling itself in its own nature." Since
this resting in presence goes beyond effort, one-pointedness, and witnessing, it is called *nonmeditation*. Although analogies can suggest what this is
like, no word or image can describe its radiant immediacy, as Lodro Thaye
points out:

> It is space, ungraspable as a thing.
> It is a flawless precious clear crystal.
> It is the lamp-like radiance of your own self-luminous mind.
> It is inexpressible, like the experience of a mute.
> It is unobscured, transparent wisdom.
> The luminous dharmakaya, buddha-nature,
> Primordially pure and spontaneous.
> It cannot be demonstrated through analogy,
> And cannot be expressed in words.
> It is the space of Dharma,
> Forever overwhelming mind's inspection.
>
> (Nalanda, 1980, p. 84)

In the state of nonmeditation it is no longer necessary to make a distinction
between conceptual mind and pure awareness, in that all mind-states are
recognized as forms of awareness and presence. It is more a question of being fully awake within thought, feeling, perception when they arise, no
longer maintaining a hair's breadth of separation from whatever arises.

This quality of pure presence reveals spontaneous clearings in the experiential stream, without any strategy or intention to create change. There
are two closely related ways in which these changes may occur: transmutation and self-liberation.

Spontaneous Transmutation

The Tantric tradition of Vajrayana Buddhism is known as the path of trans-formation, in which "impure" experience—marked by ignorance, dualism, aggression, grasping—is transmuted into "pure" experience—illumined by awareness, openness, nongrasping, and spontaneous appreciation. The basic Vajrayana methods of visualization, mantra, mudra, and symbolic ritual eventually lead to the more advanced, utterly direct approach of Mahamu-dra/Dzogchen, where the practitioner finally cuts through the separation between pure and impure by completely meeting and opening to the raw immediacy of experience on the spot.

In this direct encounter, the thick, heavy, fixated quality of experi-ence falls away, revealing a deeper, living intelligence contained within it. Chögyam Trungpa (1973) describes this kind of change:

> At this point whatever is experienced in everyday life through sense perception is a naked experience, because it is direct. There is no veil between [you] and "that." . . . Tantra teaches not to suppress or destroy energy but to transmute it; in other words, go with the pat-tern of energy. . . . When [you] go with the pattern of energy, then experience becomes very creative. . . . You realize that you no longer have to abandon anything. You begin to see the underlying qualities of wisdom in your life-situation. . . . If you are highly in-volved in one emotion such as anger, then by having a sudden glimpse of openness . . . you begin to see that you do not have to suppress your energy . . . but you can transform your aggression into dynamic energy. . . . If we actually feel the living quality, the texture of the emotions as they are in their naked state, then this experience also contains ultimate truth. . . . We discover that emo-tion actually does not exist as it appears, but it contains much wis-dom and open space. . . . Then the process of . . . transmuting the emotions into wisdom takes place automatically. (pp. 218–219, 221, 222, 234, 235–236)

Here there is no deliberate effort to transmute the emotions; rather, trans-mutation happens spontaneously through opening fully to them:

> You experience emotional upheaval as it is but . . . become one with it. . . . Let yourself be in the emotion, go through it, give in to it, experience it. You begin to go toward the emotion rather than just experiencing the emotion coming toward you. . . . Then the most powerful energies become absolutely workable . . . . What-

ever occurs in the samsaric mind is regarded as the path; everything is workable. It is a fearless proclamation—the lion's roar.
(Trungpa, 1976, pp. 70–71)

As a student in this tradition, with a few budding glimpses of what the previous words might actually refer to, I began to feel that even Focusing—
which was the simplest, most penetrating, experience-near therapeutic
method I knew—still did not go far enough.

Focusing involves attending to an unclear bodily-felt sense, while remaining extremely respectful, gentle, and attentive toward every nuance of
experience that arises from it. Seeing how concrete steps of experiential
change can emerge from attending to a felt sense is an important discovery—something that people who use spiritual practice to avoid their feelings and personal experience would do well to learn. Yet as Focusing is
commonly practiced, there is often a bias toward unfolding meaning from
a felt sense, toward resolution, toward looking for a felt shift. In this way, it
can become a form of "doing" that maintains a subtle I-It stance toward
one's experience. The bias here can be very subtle. Wanting our experience to change usually contains a subtle resistance to what is, to nowness,
to what I call *unconditional presence*—the capacity to meet experience fully
and directly, without filtering it through any conceptual or strategic
agenda (Welwood, 1992).

The subtle spiritual pitfall of psychological work is that it can reinforce
certain tendencies inherent in the conditioned personality: to see ourselves
as a doer, to always look for the meaning in experience, or to continually
strive for "something better." Although psychological reflection can certainly help people move forward in important ways, at some point even the
slightest desire for change or improvement can interfere with the deeper
letting go and relaxation that are necessary for moving from the realm of
personality into the realm of being, which is only discoverable in and
through nowness—in moments when all conceptualizing and striving cease.

When we let experience be as it is, instead of seeking to alter it in any
way, the focus of inner work shifts in an important and powerful way. No
longer is our experience something apart from us that we need to change
or resolve; instead, the focus widens to the larger field: *how-we-are-with-our-
experience.* And when we relate to our experience in a more spacious, allowing way, it becomes less problematic, because we no longer exist in an I-It,
subject-object tension with it.

Although the main aim of psychotherapy is to reduce psychological distress and increase self-understanding, rather than to overcome divided consciousness, I nonetheless felt a need to practice therapy in a way that was
more congruent with the nondoing quality of meditative presence. I was

also inspired in this vision by moments in my own personal work when opening to my experience just as it was brought me into a fuller sense of presence—a kind of "being-without-agenda," which led to a powerful sense of stillness, acceptance, and aliveness. Such moments afforded a glimpse of what lay on the other side of divided consciousness: being at-one with myself in a new and deeper way.

Of course, there is a time for actively trying to penetrate the veils of experience, as well as a time for allowing experience to be as it is. If we are unable or unwilling to actively engage with our personal life issues, then letting-be could become a stance of avoidance, and a dead-end. Yet if we are unable to let our experience be, or to open to it just as it is, then our psychological work may reinforce the habitual tendency of the conditioned personality to turn away from nowness. While Focusing showed me a way out of the first pitfall, meditation—which taught me about the wisdom of nondoing—showed me a way beyond the second pitfall.

In training professionals, I also found that the investment in change can introduce a subtle bias into therapists' responses, thereby communicating to their clients: "You're not all right the way you are." And this can reinforce the alienated attitude most people already suffer from: "I should be having a better experience from the one I'm having—what's wrong with me?" When clients pick up this bias from their therapists, it can create a fundamental obstacle in the therapeutic process and relationship. Clients either try to go along with the therapist's agenda, which can disconnect them from their own being, or else they resist the therapist's agenda, which keeps them stuck.

The more I trained therapists, the clearer it became that the most important quality in a therapist was the capacity for unconditional presence—which, oddly enough, is hardly mentioned or taught in most therapy training. When therapists are present with a client's experience in this way, something inside the client can begin to relax and open up more fully. What I have found, again and again, is that unconditional presence is the most powerful transmuting force there is—precisely because it is a willingness to be there with our experience, without dividing ourselves in two by trying to "manage" what we are feeling.

The nondoing of unconditional presence is compatible with a wide range of therapeutic methods, both directive and nondirective. It is not a passive stance, but rather, an active willingness to meet and inquire into felt experience in a totally unbiased, nonreactive, noncontrolling way.

In teaching unconditional presence, I have found it helpful to delineate different stages of this coming-into-contact. First of all, there needs to be a *willingness to inquire,* to face directly into our felt experience and see what is there. Then we can begin to *acknowledge* what is happening inside us: "Yes, this is what I'm experiencing right now. I'm feeling threatened . . .

hurt . . . angry . . . defensive." Acknowledging involves recognizing and naming what is going on, seeing how it feels in the body, and inviting it more fully into awareness. The power of bare acknowledgment should never be underestimated. To help clients linger here and not rush on toward some hoped-for resolution, I often say something like, "Notice what it's like right now *just to acknowledge* what you're feeling." Attending to the felt quality of this recognition cuts through the impulse to react to the content, allowing the client to be more present with it.

Once we acknowledge what is there, it becomes possible to meet it more fully by *allowing* it to be there as it is. This does not mean wallowing in feelings or acting them out. Instead, allowing means giving our experience space and actively letting it be as it is, putting aside any urge to manage or judge it. Often what interferes with this is either identifying with the feeling ("this anger is me") or resisting it ("this anger is not me"). A certain amount of time and concentration is often necessary before we can let our experience be there in this more allowing way.

Having allowed our experience to be as it is, we can then let ourselves *open to it* more fully, no longer maintaining any distance between it and ourselves as observer, judge, or manager. This is the point where unconditional presence diverges from Focusing and other reflective methods. There is a complete opening to, entering into, and becoming one with the felt experience, without any attempt to find meaning in it, or to do anything with it, to it, or about it. What is most important here is not so much *what* we are feeling, but the *act of opening* to it.

For example, a client fears that he is nothing—that if he looks inside, he won't find anything there. Although I first ask him to pay attention to this "fear of being nothing" in his body and we discuss how it relates to situations from his past (this is still reflective inquiry), eventually I invite him to open directly to the sense of being nothing—to enter fully into it and let himself *be* nothing. (Here reflection gives way to presence.) After a while he says, "It feels empty, but there's also a fullness, and a kind of peace." He feels full because he is present now, rather than disconnected. It is his being that feels peaceful and full. And he starts to realize that his sense of nothingness was actually a symptom of being cut off from himself—a disconnection reinforced by stories and beliefs he had about the dreaded void at his core. Of course, feelings don't always transmute this easily. It depends entirely on the client and our relationship. Yet for clients who have experienced this a number of times, it can happen more and more readily.

Feelings in themselves don't necessarily lead to wisdom, but the process of opening fully to them can. When we no longer maintain distance from a feeling, it cannot preserve its apparent solidity, which only crystallizes when we treat it as an object separate from ourselves. In the example, the client's fear of being nothing only persisted as long as he resisted that experience. But when he opened unconditionally to being nothing, this inner division ceased, at least for a while, as he stepped out of the fixed stance/attitudes/associations he held toward "being nothing," with their long history dating back to childhood. In becoming present in a place where he had been absent, he experienced his being, rather than his nothingness. "Being nothing" transmuted into the empty fullness of being— where the fear of being nothing no longer had a hold on him.

When the focus of awareness shifts from a feeling—as an object of pleasure or pain, like or dislike, acceptance or rejection—to our state of presence with it, this allows us to discover new resources and wisdom hidden within it, as we move from the realm of personality into the larger space of being. Out of presence with anger, strength often emerges; out of presence with sorrow, compassion; out of presence with fear, courage and groundedness; out of presence with emptiness, expansive spaciousness and peace. Strength, compassion, courage, spaciousness, peace are differentiated qualities of being—different ways in which presence manifests.

In this way, being fully present with ourselves overcomes the inner war, at least for a moment, between self and Other, between "me" and "my experience." And from there, everything looks and feels different. A felt shift happens, but this is more than the "content mutation" that Gendlin (1964) describes as a result of reflective unfolding. An example of content mutation would be anger unfolding to reveal fear, which in turn might unfold further, revealing itself as a desire to be loved, and then a sense of relief at realizing that one's anger was pushing away the love one wanted. I call these "horizontal" felt shifts, because even though deeper feelings and realizations may unfold, the process remains mainly within the realm of personality. But the transmutation that often occurs through unconditional presence is a "vertical" shift, where one moves from personality into a deeper quality of being, as a fixed constellation of observer/observed dissolves, along with all reactivity, contraction, or striving.

Of course, this kind of deepening may not happen quickly or easily, or by itself lead to lasting personal transformation. Often a long sequence of horizontal unfolding must occur before a vertical shift happens, and a long period of integration is necessary before these shifts can lead to real differences in the way one lives. Nor am I suggesting that Focusing and other reflective methods cannot also lead to vertical shifts. But when someone opens completely to what they are experiencing, the personality—which is an activity of judgment, control, and resistance—disappears for a moment. Therapists without some background in meditation may have difficulty fully appreciating this or allowing it to unfold.

I make a point of helping clients recognize the nature and significance of this shift into being when it occurs. I encourage them to rest there, appreciate the new quality of presence that has become available, and let it move freely in their body, without having to go on to another problem or anything else. The sense of presence might deepen and new aspects or implications might reveal themselves. Or perhaps the client starts to feel uneasy, resist, or dissociate. In that case, we might move back into reflective inquiry, to see what is going on—what old beliefs, object relations, or identities may be interfering. We might then explore these obstacles reflectively until at some point, I again invite the client to be present with his or her experience in the way just described. In this way, the capacity for presence expands, while obstacles standing in its way are also worked through.

This contemplative approach to psychological work differs from conventional therapy in being more concerned with recovering the presence of being—accessed through opening directly to experience—than with problem-resolution. The problem-solving mentality reinforces the inner division between a reformer self and a problematic "me" it wants to change. By contrast, the vertical shift facilitated by unconditional presence is a change of context that alters the whole way a problem is held. People often discover that their alienated, controlling, or rejecting attitude toward the problem at hand is in fact a large part of the problem itself. This allows them to see and consider new ways of relating to the problematic situation.

Unconditional presence is more radical than psychological reflection in that it involves *giving in* to our experience (as in Trungpa's statement, "Let yourself be in the emotion, go through it, give in to it . . ."), while learning to ride the energy mindfully, without becoming overwhelmed by it. This approach is clearly not for people lacking in ego strength—those who are unable to step back and reflect on their feelings, or whose primary task is to establish a stable, cohesive self-structure. Focusing, by contrast, helps strengthen the observing ego by helping clients find the right distance from their emotional upheaval. But here one simply dives in, radically erasing any separation from one's experience.

Transmutation through unconditional presence happens somewhat differently in psychological and in meditative practice. In therapy, it is part of a dialogical process, and therefore always develops out of and returns to a reflective interchange. Reflecting on what has happened in a vertical shift also helps integrate the new quality of presence into ongoing daily functioning. In meditative practice, by contrast, mind-states can transmute in a more immediate, spontaneous way, without reference to a prior or subsequent reflective process. By not engaging in reflective articulation, the meditator can often move beyond divided consciousness in a deeper, more sustained way. The challenge here, however, lies in integrating this deeper awareness into daily life and functioning.

Ongoing Self-Liberation

Transmutation, as just described, still involves a slight sense of duality, at least initially, in that one makes some effort to go toward experience, go into it, open oneself to it. Beyond transmutation lie still subtler possibilities of nondual presence, usually only realized through advanced meditative practice. In the Mahamudra/ Dzogchen tradition, this is the way of self-liberation. Here one learns to remain continually present within the movement of experience—whether thought, perception, feeling, or sensation. In the words of a great Dzogchen master, Paltrul Rinpoche, "It is sufficient to simply let your mind rest in the state of whatever takes place, in whatever happens" (Kunsang, 1993, p. 120). This kind of naked awareness—where there is no mental or emotional reaction to whatever arises—allows each experience to be just what it is, free of dualistic grasping and fixation, and totally transparent. Pure presence makes possible the *self-liberation* of the mindstream. This is Mahamudra—the supreme mudra, the ultimate seeing that "lets beings be as the beings which they are."

What is this supreme mudra? In the words of Tilopa, one of the grandfathers of Mahamudra, "When mind is free of reference points, that is Mahamudra." Not to rely on reference points—attitudes, beliefs, intentions, aversions, self-concepts, object relations—to interpret our experience or evaluate who we are in relation to it is to rest in the "core" of being, "at the still point of the turning world, neither from nor towards." This sense of "resting in the middle of one's experience" is not a "position" in any determinate "place." This use of the term *middle* is taken from Nishitani (1982), who describes it as the

> mode of being of things as they are in themselves—namely, the mode of being wherein things rest in the complete uniqueness of what they themselves are. . . . It is immediately present—and immediately realized as such—at the point that we ourselves actually are. It is 'at hand' and 'underfoot'. . . . All actions imply an absolute immediacy. And it is there that what we are calling the 'middle' appears. (pp. 165–66)

Resting in the middle of being means standing in pure presence.

Normal divided consciousness places us on the perimeter of the field of experience, stepped back from whatever we are observing. When resting in the middle, by contrast, "the standpoint of the subject that knows things objectively, and likewise knows itself objectively as a thing called the self, is broken down" (Nishitani, 1982, p. 154). The self-knowing that arises here is immediate and nonobjectifying.

> It is not a 'knowing' that consists in the self's turning to itself and refracting into itself. It is not a 'reflective' knowing. . . . This self-awareness. . . is a knowing that comes about not as a *refraction* of the self bent into the self but only on a position that is, as it were, absolutely straightforward. . . . This is because it is a knowing that originates in the 'middle.' It is an absolutely nonobjective knowing of the absolutely nonobjective self in itself; it is a completely non-reflective knowing. . . . On all other fields the self is at all times reflective, and caught in its own grasp in the act of grasping itself, and caught in the grasp of things in its attempt to grasp them. . . . It can never be the 'straight heart' of which the ancients speak. (pp. 154–55)

The ultimate practice here is learning to remain fully present and awake in the middle of whatever thoughts, feelings, perceptions, or sensations are occurring and to appreciate them, in Mahamudra/Dzogchen terms, as Dharmakaya—as an ornamental display of the empty, luminous essence of awareness. Like waves on the ocean, thoughts are not separate from awareness. They are the radiant clarity of awareness in motion. In remaining awake in the middle of thoughts—and recognizing them as the luminous energy of awareness—the practitioner maintains presence and can rest within their movement. As Namkhai Norbu (1986) suggests:

> The essential principle is to . . . maintain presence in the state of the moving wave of thought itself. . . . If one considers the calm state as something positive to be attained, and the wave of thought as something negative to be abandoned, and one remains caught up in the duality of grasping and rejecting, there is no way of overcoming the ordinary state of the mind. (p. 144)

It is dualistic fixation, the tension between "me"—as self—and "my thoughts"—as other—that makes thinking problematic, tormenting, "sticky," like the tarbaby to which Brer Rabbit becomes affixed by trying to push it away. Thoughts become thick, solid, and heavy only when we react to them. Each reaction triggers further thought, so that the thoughts become chained together in what appears to be a continuous mind-state. These thought-chains are like a relay race, where each new thought picks up the baton from the previous thought and runs with it for a moment, passing it on again to a subsequent thought. But if the meditator can maintain presence in the middle of thinking, free of grasping or rejecting, then the thought has nothing to pass the baton on to, and naturally subsides. Although this sounds simple, it is advanced practice, usually requiring much preliminary training and commitment.

When one can rest in presence even in the midst of thoughts, perceptions, or intense emotions, these become an ongoing part of one's contemplative practice, as opportunities to discover a pervasive quality of even awareness in all one's activities. As Tarthang Tulku (1974) describes this:

> It's possible to make thought itself meditation. . . . How do we go into that state? The moment you try to separate yourself from thought, you are dealing with a duality, a subject-object relationship. You lose the state of awareness because you reject your experience and become separate from it. . . . But if our awareness is in the center of thought, the thought itself dissolves. . . . At the very beginning . . . stay in the thoughts. Just be there. . . . You become the center of the thought. But there is not really any center—the center becomes balance. There's no 'being,' no 'subject-object relationships': none of these categories exist. Yet at the same time, there is . . . complete openness. . . . So we kind of crack each thought, like cracking nuts. If we can do this, any thought becomes meditation. . . . Any moment, wherever you are, driving a car, sitting around, working, talking, any activities you have—even if you are very disturbed emotionally, very passionate, or even if your mind has become very strong, raging, overcome with the worst possible things and you cannot control yourself, or you feel depressed . . . if you really go into it, there's nothing there. Whatever comes up becomes your meditation. Even if you become extremely tense, if you go into your thought and your awareness comes alive, that moment can be more powerful than working a long time in meditation practice. (pp. 9–10, 18)

Here no antidote need be applied: no conceptual understanding, no reflection, no stepping back, no detachment, no witnessing. When one is totally present in the thought, in the emotion, in the disturbance, it relaxes by itself and becomes transparent to the larger ground of awareness. The wave subsides back into the ocean. The cloud dissolves into the sky. The snake naturally uncoils. These are all metaphors that say: It self-liberates.

Self-liberation is not a dialogical process, but a "straight heart" realization of being-emptiness. It makes possible an intimate knowing of reality, as Nishitani suggests when he writes that "things reveal themselves to us only when we leap from the circumference to the center, into their very [suchness]" (1982, p. 130). This "knowing of not-knowing" is a complete openness and attunement to the self-revealing qualities of self, world, and other beings.

For one who can remain fully present even in the middle of deluded thoughts and emotions, the distinction between samsara and nirvana, conventional and awakened consciousness, duality and nonduality is no longer of great concern. This is known as the awareness of *one taste.* When one is no longer trapped in divided consciousness, the relative duality, or play of self and other, in daily life is not a problem. One can play by the conventional ground rules of duality when appropriate, and drop them when they're not useful. The interplay of self and other becomes a humorous dance, an energetic exchange, an ornament rather than a hindrance.

Summary and Conclusion

Most of us live caught up in prereflective identification most of the time, imagining that our thoughts, feelings, attitudes, and viewpoints are an accurate portrayal of reality. But when awareness is clouded by prereflective identification, we do not yet fully *have* our experience. Rather, *it has us:* We are swept along by crosscurrents of thought and feeling in which we are unconsciously immersed. Driven by these unconscious identifications— self-images, conflicting emotions, superego commands, object relations, recurring thought-patterns—we remain asleep to the deeper import of our experience. We remain angry without even knowing we are angry, anxious without understanding why we are anxious, and hungry without realizing what we are truly hungry for. This is the condition that Gurdjieff called "the machine."

Reflective attention helps us take a major step forward from there. Conceptual reflection allows us to make an initial assessment of what is going on and why. Beyond that, subtler, more direct kinds of phenomenological reflection can help us finally start to *have* our experience. In psychotherapy, it is a major advance when clients can, for example, move from just being angry to *having* their anger. This means that their awareness can hold the anger and reflect on it, instead of being overwhelmed or clouded by it. Beyond that, mindful witnessing allows us to step back from our experience and let it be, without being caught up in reaction or identification.

A further step on the path of awakening involves learning to *be with* our experience in an even more direct and penetrating way, which I call *unconditional presence.* Here the focus is not so much on *what* we are experiencing as on *how we are with it.* Being fully present with our experience facilitates a vertical shift from personality to being. Being-with anger, for instance, involves opening to its energy directly, which often affects a spontaneous transmutation. The anger reveals deeper qualities of being hidden within it, such as strength, confidence, or radiant clarity, and this brings us into deeper connection with being itself. From this greater sense of inner connectedness, the original situation that gave rise to the anger often looks quite different.

Beyond transmutation there lies the still subtler potential to self-liberate experience through naked awareness. Instead of going into the anger, this would mean simply resting in presence as the anger arises and moves, while recognizing it as a transparent, energetic display of being-awareness-emptiness. This possibility is discovered not through a dialogical process like psychotherapy, but through contemplative practice.

To summarize the progression described here: It is a movement from unconscious, prereflective immersion in our experience (identification), to thinking and talking about experience (conceptual reflection), to having our experience directly (phenomenological reflection), to nonidentified witnessing (mindfulness), to being-present-with experience (unconditional presence, leading to transmutation), to a trans-reflective resting in open presence within whatever experience arises, which is no other than pure being/emptiness (self-liberation).

If we use the analogy of awareness as a mirror, prereflective identification is like being captivated by and lost in the reflections appearing in the mirror. Reflection involves stepping back from these appearances, studying them, and developing a more objective relationship with them. And trans-reflective presence is like being the mirror itself—that vast, illuminating openness and clarity that allows reality to be seen as what it is. In pure presence, awareness is self-illuminating, or aware of itself without objectification. The mirror simply abides in its own nature, without either separating from its reflections or confusing itself with them. Negative reflections do not stain the mirror, positive reflections do not improve on it. They are all the mirror's self-illuminating display.

Psychotherapy as a dialogical process is essentially reflective, although when practiced by a therapist with a contemplative background, it can also include moments of nonreflective presence that facilitate a shift into a deeper dimension of being. In the spiritual traditions, disciplined reflection also serves as a stepping-stone on the way toward greater presence. In Gurdjieff's teaching, for instance, focused self-observation is what allows people to step out of "the machine" and become available to the more pointed presence that he terms "self-remembering." While psychotherapy and spiritual practice may both incorporate reflection and presence, the home base of therapy is reflection and the home base of spirituality is presence.

I would like to close with a few final considerations for Western students of the further reaches of contemplative awareness. From anecdotal evidence, stabilizing the pure presence of *rigpa* in the ongoing realization of self-liberation appears to be quite rare, even among dedicated students of Dzogchen/Mahamudra. This tradition flowered in Tibet, a far simpler and more grounded culture than ours, which also provided a social mandala, or cohesive cultural context, that supported thousands of monasteries and hermitages where meditation practice and realization could flourish. Yet even there, years of preliminary practice and solitary retreat were usually recommended as the groundwork for full nondual realization, which was sometimes described as the golden roof that crowns the entire spiritual enterprise.

The question for modern Westerners, who lack the cultural supports found in traditional Asia and who often find it hard to spend years in retreat or even to complete the traditional Tibetan preliminary practices, is how to build a strong enough base on which this golden roof can rest. What kind of preliminary practices or inner work are most relevant and useful for modern people as a groundwork for nondual realization? What special conditions may be necessary to nurture and sustain nondual presence outside of retreat situations? And how can this spacious, relaxed quality of presence be integrated into everyday functioning in a speedy, complex technological society like ours, which requires such high levels of mental activity and mental abstraction?

Since unresolved psychological issues and developmental deficiencies often present major hurdles to integrating spiritual realizations into daily life, spiritual aspirants in the West may also need to engage in some degree of psychological work, as a useful adjunct to their spiritual work, and perhaps as a preliminary practice in its own right (Welwood, 1984, 2000). Perhaps for Westerners genuine nondoing and letting-be can only be fully embodied in a healthy, integrated way once one has learned to attend to bodily feelings and grapple with one's personal experience in a Focusing-style reflective manner. That is why it is important to understand the uses and limitations of psychological reflection, and to study its role as a stepping-stone both toward and "back" from nondual presence—as a bridge, in other words, that can begin to unlock deeper qualities of being and help to integrate them more fully into everyday life.

References

Gendlin, E. T. (1964). A theory of personality change. In P. Worchel & D. Byrne (Eds.), *Personality change* (pp. 101–148). New York: Wiley.
Gendlin, E. T. (1981). *Focusing.* New York: Bantam.
Gendlin, E. T. (1996). *Focusing-oriented psychotherapy.* New York: Guilford Press.
Guenther, H. (1977). *Tibetan Buddhism in Western perspective.* Berkeley, CA: Dharma Publishing.

Heidegger, M. (1977). On the essence of truth. In D. F. Kreel (Ed.), *Martin Heidegger: Basic writings* (pp. 113–141). New York: Harper.

Izutsu, T. (1972). *Toward a philosophy of Zen Buddhism.* Teheran: Imperial Iranian Academy of Philosophy.

Koestenbaum, P. (1978). *The new image of the person.* Westwood, CT: Greenwood Press.

Krishnamurti, J. (1976). *Krishnamurti's notebook.* New York: HarperCollins.

Kunsang, E. P. (Trans.). (1993). *The flight of the garuda: Five texts from the practice lineage.* Kathmandu: Rangjung Yeshe.

Marcel, G. (1950). *The mystery of being: Vol. 1. Reflection and mystery* (G. S. Fraser Trans.). Chicago: Henry Regnery.

Merleau-Ponty, M. (1968). *The visible and the invisible* (A. Lingis, Trans.). Evanston, IL: Northwestern University Press.

Merrill-Wolff, F. (1994). *Experience and philosophy.* Albany: State University of New York Press.

Nalanda Translation Committee (1980). *The rain of wisdom.* Boston: Shambhala.

Nishitani, K. (1982). *Religion and nothingness.* Berkeley and Los Angeles: University of California Press.

Norbu, N. (1982). *The song of the vajra.* Conway, MA: Dzogchen Community.

Norbu, N. (1986). *The crystal and the way of light.* New York and London: Routledge & Kegan Paul.

Nyima, C. (1991). *The bardo guidebook.* Kathmandu: Rangjung Yeshe.

Poonja, H. W. L. (1993). *Wake up and roar.* Vol. 2. Maui, HI: Pacific Center Publishing.

Tulku, T. (1974). *On thoughts.* Crystal Mirror, 3, 7–20.

Trungpa, C. (1973). *Cutting through spiritual materialism.* Boston: Shambhala.

Trungpa, C. (1976). *The myth of freedom.* Boston: Shambhala.

Welwood, J. (1979). Befriending emotion: Self-knowledge and transformation. *The Journal of Transpersonal Psychology, 2*(1), 141–160.

Welwood, J. (1982). The unfolding of experience: Psychotherapy and beyond. *Journal of Humanistic Psychology, 22*(1), 91–104.

Welwood, J. (1984). Principles of inner work: Psychological and spiritual. *The Journal of Transpersonal Psychology, 16*(1), 63–73.

Welwood, J. (1992). The healing power of unconditional presence. In J. Welwood (Ed.), *Ordinary magic: Everyday life as spiritual path* (pp. 159–170). Boston: Shambhala.

Welwood, J. (2000). *Toward a psychology of awakening: Buddhism, psychotherapy, and the path of personal and spiritual transformation.* Boston: Shambhala.

6

Dissolving the Center

Streamlining the Mind and Dismantling the Self

FRED J. HANNA

A lthough the term has been in use for decades, being "centered" has become an especially common expression in the last decade. The term is utilized by Gestalt, existential, humanistic, and cognitive therapists, as well as transpersonal psychologists, martial artists, and those studying and practicing various meditative or other spiritual disciplines. This chapter is an attempt to describe the scope and limits of centeredness in the context of my own experience over the course of three decades of sustained meditative and introspective practices. What follows is not based on theory but descriptions of actual events and experiences. The focus is on exposing the nature of the "center" of consciousness. From a different perspective, this inquiry is an examination of changes at the core level of self and mind as a result of meditative practice.

Looking back on my experience, and on the many interviews I have done with others, I have come to regard the notion of a center as a pivotal point in which to regard the progression and momentum of meditative practice. For the sake of illustration and discussion, the idea of a center and the self are often considered to be somewhat synonymous. A common expression, for example, is when a person speaks of "being centered in myself." If the self or ego is considered to be at the center of the human psyche, as some developmental psychologists have claimed (e.g., Loevinger, 1976), then self and center may well be different labels for what is largely the same general region of experience. Both self and center may also be functionally understood as the origin point of awareness. Each seems to serve as a source point from which, at a mundane level, consciousness

113

seems to spring. Of course, there are many ways of looking at this but it is precisely the nature of this center that has held my fascination for thirty years. I consider the center to be one possible focal point for the measurement of progress on the contemplative path to personal and psychospiritual growth and development.

In this chapter I describe three major stages and several substages that may be identified in the transformation of the center of consciousness. I would like to clarify that these stages are descriptive of my own path and development. Unlike most developmental stage schemes, I make no claims that my experience also applies to the experience of others. The major stages are that of being precentered, centered, and decentered. Each of these three stages, along with their respective substages, will be defined and described in terms of my own experience, with occasional references to the experiences of others. My purpose is to show the complexity of the psychospiritual path and to outline this somewhat different approach to spiritual development based on events that occur at the center of consciousness. An appendix is provided that lists all the stages and substages.

Let me reiterate that there are no claims made here that all practitioners experience or should experience these stages in their psychospiritual growth. These stages are my own. I delineate only the stages that I have experienced. Thus, when I do refer to stages, I ask the reader to bear in mind that I am not implying that these stages are the same for everyone. What follows is a condensed narrative of a personal history of psychospiritual exploration and growth. Put in a different way, this is a report of my own phenomenological investigations over a period of more than three decades.

Defining Centeredness

In view of the fact that this chapter is built on and around the notion of centeredness, and what it means to be centered and decentered, it may be helpful to define the term before exploring the stages. Centeredness is an experiential sense of being that is intimately related to the idea of "I-am-ness"—that sense of being aware, alive, and at the center point—the source point and receiving point—of conscious experience. In the context of this chapter, it is a sense that is usually brought about by various introspective, contemplative, or meditative endeavors. *It is important to note that being centered does not require any transcendent or mystical experience.* It is simply being settled into one's inner nature without being displaced, confused, or lost in mental images, memories and thoughts, or thrown off by strong feelings that disturb awareness. It could be said that the center is a "locale" in one's inner landscape with which a person becomes familiar and knows how to find. Exposing that center, however, is an extraordinary challenge and requires transcendence of and dismantling the center itself.

A Note on Dismantling Mind and Self

This chapter represents a somewhat radical approach to psychospirituality, incorporating and integrating the knowledge of psychotherapy, psychopathology, spirituality, and meditative pursuits. It asserts, based on experiential investigations, that there is neither a self nor a Self, and that most mental functions are a liability on the path to psychospiritual insight. These are not stated as Truth. Nor are they new ideas. But the approach taken is from a slightly different perspective. Also, a critical attitude is taken toward the mind and how it has become so cumbersome, fragmented, and conflicted that it is an obstacle to growth and development. The Chinese Zen master Huang Po, for example, said that learning to halt the concept-forming activities of the mind is the key to realization. This chapter is about divesting and streamlining the mind so that it becomes permanently less active. It is also about about dismantling and disposing of a rather useless psychological entity—the self. This is not at all an issue of self-esteem or self-negation. As Engler (1986) said, "You have to be somebody before you can be nobody" (p. 24).

The Precentered Stage

This stage begins with the first experience of being centered. Only after I had experienced centeredness did it become clear to me that almost all of my life was lived without being centered. But because this centeredness was not permanent, I have called this stage "precentered." In 1966, at the age of sixteen, I began a series of introspective experiments that have continued for well over thirty years. My first experiments began with using techniques I found in a book on self-hypnosis. My interest was not so much in autosuggestion as much as to examine the fascinating trance states that I found could be brought about using these techniques. I found trance to be very peaceful and relaxing, especially when combined with the progressive relaxation techniques that were included in the book. Eventually, I was able to arrive at what I considered to be levels of considerable "depth." What I found particularly valuable was the feeling of having submerged myself far below the surface activity of the mind by diving beneath it and resting in what appeared to be an inner region of silence and peace. It was like floating on an underground river, aware of the activity on the surface but being wonderfully alone, peaceful, and centered for the first time. I did not know at the time that this was the beginning of what was to become the single greatest interest and passion of my life.

In late 1967 I discovered a now out of print book that described the technique of meditation from the perspectives of each of the world's major religions, as well as from a nonreligious perspective. It was called, *The Teachings of the Mystics* by Walter T. Stace (1960). The book consisted of an anthology along with Stace's invaluable commentary. After studying these techniques, which consisted mostly of concentrative meditation, I was initially daunted by the improbability of ever transcending mind and thought processes, as the ancient texts seem to require. However, my experience with self-hypnosis suggested that the difficult task of transcending the mind could be alleviated somewhat by placing myself in the deepest trance possible and then beginning to meditate while in that self-induced trance. This involved the body becoming completely relaxed and disconnected from my immediate conscious control through autosuggestion. It also involved submerging myself far below the surface activity of the everyday rush of thought and mental processes, finding that peaceful centered feeling, and then commencing with the technique. It worked surprisingly well.

Without a teacher, and without any specific goals or expectations, I enthusiastically began to meditate by silently repeating the syllable "OM," that I had picked up from reading the ancient Hindu texts called the *Upanishads* (Nikhilananda, 1963). I was very excited. I felt as though I had found a secret pathway into the inner caverns of the mind and self. I told no one of this activity. Thus, no one gave me expectations that meditating was difficult, that the activity was silly, or that success was likely to be out of my reach.

My only purpose was to explore the inner landscapes that meditation revealed and to practice it to the best my ability. I took the same experimental approach that I had with self-hypnosis. That I was also undergoing a religious conflict at the time was of great help in motivating my practice even though I was not expecting any major answers or, least of all, transcendence. Although I found out later that I was incorrectly pronouncing the sacred sound of OM, it did not seem to matter. I soon had experiences in meditation of intensely vivid scenes ranging from galaxies to surreal landscapes. I emerged from these experiences feeling greatly refreshed and energetic. But I knew from reading the texts that these were not significant in themselves. Eventually I had several more intense experiences of clear, expanded awareness well beyond familiar modes of perceiving and knowing.

Then, on a fortunate day in January of 1968, a thoroughly remarkable major event occurred. I was silently repeating OM in my usual incorrectly pronounced fashion, in the way the *Upanishads* had described the method. Looking back, I recall that I sometimes visualized the mantra as described in the ancient texts: the "raft of Brahman" moving across the waters of the mind and through the winds of the world, toward the shores of transcendent reality. In this session, I achieved a state of transcendence, arriving at what I considered at the time to be the "core of reality." This also seemed to be the wellspring of consciousness itself and I had seen it. Brahman, of course, is the ultimate reality in that classic text and in the Vedanta school of Hinduism. I instantly realized that I had moved beyond the world of phenomena and arrived at what I characterized as "timeless infinity," in a primordial and fundamentally unique way of knowing. I had directly encountered what I instinctively recognized as the "source of all things." After this experience I recall thinking to myself that I now better understood what the sages in the *Upanishads* had been talking about. I had gained personal insight into the meaning of the phrases, "the One without a second" and "Thou art That."

A Taste of Centeredness

Following this experience and for the next three months, I found myself truly centered for the first time in my life. The tone, temper, and tenor of my life had changed profoundly, pervasively, and positively. The structure of my thinking had been reorganized at deep levels and included deep appreciation for global meanings and realities. I recognized and perceived that "source of all things" everywhere I looked, and everything I saw with my eyes sparkled with intrinsic beauty. I felt connected to, identified with, and in communion with all beings and things. I found myself in astonishment as new understandings blossomed before me in a series of continuous spontaneous insights that lasted at least three months. Eventually, these insights stabilized, leading to my coasting on the "high" feeling that accompanied them and eventually reached a plateau. In a word, I was happy beyond any expectations I had ever had of life at that tender age of eighteen. I never dreamed I could be so damned happy. Life seemed filled with intrinsic meaning—it made sense. This elation finally subsided after about six months. I now regard this experience as opening the door to what I call the first substage of precenteredness—the glimpse of the transcendent reality beyond perception of the world, and unavailable to access through mundane cognitive processes.

However, at another level that I would not have admitted to myself at the time, some disturbing and unbalanced feelings and thoughts were brewing, soon to rise to the surface. At a subtle level, I began to feel special, somehow privileged, and amazed that such a thing would have happened to me—ME. I mistakenly began to think that I had risen beyond the mundane concerns of life. Of course, these were issues rooted in a narcissistic psychopathology that I would have to deal with later, as we shall see.

In any case, after the "glow" of the experience wore off, certain life events took place that diminished that sense of centeredness. After about seven months had passed, I found myself off-center and confused. Although my transcendent experience continued to serve as a "cushion" for life's hardships, depressions, and disappointments, I was feeling many intensely negative emotions along with mood swings of great magnitude. It was a time of deep pain. As the saying goes, "you don't know what you've got till it's gone." This certainly proved true for me. Years later I realized that this was my version of the dark night of the soul spoken of by Saint John of the Cross (1959). This episode of the dark night remains the most severe that I have experienced since.

I had just begun to realize the nature of happiness, fulfillment, and joy when I found that I was no longer centered and that I was being buffeted by the winds of negative emotions and psychological manifestations that were quite new to me. Much to my bewilderment, I longed for an experience as powerful as the one in January to remedy my emotional instability and the cognitive confusion. Unfortunately, the meditation on OM that had worked so well for me was much less productive, almost useless. I felt I had to find something else to continue on my path or remain in this unpleasant state of rollercoastering between buoyant joy, pervasive apathy, deep sadness, and a heavy despondency. I felt stymied, obstructed, weighted down, and stopped cold.

My initial passion during this time was to more fully extend my experience of that "core of reality" or "source of all things" in such a way as to reach a closure with that reality. In other words, I knew intuitively and had inferred from my readings that the next step was to merge or "become one" with it. The problem was that OM was not working and I did not have a clue as how to bring this about. I was saved by that same intuitively driven, psychoexperimental attitude that originally got me there. But it took a couple of years.

One of the insights that regularly manifested during meditation was the realization that I, as a manifestation of pure being and pure consciousness, was not limited to any particular identity or viewpoint or belief. In fact, I came to understand that I, as consciousness, was in fact a source of identities and viewpoints. Early in 1970, as a result of these insights, I developed an exercise consisting of seeing the world as if through the eyes, ears, and feelings of other persons and entities such as birds and animals. I eventually formalized this into a set of exercises that were aimed at expanding viewpoints and becoming free of the need for an identity. I had realized that ultimately I had no intrinsic identity and that any identity is merely an illusory defense against the vastness of the universe.

The exercise itself involved systematically assuming the perspectives and viewpoints of people, communities, animals, and physical objects. The essence of the exercise was to "be" those objects and entities until I had a sense of what they were about. This was not a mere intellectual exercise. Actually, it was an exercise in empathic relating, experiencing each object or entity as fully as possible. Eventually, I experimented with being entire communities, nations, and ecological systems. It was an exhilarating endeavor and one that I took great pleasure in practicing. Once again, I did not expect what was to take place.

True Center. In July of 1970 I was performing this exercise and its final phase, which involved assuming the viewpoint of all existence. I was sitting in a living room chair when instantly all worldly perception, thinking, and feeling ceased. There was, once again, only the "source of all things—the "One without a second." Then in an instant and for no apparent reason, I suddenly became that "core of reality," and I was a self no more. I was now the Self, the "I" of all of existence—all that was and all that ever could be. It lasted several seconds before "normal" worldly perception slowly reasserted itself. But now things were very different. I was literally no longer the same person that I was before. I fully saw that "I" was the "Self—the whole of existence and that my egoic self was an illusion of considerable proportions. I realized even more deeply the meaning of the classic statements, "One without a second" and "All this is That." The world—with all of its wonders, vagaries, and evil—was my friend and I have trusted it ever since. I realized that all I had to do to be happy was "to be" and "to do" according to That, my true nature.

I had finally merged with the transcendent reality and in the process had, for that moment, completely transcended the egoic self. During this moment, there was no thought, no body, no perception of worldly objects or mental images. There was only that "undifferentiated aesthetic continuum" (Northrop, 1946). When I finally returned to normal perception and functioning, the entire world was shining brightly from within and I experienced the joy and light that I had in 1968 but now with even more intensity and magnitude. The volume of my joy had hit dizzying heights of euphoria and bliss. I was even relearning how to walk and talk. I knew what the Sufis had meant by the term, "god intoxication."

In any case, I was now convinced that I could never be anything other than centered and in complete communion with the universal. I was mistaken, of course. I did not know that much of this delicious bliss would pass, and that the illusion of self was alive and well, and waiting for its moment to rise again. Nevertheless, for the moment, I had attained a centeredness so global and all-encompassing that both center and perimeter were indistinguishably the same. All the perceived universe was the center and there was no more "me" to trip and stumble over.

This transcendence and resulting insight was a clear pivot point that I now regard as the second substage of precenteredness—merging with that transcendent reality to the point of full identification with it. After about six months, the dizzying heights once again settled down to become a new plateau. The influence of mind that I referred to earlier returned, but this time without the dramatic mood swings, dark nights, and depths of despair. They were there to be sure but not quite as pronounced. Nevertheless, by this time I was acutely tuned to the dynamic forces and seductive power of the mind and my thinking and imaging patterns. I soon learned a sobering lesson. As powerful as the transcendent experience was, it was not as powerful as the mental activities that soon took control. After all, I only fully escaped the mind for a few moments, glorious as they were. Why did I not remain transcended for much longer? Why was it only for a few moments? It did not make sense. But there was an answer.

I was more aware than ever of the need to attend to my mundane psychological issues and problems, which now seemed to be uncovered and surfacing at a rate that demanded attention. To put it plainly, I became increasingly aware that I had personal issues that I had blithely ignored. After the glow wore off, I was again alternating dangerously between depression and joy, on an emotional roller coaster. I was convinced that following some kind of psychotherapeutic path was necessary to stabilize the center. Even though I was no longer the same self that I was, I vowed to continue to find the entrance point to the mind and maintain a state of freedom from its negative influences. I eventually learned that the mind is quite okay in itself, but that it contains negative programming, automaticities, and irrational beliefs that are profoundly destructive to any sense of well being. These useless aspects of mind, in addition to the much maligned ego, need to be divested and discarded before any stability can be attained. In short, as long as the mind remained out of control, I remained its slave.

Precenteredness and Psychopathology

I also discovered that in this Precentered Stage, the self, or center, is not fully formed in the developmental sense. Even though full transcendent knowing can take place momentarily at this stage, there is still the imminent possibility of the person returning to primitive narcissistic, borderline, schizotypal, or histrionic traits that remain untouched. As Thera (1964) noted, even the highest meditative attainments "cannot penetrate deep enough into the recesses of the mind for a removal of moral and intellectual defilements" (p. 27). Many therapists have pointed out that nearly all human beings have deep rooted, primitive hostility and hate that they have suppressed. With the removal of many inhibitions brought about by this powerful experience, I was seeing my own deeper issues roaring to the surface. The transcendent experience was so powerful that I was fooled into thinking that my personal issues had been wiped clean. It was not all negative. I was amazed at how much more empathic I had become. The inner worlds of others now seemed to open before me and I was curious and interested in exploring those worlds. It was easy to ignore the negative impulses, desires, and ambitions that were simultaneously awakened by this grand experience.

A pivotal question seems to be whether a person's transcendental experience leads to compassion and empathy with others, and whether there is a reduction in egocentric, selfish preoccupations. As these latter traits are also major characteristics of certain personality disorders, the alleviation of such problems becomes central to the development of the self. Indeed, egocentrism and lack of empathy are classic indicators of the lack of development of an authentic self. I am now convinced that transcendental experiences can occur to persons with serious personality disorders. Such persons often become dangerous teachers due to their lack of empathy and compassion for their students.

Thus, the mind can be transcended through a psychospiritual "escape hatch," but the deeper emotional issues and problems will still be there when one returns to ordinary life. This cannot be overemphasized. I have met several persons who claimed to be spiritual teachers who seem to have genuinely experienced transcendence, but remain chronically unempathic, much to the detriment of their students. They talk at at length about compassion and love but by their actions seem to be more interested in the love of sex and the love of self, and sometimes, the love of money or alcohol. Much has been written of this in recent years (see Feuerstein, 1990; Walsh & Vaughan, 1993). In such cases, psychotherapy would be a proper prescription (Kornfield, 1993) as these persons tend to be destructive to those around them.

It is likely that these experiences may have bypassed the essential step of reorganizing the core self so that one can address and work through his or her narcissistic or borderline issues. Only then can one stabilize the capacity for empathy and compassion. In other words, the empathy and compassion that one experiences through meditation and transcendence may only be temporary, felt concomitantly with the glow from the transcendent experience—and wears off soon after. It may also be that in such cases, after the glow diminishes, a person becomes infatuated with the fact of having been "chosen," or privileged to have reached beyond the mundane. The person may now feel that he or she has become somehow superior or special—beyond mere ordinary persons. Such a person then subtly, un-knowingly, and indirectly, projects himself or herself as a new standard for humanity. This is, of course, dangerous, especially to those who trust them-selves to the "wisdom" of such persons. It is unfortunate that, with all the literature on meditation and transcendence, this connection with psy-chopathology is almost never mentioned. If it were, both teachers and stu-dents could more readily recognize such manifestations and realize that they are natural consequences of transcendence that need to be resolved.

In my own case, I observed that I was given to illusory beliefs, magical thinking, and self-aggrandizement. This was very subtle and was probably never noticed by others as I knew better than to display such impulses. My saving grace was that I eventually recognized these as psychopathological. I see now that transcendence has a way of bringing these issues out in a per-son as part of the cognitive reorganization and the intense emotions aroused. The sanity of a person depends on whether these issues are ade-quately confronted and worked through. Thus, like the self, many of the grand insights at the Precentered Stage can, sadly, be considered transitory, vague, fragmented, erratic, unreliable, and alloyed with needs and disor-ders of the personality. No wonder I could not stay centered. I also learned another humbling lesson: So-called knowledge arising from transcendence is similarly unreliable, often impulsive rather than intuitive, and drawn from memory reconstruction of the transcendent moment rather than the spon-taneous experiencing and knowing in the here and now.

In retrospect, this was a period in my life where I learned of the diffi-culties of staying centered and of the power of the mind to undermine and knock me off-center. Indeed, it was the mind that colored, influ-enced, and destabilized that clear conscious awareness that at other times seemed so poised and unshakable. I began to intensively study a wide va-riety of sources, ranging from the *Yoga Sutras* of Patanjali (Aranya, 1983; Deshpande, 1978; Feuerstein, 1989) to theosophy, the occult, and various forms of existential psychology. I had no biases toward anything that might offer an avenue. This was a serious attempt to discover a way to sta-bilize and enhance that way of being that I had come to realize was "true normal"—the way we should be at all times. Up to this point, although I had experienced being centered hundreds of times, I still had not stabi-lized it. The inquiry continued.

The Centered Stage

The next fourteen years were dedicated to finding the secret of stabilized centeredness. It was my good fortune to have acquired a reliable, intuitive, inner source that served me well from the time I was eighteen. Curiously, I had little inclination toward finding a guru although I found many teachers and learned much from many books during this time. I faithfully followed that intuitive sense that seemed to "know" what was appropriate and fruitful for my development at a given time. This intuition persisted in spite of many confusions and embroilments in my life at different times. I found out years later that Theravada Buddhists refer to this intuition as the "knowledge of path and not path."

I continued to meditate and to study a wide variety of disciplines and subjects. Many of these subjects were mainstream and many were far removed from the conventional. I did not care. I was interested in whatever might help. An indispensable tool was my earlier study of dialectical philosophy, which enabled me to acquire an intuitive wariness of packaged presentations of truth by various groups, cults, and disciplines. I tried all manner of techniques and strategies to become free of the snares and entrapments of the mind. My goal was to become centered and stay that way.

My experiments with the methods of the phenomenological philosophy of Edmund Husserl (1931) along with my continued readings of Patanjali's methods and the Indian philosopher, Shankaracharya (Prabhavananda & Isherwood, 1970) brought me a deep understanding of the phrase, "pure consciousness." The full understanding of this phrase, I was to learn, was the key to the Centered Stage. In my meditations, I had several encounters with elusive, almost intangible, aspects of the mind that served to cloud or dim awareness in extremely subtle ways. I sought to free consciousness of such admixtures. This kind of pursuit was not a matter of, nor it did it require, transcendence. It was closer to psychotherapy than meditation. Importantly, it made meditation easier and more efficient. Nevertheless, using various techniques to purify awareness directly led to my realizing that consciousness could be free of any anxiety, depression, hostility, or delusion. I learned how to disidentify with subtle images, mental constructs, ego remnants, and self-concepts. I learned that these aspects of mind obstruct transcendence and may well be the chief reason that people need to meditate at all. I found that to the degree these mental phenomena are removed or divested, transcendence takes place more naturally and spontaneously. When consciousness is "pure" in the unclouded sense, there is always a sense of centeredness and connectedness to the transcendent, in spite of any turmoil and agitation that may be arising from the mind or the environment.

Cleansing or Purifying Consciousness

While in early pursuit of pure consciousness, a thoroughly remarkable experience occurred to me that firmly established me on my quest to become stably centered. In the fall of 1970, a chemistry-major friend approached me with what he called chemically pure mescaline. He told me in no uncertain terms that everything I had sought through meditation could be supplied in one sitting with this drug. I told him that I had quit using drugs in 1968. He insisted that I try one more time and was quite sincere about it. He even said that he felt a bit sorry for me, seeing me working so hard on my meditative endeavors. I finally agreed to try it if he were willing to hear what I actually thought of the experience. He agreed and that weekend we went to a outdoor movie theater and took the pills together.

The first three hours of this experience were wholly remarkable for the vivid hallucinations, colors, racing thoughts, and blazingly bright perceptions that the drug caused. I was enjoying myself when something quite unexpected took place. I recall thinking to myself at the time that this euphoria made it easy to understand why some persons are so taken with hallucinogens. When he asked, I told my friend that I was having a good time but that this was not at all comparable to the joy and bliss that transcendence in meditation provides. He was incredulous but listened with respect. An hour later, just as I was beginning to "peak," I remember having the thought that I could enter magical worlds and see the magical beings that live there. The euphoria had intensified by this time. At that moment, this thought arose: "I wonder what would happen if I left my body."

I instantly felt myself leave my body and "float" out through the car and into the cool October night. It was a classic example of those dissociative experiences that commonly occur under the influence of this class of drugs. But what I observed was absolutely remarkable. In that one instant of seeming to leave the body *I was no longer under the influence of the drug.* The drive-in theater looked entirely normal to me. No more racing thoughts, buzzing sensations, or altered perceptions, and no more fantasizing about magical worlds. The quality of my awareness was as normal as it ever could have been. It was as if I had never taken the drug at all. Then, just as spontaneously, I reentered my body and was instantly deluged by all the altered, bizarre perceptions, the rushing thoughts, and the intensely varied colors that had been previously coursing through my awareness. I was quite literally astounded. I decided to detach consciousness from the body one more time. As I did so, once again everything was completely normal. What I had seen as diamonds on the ground were once again stones. The movie screen no longer poured forth colors as though from an enchanted pitcher. Everything was completely normal. The irony was that I had to detach from almost all bodily awareness to know that.

As a result of this, I dramatically and poignantly realized that consciousness is not confined to the mind, brain, or body. Please note that I am not making a metaphysical case for out-of-body experiences or mind/body separatism here. What I am saying is that once consciousness seemed to be free of the body, it also seemed to be free from the influence of a very powerful drug that seemed to have set my brain "on fire." I learned an indelible lesson in that moment. Specifically, that consciousness could disidentify and consciously detach itself from the senses and mental processes, and not only does it remain intact but it becomes pure in the process. In Yoga this is called *pratyahara* (Aranya, 1983).

In addition to the lesson of pure consciousness, I learned that drugs are limited to sense and sensation. They directly affect the brain and perception, and what consciousness is aware of, but only indirectly do they affect consciousness itself—and not enough to bother with them. I should mention that I never again tried a hallucinogen and smoked hashish only one time after that, about six months later in early 1971. I have not since taken a mind-altering drug of any kind other than alcohol. Paradoxically, my one, rather pleasant, experience with mescaline taught me the futility of all psychoactive drugs as a means to psychospiritual growth.

It is fascinating to me that this experience with mescaline occurred during a time when I was intensely interested in observing the activity, operation, and dynamics of mind and thinking. I was especially interested in deconditioning automatic behaviors and thought patterns of reaction and association. These are the source of so many hidden stressors and problems in life. Curiously, I was more capable of applying experiential techniques designed to release repressed feelings of pain and stress that I had habitually buried as part of my early lifestyle and as part of the stereotypical role of my gender. I became deeply committed and involved in this self-therapy. This arduous and often deeply painful work was akin to certain forms of psychotherapy, especially of the Gestalt and experiential schools. However, the techniques were aimed at the interface between consciousness and mind. The effects were a deep and satisfying sense of cleansing and purging of mind and emotions that made transcendent experiences even more accessible.

From the viewpoint of Yoga, this work was devoted to dissolving the *samskaras* (mental impressions). These are literally the fundamental element of the conditioned mind. This is an essential aspect of yogic practice. Years of this practice combined and balanced with further transcendental experience eventually yielded an understanding of an essential life force that moves through the body and mind and all living beings. In Yoga this life force is called *prana*, while in China it is referred to as *chi* (Worthington, 1982). Initially, I simply referred to this as "energy" until one day it dawned on me that this must be the life force of which I had read. I have since learned to use this life force in a variety of ways to maintain the health of both body and mind. I will return to this at the Decentered Stage.

By 1974, I had reached what I consider to be descriptive of a first sub-stage of centeredness. In this substage, consciousness is established as the center of all activity, largely freed of mental processes and reactions. This is not to say that these processes and reactions do not take place, only that consciousness is ever observant and aware of the tides, flows, and eddies of mental processes, reactions, and emotions. Put a bit differently, it might be said that consciousness is released to some degree from the "shell" of one's personality and is able to recognize itself as always being at the center. Of course, personality traits still need to be dealt with, as well as the deeper issue of the self. One is at risk to the degree that one believes that these traits are harmless or of little consequence in terms of psychospiritual development. In fact, this may be why the Buddha incorporated the technique of mindfulness meditation into the Buddhist path (Thera, 1964). The most glorious meditative experiences do not touch the root causes of psychopathology (see also Feuerstein, 1990).

In Yoga these are called the defilements or klesas. These need to be dealt with directly through techniques such as Buddhist mindfulness or those specific techniques prescribed by Patanjali. The klesas simply do not get eliminated without such techniques. I have seen them temporarily disappear accompanied by a feeling of purging and inner purification, but this is only temporary. Patanjali (Aranya, 1983) said that klesas can go into a dormant state. Unfortunately, this also means that klesas do return when the right situation triggers them. What is confusing is that the person often believes that they are gone and acts as if this were true. For example, I once knew a male meditation teacher, with a strong inclination toward unethical sexual activity, who had undergone a transcendent experience that led him to believe that he now valued relationships over raw sexual sensation. However, when he was soon presented with an opportunity to seduce a young woman, he believed that his inclination toward sexuality had somehow become pure because of the earlier transcendent experience. The net result was that the young woman felt exploited and betrayed.

This is a serious error and comes from the fact that the klesa had not disappeared. It had only gone dormant (see Aranya, 1983) and can come back again. The man in the example ended up doing the same thing as he had before but even worse, because he then believed that he was pure and untainted in the manner of his seduction. I have seen too much and interviewed too many people to believe that klesas just disappear for no apparent reason. Yet, many persons believe exactly that. An unfortunate result of this viewpoint is that a person comes to erroneously believe that transcendent experiences provide permanent psychotherapeutic change for mental and emotional disorders. This can lead to a person doing mediation with the goal of escaping the world and problems rather than growing through real-time experience within it (see Feuerstein, 1990).

At this substage, consciousness and knowing appear to arise out of the same inner point that the self occupies. It would be as though the pit of a peach (consciousness) was clearly embedded in the center of the fruit surrounding it (personality shell) and just as clearly differentiated. Transcendental knowledge arising as a result of meditation or spontaneous experience seems to arrive or take place through this central point of consciousness. Functionally, a person at this substage no longer chronically or habitually engages in thinking. Rather, his or her modus operandi is characterized by the sustained action of looking, observing, and discerning. This is not to say that thinking does not occur, it just no longer occurs at the center of one's being. The center is now pure awareness. An important point is that at this stage consciousness remains partially embedded in the personality shell—which still contains unseen egoic and samskaric manifestations, in spite of previous occurrences of transcendence.

Releasing the Center

Of the wide range of subjects that I studied in my attempt at freedom from negative influences of mind, the Yoga Sutras contained the ideas that provided the key to freedom. This ancient text is considered the most important source for the psychological theory and practice in all of Indian philosophy. It also has had wide influence upon other schools such as Buddhism, Taoism, Vedanta, and Jainism (Worthington, 1982). Patanjali's aphorisms about the mind are quite conducive to practical application. These also foster the experimental spirit that Bharati (1974) noted to be so important.

The chief lesson I learned from Patanjali and his Yoga Sutras was that the self is an aspect of and a construction of mind, and that both self and mind are of a different order of existence than consciousness. In the Yogic scheme, there are two primary constituents—*prakriti,* or materiality and *purusha,* or consciousness. Both mind and self are a subtle form of prakriti or materiality. This was borne out in my own explorations in meditation where I found repeatedly that consciousness, or the faculty of seeing or looking, is much more subtle than any mental manifestation such as an image, thought, or desire. And sure enough, according to Patanjali, mind is of the nature of the perceived while consciousness is of the nature of the perceiver. Indeed, the self, being a construct, can also be directly perceived as an object of consciousness, although this sometimes takes years to see. According to Patanjali, mind is of the same nature as physical objects. My insight was that if this is true, then mind can be reduced to energy just as physical matter can be transformed into physical energy. I soon became involved in experiments wherein I was attempting to dissolve mental obstructions that are at the bottom of states of lethargy and depression, releasing them into the pure mental energy of which they seem to be composed. It worked for myself and for others as well. The complete procedure is documented in two articles (Hanna, 1991; Puhakka & Hanna, 1988).

Confounding the process of converting mental constructions into energy is the issue of identification. According to Patanjali, consciousness becomes confused and entrapped when it identifies itself with mind and body. This was one of the most significant insights of my life. My investigations indicated to me that to the degree that consciousness identifies with a mental construction it will to that degree become unlikely to ever come to observe it. In other words, what should be in the realm of the perceived is now hidden in background of the realm of the perceiver. The perceiver has identified with these constructions as intrinsic characteristics. For example, a young girl may have been convinced that she is immoral due to her cruel father's verbal abuse. In this case, she has identified with this belief, image, or mental construction as the case may be. Before she can rid herself of the problem, she first has to disidentify from it so that she can come to view it directly.

In this same way, various psychopathological traits such as arrogance and lack of empathy never become examined as part of the psychospiritual quest, largely because they have become infused into that which is doing the seeing. It would be like a human eye attempting to turn around and see itself. The trick is to extract consciousness from the mind and its creations and to stop identifying with them. The aforementioned techniques effectively deal with this process (see Puhakka & Hanna, 1988).

In due time, I was routinely disidentifying consciousness from mind and its manifestations. After a little practice, I realized that consciousness could eventually come to confront, envelop, and pervade virtually any issue or source of mental or emotional conflict or pain. The personality shell or husk that surrounded me was beginning to slowly dissipate as I continued to observe it and dissolve it. After several years of trial and experimentation, I clearly saw that consciousness can affect, rise above, and/or dissolve any mental construction, image, thought complex, memory, or emotional pain. This is a liberating insight. The net result is that no depression, anxiety, or impulse can contain the penetrating influence, and joy, of pure consciousness. Making use of this insight provides a key to lasting joy.

In fact, it was in 1974 that a host of meditative insights and experiences combined to give me the certainty that consciousness was primordially and ultimately the master of mind and perception. Indeed, consciousness creates and constitutes the inner world. Through my study and practice I eventually learned to undo anything that the mind created. Of course, I still managed to make foolish mistakes, and occasionally become confused. But I had realized beyond any reasonable doubt that consciousness had the capability to alter and dissolve virtually any image, complex, thought, or trait. Indeed, it became obvious that consciousness was the ultimate source of all such mental constructions. In my practice-inspired interpretation of Patanjali's Yoga, this action is called *pratiprasava*. After seven years, I had found an effective tool to approach centeredness I had sought for so long. I simply uncreated, deconstructed, or dismantled any mental construct that intruded into awareness. I now had attained a degree of mastery over mind and self.

This mastery was the second substage of centeredness. When consciousness is integrated, settled, and established in itself with no need for mental ideas or constructions as props and supports, it become liberated from being chronically absorbed or lost in mental processes. It can exert direct influence on the mind and can change any of its manifestations. It no longer needs thoughts in order to feel alive and aware. The pith is removed from the peach.

Consciousness is now seen as separate from self, more primal than self and inherently absolute. This is not to say that consciousness no longer becomes buffeted and blown about by internal mental forces; indeed it does. The difference is that awareness of the clean and pure nature of consciousness is maintained throughout and that consciousness can directly act to change and diminish virtually anything in the mind. Just as one knows that the dirt that accumulates on the body is not of the true nature of the body, so one knows that the mental debris that compiles and compounds in the mind is not a part of consciousness. This is not an occasional occurrence as it is in the previous stages. It is permanent. Pratiprasava, or the uncreating, is the key to this purification.

Exploding Outward from the Center

This realization was graphically played out as a result of an experience in May of 1977. I was traveling alone, contemplating the rugged desert country of southern Idaho near the area known as the Craters of the Moon. As I surveyed the desert, I realized that I felt somewhat awed and a bit threatened by the vast inhospitable landscape that rolled on before me from horizon to horizon. I then realized with something of a start that my concern was based on my body's inherent survival instincts. A simple insight flowed from this, which indicated to me that concern for the survival of consciousness was absurd and that my concern was actually for the body. Images flowed before me, times and actions that were dictated by the need to protect the body. Soon the insight became more global. In a flash, I saw hundreds of memories of my locking doors, stopping at red lights, taking karate lessons, and eating healthy. I recognized how much time was spent protecting the body and how little time was devoted to psychospiritual growth. It was clear to me that for most of my life, I had compromised my spiritual integrity. This in and of itself was a minor insight at best. It was what followed that had lasting effects.

At that point, consciousness expanded and seemed to pour out of the center to fill my body and the environment—engulfing all horizons and beyond. I was acutely aware as I watched this billowing of presence. Even though it was a highly serene experience, I yet sensed the power inherent in this expansion of being. Then I was suddenly hit by a peculiar, almost bizarre, insight. I recognized this released core of consciousness as somehow familiar. Instantly I saw images of myself praying to God as a very young boy. I realized then, intuitively, that the God that I prayed to back then and throughout my childhood was nothing other than this expanding core of my own being. Although there was no transcendence involved in this experience, I was nevertheless astounded. As a child I must have sensed the power of this aspect of consciousness and was so much in awe of it that I thought it must be nothing other than the God that I was taught to believe was in my heart. But the most remarkable aspect of this experience was the vision of my "personality."

After getting a sense of the God that I prayed to as young boy, my perception then shifted to my personality—that which everyone referred to as "Fred." I saw my entire personality laid out before me as objectively as I would view a rock or a tree. I saw my personality as a host of images, memories, feelings, and thoughts, intertwined and held together in a definite fluid structure that was literally pervaded by what I had come to know as prana or life force. I saw all of my characteristic personality traits, reactions, preferences, values, aversions, and aspirations—not as ideas but as actual mental objects. I even vividly experienced the quality or palpable sense of "Fredness" just as I was known by my friends and family. But, of course, none of this was the real me.

Upon seeing this I recognized that my personality was functioning as a prison through my identifying with this "Fred" entity. I knew that my quest for freedom led toward directly dismantling it and disidentifying with it. I saw that I no longer needed to be, or to have, the "Fred" that I had presented myself as and identified with for so long. The "Fred" entity was clearly a mental construct that was literally using up life force, wasting energy, and was used as a prop or crutch for being-in-the-world. This was a liberating experience. So intricate and complex was the "Fred" entity that I spent the next several years deconstructing it. This represented a significant move toward feeling comfortable about being alive and being-in-the-world. I felt freed of a major burden. I also found that I could expand my presence almost at will, even at the most difficult and challenging moments.

I now point to this experience as the culmination of movement toward the third substage of centeredness. The center explodes outward and stabilizes as an expansive beingness. Since that time, Consciousness was never again experienced as a center or point confined to being within the skull. There was now a sense of size or spaciousness (see Govinda, 1960) at the center, as though consciousness was pervasive and encompassing. I should mention that I did various exercises along these lines as early as 1969, but it all stabilized at this moment in the Idaho desert. Once again, there was nothing transcendent here—only a dynamic, supple, fluid, and expansive release of being. Since then I have become acutely aware of how one's presence expands and contracts in direct proportion to the severity of challenges and difficulties in the environment. I continued this line of inquiry of deconstructing the mind and self for the next five years.

The Decentered Stage

The Decentered Stage is largely new territory with many years of exploration remaining. Several early substages can be described, however. Although transcendent experiences seem to have had a way of enhancing levels of compassion, empathy, and concern for ecological issues (on this latter trait, see Smurthwaite & McDonald, 1987), during this stage these traits began to manifest in earnest. I continued to experience transcendence at rather regular intervals, but by this time I did not consider these to be central to the stabilization of awareness. At this stage I finally began to understand "true normal." There were several liberating insights that manifested during this time, *not the least of which was a steadily increasing disinterest in the state of centeredness.*

Subpersonalities

As mentioned so often in the Precentered and Centered stages, I focused on balancing practice between transcending and meditation-based psychotherapy derived from Patanjali's Yoga. By this time, the mental constructs mentioned in earlier stages had been largely reduced and I was routinely encountering a new kind of phenomenon. I was now working with fragmented consciousness rather than purely mental objects such as images, thoughts, and desires. My first experience of this came with a shift in my meditations and practices toward understanding and working with the phenomenon known as "subpersonalities" (see Assagioli, 1965; Rowan, 1990). Subpersonalities can be seen as minor selves, or fragmented consciousness, which operate within us constantly and in a more or less automatic fashion that is usually removed from our awareness. Ornstein (1986) referred to these as "small minds" that have their own agenda and function, and although highly automatic, are ultimately under the control of the self, which he described as "awareness of awareness." This phenomenon was also known to Tibetan Buddhists and was described by Alexandra David-Neel (David-Neel & Longden, 1967) who adequately captured the subtlety and cunning that these aspects of mind can manifest in staying hidden. I also believe that these were described in the Yoga-Sutras (see Hanna, 1994). All of these sources agree that virtually all of us have this phenomenon but that we are seldom if ever aware of it.

Perhaps the most remarkable feature of subpersonalities is that they have their own sense of "I-ness" as part of possessing their own cognitive processes, feelings, and rudimentary, mundane awareness. I first discovered the sheer breadth of this phenomenon in October of 1982. I would not have believed it before then. Dealing with subpersonalities became the major focus of my psychospiritual quest for the next seven years, although I balanced this intense work with various techniques for transcendence. Many of my most subtle neuroses and psychological issues stemmed from these remarkable estrangements of consciousness. My first encounters with subpersonalities was along the lines of what Jung called the "shadow." In other words, I found myself confronting and dealing with "dark" attitudes and beliefs that were extremely subtle and were not easily acknowledged. Among my first insights was how hard I had worked to suppress these and relegate them to the outer edges of my awareness. My ultimate purpose in following this approach was to completely and utterly silence the internal dialogue of the mind. Most of our internal conflicts, negative self-talk, and automatic negative thoughts stem from subpersonalities (see David-Neel & Longden, 1967). These make up a significant portion of what is called the unconscious, and there is often a tremendous sense of relief when these subpersonalities are dissolved. By the way, the few persons who do write about this phenomenon do not mention that subpersonalities can be dissolved and indeed do not even believe it. However, I have taught many to do so, and they do with little effort and with a great sense of relief and an integrated sense of well-being.

After years of experimenting with these schisms of consciousness, I finally began to understand their nature—an insight that proved to be both revealing and integrating. I have already mentioned chi and prana in this article. It was in these terms that I could best make sense out of this fascinating phenomenon. This fundamental life force seems to be intimately involved with mundane consciousness. I discovered that in my own case, whenever I encountered an experience, such as a moment of trauma that I could not easily integrate, I subtly and unknowingly split off part of my own conscious life force to deal with it. This is, of course, an unconscious process and is related to the defense mechanism of repression. My assumption, based on working with these issues with many clients, is that this phenomenon is common to most human beings. After decades of upsets, disappointments, and trauma, subpersonalities begin to accumulate in a way that takes up tremendous amounts of energy and unconscious effort. After seven years of working to reintegrate these wayward conglomerates of life force, I was continuously amazed at the subtlety and intricacy of this phenomenon. A good portion of my sense of self or "I" was actually originating from subpersonalities. The approach to dealing with them is to return these entities back into pure life force of which they are composed through the use of the technique of pratiprasava. At the end of those seven years, I had reached a fairly continuous state of psychological quiet, lightness, and inner harmony—and high energy.

The effects of this therapy on the center point was quite profound. The center of consciousness began to appear as being no longer at the center of anything. This was quite a contrast compared to the relative clarity that occurred at all levels of the Centered Stage. Still, the benefits of reintegrating subpersonalities were considerable and at times monumental. I had expected to become even more centered when in fact I was becoming less so. The center itself now appeared to be somewhat disorganized, as though there were a whirlpool there that had begun to swallow up my sense of "I." Indeed, because subpersonalities contribute to a sense of "I," I began to feel somewhat disoriented as the "I-ness" began to literally disappear. At first this was a mystery to me, but eventually I began to see the positive benefits. Thus, the first substage consists of a breaking down of centeredness as a result of the decomposition of confining self-structures such as subpersonalities. This is accompanied by a vague, mildly pleasant sense of disorganization at the center. My psyche was changing along with some bedrock beliefs about what it means to be stable, sane, and normal. In other words, being centered was now beginning to be unpleasant and limiting.

Fading In and Fading Out

Buddhist mindfulness meditation became an occasional focus of my meditations beginning in 1979. The direct and highly descriptive writings of Mahasi Sayadaw (1976, 1978) were most helpful in understanding how to achieve some of the more difficult insights. By 1989, as I was phasing out of the Centered Stage, mindfulness was directly on my path to further development and was incorporated into my array of active exercises. However, I am convinced that without practicing the earlier meditation, my mindfulness experiments would have been far less productive. In any case, I studied a variety of sources and experimented with a number of applications of this powerful technique before settling on three specific approaches that seemed well suited to my particular growth needs. Three areas of application were particularly fruitful: (1) mindfulness of the self, (2) mindfulness of the will, and (3) mindfulness of the field of body-mind. Each of these produced lasting and invaluable insights.

Practicing mindfulness of the self in 1990 brought me to a new plateau. I had been convinced that I had reduced the self to a mere skeletal construction of mind, loosely hung together as a more or less necessary aspect of being-in-the-world and interacting with others. Put a little differently, I had come to the point of perceiving the self only as an apparatus for organizing perceptions, thoughts, feelings, and interactions with others—nothing more. Even though I attributed *nothing in the way of identity* to this apparatus, my understanding was soon to be revealed as woefully incomplete. I had shaved the self down to its bare-boned structure and had extracted from it virtually all of its active life energy, but it was more powerful and deeply rooted than I had thought. After continued mindfulness meditation on it, an entirely new dimension of it was revealed. It was now clear that its very foundation was built on pain, insularity, and intolerance. I realized that the self was a kind of serious disorder or psychopathology in its own right. The self now appeared as an amazingly complex almost unperceivable construction of the mind, well beyond personality, but there as an ontological crutch, upon which one leans the weight and weariness of life. I had thought that I had worked through all this, but here it was again at a more subtle level, operating automatically, believing it was both separate and eternal. I had earlier learned that I was dependent on the thought process to keep me company and to protect me from the existential anxiety that stems from the dread of nothingness. Now I saw that the very purpose of the self was to do the same thing and that this was a much more profound way of doing so.

The most surprising aspect of this new layer of the self was seeing that it was founded upon emotional pain and desire. By 1993, the self was plainly revealed as a great gaping wound in the fiber of being, intimately bound up with pain and suffering. Mindfulness of it was an excruciatingly painful enterprise, involving the confronting of deep anguish and suffering. These meditations revealed the self as a global defense mechanism against the intolerable threat of a vast, infinitely complex and impersonal cosmos that ultimately had neither meaning nor substance. Having by this time become fairly well read in a variety of Buddhist, Hindu, and Yogic sources, it did not take me long to see where this line of exploration was headed. The void, *sunyata*, lay at the end of this path. I was both excited and somewhat shaken. I had not anticipated this. Up to this point, I had mistakenly believed that Brahman, or the One, was quite the same thing as the Buddhist void or sunyata. I saw my naiveté. In one sense they are indeed the same, and in another sense that I cannot quite explain, they are not at all.

Although I intuitively recognized that the end of the self was looming along this path, it was okay. I knew that the self is not a necessary aspect of life. Being attached to it is rather like being absorbed in painful memories and needlessly wallowing in them, thinking them an indispensable part of life. Similarly, without a self, the way is cleared to wake up and live spontaneously. I also began to see that sunyata reveals itself when the self is not merely transcended, but dismantled through mindfulness.

As I continued the exercise, the notion of the self as a defense and as a wound or tear in the fabric of being appeared ever more valid. I began to see that it was intimately involved with virtually all forms of psychological problems and issues (that are not congenital, of course). From the viewpoint of the self, the infinite is intolerable. Infinite existence is something that the self struggles mightily against. Through the mind, it divides and separates all of life into dichotomous fundamental categories such as here/there, this/that, near/far, now/then, and self/other. I saw that in order to maintain itself, the self demands that things must not be perceived as they really are but must instead conform to any desires, needs, and expectations that further its illusion. And amazingly, I saw that the fundamental nature of the self is pain and that being without one was to enjoy an even deeper sense of well-being and natural joy—a natural consequence of psychospiritual development (Loevinger, 1976).

I utilized experiential techniques as part of mindfulness of all that pain and anguish. At times it seemed as though the self had been exhausted or dissipated. Eventually, I reached a point where I would go for several days at a time with no conscious awareness of a self at all. I experienced no categorical differentiations even in my environment and everyday interactions with people. The self really did drop away, and with it came a recognition of the voidness or emptiness of all life. But rather than being gloomy, grave, or grim, this emptiness was a grand source of both serenity and high-energy animation. It was so remarkably natural that I hardly noticed that the self wasn't there anymore. But I did notice. I had, of course, briefly experienced this many times in meditation but never to this consistent degree, and never so much in everyday functioning as well. After a few weeks the self would return. When it returned I would again meditate on it until a new realization would dissipate another chunk of it I had not seen before. I had known for many years that these subtle manifestations of self were there. Now I was seeing what I already knew, but at a depth that I never suspected.

This was the second substage of Decenteredness. The self fades in and out for short periods of time leaving an awareness of no category distinctions in everyday life. During times when the self is faded out, there are great feelings of empathy, compassion, perception, and spontaneity. A recognition grows of a luminous pervasive awareness of the void as consummate and all-encompassing. In fact, it might be better said that the void is all that there is, and that awareness is ultimately the void as well. In any case, the self is now clearly seen as a defense against or a false haven from voidness. Voidness is the true nature of all existence. It is only apparent without a self. When there is no self to alter, modify, qualify, compromise, and inhibit perception, the world becomes as though washed clean—fresh, bright, and shimmering with light. Even the most mundane scenes are amazingly new and glow from within. This includes far more than the routinely beautiful flowers, forests, and clouds of the world. It also includes cockroaches, feces, and garbage.

Amazing as it may seem, the world was even more clean and beautiful now than in the days of the Centered Stage. Without the self, there is a stark, breathtaking, *impersonal* majesty in all things that I did not encounter at earlier stages. The incredible fact is that I was simply seeing the world closer to how it is in actuality. Perhaps most remarkable is that there was no longer any sense of I-ness or me-ness or selfhood. I realized that the self is that part of the mind that manipulates the rest of the mind into serving its purposes of desire and avoidance. I also realized that a primary purpose of the self is to defend the entire mental structure from the anxiety and instability that it fears would result from seeing the vastness, emptiness, and raw simplicity of the world as it is in itself. The self usually supplies a host of mental filters and cushions that help to avoid this stark apprehension. The mere fact of desiring implies and declares that the world is not okay as it is in itself. The incredible irony is that with the deconstruction of the self comes a greater sense of "security" and pure radiant joy than could ever be possible with a self. Each of the stages and substages described seem to bring more intense levels of joy.

No More Center: Disengaging the Will

Once the self had begun to fade in and fade out I found myself contemplating more and more a phrase that many Buddhist sources had mentioned concerning the realization of *nirvana* (or *nibbana* in the Pali language). Sayadaw (1976), for example, stated that nibbana is the end of sankhara or mental formations—especially volitions. More and more I became intuitively drawn to and fascinated with the phenomenon of the will. Finally, in November of 1994, I made the will the focus of my mindfulness meditations—watching every act of will from moving limbs of the body to making decisions, to choosing and forming the words of conversations. Eventually, I became adept at watching thoughts come into being and what's more, *watching the subtle aspects of will that bring those thoughts and images into being.*

Then a thoroughly fascinating event occurred. In March of 1995, during a mindfulness session on the will, I found that the will itself had become disengaged and that it was being observed as plainly as though it were a mental image of a tree. For twenty-five years I had believed that the will was intrinsic to consciousness itself. I was amazed to see that this was clearly not the case. After a few minutes of settling into meditation there arose a pure, uninterrupted contemplation of the will in operation. I began to understand that the basis of human nature was without any kind of volition. Most significant was the insight that the will is the cradle of and mother to, the self. In other words, it is not the self that does the willing, as we might normally conceive it. It now seemed that it is willing that actually creates the self. Will, as ontologically prior to the self, is driven by desires and cravings, and these tendencies create surges in the mind that produce mental currents and backwaters that eventually end up performing volitional acts. When there is no desire, the will is disengaged. When the will is disengaged, awareness becomes even more pure and cleansed. I saw it now. The philosophers of Samkhya and Yoga were right—the will is part of *prakriti* (material) and not of *purusha* (consciousness) (see Bahadur, 1978). The steady rush of thoughts in the mind are continuously, moment by moment, maintained and nurtured by the will. So is the self. Without will, there is no self; the mind ceases its needless operations. Once again I saw that a self is not necessary in order to function at optimum levels.

This was the third of the substages in the Decentered Stage. The insight about the nature of will freed me with more revolutionary intensity than any experience I had had to date. It was wholly astonishing. When I now looked "within" for a center of awareness, nothing was to be found. There was now an almost palpable chasm or gap or emptiness where once there had been a self. Unlike fading in and fading out, this is a revolution at the centerpoint of awareness—a metamorphosis. An essential core aspect of the self had been removed and been joyously replaced by the void. Ties and bonds to the self had been spontaneously cut. Both the pith and the peach were gone. There was no more "I," and when I looked it was nowhere to be found. There was no more center from which to orient the rest of the world and mind.

Perhaps most remarkable is that I discovered what it is to function without willing. This is where spontaneous intuition guides one's actions without engaging the will. I believe that this is the essence of the concept of *wu-wei* found in the Taoist writings of Lao-Tzu (Chang-yuan, 1975) or Chuang-Tzu (Watson, 1964). The phrase is usually translated as actionless action—action that is rooted in being rather than having or doing. I would phrase it as action without will. Life at that point was nothing other than the void, perceiving and interacting with itself. I realized that the infinite cosmos is always there, it is the will that constantly shifts the lenses, providing various beliefs, distinctions, and interpretations. Each of these views, however, is an alteration of what truly is. As Nagarjuna (200/1970), the great Buddhist dialectician observed, it is the flawed nature of the mind and thought that impedes seeing things as they are in actuality.

I would like to add that there seems to be no evidence for the popular ideas of the Universal Self and the Universal Will. In younger days, I was once very fond of such characterizations. These are attractive ideas but arise from dependence on self and mind. In other words, such concepts are conceptually "pretty" in that they are harmonious, symmetrical, and balanced with great intellectual and conceptual appeal. Much like certain religious beliefs, they even bring a certain amount of comfort. However, they actually represent the concept-forming activities of the mind, warned against by Huang Po and so many others. Concepts as these and others such as cosmic evolution make good sense at earlier stages, but as the self becomes dismantled and the mind divested, such concepts lose their attractiveness, become less important, and are spontaneously abandoned.

In any case, this state of "willess activity" lasted for approximately a year, and once again, even though it diminished there was another new plateau that had been achieved. For the first time since I began my quest, I did no sitting meditation during that year. My meditation was now done spontaneously and in the moment as life presented itself. I had no illusions, however, I knew that there was much more work to do. I had been around the meditative block too many times to get fooled again. After the glow wore off I found myself meditating once more on the will and other new areas that needed attention. But that center has not returned. There is no center of consciousness anymore and that feels quite natural and appropriate. It is hard to remember what it was like to have one. To experience the lapse of a self under healthy circumstances is, paradoxically, to understand what it means to be a normal human being, that is, "true normal." Indeed the more the meditation and growth continue, the more normal and insignificant this person becomes. It is quite liberating to be rid of this needless significance.

Seeing Consciousness Arise Out of Nothing

As of this writing, I am still quite in the middle of the Decentered Stage, and the meaning of true normal continues to unfold. A fourth substage manifested recently while meditating on consciousness itself. This meditation can be described as following or tracing consciousness back to its origin point, well beyond mind and perception of the world. I was doing this exercise as a result of the influence of Zen. There came a point at which, amazingly enough, I saw that consciousness itself is actually quite substantial, much more so than the void or sunyata. And as the void, I saw consciousness itself coming into being out of nothing at all. In some deep chamber of inner life, I saw it there, springing from the eternal dialectic between absolute somethingness and absolute nothingness, and arising as the wondrous compromise between the two. Consciousness actually appeared as a gossamer substance, alive and fluid, aware, pure, and somehow clean and "innocent." *The wholly astonishing aspect was that consciousness, that which does the seeing, was actually being seen and watched, as both subject and object.* Please believe me when I say that I know this makes no sense at all. I am only reporting what seemed to me to happen. Perhaps equally strange, I also felt released from consciousness, with a resulting sense of being unburdened and somehow freed.

There was no "I" in this experience, only the void itself. A deep certainty arose that the void is not consciousness but encompasses consciousness as it does everything else. I know that this flies directly in the face of popular transpersonal writings, for there we find consciousness glorified and exalted as the supreme, ultimate, perfect, utmost, transcendent reality. Not so to this investigator. It is wonderfully freeing to be released from this limiting perspective. Paradoxically, it seems that even transcendental consciousness has its limits. This insight taught me to appreciate Zen more than ever. I should also mention that the effect was largely temporary but the lesson lives on.

Transcendent Experiences Functioning as a Kind of Trauma

Although not a substage unto itself, I should mention that at some point it is important to treat the powerful transcendent experiences of the type described in this article as a kind of trauma. In a convoluted sort of way, these experiences have a lasting effect on a person just as would any other moments of high impact. It is rather like winning the lottery for a person who is unprepared to deal with the shock, however pleasant. Even though these are moments of pleasure and insight, they nevertheless have a way of silently shaping beliefs, thoughts, and personality patterns. I have recently learned that these need to be treated in a psychotherapeutic fashion so that they lose their influence in forming, fashioning, and continuing the self.

I will not venture to comment on any remaining substages in the Decentered Stage or the further stages that lie beyond. I can only speculate, and there is not much point in that as I have been so often wrong about such things in the past. I do know intuitively that they are there. I just have no idea what these stages and substages might be. For the record, I continue to discover issues to work through and resolve. I also find that existential anxiety has become my friend, and that it is a source of excitement and wonder rather than insecurity, dread, and foreboding. Before concluding, however, it may be appropriate to give a more elaborate description of the void, based on my limited acquaintance with it.

The Nature of the Void

Describing the void is a futile endeavor but then so is describing transcendent bliss, or the Himalayas under a full moon. Since it has been mentioned here so often, it may be of help to the reader to attempt a description anyway, if only to convey a flavor of it. The irony is that there is nothing more obvious and at the same time more hidden from view. Unfortunately, I have only limited experience with it and only rarely have I witnessed its full splendor. I believe that those who are truly advanced in their development have the honor of witnessing its grand majesty for extended periods of time. I can only speculate on what that is like. Nevertheless, I will try to do this justice, knowing full well the limits of language.

The void, or emptiness, or *sunyata*, is an ancient Buddhist concept that is easily misunderstood. There are several key points to consider. The void is not the same as nothingness. Unlike what often happens in full union with Brahman, it does not have to occur in a trance. The void is what is left when the self is completely absent (see Buddhadasa, 1994). Another important and related point is that the void is what is apprehended by the highest intuitive knowledge—where there are no views, conceptions (Murti, 1960), ideas (Hanh, 1992), or thoughts (Suzuki, 1969). The world is seen as it is in its actuality and primordiality—with no more filters, modifications, interpretations, qualifications, goals, or purposes to obscure its radiant existence. In other words the world is as it is in itself, completely empty and totally full. Without a self, all of life is interconnected, intersubjective, and sharing consciousness. The entire world is brimming with aliveness in the organismic sense mentioned by the great philosopher Alfred North Whitehead (1978).

There is a multiple loci of consciousness—that is, a distinct sense that one is seeing things from many spatial locations simultaneously. There is a similar sense of multiple foci, in which there is a simultaneous sense of being focused upon myriad points at one and the same time. The combination of multiple loci and foci may give some idea of why it is so difficult to describe this intuition. Thinking is at a standstill and is replaced by an encompassing intuitive knowing that is dialectical rather than logical or rational. Mental images are absent—no longer an aspect of mental activity, and thus these no longer serve as unconscious filters or templates for perceptions and preconceptions of a world that now appears primordially cleansed. Strange as it may seem, mental images actually inhibit the contemplation of the void. In the void, the world brilliantly announces itself in its primeval actuality. The routine processes of the mind are halted whether one is walking at the mall or deep in meditation.

Another salient aspect of what manifests in the absence of a self is a pervasive, global, intersubjective empathy. This is empathy from a decentered perspective and is amazingly intense when transcendence is experienced at this stage. In everyday living, this manifests as a sense of all beings and things in touch with and interpenetrating all other beings and things. Compassion, although sometimes well developed as a result of transcendent experiences, is greatly enhanced when a self is not there to render it ever so slightly alloyed or compromised by self-interest.

The void is vastness without space, eternity without time, infinity without quantity, totality without substance, and nothingness without absence or lack. It is all encompassing without having anything to include or enclose. It is pure being without existence. It is total, complete primeval awareness without having anything being apprehended. Amazingly difficult to describe, the void is more primeval and primordial than consciousness itself. Paradoxically, *the presence of a self is actually more of a dearth or deficiency than is the void.* And as Huang Po said, the void has no center. Awareness that is oriented around a center is not yet capable of appreciating the void. Whatever is lost through the reduction and dismantling of the self is more than made up for by the discovery of a cosmic joy of incredible magnitude that penetrates, pervades, and fills everything. Although we humans call it joy or bliss, in the intuition of the void, one realizes that this is, in reality, merely the primordial feeling that the universe itself constantly experiences.

Heart Sutra of Buddhism is well known for its simple statement of the nature of the void. The Heart Sutra is so named because it claims to have captured the essence of Buddhism. It states: "Form is nothing other than Void. Void is nothing other than form." As a result of the insights mentioned here, this sutra can be restated in another more all-encompassing way, using insights from the radical empiricism of William James (1904/1977), which bears many parallels to Buddhism (Kalupahana, 1987). According to James, the ultimate "stuff" of all of life is experience and that there is really nothing beyond experience. Experience includes both form and idea. Meditation teaches us that the deepest exploration of experience leads directly to the void. Reframed, the Heart Sutra might be put this way: Experience is nothing other than void; void is nothing other than experience. When experience is seen at its most fundamental level, the void appears. Put yet another way: There is nothing other than void. In other words, the void is the most obvious thing there is.

Conclusion

The various stages and substages of one person's psychospiritual quest for the center have now been outlined. Although many details and techniques have been left out, it may be clear by now that current theories of spiritual development do not take into account much of the sequence or the content of the experiences described here. Likewise, the development that I have experienced may not be applicable to that of others. In any case, I would like to make it clear that I have not progressed far enough on the path of psychospiritual development to claim any status such as being a guru, an arhant, a master, a saint, adept, or jivanmukta. After over thirty years of introspective experience, I have come to believe that so-called "enlightenment" is so relative that the term is almost useless. Furthermore, there is nothing noble, superior, or evolutionary about this quest, in spite of popular literature that glorifies the subject. This is hard work—effortless at times perhaps, but at other times the most difficult, painful, and demanding work I have ever done. Granted it has wonderful side benefits in terms of fulfillment and joy, but my inquiry and practice is based on attaining true normal, and I am still discovering what that means. I am certain that there remains so much more for me to know that given many more decades of work, I will likely remain much more ignorant than I am knowledgeable.

If there is anything different about the path presented here, it is that I have spent many, many years exploring the subtle effects of the mind and psychopathology on the stabilization of psychospiritual realization. Suzuki (1969), Hanh (1992), and Nagarjuna (200/1970) have noted the seductiveness of the mind and how its conceptualizing obstructs and detours the progress of insight. However, the factor of psychopathology—depression, anxiety, hostility, narcissism, as well as obsessive-compulsive, avoidant, and antisocial tendencies—profoundly affect and hinder psychospiritual development. This is where the study and practice of Patanjali's yogic methods can be of great benefit. This aspect of Patanjali is usually ignored or downplayed in the more popular interest of producing transcendence and samadhi. However, when the personal issues are confronted and worked through, and the psychological baggage is dropped, transcendence is much more effortless and more easily achieved.

In conclusion, I would like to briefly summarize what I have learned from thirty plus years of inquiry and practice based on emptying the mind and self, and attempting to phenomenologically investigate what is ultimately real. To transcend name and form one must have the knowledge that names arise from mind, and form is a product of the senses. Pure, transparent awareness transcends both mind and senses. Pure awareness generates no names and adds nothing to perception in the way of compounding and solidifying forms. When one experientially recognizes this, the self is emptied and the void shines in its fullness.

Appendix
A Summary of the Stages and Substages

The Precentered Stage

The Precentered Stage begins with the first experience of being centered. It is only the beginning. Some persons have many transcendent experiences and never get past this stage. Continued practice in the Precentered Stage produces the insights that lead to becoming centered and the stability that comes with it.

Substage 1: Precenteredness begins with a glimpse of a transcendent reality beyond ordinary perception of the world and mundane cognitive processes. The reality glimpsed is recognized as being beyond ordinary subject/object distinctions.

Substage 2: Merging with that transcendental reality to the point of full identification with it. Once again, this involves transcending the world of phenomena and moving beyond subject/object distinctions.

The Centered Stage

At this stage a person intuitively understands the meaning of the term "pure consciousness." Consciousness is understood as the center, focus, and origin of reality. It is seen as separate from mind and self, which serve only alloy and debase its pure character and quality. Consciousness is established in itself, freed from psychopathology, and ultimately tied to transcendental reality.

Substage 1: Consciousness is established as the center, largely free of mind and reactions. This is not to say that reactions do not take place, only that consciousness is ever observant and aware of the tides, flows, and eddies of mental processes and emotions. Put a bit differently, it might be said that consciousness exits or is released to some degree from the "shell" of one's personality.

Substage 2: Consciousness becomes integrated, settled, and established in itself with no need for mental ideas or constructions as props and supports. It is liberated from being chronically absorbed or lost in mental processes, including personality issues and structures. Consciousness is seen as separate from mind, more primal than mind, and as absolute. It can also master and change any construction of mind, although not its total master.

Substage 3: The center expands outward and stabilizes as extended being. Consciousness is no longer and never again experienced as a central point confined to being within the skull. There is now a continuous sense of size or grand spaciousness that becomes a part of one's being.

The Decentered Stage

In the Decentered Stage the center begins to corrode or decompose as if from within. The self begins to literally disappear not only in transcendent experiences but in everyday life—which begins to become more and more transcendent. The "I" becomes less pronounced.

Substage 1: Centeredness begins to break down as a result of the decomposition of confining self-structures. This process results in a not unpleasant lack of a sense of center, which is now replaced by a sense of a mildly pleasant disorganization.

Substage 2: The self is clearly seen as a defense against or a haven from the stark reality of the void, and as a wound in the fiber of one's being. The self fades in and out for short periods of time leaving a lack of category distinctions in everyday life. During times when the self is faded out, there is a recognition of a luminous, pervasive awareness of the void as primordial and what all things are.

Substage 3: The center ceases to exist, along with a sense of self. There is an almost palpable chasm or gap where once there was a self. Unlike fading in and fading out, this is a revolution at the center of awareness—a metamorphosis. An essential core of the self is removed and is joyously replaced by the void.

Substage 4: Consciousness itself is seen, in and by the void, coming into being. For the first time, consciousness seems almost substantial and limited by comparison to the void. One is momentarily freed from consciousness.

Substage 5: No inkling, no clue. There remains much, much more to learn.

References

Aranya H. (1983). *Yoga philosophy of Patanjali.* Albany: State University of New York Press.

Assagioli, R. (1965). *Psychosynthesis: A manual of principles and techniques.* New York: Penguin.

Bahadur, K. P. (Trans.). (1978). *The wisdom of Saankhya.* New Delhi: Sterling Publishers.

Bharati, A. (1974). *The light at the center: The context and pretext of modern mysticism.* Santa Barbara, CA: Ross-Erikson.

Buddhadasa, B. (1994). *Heartwood of the bodhi tree*. Boston: Wisdom Publications.

Chang-yuan, C. (Trans.). (1975). *Tao: A new way of thinking*. New York: Harper & Row.

David-Neel, A., & Longden, L. (1967). *The secret oral teachings in Tibetan Buddhist sects*. San Francisco: City Lights Books.

Deshpande, P. Y. (1978). *The authentic Yoga: Patanjali's Yoga sutras*. London: Rider.

Engler, J. (1986). Therapeutic aims in psychotherapy and meditation: Developmental stages in the representation of self. In K. Wilber, J. Engler, & D. Brown (Eds.), *Transformations of consciousness* (pp. 17–51). Boston: New Science Library.

Feuerstein, G. (1989). *The Yoga-sutra of Patanjali*. Rochester, VT: Inner Traditions International.

Feuerstein, G. (1990). *Holy madness*. New York: Paragon House.

Govinda, A. G. (1960). *Foundations of Tibetan mysticism*. Bombay, India: B. I. Publications.

Hanh, T. N. (1992). *The diamond that cuts through illusion: Commentaries on the Prajnaparamita Diamond Sutra*. Berkeley, CA: Parallax Press.

Hanna, F. J. (1991). Processing mental objects directly: A therapeutic application of phenomenology. *The Humanistic Psychologist, 19*(2), 194–206.

Hanna, F. J. (1994). The confines of mind: Patanjali and the psychology of liberation. *Journal of the Psychology of Religion, 2–3*, 101–126.

Husserl, E. (1931). *Ideas: General introduction to pure phenomenology*. New York: Collier Books. (Original work published 1913)

James, W. (1977). Does consciousness exist? In J. J. McDermott (Ed.), *The writings of William James: A comprehensive edition*. Chicago: University of Chicago Press. (Original work published 1904)

John of the Cross, St. (1959). *Dark night of the soul*. Garden City, NY: Image Books.

Kalupahana, D. J. (1987). *The principles of Buddhist psychology*. Albany: State University of New York.

Kornfield, J. (1993). Even the best meditators have old wounds to heal: Combining meditation and psychotherapy. In R. Walsh & F. Vaughan (Eds.), *Paths beyond ego: The transpersonal vision* (pp. 67–69). Los Angeles: Jeremy Tarcher.

Loevinger, J. (1976). *Ego development*. San Francisco: Jossey-Bass.

Murti, T. R. V. (1960). *The central philosophy of Buddhism*. London: George Allen & Unwin.

Nagarjuna. (1970). *Nagarjuna: A translation of his Mulamadhyamikacarika with an introductory essay*. (K. K. Inada, Trans.). Tokyo: Hokuseido Press. (Original work circa 200)

Nikhilananda, S. (Trans.). (1963). *The Upanishads.* New York: Harper & Row.

Northrop. F. S. C. (1946). *The meeting of East and West.* New York: The MacMillan Company.

Ornstein, R. (1986). *Multimind: A new way of looking at human behavior.* London: MacMillan.

Prabhavananda, S., & Isherwood, C. (1970). *Shankara's Crest Jewel of Discrimination.* New York: New American Library.

Puhakka, K., & Hanna, F. J. (1988). Opening the pod: A therapeutic application of Husserl's phenomenology. *Psychotherapy, 25*(4), 582–592.

Rowan, J. (1990). *Subpersonalities: The people inside us.* London: Routledge.

Sayadaw, M. (1976). *Practical insight meditation: Basic and progressive stages.* Kandy, Sri Lanka: Buddhist Publication Society.

Sayadaw, M. (1978). *The progress of insight.* Kandy, Sri Lanka: Buddhist Publication Society.

Smurthwaite, T. J., & McDonald, R. D. (1987). Examining ecological concern among persons reporting mystical experiences. *Psychological Reports, 60,* 591–596.

Stace, W. T. (1960). *The teaching of the mystics.* New York: New American Library.

Suzuki, D. T. (1969). *The Zen doctrine of no mind.* London: Rider.

Thera, N. (Ed.). (1964). *The simile of the cloth and the discourse on effacement: Two discourses of the Buddha.* Kandy, Sri Lanka: Buddhist Publication Society (Wheel Series No. 61/62).

Walsh, R., & Vaughan, F. (1993). Problems on the path: Clinical concerns. In R. Walsh & F. Vaughan (Eds.), *Paths beyond ego: The transpersonal vision* (pp. 131–137). Los Angeles: Jeremy Tarcher/Perigee.

Watson, B. (Trans.). (1964). *Chuang Tzu: Basic writings.* New York: Columbia University Press.

Whitehead, A. N. (1978). *Process and reality.* New York: The Free Press.

Worthington, V. (1982). *A history of yoga.* London: Arkana, Penguin Group.

7

Illuminative Presence

ZIA INAYAT KHAN

What is meant by "enlightenment?" The preponderance of those who claim to have tasted some savor of spiritual realization or enlightenment insist that it cannot be expressed in words. Though the human soul is distinguished as a "speaking soul" (*nafs natiqa*), it would seem that not all experiences are equally susceptible to discursive expression.

> The winged words on which my soul would pierce
> Into the height of Love's rare Universe,
> Are chains of lead around its flight of fire.—
> I pant, I sink, I tremble, I expire!
> —Percy Bysshe Shelley, *Epipsychidion* (1921, p. 20)

Language communicates representations, not sheer realities. The immediate, nonrepresentational apprehension of an object in its essence, which is intensified and expanded in mystical awareness, is on this account ineffable. Yet over the ages a deluge of ink has been spilled in inscribing spiritual experiences. We may well ask, if unitary consciousness is truly ineffable, is all of this literature in vain?

The Sufis call our attention to a "science of allusion" (*'ilm al-ishara*), whereby mystical experience can be encrypted in words. This science involves an epistemic "translation" of experience from unitive knowledge to phenomenal knowledge through an act of critical introspection. The outcome is a body of knowledge that can be subjected to rational critique in its expression (*'ibara*), but can be intuitively understood only in its allusion (*ishara*).

In the innermost heart of words are concealed the sharp edges of
a sword, but they can be perceived only by inner vision.
— Shaykh Ahmad Ghazali (1986, p. 15; 1991, p. 113)

Since the discursive expression of immediate unitary experience is necessarily relative, the idioms of mystical allusion are many and diverse. This
chapter looks at one such idiom, with a view to highlighting its epistemology of mysticism. Its exponents refer to it as the illuminative philosophy
(*hikmat al-ishraq*). It is a school of thought that reconstructs the experience
of enlightenment on the model of a "science of lights." By means of a
method informed by Aristotelian logic, but open to judgments of intuition,
the illuminative philosophy arrives at a coherent understanding of knowledge that lucidly accounts for mystical apprehension.

The Science of Lights

God is the Light of heaven and earth.
— Qur'an, 24:35

The illuminative philosophy was originally systematized by the itinerant Persian sage Shihab al-Din Yahya Suhrawardi (d. 1191). Suhrawardi guided an
intimate group of disciples and put forward his ideas in an extensive body
of doctrinal works, visionary narratives, and cosmic orisons. Tragically, the
"Master of Illumination" (*shaykh al-ishraq*) was put to death at the age of
thirty-six by order of Sultan Salah al-Din, the Saladin of the Crusades.[1]
Suhrawardi's thought clearly represented a threat to the intellectual and political status quo (Ziai, 1992).

Woe to lovers; they try to keep the secret of love, but their passion reveals it. Now, if they give away their secret, their blood becomes lawful (to shed). Thus is the blood of those who give it
away given up . . .
— Shihab al-Din Suhrawardi (Massignon, 1982, p. 416)

But it is not the drama of Suhrawardi's meteoric life that concerns us
here, but rather the special insights of his illuminative (*ishraqi*) doctrine.
The Arabic verbal noun *ishraq* denotes the radiant splendor of the rising
sun. Suhrawardi and his followers use this term to invoke a perennial Hermetic wisdom tradition with roots in ancient Egypt, Greece, and Persia
(Suhrawardi, 1993b, pp. 10–11). What distinguishes its initiates as "oriental"
(*mashriqi*) is their intellectual and spiritual orientation toward the cosmic
Orient, the unveiling-place of light, and hence of "witnessing" (*mushahada*),
par excellence.

This mystical symbolism is not without firm philosophical footing. Suhrawardi was intent on using rational proofs to demonstrate realities beyond the purview of the rationalists.[2] With this in view he treated the problem of definition as a fundamental methodological consideration (Ziai, 1990, pp. 77–128). In his critique of prevalent methods of definition, he emphasized that definition ultimately depends on the identification of a self-evident reality. This being the case, the question arises as to what is the most prior and intelligible, and thus most axiomatic, phenomenon. In the ken of the illuminative philosophy, this can only be light (*nur*): "If there is anything in existence that does not require definition and explanation, it is that which is apparent (*zahir*). And there is nothing more apparent than light. Thus there is nothing in less need of definition than light" (Suhrawardi, 1993b, p. 106). Light needs no definition because its very nature is definitive. Nothing can make it more apparent than it already is, whereas it makes everything else apparent. "Light is that which is apparent in its own reality and makes other things apparent by its essence" (Suhrawardi, 1993b, p. 113).[3]

By apparency is meant the "knowability" of things, which the illuminative philosophy treats as indistinguishable from their act of being. Conceived in this way, light is not restricted to visible light. Objects of sensory perception are by no means the only things that are apparent to the knowing mind. Visible luminosity is only the most empirically tangible example of apparency. In fact, physical light is only to be regarded as light in a derivative sense, since, in view of its dependence on a corruptible substratum, its apparency is a matter of accident rather than essence (Suhrawardi, 1993b, p. 108). But by the principle of sufficient reason, which holds that everything has a distinct and sufficient cause for its existence, it can be inferred that if there is such a thing as accidental light (*nur 'arid*) there must also be pure light (*nur mahd*). In this way illuminative ontology segues from light that subsists in something else to light that subsists in its own essence, or immaterial light (*nur mujarrad*).

Like material light, immaterial light is "light in itself" (*nur fi haqiqat nafsihi*), but unlike its accidental counterpart it is also "light to itself" (*nur li nafsihi*), meaning it makes itself apparent to itself, rather than merely to something else. In other words, light in its immaculate state is identical with consciousness. Hence, everything that apprehends its own essence is an immaterial light (Suhrawardi, 1993b, pp. 10–11).

All immaterial lights are continuous and without disjunction in their essence, as follows from having the same luminous reality (Suhrawardi, 1993b, pp. 119–120). They vary only in degree of intensity. The most intense light is the "Light of Lights," the necessary being (wajib al-wujud) whose infinite luminosity is the ultimate sufficient cause (Suhrawardi, 1993b, pp. 121–24). Each light is illuminated in proportion to its onto-logical proximity to this radiant core of being. Thus proceeds a hierarchy of luminous emanations, pouring out to the horizon of "darkness in it-self." But by darkness is meant nothing other than the absence of light.[4]

Self-Knowledge

I am all that I have revealed of being.
                    —Zu'l-'ulum Azar Kayvan (Khuda-jui, 1848, p. 27)

The mystic does not possess knowledge, for he is knowledge himself.
                                      —Hazrat Inayat Khan (1989, p. 407)

Inasmuch as the human subject intuitively posits its own "I-ness" (*ana'iyya*) it may be said to be aware of itself. All other knowledge presupposes this ba-sic self-awareness, since one could not attribute knowledge of another to oneself without being aware of oneself in the first place. Accordingly, the in-ner self or individual "essence" (*dhat al-nafs*) is recognized in the illumina-tive philosophy as an immaterial light. That which is essential to one's personal identity is thus seen to shine forth as a luminous monad manifest-ing all of the qualities of pure light, such as life, apparency, simplicity, indi-visibility, and indefinability. Its inalienable nature is to know itself and others. But how is this knowledge achieved?

The question of knowledge is central to the illuminative philosophi-cal project. Suhrawardi recounts having agonized over epistemological problems, feeling unsatisfied with the accounts found in the standard sources. He continuously practiced contemplation and spiritual exercises, until at last one night he was overtaken by a visionary rapture in which Aristotle appeared. A dialogue commenced, in the course of which the Greek master introduced the theory of knowledge by presence (*'ilm huduri*), thereby laying the cornerstone of illuminative epistemology (Suhrawardi, 1993a, pp. 70–74).[5] The encounter began in this way:

Suddenly I was wrapped in gentleness; there was a blinding flash, then a very diaphanous light in the form of a human being. I watched attentively and there he was: Helper of souls, Imam of wisdom, Primus Magister, whose form filled me with wonder and whose shining beauty dazzled me. He came toward me, greeting me so kindly that my alarm gave way to a feeling of familiarity. And then I began to complain to him of the trouble I had with this problem of knowledge.

"Come back (awaken) to yourself," he said to me, "and your problem will be solved."

"How so?" I asked.

"Is the knowledge which you have of yourself a direct perception of yourself by yourself, or do you get it from something else?" (Corbin, 1977, pp. 118–119; Suhrawardi, 1993a, p. 70)

Aristotle proceeded to explain that one's awareness of oneself can only be by way of oneself. Self-awareness means that the self is both the subject and the object of its own knowledge. There can be no other knowing subject or acting power in this knowledge. Likewise, it is precisely the self that must be known, not an effect produced within it. Even if an effect were a true representation of the self, it would still be something other than the self (Suhrawardi, 1993a, p. 70).

All intellectual representations are universal, in that they are composed of qualities that may be shared by any number of individual objects. In view of its general applicability, the abstract concept of "I" is universal. But this objectified "I" is clearly distinguishable from the private apprehension of "I," which in its exclusivity cannot be other than particular, and thus cannot be a representation (Suhrawardi, 1993a, pp. 70–71).

To put this another way, within the anatomy of knowledge "I-ness" always remains fundamentally distinct from "it-ness" (Yazdi, 1992, pp. 75–82). External objects may be satisfactorily apprehended through representations since both belong to the realm of "it-ness." But the "I" belongs to another realm altogether. If one were to objectify one's "I-ness," the resulting representation would be an "it" in relation to one's "I," which means that one's presumed knowledge of oneself would actually be knowledge of another, and thus could not be properly understood as self-knowledge (Suhrawardi, 1993b, p. 111).

The illuminative philosophy further contends that it would be impossible in any case to conceive a representation of oneself without already having a precognitive apprehension of oneself. Otherwise, how would one know that the representation represented oneself rather than something else?[6] In accordance with the priority of essence over attribute, knowledge of an attribute, such as a representation, presupposes knowledge of the essence to which it is attributed (Suhrawardi, 1993b, p. 111).

These arguments inexorably lead to the conclusion that the self knows itself by itself. This means that one's knowledge of oneself cannot be other than the very reality of oneself. As the apparition of Aristotle put it, "Your essence is (at once) self-knowledge, the self-knowing subject, and the self-known object" (Suhrawardi, 1993a, p. 71). Knowledge in this unitary state is intuitive rather than predicative. There is no question either of conceptual content or truth value (Yazdi, 1992, pp. 45–47). One simply knows oneself experientially by being present to the sheer luminous reality of oneself. Hence this knowledge is designated as "knowledge by illumination and presence" (*'ilm ishraqi huduri*).

Knowledge by Presence

Within the illuminative system, the self-objectivity of the knowing subject is the primordial mode of knowledge by presence. But presential knowledge also extends to other acts of knowing. All knowledge that is constituted by an immediate encounter with the known object, rather than with a representation corresponding with it, falls under the rubric of knowledge by presence.

The empirical awareness that one has of one's feelings and sensations is a clear example. One feels pain by dint of the immediate presence of the pain, rather than through any mental image. In other words, one's awareness of one's pain is indistinguishable from the pain itself. One could not be any more certain of being in pain than by simply feeling pain (Yazdi, 1992, pp. 67–68).

Sensations do not need to be represented in the mind because they are immediately present within it. One directly apprehends one's body and all of its external senses and internal senses (*viz.*, sensus communis, representation, active imagination, estimation, and memory) (Ibn Sina, 1990, pp. 30–31; cf. Suhrawardi, 1993c, pp. 87–88) without recourse to epistemic intermediaries. Since one's mental and physical faculties are logically particular, in that they are private to oneself, it would be impossible to apprehend and operate them through intellectual representations, which are by nature universal (Suhrawardi, 1993a, pp. 71–72).

Ultimately, all knowledge is grounded in knowledge by presence. In the case of conceptual knowledge, an external object is conceived by correspondence to an internal representation. While the external object remains absent, the internal representation is known by its presence within the mind (Suhrawardi, 1993a, p. 72). Otherwise, to know a representation conceptually would require another representation, which would in turn require another, ad infinitum. Thus even when something is known by correspondence, the representation by which it is known is known by presence.

The World of the Image

When you learn from the writings of the ancient Sages that there
exists a world possessed of dimensions and extent, other than the
pleroma of Intelligences and the world governed by the Souls of
the spheres. . . do not hasten to proclaim it a lie.
> —Shihab al-Din Suhrawardi (Corbin, 1977, p. 118;
> Suhrawardi, 1993a, p. 109)

The advice to see well, which is the basis of the realists' education,
easily overshadows our paradoxical advice *to dream well.*
> —Gaston Bachelard (1987, p. 13)

The recognition that representations are known by presence opens out into
one of the most distinctive contributions of the illuminative philosophy,
namely the doctrine of "the World of the Image" (*'alam al-mithal*) (Corbin,
1977; Rahman, 1966; Walbridge, 1992). This doctrine invites us to recon-
sider the logical-positivist assumption that the experiences of the imagination are "imaginary" in the common sense of the word, implying fictitious
or arbitrary. On the contrary, it is suggested that the presential awareness
that we have of what we might instead call "imaginal" phenomena evinces a
dimension of being that is ontologically no less real than the sensible
world.[7]

In his visionary narratives Suhrawardi refers to the World of the Image
as *"na-koja-abad,"* or "the land of nowhere" (Suhrawardi, 1982, pp. 27, 65;
1993c, pp. 211, 273). What this paradoxical name implies is that the topog-
raphy of active imagination belongs to a place, endowed with dimensions
and extent, which is nonetheless placeless, in that it is not embodied in matter. It is thus identifiable neither with the intelligible world of abstract ideas
(wherein are found the Platonic forms or archetypes) nor the sensible
world of physical forms, but rather constitutes an isthmus (*barzakh*) or interworld that intervenes and mediates between the two.

The phenomena of this interworld are "in suspension" (*mu'allaqa*),
which is to say, they subsist independently of any corruptible substratum,
but nonetheless quasi-corporeally. The manifestation of these autonomous
images is thus more akin to the apparitional appearance of reflections on
the surface of a mirror than, for example, the inherence of color in an object. But rather than a physical object or organ of sensory perception, their
natural place of appearance (*mazhar*) is the active imagination, the cognitive faculty that is able to touch them because it participates in their order
of being (Suhrawardi, 1993b, pp. 211–213).

The active imagination accommodates the forms of this world to the World of the Image by mirroring sensory data with the light of consciousness. In this concurrence of matter and spirit a liminal dimension of cognition comes into focus, within which "spirits are corporealized and bodies spiritualized" (Corbin, 1977, p. 177). This is the perceptual threshold that allows intellectual concepts and material forms to be experienced in direct mutual symbolization. The myriad entities that populate the landscape of this world are unique in being both immaterial and logically particular. For every existing thing in our world an apparitional counterpart is configured and typified there. These autonomous images are fully animate and interactive, and are palpable to the five senses of the imagination. Unstraightened by matter, they live and move with a freedom that makes possible the incredible.

We experience the World of the Image to the degree that it is present to us by our withdrawal from the exigencies of material life. The dreams and reveries that come with closing or downplaying the external senses are none other than the events of this world. Its contours come into clear resolution in the vivid experience of lucid dreaming. For the poet and the prophet, this world of "poetic facts" (Wilson, 1988, p. 31) and visionary initiations is a second home.

Witnessing

Who knows himself knows his Lord.
                              —Hadith of the Prophet Muhammad

The scenery of the World of the Image is perceived by virtue of its being present to the imagination, over which the essential self (*dhat al-nafs*) has an innate authority. In its role as a "governing light" (*nur ispahbad*), the self is the "sense of the collectivity of senses." The particular faculties of perception and cognition cannot apprehend themselves, but are apprehended and encompassed by the self. The body, viewed holistically, is its "temple" (*haykal*) (Suhrawardi, 1993b, p. 214–215).

The more actively the authority of the self is exercised over the imagination, the more effectively the objects of the imagination are grasped. Thus illuminative oneirology distinguishes between the distorted dreams of impish imaginations and the lucid imaginal visions enjoyed by strong souls. The former require interpretation, while the latter speak for themselves (Khuda-jui, 1848, p. 6; Suhrawardi, 1993b, pp. 236–237).

The authority of the self over its faculties of perception and cognition is ultimately a function of its presence to itself, since they are known by their presence to it. By disidentifying with matter, and in this way intensifying and deepening its apprehension of itself, the self stands to enhance all of its direct perceptions, which are in fact effusions of itself (Suhrawardi, 1993a, p. 72). This was explained to Suhrawardi by the apparition of Aristotle: "As long as you remain in your (material) world, you are veiled (and disconnected). But as soon as you leave that world (provided that) you have become perfected, you will enter (into the state of) identity and eternal continuity" (Suhrawardi, 1993a, p. 73; Yazdi, 1992, p. 118).

The basis of this identity (*ittihad*) and continuity (*ittisal*) is the essential unity of all light, for as has been observed, all luminous beings are alike in their "light-ness." This is the case because every light emanates from, and in like measure is absorbed in, the Light of Lights. The Light of Lights is the overmastering reality to which the totality of existence is immediately present by immersion. Thus the luminous subject's act of presence to itself is also an act of presence to the Light of Lights, and by extension to all beings.

Mystical perception, or witnessing-illumination (*mushahada-ishraq*) takes place in this context, when a luminous subject comes into direct contact with a luminous object, and both subject and object are bathed in the light of the Light of Lights (Ziai, 1990, pp. 155–161). The subject makes its object known in the light of its own self-consciousness, which is purely an epiphany of the presence of the Light of Lights, within which the object is immersed. Knowledge in this presential mode utterly transcends the subject-object dichotomy that characterizes representational knowledge. In this manner an "illuminative relation" (*idafa ishraqiyya*) is obtained, an epistemic event that is nothing more or less than an instantaneous unmediated encounter and identification between sheer realities (Suhrawardi, 1993a, pp. 486–487).

The fullness of witnessing is commensurate with the degree to which the essence of the self apprehends itself in its principle and accordingly partakes of the illumination of the Light of Lights. Essential self-awareness is increased by withdrawing from preoccupation with sensoria and conceptual thinking, and turning within. By meditating on its own consciousness, the self is able to retrace its emanation through the converse principle of absorption (*fana*).

The process of inner illumination is incremental. Suhrawardi (1993b) describes fifteen experiences of light that transpire in gradual succession (pp. 252–254). In his poetic spiritual autobiography, the Mazdean Illuminationist mystic Azar Kayvan (d. 1617–18) offers a still more comprehensive view. He relates that withdrawal from the outer senses first confronts the meditator with his crude creaturehood, perceived as a terrifying black fire. Only by overcoming its tyranny can he move on to the purification of his elemental nature. Then, by transcending his "satanic" egoism, which calls out "I and no other!" until it is subsumed in the lucid fire of the remembrance of pre-eternity, one by one he experiences the unveiling of the organs (*lata'if*) that make up his subtle anatomy: the soul (*nafs*), the heart (*qalb*), the "secret" (*sirr*), the spirit (*ruh*), and the arcanum (*khafi*).[8] These successive illuminations ultimately lead to an inner realization of the essential continuity and identity of the self with the source of all being, experienced as absorption (*fana*) and subsistence (*baqa*) in the Truth (Khuda-jui, 1848, pp. 8–20).

It bears emphasizing, however, that the experience of *unio mystica* does not objectively constitute an ontic nullification of the subject's distinct act of being. Light is both that which unites and that which differentiates beings. Unitive experience simply involves shifting the focus from difference to unity. The son and spiritual successor of Azar Kayvan explains:

> According to the eminent Illuminationists of Iran, union (*vusul*) with the source, which the Sufis interpret as absorption and subsistence, does not mean that the possible mixes with the necessary being, or that possible beings cease to exist. Rather, when the necessary being renders itself apparent (*zuhur*), all possible beings are seen as enfolded in that light like stars. If one should happen to remain in that state, one would discover that they are enfolded in the victorious power of the apparency of the Sun—or otherwise one would simply see everything as nothing. (Kay-Khusraw Isfandiyar, 1963, p. 29)

Conclusion

The illuminative theory of knowledge by presence succeeds in rationally explaining unitary experience by demonstrating continuity between ordinary and mystical awareness. All knowledge, even conceptual thinking, ultimately involves an immediate apprehension of presence. The knowing self is in itself a perpetual reflexive act of presential knowledge. In this light, unitive consciousness can be explained simply as an intensification and expansion of the most basic mode of knowledge.

In the process, this theory also goes far in contributing to the rehabilitation of imagination. If apparency bespeaks reality, the modern logical-empiricist deprecation of imagination—and of the symbols, myths, and rituals that respond to it—requires urgent rethinking.

But for all its dialectic dexterity, like any science of allusion, the illuminative philosophy can finally do no more than to systematically allude to realities that must be experienced first-hand. Like the role of observation in astronomy, mystical experience is crucial to a proper understanding of mystical theory. Without it even the most sympathetic inquirer remains a toy with which doubts play (Suhrawardi, 1993b, p. 13).

Notes

1. The fullest source of information on Suhrawardi's life is his follower Shahrazuri's (d. 1282) account of him in his *Nuzhat al-Arwah wa Rawdat al-Afrah*, which has been translated by Wheeler M. Thackston Jr. (Suhrawardi, 1982, pp. 1–4).
2. Suhrawardi (1993b) writes in the Introduction to his magnum opus *The Philosophy of Illumination*, "I did not in the first place obtain (this knowledge) through cogitation, but rather it was obtained by other means. Then I sought proof for it, such that were I, for example, to put aside my vision, still no one could dissuade me" (p. 10).
3. This formula is found in Abu Hamid Ghazali's (d. 1111) famous treatise on the Quranic light verse (1988, p. 46).
4. In this regard, the illuminative interpretation of ancient Persian dualism is comparable with the theology of the canonical Pahlavi work *Dinkard*, which holds that, essentially, Yazdan (the divine power, light) is "existent" and Ahriman (the satanic power, darkness) is "nonexistent" (Aturpat-i Emetan, 1979, pp. 198–199; cf. Suhrawardi, 1993b, pp. 10–11).
5. The attribution of this very un-Peripatetic theory of knowledge to the spirit of Aristotle is a matter of some irony. But it must be remembered that in Islamicate circles the Stagirite was associated with the so-called Theology of Aristotle, which was in fact an epitome of the last four Enneads of Plotinus.
6. The essence of this argument—viz., that one can only recognize that which one already inherently knows—an idea that goes back to Plato, is whimsically redeployed in a popular Mulla Nasr al-Din story: *Nasr al-Din walks into a shop. He asks the shopkeeper, "Did you see me come in?" "Yes," the man replies. "Have you ever seen me before?" "No." "Then how did you know it was me?"*
7. The term "imaginal" was coined by Henry Corbin (1995, p. 19) to avoid the negative valence of "imaginary" in the context of introducing the World of the Image.
8. For an in-depth discussion of Sufi doctrines of subtle physiology, see Corbin (1994).

References

Aturpat-i Emetan. (1979). *The wisdom of the Sasanian sages* (S. Shaked, Trans.). Boulder, CO: Westview Press.

Bachelard, G. (1987). *On poetic imagination and reverie* (C. Gaudin, Ed. and Trans.). Dallas: Spring Publications.

Corbin, H. (1977). *Spiritual body and celestial earth.* Bollingen Series no. 91:2. (N. Pearson, Trans.). Princeton, NJ: Princeton University Press.

Corbin, H. (1994). *The man of light in Iranian sufism* (N. Pearson, Trans.). New Lebanon, NY: Omega Publications.

Corbin, H. (1995). Mundus imaginalis: Or the imaginary and the imaginal. In L. Fox (Trans.). *Swedenborg and esoteric Islam* (pp. 1–33). West Chester, PA: Swedenborg Foundation.

Ghazali, Abu Hamid Muhammad. (1988). *Mishkat al-Anwar* (W. H. T. Gairdner, Trans.). New Delhi: Kitab Bhavan.

Ghazali, Ahmad. (1986). *Sawanih: Inspirations from the world of pure spirits* (N. Pourjavady, Trans.). London: Kegan Paul International.

Ghazali, Ahmad. (1991). *Majmu'a-yi Asar-i Farsi* (A. Mujahid, Ed.). Tehran: Intisharat-i Danishgah-i Tehran.

Ibn Sina, Abu 'Ali. (1990). *Avicenna's psychology* (F. Rahman, Trans.). Westport, CT: Hyperion Press.

Kay-Khusraw Isfandiyar bin Azar Kayvan. (1963). *Dabistan-i Mazahib* (R. Rizazada Malik, Ed.). (Vol. 1). Tehran: Kitab-khana-yi Tahuri.

Khan, I. (1989). *Complete works of Pir-o-Murshid Hazrat Inayat Khan, original texts: Sayings, part I* (M. van Voorst van Beest, Ed.). London: East-West Publications.

Khuda-jui bin Namdar. (1848). *Jam-i Kay-Khusraw.* Bombay: Matba'-i Fazl al-Din Kahamkar.

Massignon, L. (1982). *The passion of al-Hallaj* (H. Mason, Trans.). (Vol. 2). Princeton, NJ: Princeton University Press.

Rahman, F. (1966). Dream, imagination, and *'Alam al-Mithal.* In R. Caillois & G.E. von Grunebaum, (Eds.) *The dream and human societies* (pp. 409–419). Berkeley and Los Angeles: University of California Press.

Shelley, P. B. (1921). *Epipsychidion.* London: Selwyn & Blount Ltd.

Suhrawardi, Shihab al-Din. (1982). *The mystical and visionary treatises* (W. M. Thackston, Jr., Trans.). London: The Octogon Press.

Suhrawardi, Shihab al-Din. (1993a). *Majmu'a-yi Musannafat-i Shaykh-i Ishraq* (H. Corbin & S. H. Nasr, Eds.). (Vol. 1). Tehran: Pazuhishgah-i 'Ulum-i Insani va Mutalafat-i Farhangi .

Suhrawardi, Shihab al-Din. (1993b). *Majmu'a-yi Musannafat-i Shaykh-i Ishraq* (H. Corbin & S. H. Nasr, Eds.). (Vol. 2). Tehran: Pazuhishgah-i 'Ulum-i Insani va Mutalafat-i Farhangi .

Suhrawardi, Shihab al-Din. (1993c). *Majmu'a-yi Musannafat-i Shaykh-i Ishraq* (H. Corbin & S. H. Nasr, Eds.). (Vol. 3). Tehran: Pazuhishgah-i 'Ulum-i Insani va Mutalafat-i Farhangi .

Walbridge, J. (1992). *The science of mystic lights: Qutb al-Din Shirazi and the illuminationist tradition in Islamic philosophy.* Cambridge, MA: Harvard University Press.

Wilson, P. L. (1988). *Scandal: Essays in Islamic heresy.* New York: Autonomedia.

Yazdi, M. H. (1992). *Principles of epistemology in Islamic philosophy: Knowledge by presence.* Albany: State University of New York Press.

Ziai, H. (1990). *Knowledge and illumination: A study of Suhrawardi's "Hikmat al-Ishraq."* Brown University Judaic Studies Series 97. Atlanta: Scholars Press.

Ziai, H. (1992). The source and nature of political authority in Suhrawardi's philosophy of illumination. In C. Butterworth (Ed.), *Political aspects of Islamic philosophy* (pp. 304–344). Cambridge, MA: Harvard University Press.

8

Spiritual Inquiry

DONALD ROTHBERG

I have pursued my apprenticeship for sixty-four years.
During these years, many, many times I have gone to the
mountains alone. Yes, I have endured much suffering during my life. Yet to learn to see, to learn to hear, you must
do this—go into the wilderness alone. For it is not I who
can teach you the ways of the gods. Such things are
learned only in solitude.
    —Matsuwa, Huichol shaman (Halifax, 1979, p. 250)

Yes, Kalamas, it is proper that you have doubt, that you
have perplexity, for a doubt has arisen in a matter which is
doubtful. Now, look you Kalamas, do not be led by reports,
or tradition, or hearsay. Be not led by the authority of religious texts, nor by mere logic or inference, nor by considering appearances, nor by the delight in speculative
opinions, nor by seeming possibilities, nor by the idea:
"This is our teacher." But, O Kalamas, when you know for
yourselves that certain things are unwholesome and
wrong, and bad, then give them up. . . . And when you
know for yourselves that certain things are wholesome and
good, then accept them and follow them.
    —Gautama Buddha (Rahula, 1974, pp. 2–3)

It is as if it were not possible to turn the eye from darkness
to light without turning the whole body; so one must turn
one's whole soul from the world of becoming until it can
endure to contemplate reality, and the brightest of realities,
which we say is the Good. . . . Education then is the art of
doing this very thing, this turning around, the knowledge
of how the soul can most easily and most effectively be
turned around.
    —Plato, *Republic*, Bk. 7, 518c (Grube, 1974, p. 171)

> When I think of the faces of that squad of armed, green-
> uniformed guards—my God, those faces! I looked at them,
> each in turn, from behind the safety of a window, and I
> have never been so frightened of anything in my life as I
> was of those faces. I sank to my knees with the words that
> preside over human life: And God made man after His
> likeness. That passage spent a difficult morning with me.
> —Etty Hillesum (1985, p. 258)

What would contemporary culture look like if the insights and methods of spiritual approaches to knowledge and inquiry, such as those of Matsuwa, the Buddha, Plato, and Etty Hillesum, among others, were taken seriously? How might educational institutions and practices, in which the ways of knowing and inquiry of a culture are developed and passed on, be transformed? How would contemporary understandings of science be changed if such ways of knowing and inquiry were recognized as legitimate and integrated?

My intention in this chapter is to lay some of the groundwork for responding to these questions by exploring the idea that there are forms of systematic "spiritual inquiry." I want, in the first part of this chapter, to establish a provisional plausibility for this idea on the basis both of a review of contemporary literature concerning the idea of a "spiritual science" and the examination of practices and texts drawn from many cultures and historical periods. These practices and texts seem to give evidence of ways of inquiry leading to resolutions of spiritual questions. There seem to be methods involving something like what we contemporary Westerners would call systematic observation, deep questioning, and/or critical analysis, qualities that are at the heart of what we generally mean by the terms "science" and "inquiry."

In the second part of the chapter, however, I step back and question a premature assimilation of these approaches through the contemporary Western categories of "science" and "inquiry." I consider critically some of the complexities and difficulties of relating these mostly premodern, and often non-Western approaches to the two main forms of contemporary Western inquiry, namely the natural and human sciences. How should we explore the idea of spiritual inquiry? Can we do this simply within the context of contemporary scholarly institutions and practices? Are new modes of inquiry necessary to explore and express spiritual inquiry in a contemporary way?

Before proceeding further, however, it is helpful to give some initial clarification of the terms "spirituality" (and "spiritual"), "religion" (and "religious"), and "inquiry." A deeper discussion of these terms, particularly of the concept of "inquiry," can only occur through following the questions in the second part of the chapter. Furthermore, it is important to say at this point that I use these terms with some reservations. They are rooted in Western traditions, have been used in very different ways historically and in contemporary discourse, and do not translate easily (or sometimes at all) into non-Western or premodern traditions.

I take *spirituality* to involve the lived transformation of self and community toward fuller alignment with or expression of what is understood, within a given cultural context, to be "sacred." This transformation may be supported by doctrines, practices, and social organization. However, I do not mean to suggest with the term that there is a separate spiritual realm, even if belief in such a realm is found in some spiritual teachings. I use the term *religion* as a broader term signifying the organized forms of doctrine, ritual, myth, experience, practice, spirituality, ethics, and social structure that together constitute a world in relation to what is known as sacred (Rothberg, 1993, pp. 105–106; Smart, 1976, pp. 6–12).

It is important to note, following these definitions, that there can be both nonreligious (i.e., nonorganized) spirituality and nonspiritual religiosity. Furthermore, neither spirituality nor religion as such is inherently good or bad. Spirituality and religion can make possible love and wisdom as well as great brutality. Religions, of course, have long been criticized for the many horrors for which they have been in large part responsible. Nazism, to give a less-obvious example, can be interpreted as involving spiritual dimensions, as a number of commentators have pointed out (e.g., Berman, 1989, pp. 253–293).

By inquiry, I understand most generally (and minimally) a response to an existential and/or intellectual question through the search for insight, knowledge, or understanding.[1] The question may be a deeply practical one concerning how to solve a problem or resolve an existential dilemma. The question may be very abstract, seemingly purely theoretical. It may be motivated mainly by inquisitiveness, curiosity, wonder, or a sense of mystery. The inquiry may be highly personal and idiosyncratic, or it may be organized within a given culture and carried out through particular practices.

To use the concept of *inquiry* rather than that of *knowledge* as a focus is to stress the *activity* and *process* that lead to knowledge, rather than the completed and abstracted *result*. Furthermore, inquiry is a much less ideologically loaded term than science, much less wedded to particular Western interpretations of knowledge (especially positivist and empiricist interpretations of knowledge as exclusively empirical). In these senses, the concept of inquiry seems more neutral and potentially useful for the kind of cross-cultural exploration required in investigating spiritual approaches.

The Idea of Spiritual Inquiry

It is not surprising that many contemporary Westerners exploring spirituality, especially in an experiential way, should be attracted to interpreting a number of spiritual practices and traditions in part through the categories of science and inquiry. These categories are of course the hallmark, in contemporary culture, of what is cognitively significant, and it is the cognitive that in modern times usually provides the way to "truth" and "reality." But even though such categories have been central to the (Western) Enlightenment critiques of religion (as superstitious, dogmatic, irrational, etc.), they have also seemed initially very applicable to many spiritual approaches, particularly those deemed mystical and contemplative.

Indeed, many recent writers have attempted to make sense of something like a "spiritual science." Some, focusing on contemplative disciplines, have spoken variously of a "science of self-investigation" (Needleman, 1976, p. 159); an "inner empiricism" (Weber, 1986, p. 7); the "inner sciences" (Thurman, 1991, pp. 53–73); "state specific sciences" (Tart, 1972); and "mysticism as a science" (Deikman, 1982). Some have attempted to reconstruct traditional Greek, Jewish, Christian, and Islamic metaphysical systems, interpreting them in their mature forms as examples of the most fundamental "sacred science" (e.g., Nasr, 1981, 1993), and also applying the term "sacred science" to traditional interpretations of disciplines such as cosmology, linguistics, mathematics, astronomy, medicine, and architecture (e.g., Bamford, 1994; Nasr, 1993, pp. 95–118). Some have begun to write about "native" or "indigenous" science (Colorado, 1988; Deloria, 1993). A number of authors have employed something like the term "spiritual science" as a synonym for a systematic approach to spiritual training (e.g., Steiner, 1904/1947), in ways similar to the ways that cognates of "science" have been used historically in many mystical texts.

Others have attempted to connect spiritual approaches more explicitly with the contemporary natural and human sciences. Several authors have, in light of "postempiricist" philosophy of science, pointed out the strong parallels between natural scientific and religious ways of knowing (Barbour, 1974; Rolston, 1987). Others have shown the similarities between empirical and more explicitly mystical ways of knowing (e.g., Smith, 1976, pp. 96–117). More controversial has been the attempt to explore apparent commonalities between the findings of contemporary science, particularly physics and various mystical traditions, and to interpret the practice of natural science as a possible spiritual path (Capra, 1975; Weber, 1986; Wilber, 1985).

A number of authors have examined the connections between contemplation, particularly Buddhist forms, and the cognitive sciences. De Wit (1991) has given the outlines of a pioneering cross-cultural "contemplative psychology." Hayward (1987, pp. 189–201) has argued that the practice of Buddhist mindfulness meditation "can be regarded as a form of scientific method" (p. 193), in that it is essentially naturalistic, universalistic, and intersubjectively testable. Rosch (1992, pp. 84–106) has distinguished the rejected project of introspection in modern psychology from the method of mindfulness meditation. Varela, Thompson, and Rosch (1991) have claimed that mindfulness meditation is preferable to the current methods in the human sciences, such as phenomenology, for the systematic examination of human experience, in large part because it combines both theoretical and practical dimensions. Thurman (1991, pp. 51–73) has maintained that Tibetan Buddhist "inner science" shares the core qualities of Western science; it is theoretically flexible and nondogmatic, open to empirical experience, critical, rational, systematic, and analytical. Yet it is also highly practical, oriented to the achievement of the deepest possible human happiness.

Wilber (1983, pp. 1–81), following and expanding on the work of Habermas (1968/1971), has given perhaps the most comprehensive (although preliminary and simplified) philosophical treatment of the idea of spiritual science. He has outlined a very general model of three distinct and paradigmatic types of sciences: (1) the "empirical-analytic" sciences of the world known through the senses; (2) the "mental-phenomenological" sciences of the human symbolic world of meanings; and, finally, (3) the "transcendental" or "transpersonal" sciences. These latter sciences, in turn, comprise what Wilber calls the "mandalic sciences," involving use of the mental-phenomenological mode in order to understand spiritual experiences and realities, and the "noumenological" or "gnostic" sciences, with methodologies designed to facilitate direct spiritual insight. These three types of sciences share a basic structure. Every science is injunctive (to know, one must carry out this or that inquiry), leads to concrete apprehensions of reality, and has its results communally confirmed.

I use the concept of spiritual inquiry in a way generally continuous with the aforementioned literature, referring to a number of spiritual approaches, outlined below, which seem to have many of the qualities of inquiry found in the natural and human sciences. On this basis, it seems plausible to hypothesize that there are general qualities of inquiry and science shared by both the contemporary sciences and forms of spiritual inquiry. That is, these spiritual approaches seem in many ways relatively open and nondogmatic, rooted in rigorous observation, methodical, systematic, critical, and/or intersubjective. Yet these inquiries also seem to go considerably beyond the contemporary sciences, in that they have to do with ways of knowing, access to domains of reality, and transformative practices not currently understood as scientific. They suggest the possibility of a significantly expanded understanding of inquiry and knowledge.

Methods of Spiritual Inquiry

I want, then, to offer a very preliminary typology of five interrelated ways or "ideal types" of spiritual inquiry: (a) systematic contemplation, (b) radical questioning, (c) metaphysical thinking, (d) the critical "deconstruction" of metaphysical and other views, and (e) the cultivation of visions and dreams. I give several examples of each type, generally presented from the perspectives of the approaches cited.

Systematic Contemplation

The form of spiritual inquiry that is probably best known today involves training to develop a relatively open and receptive contemplative or meditative awareness. The inquirer cultivates the ability to be "present" with the phenomena of human experience in their breadth and depth, often in a primarily nondiscursive way, and commonly uses exercises and conceptual models to help initially access particular dimensions of experience. This contemplative process purportedly gives insight into the surface patterns and deeper nature of these phenomena and potentially opens up awareness to the most fundamental spiritual insight, however this is understood.

Forms of contemplative inquiry can be located as particular approaches or schools particularly within Asian and Western metaphysical and religious traditions. I want to discuss two examples of living traditions, Buddhist mindfulness meditation and Christian contemplation, while recognizing the large range of similar examples that might be drawn from Hindu, neo-Confucian, Taoist, Greek, Jewish, and Islamic sources, among others.

The basic method of mindfulness meditation has been developed in a variety of forms in Theravāda and Mahāyāna Buddhist traditions (e.g., Hanh, 1976; King, 1980; Kornfield, 1977; Nyanaponika, 1965). A number of contemporary practitioners have applied this method of inquiry to, for example, death and dying (Levine, 1982); stress, pain, and illness (Kabat-Zinn, 1990); social transformation (Hanh, 1987; Macy, 1983); and intimate relationships (Welwood, 1990).

The mindfulness meditator generally begins in a communal context, guided by a teacher, and with a basic grounding in ethical behavior and understanding of Buddhist teachings. One typical sequence in the Theravāda tradition is first to train the meditator's attentional abilities by cultivating the ability to concentrate on one object, often initially on the sensations of breathing, through practice of a formal exercise. The meditator then is urged, in both formal meditation and everyday activity (as, for instance, a monk or nun), to be aware of any content of consciousness, as much as possible from the attitude of a present-centered, nonjudgmental, "bare attention." The stance is that of a radical openness to whatever content presents itself, pleasant or unpleasant, wanted or unwanted; thoughts about Buddhist teachings and experiences of qualities such as compassion, equanimity, and even mindfulness itself have, strictly speaking, no privileged status.

From this basic contemplative stance, the Buddhist meditator is initially aware of a wide range of ordinary experiences—bodily sensations and sensory data, and mental and emotional states—and may discern habitual patterns of these experiences. If the meditator continues to "progress," there are further general developmental shifts, both in the way of knowing and in the contents of consciousness. The meditator experiences in an immediate way insights into the nature of ordinary experience and phenomena as *anicca, dukkha, anattā*: as impermanent, unsatisfactory, and selfless. As concentration increases, temporal and gross cognitive constructions decrease significantly. The gap decreases between knower and known, between consciousness and its content. The lived experience may be more and more that of a continually changing flux, without an active and independent knower. The "experience" of *nibbanā* (Sanskrit: *nirvāṇa*) provides the final, liberating insight into the nature of all phenomena.

Christian contemplation, according to the work of Thomas Merton (1959, 1948/1978; Shannon, 1981), perhaps the most prominent Western Christian contemplative of this century, can be classified, following the teachings of the early Greek fathers, into three types: active contemplation, natural contemplation, and mystical theology, sometimes called "infused" contemplation. Active contemplation, the mode of contemplation most accessible to nonmonastics, is an inquiry through which the contemplative aims to discover and be aligned with the will of God in everyday life. For Merton (1959), it means being in touch with several dimensions of life: with the essential (outer) events and movements of one's epoch; with one's own (inner) life and deeper intentions, activated particularly through liturgy, reading, and meditation on important themes; and with reality as a whole, contemplated with a sense of awe. Such contemplation is practiced with some effort, and with the aid of conceptual models, discriminating judgments, and acts of faith. The intention of active contemplation is, as in infused or "passive" contemplation, union with God in love; indeed active contemplation may at times become infused.

Natural contemplation (*theōria physikē*) is the "intuition of divine things in and through the reflections of God in nature and in the symbols of revelation" (Merton, 1959, p. 66). It presumes considerable ascetic training, so that the contemplative is no longer attached to objects and nature, but can instead discern their essential natures and their symbolic relation to God.

The third form of contemplation, mystical theology (*theologia*), is defined as "pure contemplation" and understood by Merton to culminate in the direct "experimental" knowledge of God, without thoughts, concepts, or images. Such contemplation is central to the long line of Christian apophatic mystics, such as Pseudo-Dionysus, Eckhart, the unknown author of the *Cloud of Unknowing*, St. John of the Cross, and Teresa of Avila. Merton, following this tradition, identifies such infused contemplation as a kind of "dark knowing" that is also an unknowing. It demands, therefore, considerable openness. Merton (1959) writes: "The great obstacle to contemplation is rigidity and prejudice. He who thinks he knows what it is beforehand prevents himself from finding out the true nature of contemplation" (p. 111).

The path of infused contemplation proceeds through a number of stages of "purification" through which love develops—most fruitfully, believes Merton, in the monastic climate of silence and solitude. One crucial initial stage is the experience of aridity and darkness, and sometimes intense conflict, in which prayer, meditation, liturgy, and contemplation lose much of their meaning; this period is interpreted as the clearer surfacing of selfishness and sin. At some point, there comes initial illumination, a sense of contact with God. This may be followed by the continued attempt to purify one's love through all of one's experiences, cultivating the kind of *apatheia* or "holy indifference" recommended, for example, by St. John of the Cross:

> Even as the bee extracts from all plants the honey that is in them
> . . . even so the soul with great facility extracts the sweetness of
> love that is in all things that pass through it. It loves God in each
> of them, whether pleasant or unpleasant. (cited in Merton,
> 1948/1978, pp. 64–65)[2]

As infused contemplation continues, the purified inmost self may be touched by God in a "dark knowing" free of all concepts (even the concept of God, as Eckhart once suggested). In such intuitive knowledge and purity of love for God, the split between subject and God is healed.

Radical Questioning

Whereas contemplative inquiries of the kinds previously described are carried out in large part nondiscursively, especially in their more advanced stages, other modes of spiritual inquiry proceed primarily through language and concepts, even if language and concepts are eventually left behind. For example, the art of asking fundamental and often unusual and unexpected questions as a path of ethical and spiritual learning leading to the deepest spiritual insights has been developed widely in both Western and Asian traditions.

For Socrates and Plato, questions, particularly in the setting of dialogue, are the main means by which to arrive at the knowledge of fundamental realities and to prepare for intuition of ultimate reality. As McGinn (1991, p. 29) suggests, there is no separation between such questioning and spirituality, for, contrary to most contemporary philosophical scholarship on Plato, philosophy is always spiritual practice for Plato and most ancient philosophers. Initially, questions might reveal our perhaps unexpected ignorance, thereby liberating our wonder and curiosity if we are not too prideful. It was apparently at this open and agnostic state that Socrates both began and frequently arrived, a state that was in Socrates' case sometimes connected with visions and other spiritual experiences.

For Plato, however, questioning could go further. As we follow the way of questions, especially as guided by a mentor like Socrates and in the context of ongoing moral purification, we move away from the overlays of ignorance toward the knowledge that is always already present in the depths of the soul and only needs to be uncovered. In this sense, we do not arrive at new answers with our questions, but rather at the universal innate and archetypal knowledge of self and cosmos. At first, such knowledge is of patterned and ordered realities, the Forms or *eidē* of the "intelligible region," and is a knowledge articulable in language. Following such intellectual preparation and knowledge may come the sudden and "unspeakable" (*arrhēton*) insight (*noēsis*) into the Form of Forms, into what Plato variously calls the Good, the Beautiful, or the One.

Western ways of asking radical questions have especially been preserved since Plato and Socrates in the philosophical traditions, even as the confidence that such questions would yield sacred knowledge has often wavered and been lost, especially in modern times. The energy of radical questioning has instead often been used to criticize religious and philosophical claims to knowledge of the sacred. There have, nonetheless, been a number of modern exemplars, such as Kierkegaard and Heidegger, of deep philosophical questioning as a kind of spiritual inquiry.

Examination of Asian traditions also reveals a number of modes of deep questioning. For example, the Buddha's address to the Kalama people (cited at the beginning of this chapter), in which he urged them to question deeply their usual beliefs based on authority, tradition, or popularity and instead seek confirmation in their own experiences, stands parallel with Socrates' exaltation of the examined life. In later Buddhist traditions, the factor of "inquiry" (*vicāra* [Pali]) was highlighted as one of the Seven Factors of Enlightenment and sometimes developed in a concentrated way as a spiritual method. Stephen Batchelor (1990) writes of the tradition of radical questioning in the Chinese, Korean, and Japanese Zen traditions.

Those practicing such questioning are guided in developing a "great doubt," a doubt to be cultivated in and out of the meditation hall through focusing continually on words like "What is it?" or "What is this?" or "Why is it?" or simply "What?" The seventeenth-century Japanese Zen master Takasui advised his students:

> You must doubt deeply, again and again, asking yourself what the subject of hearing could be. Pay no attention to the various illusory thoughts and ideas that may occur to you. Only doubt more and more deeply, gathering together in yourself all the strength that is in you, without aiming at anything or expecting anything in advance, without intending to be enlightened and without even intending not to be enlightened; become like a child within your own breast. (Batchelor, 1990, p. 15)

The twentieth-century Indian sage Ramana Maharsi developed a well-known method of questioning, with roots especially in the Hindu traditions of *jñāna* yoga and Advaita ("nondual") Vedanta, that he called "Self-inquiry" (also *vichara* [here in Sanskrit]). Ramana Maharsi advised the seeker continually to ask the question, "Who am I?," examining the supposed sources of the self, until the more conditioned aspects of self disappear and the deeper "Self" is known:

> Trace, then, the ultimate cause of "I" or personality. . . . From where does this "I" arise? Seek for it within; it then vanishes. This is the pursuit of wisdom. When the mind unceasingly investigates its own nature . . . [t]his is the direct path for all. (Godman, 1985, p. 50)

Metaphysical Thinking

In the various traditions of spiritual inquiry examined, we can note a certain tension between those who claim that contemplation or questioning can reach determinate "answers," articulable in language, and those who claim that no methods can produce and no language can adequately express the core spiritual understanding; for the latter, in an important sense, there are no answers (Fenner, 1994). This tension between spiritual inquiry as a path of knowing and spiritual inquiry as unknowing also appears when we consider (in this and the next section) two further methods of spiritual inquiry: metaphysical thinking, and the "deconstruction" or suspension of metaphysical thinking.

In the world's religions and in Western philosophy, there have been attempts to further spiritual understanding through intellectual analysis, synthesis, and speculation concerning the nature of human experience, the nature of the mind and knowing, the structure of reality, and spiritual development; I speak of such inquiry generally as "metaphysical thinking." Thinking of this sort is typically the attempt to understand and systematize earlier spiritual insights, in the interest of guiding future spiritual development. Platonic contemplation, questioning, and intuition of Forms, for example, led to rich traditions of further speculation and spiritual experience. Jewish, Christian, and Islamic philosophers and theologians have taken the founding religious revelations of their traditions as starting points and articulated, in Christian terms, "faith seeking understanding" (*fides quaerens intellectum*).

Metaphysical exploration is often a starting point for further contemplative inquiry, as the seeker receives and studies a kind of "road map" of the spiritual path. For Ibn al-'Arabi (Chittick, 1989), metaphysical reflection and reason typically help make possible the deeper insights of "gnosis" (*kashf*) and "the heart" (*qalb*). In Jewish mysticism, study of the Torah and of the structures of the higher worlds, as outlined in the Kabbalah, may not only facilitate further contemplative practice, but may sometimes in itself lead to mystical ecstasy. For Aquinas, inquiry through the "natural" intellect brings the individual to many truths, although "supernatural" truths are revealed through other modes of knowledge. Study of the Abhidhamma "psychology," and of other epistemological and metaphysical models, often precedes Buddhist contemplative practice.

Metaphysical thinking may also be used coupled with contemplation or radical questioning, as a guide to illuminate everyday experience and deepen understanding. A Hindu *jñāna* yogi might reflect on his or her assumptions about the nature of the self, considering the thesis found in the Upanishads, that the deepest aspect of the self, the atman, is being or ultimate reality itself. A Buddhist might use the teaching of "dependent origination" (*paṭicca samupāda*) to help structure mindfulness meditation, examining how that teaching can be observed as operative in moment-to-moment experience. A Jew might reflect on a given passage of the Bible in relation to some aspect of daily life, as, in an extreme example, Etty Hillesum, in the passage given at the beginning of the chapter, brought scriptural understanding to bear on her experience in the Nazi camps.

The Critical "Deconstruction" of Metaphysical and Other Views

We can also speak of methodical inquiries in which the focus is on an undoing of established metaphysical and other belief systems, in the interests of making possible the deepest spiritual insights. In these (in Christian terminology) apophatic inquiries of a *via negativa*, there is an openness to questioning or suspending even those core principles or teachings of the very tradition of the inquirer. The inquirer leaves behind the familiar and safe territory in order to know in a different way. In Christian theology and practice, methods of systematically suspending core beliefs have been developed in the tradition of "negative theology" that dates from the work of Pseudo-Dionysus and have been linked with the claim of infused contemplation that concepts are absent in the most profound knowing.

In Asian traditions, it is the Buddhist Mādhyamika method of "deconstructing" core concepts (Buddhist concepts included) that is perhaps paradigmatic as a path of spiritual inquiry in this mode. In that approach (Fenner, 1991, 1994; Sprung, 1979; Thurman, 1984), the inquirer examines thoroughly, in a formal way, every logically possible alternative on a given issue or topic, ultimately finding that none of the alternatives meets the anticipated requirement of noncontradiction (i.e., that a statement and its contradiction cannot both be true). All possible metaphysical views (*dṛṣṭi*), including the most central Buddhist tenets about causality, *nirvāṇa*, the spiritual path, and so on, are, when probed, self-contradictory; they imply their opposites. All intellectual attempts to claim some kind of absolute truth, complete adequacy or determinacy of thought to reality, or full intelligibility, are doomed to failure because of the intrinsically dualistic structure of such claims. Guided by this understanding, such a deconstructive inquiry, when coupled with contemplative practices, it is claimed, leads the inquirer to "nonconceptual" and freeing spiritual insights into "emptiness" (*śūnyatā*) (i.e., the nature of reality as known without metaphysical views). It is furthermore the claim (e.g., of the main Mādhyamika thinker, Nāgārjuna) that, far from such inquiry leading to nihilism, only such an understanding and practice makes possible ethical and spiritual life.

This form of spiritual inquiry is particularly interesting and important in that there are significant parallels with modern (and some postmodern) critiques of metaphysics. Inquiring at a time when practical spiritual contexts had largely been separated from intellectual inquiry, for a variety of reasons, modern Western secular critics of classical metaphysics often found only mere dogma, a lack of contact with experience and evidence, and, from a purely intellectual perspective, numerous problems and internal contradictions. For some of these critics, beginning with Nietzsche and leading on to contemporary deconstructionist postmodern interpreters, the prospect is of a kind of nihilism; the old metaphysical, ethical, and political grand narratives and systems do not hold, even on their own terms. Thus it is important to note that, with these forms of spiritual inquiry, a deeply reflexive view of language and conceptual systems can be articulated in an ethical and spiritual setting (i.e., not at the cost of nihilism).

The Cultivation of Visions and Dreams

In many traditions, particularly indigenous traditions, the resolution of spiritual questions or problems may occur through practices culminating in visions or dreams bringing spiritual knowledge. Interestingly, few contemporary Westerners have spoken of these practices as sciences or forms of inquiry. Perhaps this is because the cultivation of visionary capabilities does not seem central to contemporary methods of the natural and human sciences, even though the use of the creative imagination has played an important role in many scientific discoveries and in phenomenology, and the exploration of dreams has been since Freud the "royal road" to self-knowledge in psychotherapy.

A number of different practices may induce the desired vision or dream. The seeker in ancient Greece and Egypt frequently went to a sacred place to sleep, or slept in contact with sacred objects, in order to "incubate" dreams that might answer a given question or problem. Diviners (e.g., in many African cultures) engage in ritual practices leading to visions or dreams, after they have first been "called" by the ancestral spirits to become diviners. There may often be an extended time of solitude in the wilderness, as in the North American "vision quest," described by Hultkrantz (1993, pp. 255–372) as "the most characteristic feature of North American [indigenous] religions outside the Pueblo area" (p. 278). Other means used include fasting and other ascetic practices, community rituals, and the use of psychedelics. Typically, these practices make possible a dream or vision in which there are revelations from spirits, either from one's own guardian spirit or from other spirits. Information revealed in trance permits shamans, for example, to heal.

An Eskimo shaman of the twentieth century, Igjugarjuk, described, in conversation with the anthropologist Rasmussen, the nature of his initiation into the life of a shaman, the life of "seeking for knowledge" (Halifax, 1979). Placed in solitude far from his village with little food and water, under severe ascetic conditions, Igjugarjuk was enjoined to think only of the helping spirit he wished to contact:

> [This] took place in the middle of the coldest winter, and I, who never got anything to warm me, and must not move, was very cold, and it was so tiring having to sit without daring to lie down, that sometimes it was as if I died a little. Only toward the end of the thirty days did a helping spirit come to me . . . whilst I had collapsed, exhausted, and was sleeping. But still I saw her lifelike, hovering over me, and from that day I could not close my eyes or dream without seeing her. (Halifax, 1979, p. 67)

In this shamanic initiation, there is a close relationship of seeking for spiritual knowledge with crisis and ordeal.[3] The individual (or collective) crisis, whether that of a severe illness or great cultural danger, or that of the more constructed crisis of ascetic wilderness solitude, seems, under certain conditions, to facilitate the opening to wisdom through inquiry.[4]

Igjugarjuk described his usual procedure as a shaman for seeking for knowledge, for inquiring into a given issue or problem:

> [T]he people of my village were called together and I told them what I had been asked to do. Then I left tent or snow house and went out into solitude, away from the dwellings of man, but those who remained behind had to sing continuously. . . . If anything difficult had to be found out, my solitude had to extend over three days and two nights, or three nights and two days. In all that time I had to wander about without rest and only sit down once in a while on a stone or a snow drift. When I had been out long and had become tired, I could almost doze and dream what I had come out to find and about which I had been thinking all the time. (Halifax, 1979, p. 68)

Understanding Spiritual Inquiry in the Contemporary Context

But how well do the concepts of science and inquiry help us to explore and interpret these spiritual approaches and traditions? On the one hand, there seem to be some very significant potential advantages to using these concepts. For example, they provide a way of responding to the (Western) Enlightenment critiques of religion without, as it were, having to choose sides between science and religion (and spirituality). We might interpret spiritual inquiry, for example, as a mode of inquiry in large part complementary to rather than in conflict with contemporary modes of inquiry, perhaps understood as in Wilber's account of three types of sciences. Speaking of spiritual inquiry also seems to help develop a discriminating response to the Enlightenment critiques. It might be argued that these critiques can be cogently applied to the dogmatism, superstition, and authoritarianism of some religious and spiritual approaches, but that these critiques are not so adequate when applied to many of the forms of spiritual inquiry discussed earlier (Rothberg, 1986a, 1986b). Third, given that spiritual inquiry involves ways of knowing, dimensions of mind and body, and domains of reality other than those that are thematized in the contemporary sciences, the possibility arises of radically transformed understandings of these areas if the findings of all modes of science or inquiry were integrated. This is currently occurring in several areas, such as transpersonal psychology and medicine.

But there are also a number of problems and dangers in integrating material from diverse cultures and epochs, which may be less obvious than the potential advantages. Some of the recent work and discussions in and concerning hermeneutics (e.g., Gadamer, 1960/1975), anthropology (e.g., Clifford & Marcus, 1986), cultural studies (e.g., Said, 1978/1979; Williams & Chrisman, 1994), philosophy (e.g., Wilson, 1970), and cross-cultural and interreligious dialogue (e.g, Kremer, 1992a, 1992b; Walker, 1987) help us to identify some of these issues.

The major danger is a tendency to project, often unconsciously, contemporary Western views and models of the natural and/or human sciences as if these understandings are universal. We may very easily tend toward a kind of cultural imperialism, toward what Said (1978/1979) has called "Orientalism," in which we assimilate the "other" (the premodern, the non-Western, apparently nonrational ways of knowing, etc.) to our categories and projects, albeit usually in far more subtle ways than in the past. (Of course, to worry about projection and cultural imperialism is often another typically Western preoccupation, and we may also uncritically assume the ideas related to these concerns to be universal as well.)

For example, in thinking about spiritual science or inquiry, we might, with many good intentions, attempt to show that the spiritual approaches discussed meet certain criteria of science or inquiry. Indeed, many of those cited in the review of current literature about spiritual science have more or less followed this tack. Claims resulting from many of the modes of spiritual inquiry (particularly contemplative modes) may be said to be based on experience (rather than mere dogma), on "evidence" and "data," and thus be generally "verifiable." Through the use of systematic methods, many of the claims of spiritual inquiry can be replicated by others and generalized. The claims seem in a number of cases to be intersubjectively confirmed by a spiritual teacher or within a community. Furthermore, there are often "critical" standards, internal to the methods of spiritual inquiry, that help to discriminate insight from pseudo-insight or confusion. Those modern critics who argue that the religious contexts of spiritual inquiry prevent a truly open and nondogmatic inquiry might be countered by pointing to the ways in which the contemporary sciences are understood to work through "paradigms," on the basis of generally unquestioned views of science, logic, and metaphysics (Barbour, 1974; Rolston, 1987).

I want to identify two main problems with this strategy of thinking about spiritual science that reflect elements of projection. First of all, we may, consciously or unconsciously, give a privileged position to contemporary, established Western concepts of science and inquiry. To interpret spiritual approaches through categories like "data," "evidence," "verification," "method," "confirmation," and "intersubjectivity" may be to enthrone these categories as somehow the hallmarks of knowledge as such, even if the categories are expanded in meaning from their current Western usage. But might not a profound encounter with practices of spiritual inquiry lead to considering carefully the meaning of other comparable categories (e.g, *dhyāna, vichara, theōria, gnōsis,* or *contemplatio*) and perhaps to developing understandings of inquiry in which such spiritual categories are primary or central when we speak of knowledge? To assume that the categories of current Western epistemology are adequate for interpreting spiritual approaches is to prejudge the results of such an encounter, which might well lead to significant changes in these categories. At best, to understand some of the examples of spiritual inquiry as meeting many or most of the general criteria of science or inquiry might establish a certain plausibility, among those who value the contemporary Western sciences, that spiritual inquiry should be taken seriously and might be integrated among the sciences.

A second problem is that to use the contemporary Western categories of science and inquiry is usually to give very selective interpretations of spiritual approaches, noticing some aspects and ignoring others. For example, if we are making use of an empiricist Western model of natural science, we may well leave out consideration of the larger context, of the ways that many if not most contemplative methods, Asian and Western, are typically grounded in communities and in ethical practices (e.g., in Patañjali's yoga, the Buddhist model of a threefold training, or the writings of Christian monastics such as Benedict and Bernard of Clairvaux). We may tend thereby uncritically to duplicate the empiricist split of science and ethics and its asocial and ahistorical perspective and consider these spiritual approaches as exclusively "psychological" or "inner." We may focus on extracting techniques to help with stress, pain, or illness, but overlook the more profound goals of spiritual inquiry.

It may be less obvious that to carry out an "encounter" between representatives of different modes of inquiry through "dialogues" and "discourses" more rooted in the human sciences often involves many of the same difficulties of projection, exclusion, privileging, and limited horizons. For many, dialogue, in the context of scholarly and public forums, seems a neutral ground for the sharing and investigation of differences, whether differences related to values, views, gender, ethnicity, cultures, or religions.

I would like to illustrate some of these dangers of projection by examining in some depth the work of Habermas, who has developed one of the most comprehensive theories of how such dialogue might proceed in the human sciences. He has given an account of the underlying structures of "communicative rationality" (communication aiming at understanding) and of the special role of what he calls "discourse" (Habermas, 1968/1979, pp. 1–68; 1968/1984a; 1973/1984b, pp. 127–183). For Habermas, discourse is an activity separate from but grounded in everyday action, in which there is consideration only of arguments concerning problematic claims to validity (to theoretical truth or normative "rightness"), conducted in a setting ideally free from various forms of domination and oppression. The participants are ideally psychologically mature so that their motivation can be entirely to search for what is true or right and not to act in ways that are consciously or unconsciously strategic, deceptive, or self-deceptive.

But what would a dialogue (and resulting discourse) look like, to give an example, between a scholar sympathetic to spiritual inquiry and a scholar of the human sciences, one who proceeds according to Habermas's model? Whatever benefits there might be, the second scholar will likely at some point say something like the following: "Yes, I've been edified some. But I have one main problem about calling what you present 'inquiry.' These spiritual insights all seem ineluctably 'private,' without there being public reasons to believe in the claims. How could we evaluate these claims? Why should I think that the shaman has contacted a spirit rather than just had an interesting dream? Why should I think that the meditator's experiences of light are anything more than a physiological response of the brain when under great stress? What are the publicly accessible reasons for thinking that Ramana Maharshi was in touch with his Self, or that Eckhart was united with God? Why should I think that 'spiritual inquiry' brings 'knowledge' rather than edifying private but nondiscursive experiences?"

A response to these questions can take several approaches. The emphasis on the giving of reasons in public discourse as the sole guarantor of validity might be questioned in a variety of related ways: as tending to exclude direct attention to the role of body, emotions, and personal experience in knowledge (e.g., Jaggar & Bordo, 1989; Scheman, 1992, pp. 61–71; Solomon, 1992, pp. 19–47); as uncritically assuming the distinction between "public" and "private" in ways that tend to obscure the dimensions of gender, class, race, and power embodied in the history and theory related to this distinction (Benhabib & Cornell, 1987); as ethnocentric, as presuming the universality of Western models (Winch, 1964/1970, pp. 78–111); or as neglecting the horizons of tradition and narrative and the ways in which dialogue may take the shape of a "fusion of horizons" (Gadamer, 1960/1975).[5]

I want to suggest a further reason. The second scholar is right to point to the ways, at this time, in Western culture, that no public reasons could conclusively establish the validity of many of the most basic claims associated with spiritual inquiry, even if some of those claims might be adequately assessed on empirical or interpretive grounds (Rothberg, 1990). As I hope to show in what follows, what is "questionable" is to project discourse as the universal horizon of knowledge.

But even before we consider this question, an immediate objection may arise. If we are questioning discourse in this way, aren't we doing so by engaging in discourse ourselves? Habermas (1983/1990, pp. 86 ff.) points out, in a kind of "transcendental" argument, that there is a "performative paradox" in questioning discourse as the main way to reach validity. In doing this, thinks Habermas, one is presumably invoking reasons and thus assuming exactly what is questioned, namely that problematic claims should be settled by discussion and giving reasons. However, the problem with Habermas's argument is that he again implicitly presumes discourse as the universal horizon, because if there are other ways of questioning and inquiry not part of communicative rationality, such as those found in forms of spiritual inquiry, then this argument doesn't work. Rather, these other ways of inquiry may suggest further horizons beyond the structures of communicative rationality.

In fact, there can be no ordinary arguments and reasons as to why one should accept discourse as an ultimate arbiter. Rather, Habermas, for example, gives two unusual kinds of arguments. First, he gives "quasi-transcendental" reconstructions (à la Kant) of the structures of communicative rationality (and discourse) as simply given in human experience (and not simply a particular cultural artifact). But even if acceptable, this in itself isn't adequate to establish the universality of these structures, unless there are no broader or complementary structures. Habermas needs therefore a further argument, and gives a "developmental-logical" one in which he claims that communicative rationality is identified as the most advanced structure of human onto- and phylogenetic development. However, in the light of his problematic reading of how religious and metaphysical traditions represent "lower" levels of development (Rothberg, 1986b), this argument also doesn't work. If forms of spiritual inquiry are not essentially immature forms of rational inquiry, then an alternative perspective may be more plausible. From the points of view of many theorists of spiritual inquiry, both traditional and contemporary, rational competences are among several basic competences, and not the endpoints of development; spiritual "competences" are similarly "given" as part of human potential and may in fact provide a more comprehensive horizon of knowledge than communicative rationality. Thus, to assume that rational discussion (as defined by Habermas) provides the basic horizon for all inquiry again prejudges the structure of an authentic encounter with spiritual inquiry.

But how might we explore the relations between the contemporary sciences and spiritual inquiry, aware of the dangers of projection and exclusion? Kremer (1992a, 1992b) speaks of the limits of the model of discourse and the need for a complementary model of what he calls "concourse." For Kremer, recognition of the limits of discourse, the ways in which discourse presumes a banished and unexplored "other" (e.g., body, emotions, the feminine, wilderness, and the spiritual), may prompt a kind of "dark night of the soul" for what he calls the contemporary "masculinized scholar." The scholar travels above and below, like a shaman, to encounter and reclaim the other, and carries back a story of the integration of what has been excluded. Concourse for Kremer is the expression of such a story as a model of multidimensional inquiry, in which all of these formerly excluded dimensions are potentially present. In a given inquiry, there might be rational discourse, along with ritual, silence, stories, spiritual practices, theater, or dancing.

I believe that Kremer's idea of concourse represents, at least in the kind of brief outline given, a more adequate model for the meeting of different modes of inquiry than the model of discourse. Indeed, some of those exploring interreligious dialogue (e.g., Walker, 1987, pp. 11–18) have found it necessary to develop expanded models of dialogue that go beyond more strictly academic discourse, including not only such discourse but also spiritual retreats, rituals, and contemplative practice.

Of course, to recognize the need for such an expanded sense of inquiry is only, as it were, to open a door. There still remain versions of all the old questions about the criteria for evaluating the validity or appropriateness of claims and practices. There also emerge newer questions about the distinctions between what we might call premodern and postmodern interpretations of spiritual inquiry (and of spirituality in general).

However, there are currently a number of significant constraints and limits to developing such multidimensional forms of inquiry, both in contemporary Western spiritual settings and in academic institutions. In contemporary spiritual settings, there frequently remain hierarchical social structures and authoritarian relationships often at odds with the contemporary democratic spirit (if not reality) of inquiry, and a cautiousness about integrating contemporary modes of inquiry. Spirituality is often interpreted individualistically and privately rather than more communally and publicly (Rothberg, 1993), making collective inquiry more difficult. There often remains a residual anti-intellectualism, in large part a reaction to the limited intellectual life presented in most schools and universities.

Within academic settings, there also are many constraints on multidimensional inquiry, especially within institutions organized around something like the idea of "rational" discourse and current models of scholarship. Despite the former influence of Dewey's pragmatism on educational models, there is little openness to the "experiential" and practical dimensions of learning in "higher" education. Typically, there is a separation of thought and reflection from in-depth examination and deepening of one's own experience, as well as from the practical ethical and political dimensions of individual and collective inquiry. One usually investigates, as a student and scholar, what is other and separate and does this individually rather than more collaboratively (although this is less true of the natural sciences). Ironically but also predictably, many of the criticisms of conventional notions of objectivity and the separation of theory and practice (such as have been inspired by Marx, Nietzsche, Foucault, critical theorists, and many feminists, among others) often can only find a (sometimes comfortable) place in the academy's discussions as purely theoretical criticisms![6]

This suggests that to take the idea of multidimensional inquiry seriously (and playfully) in a particularly contemporary way demands critical transformations of the present ideas of spirituality, scholarship, and educational institution. Only such shifts will let the intentions of spiritual inquiry infuse and be influenced by other forms of inquiry. In this sense, the exploration and understanding of spiritual inquiry is only at a beginning.[7]

Notes

1. Inquiry is an important category, particularly in the American pragmatist tradition. Dewey (1938, pp. 104ff.), for example, thought of inquiry as a response to an actual indeterminate, doubtful, or perplexing situation, a response that leads, if successful, to a determinate, resolved situation.

   Of course, most of contemporary writers about such honorific terms such as "inquiry," "science," and "rationality," including Dewey, would not be satisfied with the rather minimal account of inquiry I have given. They would typically want to include discussion of criteria that are characteristic of the contemporary natural and/or human sciences, for example, that inquiry is replicable, verifiable, systematic, critical, self-reflective, based on evidence and reasoning, and so on. However, my strategy is to give minimal initial definition, so that some of the issues that arise in looking at the relations between different forms of inquiry (i.e., in the second part of the essay) are not prejudged, so that contemporary criteria of inquiry are, as much as possible, not given a privileged place.

2. I have removed italics and capitalizations that appear in Merton's quotation.

3. I thank Mat Schwarzman for this insight.

4. Under other conditions, of course, crisis, danger, and suffering can lead to fanaticism and brutality.

5. I am leaving out discussion of the frontal assault on this model by some postmodern critics. Nonetheless, to a large extent, many postmodernists

still assume an exclusively textual and intellectual model of knowledge, even if claims to "the truth" are given up; the model of discourse changes but discourse still remains the basic framework of understanding.

6. There are nonetheless many persons exploring and implementing more dynamic and dialectical versions of the theory-practice relationship from these perspectives, as well as, significantly, from the perspectives of a "critical pedagogy" (e.g., Freire, 1970), and experiential and collaborative learning (e.g., Boud, Cohen, & Walker, 1993).

7. The author would like to thank Dennis Friedler, Bonnie Morrissey, Ken Otter, Joseph Prabhu, and Tony Stigliano for their helpful comments on earlier drafts of this essay.

References

Bamford, C. (Ed.). (1994). *Homage to Pythagoras: Rediscovering sacred science.* Hudson, NY: Lindisfarne Press.

Barbour, I. (1974). *Myths, models, and paradigms: A comparative study in science and religion.* New York: Harper & Row.

Batchelor, S. (1990). *The faith to doubt: Glimpses of Buddhist uncertainty.* Berkeley: Parallax Press.

Benhabib, S., & Cornell, D. (Eds.). (1987). *Feminism as critique: On the politics of gender.* Minneapolis: University of Minnesota Press.

Berman. M. (1989). *Coming to our senses: Body and spirit in the hidden history of the West.* New York: Simon & Schuster.

Boud, D., Cohen R., & Walker D. (Eds.). (1993). *Using experience for learning.* Buckingham, England: The Society for Research into Higher Education and Open University Press.

Capra, F. (1975). *The tao of physics.* Boulder, CO: Prajna Press.

Chittick, W. (1989). *The Sufi path of knowledge: Ibn al-'Arabi's metaphysics of imagination.* Albany: State University of New York Press.

Clifford, J., & Marcus, G. (Eds.). (1986). *Writing culture: The poetics and politics of ethnography.* Berkeley: University of California Press.

Colorado, P. (1988). Bridging native and Western science. *Convergence, 21*(2/3), 49–67.

Deikman, A. (1982). *The observing self: Mysticism and psychotherapy.* Boston: Beacon Press.

Deloria, V. (1993). If you think about it, you will see that it is true. *Noetic Sciences Review, 27,* 62–71.

Dewey, J. (1938). *Logic: The theory of inquiry.* New York: Henry Holt & Company.

De Wit, H. (1991). *Contemplative psychology.* Pittsburgh: Duquesne University Press.

182 Rothberg

Fenner, P. (1991). *The ontology of the middle way.* Dordrecht, Holland: Kluwer Publishing Company.

Fenner, P. (1994). Spiritual inquiry in Buddhism. *ReVision, 17*(2), 13–24.

Freire, P. (1970). *Pedagogy of the oppressed.* New York: Herder & Herder.

Gadamer, H.-G. (1975). *Truth and method.* New York: Seabury. (Original work published 1960)

Godman, D. (Ed.). (1985). *Be as you are: The teachings of Sri Ramana Maharshi.* London: Arkana.

Grube, G. (Trans.). (1974). *Plato's Republic.* Indianapolis, IN: Hackett Publishing Co.

Habermas, J. (1971). *Knowledge and human interests* (J. Shapiro, Trans.). Boston: Beacon Press. (Original work published 1968)

Habermas, J. (1979). *Communication and the evolution of society.* (T. McCarthy, Trans.). Boston: Beacon Press. (Original work published 1968)

Habermas, J. (1984a). *The theory of communicative action, Vol. 1: Reason and the rationalization of society* (T. McCarthy, Trans.). Boston: Beacon Press. (Original work published 1968)

Habermas, J. (1984b). Wahrheitstheorien [Theories of truth]. In J. Habermas, *Vorstudien und Ergänzungen zur Theorie des kommunikativen Handelns (Preparatory studies and supplements to the theory of communicative action)* (pp. 127–183). Frankfurt: Suhrkamp. (Original work published 1973)

Habermas, J. (1990). *Moral consciousness and communicative action* (C. Lenhardt & S.W. Nicholson, Trans.). Cambridge, MA: MIT Press. (Original work published 1983)

Halifax, J. (1979). *Shamanic voices: A survey of visionary narratives.* New York: E.P. Dutton.

Hanh, T. N. (1976). *The miracle of mindfulness: A manual on meditation.* Boston: Beacon Press.

Hanh, T. N. (1987). *Being peace.* Berkeley: Parallax Press.

Hayward, J. (1987). *Shifting worlds, changing minds: Where the sciences and Buddhism meet.* Boston: Shambhala.

Hillesum, E. (1985). *An interrupted life: The diaries of Etty Hillesum 1941–43.* New York: Pocket Books.

Hultkrantz, A. (1993). Native religions of North America: The power of visions and fertility. In H. Earhart (Ed.), *Religious traditions of the world* (pp. 255–372). San Francisco: Harper San Francisco.

Jaggar, A., & Bordo, S. (Eds.). (1989). *Gender/body/knowledge: Feminist reconstructions of being and knowing.* New Brunswick, NJ: Rutgers University Press.

Kabat-Zinn, J. (1990). *Full catastrophe living: Using the wisdom of your body and mind to face stress, pain and illness.* New York: Delacorte Press.

King, W. (1980). *Theravāda meditation.* University Park: Pennsylvania State University Press.

Kornfield, J. (1977). *Living Buddhist masters.* Santa Cruz, CA: Unity Press.

Kremer, J. (1992a). The dark night of the scholar: Reflections on culture and ways of knowing. *ReVision, 14* (4), 169–178.

Kremer, J. (1992b). Whither dark night of the scholar? Further reflections on culture and ways of knowing. *ReVision, 15*(1), 4–12.

Levine, S. (1982). *Who dies? An investigation of conscious living and conscious dying.* New York: Anchor Books.

Macy, J. (1983). *Despair and personal power in the nuclear age.* Philadelphia: New Society Publishers.

McGinn, B. (1991). *The presence of God: A history of Western Christian mysticism, vol. 1: The foundations of mysticism: Origins to the fifth century.* New York: Crossroad.

Merton, T. (1959). *The inner experience.* Unpublished manuscript.

Merton, T. (1978). *What is contemplation?* Springfield, IL: Templegate. (Original work published 1948)

Nasr, S. (1981). *Knowledge and the sacred.* New York: Crossroad.

Nasr, S. (1993). *The need for a sacred science.* Albany: State University of New York Press.

Needleman, J. (1976). *A sense of the cosmos: The encounter of modern science and ancient truth.* New York: Doubleday.

Nyanaponika. (1965). *The heart of Buddhist meditation.* New York: Samuel Weiser.

Rahula, W. (1974). *What the Buddha taught.* New York: Grove Press.

Rolston, H. (1987). *Science and religion: A critical survey.* New York: Random House.

Rosch, E. (1992). Cognitive psychology. In J. Hayward & F. Varela (Eds.), *Gentle bridges: Conversations with the Dalai Lama on the sciences of mind* (pp. 84–106). Boston: Shambhala.

Rothberg, D. (1986a). Philosophical foundations of transpersonal psychology: An introduction to some basic issues. *The Journal of Transpersonal Psychology, 18*(1), 1–34.

Rothberg, D. (1986b). Rationality and religion in Habermas' recent work: Some remarks on the relation between critical theory and the phenomenology of religion. *Philosophy and Social Criticism, 11,* 221–243.

Rothberg, D. (1990). Contemporary epistemology and the study of mysticism. In R. Forman (Ed.), *The problem of pure consciousness: Mysticism and philosophy* (pp. 163–210). New York: Oxford University Press.

Rothberg, D. (1993). The crisis of modernity and the emergence of socially engaged spirituality. *ReVision, 15*(3), 105–114.

Said, E. (1979). *Orientalism.* New York: Vintage Books. (Original work published 1978)

Scheman, N. (1992). Who is that masked woman? Reflections on power, privilege, and home-ophobia. In J. Ogilvy (Ed.), *Revisioning philosophy* (pp. 61–71). Albany: State University of New York Press.

Shannon, W. (1981). *Thomas Merton's dark path: The inner experience of a contemplative.* New York: Penguin Books.

Smart, N. (1976). *The religious experience of mankind* (2nd ed.). New York: Charles Scribner's Sons.

Smith, H. (1976). *Forgotten truth.* New York: Harper & Row.

Solomon, R. (1992). Beyond reason: The importance of emotion in philosophy. In J. Ogilvy (Ed.), *Revisioning philosophy* (pp. 19–47). Albany: State University of New York Press.

Sprung, M. (Trans.). (1979). *Lucid exposition of the middle way: The essential chapters from the Prasannapad ̄a of Candrak ̄ırti.* Boulder, CO: Prajñ ̄a Press.

Steiner, R. (1947). *Knowledge of the higher worlds and its attainment.* New York: Anthroposophic Press. (Original work published 1904)

Tart, C. (1972). States of consciousness and state specific sciences. *Science, 176,* 1203–1210.

Thurman, R. (1984). *The essence of true eloquence: Reason and enlightenment in the central philosophy of Tibet.* Princeton, NJ: Princeton University Press.

Thurman, R. (1991). Tibetan psychology: Sophisticated software for the human brain. In D. Goleman & R. Thurman (Eds.), *MindScience: An East-West Dialogue* (pp. 51–73). Boston: Wisdom Publications.

Varela, F., Thompson, E., & Rosch, E. (1991). *The embodied mind: Cognitive science and human experience.* Cambridge, MA: MIT Press.

Walker, S. (Ed.). (1987). *Speaking of silence: Christians and Buddhists on the contemplative way.* New York: Paulist Press.

Weber, R. (1986). *Dialogues with scientists and sages: The search for unity.* London: Routledge & Kegan Paul.

Welwood, J. (1990). *Journey of the heart: Intimate relationships and the path of love.* New York: HarperCollins.

Wilber, K. (1983). *Eye to eye: The quest for the new paradigm.* Garden City, NY: Anchor Books.

Wilber, K. (1985). *The holographic paradigm and other paradoxes: Exploring the leading edge of science.* Boston: Shambhala.

Williams, P., & Chrisman, L. (Eds.). (1994). *Colonial discourse and post-colonial theory.* New York: Columbia University Press.

Wilson, B. (Ed.). (1970). *Rationality.* New York: Harper & Row.

Winch, P. (1970). Understanding a primitive society. In B. Wilson (Ed.), *Rationality* (pp. 78–111). New York: Harper & Row. (original work published 1964)

9

Transpersonal Cognition in Developmental Perspective

MICHAEL WASHBURN

Much has been said about possible forms of postoperational cognition (Commons, Richards & Armon, 1984; Miller & Cook-Greuter, 1994).[1] Some theorists have focused on holistic, dialectical thinking (e.g., Basseches, 1980, 1984a, 1984b, 1989; Riegel, 1973; Wilber, 1990, 1995), others on imaginal, inventive, or creative intuition (e.g., Arieti, 1976; Arlin, 1975, 1977, 1984, 1989), and still others on contemplative absorption, insight, or rapture (e.g., historical figures such as Patanjali [Aranya, 1983]; Buddhaghosa [1975]; and St. Teresa of Avila [1980a, 1980b]) as possible higher types of cognition. All of these types of cognition likely play a role in postoperational cognition if not in transpersonal cognition as well, as I try to explain in the ensuing discussion.

In this chapter I discuss three basic types of cognition: agentic (ego-initiated, sequential) cognition and two types of intuitive (spontaneous, holistic) cognition: imaginal intuition and mental intuition.[2] Pursuing a developmental perspective, I trace the prepersonal, personal, and transpersonal forms of these three types of cognition. Two principal conclusions emerge from this developmental survey: (1) that the transition from prepersonal to personal stages is marked by a disappearance of imaginal intuition (based on concrete symbols), and (2) that the transition from personal to transpersonal stages is marked by a reemergence of imaginal intuition on a higher level. On the basis of these conclusions, I propose that the development of transpersonal cognition can be understood as a progressive integration of reawakened imaginal intuition with the agentic cognition (especially formal operational cognition) and mental-intuitive cognition (understanding of conceptual meanings and postoperational intuition of higher holistic patterns) of personal stages. I also propose that the development of transpersonal cognition should be understood as but one dimension of a more complex process, a process that culminates in a higher union of the ego with the nonegoic potentials of the deep psyche.

In the first section I introduce the general notions of agentic and intuitive cognition and then briefly explain the distinctive ways in which these types of cognition are expressed in prepersonal stages of development, namely, as sensorimotor cognition (agentic cognition) and as preconceptual cognition or, to use Freud's term, the primary process (imaginal intuition). In the second section I explain the distinctive ways in which agentic and intuitive cognition are expressed in personal stages, namely, as the preoperational cognition of the four-to-seven-year old (mental intuition), as concrete and formal operational cognition (agentic cognition), and as dialectical-holistic thought or, to use an expression introduced by Ken Wilber, "vision-logic" (mental intuition). In the third section I present a brief cross-cultural survey of three mainstream contemplative traditions, focusing on contemplative practice as a discipline that seeks to awaken psychic and spiritual potentials integral to or associated with transpersonal cognition. Then, in the fourth section I discuss how the potentials awakened during contemplative practice—and how reactivated imaginal intuition in particular—are progressively synthesized with the agentic and mental-intuitive cognition of personal stages as development moves toward the ideal of transpersonal integration.

Prepersonal Stages of Development:
Initial Forms of Agentic and Intuitive Cognition

Agentic cognition is any type of thinking that is executed by the subject of cognition, usually called the ego. In agentic cognition the ego is a cognitive agent with tasks to accomplish. The ego pursues knowledge of a specific sort and undertakes the steps necessary to arrive at the knowledge desired. Agentic cognition, in following a step-by-step procedure in pursuit of a cognitive goal, is linear and sequential in character. The type of knowledge sought by agentic cognition and the steps followed to arrive at it change as development unfolds. The common denominator is the working through of a cognitive agenda in a procedural, step-by-step manner.

Intuitive cognition, in contrast, is cognition that is direct and immediate. In intuitive cognition the ego is a seer rather than a doer; the ego discerns a meaning or truth or "just knows" (or at least feels authoritatively confident) that something is so and, therefore, does not need, agentically, to produce, derive, or demonstrate a result. In its directness and immediacy, intuitive cognition has an all-or-nothing character; one either sees or does not see. Whereas agentic cognition is arrived at sequentially, step by step (or part by part), intuitive cognition emerges, if at all, as a whole, albeit in varying grades of obscurity or clarity. Sometimes intuitive understanding emerges not only as a whole but also in dramatic flashes or seeming revelations. Intuitive understanding, however, can emerge inconspicuously and even unbeknownst to the intuiting subject. Upon reflecting or being questioned, one can discover that one already "just knows" something without, earlier, having been conscious of a new insight.

The earliest form of agentic cognition is the sensorimotor cognition of the infant and toddler. In sensorimotor cognition the fledgling ego is in charge as the child explores the physical environment with all sense modalities and constructs rudimentary schemata for understanding physical objects, their causal powers, and their interrelationships. Sensorimotor cognition is the earliest form of reality testing. The infant physically tests reality not only by visually observing the properties and behaviors of things but also by tasting and poking things and moving them about. Sensorimotor cognition is in these ways a step-by-step process by which the fledgling ego uses its sensorimotor instruments to achieve a desired cognitive goal.

The earliest form of intuitive cognition is the primitive imaginal cognition of the infant and toddler. This type of intuition is imaginal rather than mental in character because it is based on spontaneously produced inner sensory experiences. In being imaginal in this sense, the intuition in question is likely not exclusively visual. It is likely intermodal and, therefore, multimodal in nature. The work of Andrew Meltzoff and his associates (see Meltzoff, 1990) has shown that infants are able to imitate the caregiver's facial expressions and are, therefore, able directly to translate visual impressions into corresponding motoric expressions (Meltzoff & Moore, 1977, 1983, 1989). Infants are also able to match speech sounds with corresponding visual impressions (Kuhl & Meltzoff, 1982) and tactile sensations with corresponding visual impressions (Meltzoff & Borton, 1979). This intermodal translation and cross-modal matching of sensory data suggests that the nascent imagination, which produces inner likenesses of perceptual materials, is itself inherently intermodal and multimodal in character. It suggests that the earliest imagination is not exclusively a visual imagination producing only inner images but is an imagination that produces complex groupings of images, inner sensations, and motoric promptings corresponding to multiple sense modalities and to innate and learned action schemes.

Theorists of cognitive development have different views on the typical age at which the imagination becomes a vehicle of cognition by producing inner representations of outer objects and action schemes. In psychoanalysis, Freud and Melanie Klein held that the imagination is active in this way from the outset of life. The imagination of the neonate, they held, produces "hallucinated" satisfiers of the instinctual drives. Other psychoanalysts (e.g., Fraiberg, 1969), following Piaget's work, have held that the imagination cannot produce such substitutes for drive objects until after the child begins to understand object permanence, which, according to Piaget, is not until about eight or nine months of age and, according to more recent studies (Baillargeon, 1987; Bower, 1982; Diamond, 1993; Mandler, 1990), is around three to five months of age. Whatever the date of first appearance, however, imaginal representations of outer objects and actions count as the first example of spontaneously arising intuitive cognition. The fledgling ego is "given" such representations as it seeks to keep in mind or as it seeks satisfaction or comfort from a desired but absent object.

Both sensorimotor cognition and imaginal intuition undergo considerable development in the first few years of life. The most rudimentary sensorimotor schemata, once mastered, become components of new, more complex schemata, which in turn become components of even more complex schemata. And imaginal representations evolve from being only stand-ins for particular objects—paleosymbols, to use Silvano Arieti's (1967) term—or only inner reenactments of outer sensorimotor actions (Piaget) to being *preconceptual symbols*, imaginal embodiments or enactments of general meanings prior to an abstract understanding of such meanings. Both sensorimotor cognition and imaginal intuition thus advance dramatically during the early years of childhood, prior to latency. Sensorimotor cognition builds an increasingly wide-ranging repertoire of abilities to interact with the physical environment, and imaginal intuition, especially when it becomes preconceptually symbolic, forges an increasingly more general and complex matrix of meanings. Moreover, these two forms of cognition work in seamless unison as the child grows in understanding, making progress from the level of rudimentary sensorimotor particularity to levels of increasingly sophisticated symbolic generality.

The more mature (preconceptual) imaginal intuition of early childhood is known as the *primary process* in psychoanalysis. Among Piagetians it is known as *preconceptual cognition* or, more precisely, as the cognition of the preconceptual substage of the stage of preoperations. Both psychoanalysts and Piagetians believe that primary process or preconceptual cognition is left behind at approximately four or five years of age, that is, in psychoanalytic perspective, at the end of the oedipal stage and the beginning of latency. In agreeing that imaginal, autosymbolic intuition is left behind at this age, however, psychoanalysts and Piagetians disagree on why and in what sense it is left behind.

Piagetians believe that imaginal intuition is left behind because the child begins to discern general meanings independently of imaginal embodiments or enactments—this advance signaling, in Piaget's scheme, the beginning of the (mentally) intuitive substage of the stage of preoperations. The child begins *mentally* to discern general meanings that before it could only *imagine*, and for this reason the child no longer needs to use the imagination as the vehicle of emerging conceptual thought. For Piagetians, then, the child at approximately four or five years of age leaves imaginal, autosymbolic intuition behind for the simple reason that this primitive sort of intuition is outgrown and replaced by a superior sort of intuition. Imaginal intuition is superseded by the first form of mental intuition, the ability to understand general meanings independently of imaginal or physical instantiation. And in thus being outgrown, imaginal intuition ceases any longer to exist. We must not misunderstand: The imagination continues to exist and to function. What disappears is the imagination *functioning as the vehicle for cognizing general meanings*. The imagination ceases being the vehicle of emerging conceptual thought. It loses for the most part its symbolic character and becomes a medium of merely particular images or of merely referential representations of particular things.

Psychoanalysts have a different understanding of the disappearance of imaginal intuition. For psychoanalysts, this type of cognition is left behind not only because the primary process is superseded by the secondary process but also because the faculty of primary process cognition, the autosymbolic imagination, is repressed and thereby excluded from consciousness. As early as *The Interpretation of Dreams* Freud held that primary process materials cannot be assimilated by the secondary process and, therefore, that a repressive elimination of the primary process occurs when the secondary process emerges. Later, after the introduction of the notion of the tripartite (id-ego-superego) psyche in 1923, Freud (1926, 1933) elaborated on the nature of this repression, explaining that the repression is a response of the developing ego to anxiety caused by the instinctual demands of the id. Freud hypothesized that the repression in question—which he termed *primal repression*—likely begins being set in place during the oedipal period and is then consolidated when oedipal conflicts are resolved and the child moves from the oedipal stage to the stage of latency. According to Freud, then, the primary process (prepersonal autosymbolic intuition) is left behind not only because it is outgrown but also because the vehicle of this kind of cognition is repressed and rendered unconscious. In the psychoanalytic view, the primary process, in being outgrown, does not thereby cease to exist; it continues to exist and to function as the cognition of the deep unconscious, the id. The primary process is lost to consciousness but continues to function when we are asleep and dreaming.

My own perspective follows the psychoanalytic account in holding that the transition from the primary to the secondary process—or from

prepersonal imaginal intuition to personal mental-intuitive and operational cognition—is a transition that not only transcends the outgrown instrument of cognition but also represses it: The creative imagination is
repressively disjoined from consciousness. The imagination that remains
is but a simulacrum of the original imagination. It is an imagination
stripped of the plenipotent energy, spontaneity, and autosymbolic creativity of the deep psyche, which is now submerged and quieted. And because
of the ego's reliance on visual perception, it is an imagination stripped of
its former intermodal and multimodal character and reduced to an exclusively image-producing function. The imagination that remains is an
imagination that has been rendered tame and compliant to the ego's will.
No longer a cognitive source rooted in the creative depths of the psyche,
it is the *ego's* imagination, an instrument the ego uses to fabricate images
for its inner theater.

We should stress that although the autosymbolic imagination is lost in
this way, the transition in question nonetheless counts as a net developmental advance. For if general meanings are to be understood in the full scope
of their generality, and if operational thinking is to achieve the full range of
its power, it is necessary that general meanings be freed from embodied particularity, no matter how richly symbolic that particularity might be. We must
wean ourselves from dependence on the imagination if we are to learn how
to think abstractly. The repressive forfeiture of the autosymbolic imagination
is, then, the price to be paid for the full development of conceptual-
operational thought. Or at least this seems to hold as a general rule.[3]

Primal repression submerges and quiets all potentials of the deep
(nonegoic) psyche, including not only the autosymbolic imagination but
also plenipotent energy, instinctuality, polymorphously hedonic bodily life,
and embodied affect. All of these *nonegoic potentials* are at least attenuated by
primal repression. Primal repression draws a fundamental dividing line between the system of the ego and consciousness on the one hand and the system of the deep, repressed unconscious on the other, as classical
psychoanalysis explains. This point is important to our subject, transpersonal cognition, because it implies that the reawakening of the autosymbolic imagination, if and when this should happen, is not an isolated,
exclusively cognitive affair. It is a part of a wider and deeper process, the
reawakening of nonegoic life generally.

When primal repression submerges nonegoic potentials, it does so
early in life when these potentials are still at a prepersonal level of expression. For this reason the deep submerged unconscious has the character of
the id as described by psychoanalysis. This "pre" character of the deep psyche, however, is not its intrinsic constitutional character; it is, rather, only a
specific developmental organization of the deep psyche. It is, therefore,

possible for the deep psyche to be liberated from this organization and, no longer quieted by primal repression, to express itself in higher, transpersonal fashion. As I (1996, 1998b) have argued elsewhere, there is no confusion of pre and trans or "pre-trans fallacy" here, as Ken Wilber (1980, 1995, 1996) has alleged. What, early in life, is repressed as pre can, later in life, be reawakened as trans—or as "on the way" to trans.

Personal Stages of Development:
Mental Intuition and Operational Cognition

Primal repression ushers in a period—a long period—during which the nonegoic potentials of the deep psyche have little or no role in cognition and, therefore, during which the ego as cognitive subject is the primary if not sole source and agent of cognition. This is a period that covers what in transpersonal theory are referred to as the *personal* stages of development, stages that follow the prepersonal stages of early childhood and precede the transpersonal stages of psychospiritual awakening and integration (should these stages emerge).

As stages of cognitive development, the personal stages begin with the intuitive substage of the stage of preoperations (early latency period, from approximately four or five to seven years of age) and continue through the stages of concrete operational thinking (middle latency until adolescence), beginning formal operational thinking (roughly coinciding with adolescence), fully established formal operational thinking (roughly coinciding with early adulthood), and, to use Ken Wilber's term, "vision-logic" (corresponding roughly to mature adulthood). The first and last of these stages—the intuitive cognition of the early latency period and the vision-logic of mature adulthood—are stages during which mental (as opposed to imaginal) intuition is in the forefront. The intervening stages are stages during which agentic cognition in the form of either concrete or formal operational cognition is in the forefront. All of the personal stages are both intuitive and agentic to some extent, so, properly speaking, the first and last of the personal stages are predominantly but not exclusively mentally intuitive and the intervening stages are predominantly but not exclusively operationally agentic.

The intuitive substage of the stage of preoperations, as noted earlier, is the stage during which the child leaves imaginal intuition of general meanings behind and begins to intuit such meanings directly, by the mind alone without the aid of the imagination or senses. The child replaces imaginal intuition with mental intuition, albeit mental intuition of a rudimentary and vague sort. Philip Cowan (1978) exposits Piaget's conception of this first form of intuition as follows:

Philosophers and mathematicians sometimes use the term "intuition" to describe a faculty of the mind which directly grasps self-evident truths. . . . Piaget adopts this term as a metaphor to describe four-to-seven-year olds' certainty about their knowledge on the one hand, and the almost complete lack of awareness about how they know what they know, on the other. (p. 144)

Four-to-seven-year olds are quite sure that they correctly understand many meanings and truths. They state with confidence that they "just know"—even though they can provide no analysis of what they claim to know or account of how they know what they claim to know.

In speaking of the mental intuitions of the four-to-seven-year old, we should be careful to avoid thinking of these intuitions as flashes of interior insight. The intuitions in question are mostly of the type, referred to earlier, that emerge unbeknownst to the person whose intuitions they are. The four-to-seven-year old usually acquires intuitive knowledge without any discrete contents emerging before the mind or any specific events (e.g., sudden experiences of clarity or vision) occurring in the mind. The reason intuitions can emerge in this unnoticed manner is that they are acquired *en masse* through language acquisition rather than one by one through inductive generalization or purely rational insight. The child only rarely needs to come up with general meanings on her or his own, for general meanings are assimilated wholesale—and, therefore, prereflectively—through the learning of language. As Wittgenstein helped us see, conceptual understanding does not presuppose any subjective contents or events; all it presupposes is the ability to use language correctly when acting in the world.

If by approximately age four the child's intuitive understanding presupposes no subjective contents or events, then, of course, it does not presuppose symbolic images serving as bearers of general meanings. And no such representations present themselves, for, as already explained, the autosymbolic imagination has by this time been disconnected from consciousness by primal repression. The intuitions of the four-to-seven-year old, then, are not imaginal intuitions embedded in particulars; they are, rather, mental intuitions free of particularity. For the four-to-seven-year old, meanings are independent of instantiations. They are not, however, independent of the language through which they are transmitted. On the contrary, they belong inherently to language and are, therefore, meanings that in principle are verbally expressible—even though the four-to-seven-year old, who "just knows," is not yet able to give verbal expression to them.

In saying that the meanings grasped by the young latency child are verbally expressible, I am not saying that these meanings can always be given "clear and distinct" definitions. For as structuralist and poststructuralist linguistics and philosophy have taught us, meanings belonging to language belong to language as a whole and cannot, therefore, be carved out as isolated units of intelligibility. The meanings understood by the four-to-seven-year old, then, although in principle verbally expressible, are not always—or even usually—verbally definable in the strict sense.

As the child's language-based intuitive understanding grows, the pieces of a widely inclusive conceptual framework gradually fall into place, and the child is ready to begin performing basic mental (as opposed to sensorimotor) operations by following out in thought the logical relationships that hold among component meanings of the framework. At first the child is able to perform such operations only by manipulating concrete instances of the meanings whose logical relationships are being considered. This thinking about logical relationships in reference to particular objects is concrete operational thinking. Later, however, the child, now typically an adolescent, begins to be able to perform such operations in the abstract. This fully abstract thinking about logical relationships is formal operational thinking, which, usually emerging during the years of adolescence, is fully established only in the years of early adulthood.

Formal operational thinking or, in Freud's terms, the secondary process is the cognition most distinctive of personal stages of development. From adolescence through early adulthood—if not throughout the rest of life—this is the type of thought that is predominant, as Piaget and most other cognitive developmental theorists attest. To be sure, people pursue education and otherwise continue to grow in the scope and depth of their (mental) intuitions during adult years; nevertheless, what is most distinctive of the cognition of most adults is the hard work of gaining mastery of the logical relationships governing the framework of culturally received meanings. To use an adage, thinking for most of us is "90% perspiration [operations] and 10% inspiration [intuition]." The 90%–10% ratio is, of course, contrived; moreover, the ratio of "perspiration" to "inspiration" can change, as we shall see. Still, the fact is that formal operational cognition is the highest level of cognition achieved by most people. The highest level of thinking achieved by most of us is abstract inferential or analytical thinking, "thinking things through" entirely on the level of thought.

But we must give intuition its due. For the achievement of formal operational cognition by no means brings an end to mental intuition and in fact prepares the ground for new, higher-order mental intuitions. Mastery of formal operational thinking at a particular level prepares the ground for mental intuitions at a higher level. Take chess as an example. One must first understand certain basic positions (mental intuition of basic general meanings) and then be able to calculate consequences of possible moves from those positions (operational thinking) before one can begin intuiting

higher-order positions, from which one can then calculate new consequences, leading to yet higher-order intuitions, and so forth. In this way intuitions prepare the ground for sequential operations, which become bases
or modules of higher-order intuitions, and so forth.

Although the ratio of operations to intuitions may be weighted more
heavily on the side of operations during most personal stages, this ratio
tends to shift toward a higher percentage of intuitions as one achieves
greater operational mastery at any level and as one moves to higher levels of
intuitive insight. For the greater one's operational mastery at a given level,
the easier it is to continue to reap new insights from earlier efforts; and the
higher one's intuitive level, the more complexly nested and inclusive is the
vantage point from which one can see not only new patterns of meaning
but also old patterns in a new way. To return to the chess example, a chess
grandmaster, although needing to perform many long-range calculations,
relies extensively on immediate intuitions of promising or unpromising
global board positions. The beginner, in contrast, must calculate almost
everything.

Given this change in the overall ratio of operations to intuitions, the
cognition of early to middle adulthood can be said to have a tendency to
evolve in an increasingly intuitive direction. According to the nineteenth-
century German philosopher G. W. F. Hegel, "understanding" (*Verstand,*
conceptual-operational cognition, the secondary process) evolves into "reason" (*Vernunft,* dialectical-holistic cognition). And according to Ken Wilber
(1990, 1995), the formal operational cognition of early adulthood evolves
into "vision-logic" (the intuition of ever more inclusive theoretical patterns). In a similar vein, Klaus Riegel (1973) and Michael Basseches (1980,
1984a, 1984b, 1989) have argued that formal operational cognition is superseded by inclusive dialectical thinking, and Francis Richards and
Michael Commons (1984) have stressed the metasystematic aspect of postformal thought. Dialectical-holistic reason, vision-logic, or metasystematic
thinking is likely achieved by only a few. The movement toward a significantly higher percentage of intuitions is only a *tendency,* a tendency that
becomes an actuality only for people who have pursued learning and reflection intensively and for a long period of time. The consensus among
cognitive developmental theorists is that formal operational cognition remains the highest cognitive level achieved by most people. For most people,
then, vision-logic or holistic intuitive thinking is an ideal rather than an actual goal toward which their thinking evolves.

Wilber holds that vision-logic is not only the highest stage of personal
cognition but also a transitional stage leading to transpersonal cognition. I
agree with Wilber on the first point but have reservations about the second.
To be sure, vision-logic, as a form of mental intuition, represents a turn away

from the one-sidedly agentic-operational cognition more characteristic of the personal stages of development. But this fact by itself does not indicate the imminence of a transition to transpersonal stages. For if the emergence of vision-logic is rare, movement into transpersonal stages is rarer still. More than vision-logic is needed to usher in transpersonal stages. As was suggested in our discussion of prepersonal cognition, what is needed, specifically, is the loosening or lifting of primal repression and the reawakening of nonegoic potentials, the autosymbolic imagination in particular.

Contemplative Practice: A Cross-Cultural Survey

We cannot know for sure why some people experience transpersonal awakening and others do not. Factors beyond the control of the will—factors falling under the theological category of grace—likely play an important role. A spiritual discipline, and contemplative practice in particular, however, can play an important role as well. In this section I present a brief cross-cultural survey of the views of three of the foremost authorities on contemplative practice: (1) Patanjali (second century B.C.E. or second century C.E.), who is the chief authority on concentrative-absorptive meditation as practiced in the classical yoga tradition of Hinduism; (2) Buddhaghosa (fourth century C.E.), who is the chief authority on mindfulness-insight meditation as practiced in the Theravada tradition of Buddhism; and (3) St. Teresa of Avila (1515–1582), who is the chief authority on contemplative prayer as practiced in the Roman Catholic tradition of Christianity. In reviewing the accounts of these three authorities, it will become evident that, despite major cultural and interpretive differences, they agree sufficiently on the phenomenology of contemplative experience that their accounts have important common implications for an understanding of transpersonal cognition.

Patanjali's *Yoga Sutras* (see Aranya, 1983) is the classic work on concentrative-absorptive meditation. According to Patanjali, the meditative process unfolds through three primary stages: *dharana, dhyana,* and *samadhi. Dharana* is the practice of unwavering attention aimed at an outer or inner object of concentration. This practice is at first unsteady; the meditator repeatedly falls prey to distraction or drowsiness. Perseverance, however, strengthens the practice so that the meditator is increasingly able to attend fully and one-pointedly to the meditation object. The meditator makes progress in this direction, I suggest, not only because sustained focusing on the meditation object strengthens the ego's "mental muscles," as it were, but also because it organizes psychic energy into a powerful, evenly flowing current which carries attention along in its flow.[4]

Moreover, this current, directed to the meditation object, invests the object with energic charge and thereby transforms it into a cathexis object, an object the charge of which attracts the meditator's attention. All objects that attract attention are cathexis objects, not only meditation objects but also objects (persons, scenes, events) of everyday life, for example, a good book we cannot put down, a person or natural view we find beautiful or unusual, a gripping event from which we cannot look away. All such objects are invested with energy that draws and tethers attention. What is different about meditation objects as cathexis objects is that the cathexis is created by concentrative practice rather than by preestablished instinctual or habitual dispositions.

As progress is made in the practice of *dharana*, then, energy resources are tapped, and an increasingly powerful current of energy flows to the meditation object, transforming it into a cathexis object. The meditation object thus becomes not only the target of attention but also an attractor of attention, and the meditator's one-pointed attention for this reason becomes increasingly strong and effortless. Consciousness begins to flow easily to the object without falling prey to distraction or drowsiness. Such a strong, easy, sustained flow of focused awareness is *dhyana*.

Continued practice of *dhyana* can lead to *samadhi*. For the continued flow of energized attention adds to the charge of the meditation object until the charge is of sufficient magnitude not only to attract consciousness but also to absorb it. *Samadhi*, then, is absorption or, to use Mircea Eliade's (1969) term, *enstasy:* The subject-object division collapses and consciousness, no longer the consciousness of a subject observing an object, *becomes* the object.

To illustrate, consider what happens when we become absorbed in a film. We lose awareness of ourselves and are drawn into the drama, as if the story and characters were real. Consciousness ceases being the consciousness of an observing subject and becomes the medium of the world of the film. The situation is similar in *samadhi* except that *samadhi* is achieved through active rather than passive, meditative rather than nonmeditative means. In *samadhi*, the meditator becomes unself-consciously absorbed in the meditation object; nothing exists except the object as enlivened and illumined by consciousness.

Depending upon how powerfully the meditation object is charged and on the nature of the object itself—for example, its character as an outer perceptual object, inner psychic content, or intelligible meaning, its degree of fineness or subtlety—the resulting *samadhi* can be more or less powerful and "pure" (i.e., free of instinctual or affective admixture). The practice of *samadhi* typically unfolds from absorptions in outer perceptual objects to absorptions in inner psychic contents or intelligible meanings, from absorptions that are coarse to absorptions that are more rarefied, from absorptions that are less powerful and pure to absorptions that are more powerful and pure. With continued practice the meditator gradually achieves higher and higher levels of *samadhi*.

At each level of practice, according to Patanjali, *samadhi* evolves through two basic stages: (1) an initial stage during which the meditator's consciousness is flooded with spontaneously arising images and other inner sensory data (*tanmatras*), with flashes of intellectual insight, and with impulses and feelings, and (2) a later stage during which these spontaneities subside and absorption stabilizes into a motionless poise. The first of these two stages is called *savitarka samadhi* when the *samadhi* is at a preliminary "coarse" level and *savichara samadhi* when the *samadhi* is at a more subtle, refined level. Initial absorption at any level of subtlety, it seems, elicits multimodal imaginal intuitions, mental intuitions, and related affective and appetitive fluctuations. More evolved absorptions at any level, in contrast, are more anchored and still. Accordingly, at coarser levels *savitarka samadhi* is superseded eventually by the more stable *nirvitarka samadhi*, and at more subtle levels *savichara samadhi* is superseded eventually by the more stable *nirvichara samadhi*.

As one masters *samadhi* at subtler levels and becomes more adept at accessing the energy that, as cathexis energy, produces *samadhi*, one eventually outgrows the need to focus on objects in practicing meditation. One is eventually able to dispense with objects and achieve "unsupported" *samadhi* (*asamprajnata samadhi*). At this point the meditator is able to tap powerful reserves of energy without the expedient of an object serving as cathexis target. The meditator, that is, is able to produce a pure power cathexis and, thereby, to enter an objectless absorption. According to Patanjali, such objectless absorptions evolve through many grades of power and clarity. The continued practice of *asamprajnata samadhi* leads to objectless absorptions of increasing brilliance and transparency until all residual obscuring psychic tendencies (*samskaras*) are "burned." Once the psyche has been purged in this way, the meditator is said to pass completely beyond phenomenal existence as we know it and to achieve oneness with his or her absolute eternal Self. This unity with the transcendent Self is liberation or, as Patanjali calls it, *isolation* (*kaivalya*).

The Buddhist tradition also employs concentrative-absorptive meditation but assigns it a less central role, using it primarily as a training exercise for the effective practice of mindfulness-insight meditation. Mindfulness meditation leading to insight (*vipassana*) is the distinctive meditation of Buddhism. This is the view already set forth in the Pali canon, and it is the view that Buddhaghosa systematized and codified in his classic *Visuddhimagga* (*Path of Purification* [see Buddhaghosa, 1975]). According to Buddhaghosa, however effective the practice of absorption (Pali: *jhana*) might be, the practice of mindfulness leading to insight is the only way to achieve deep intuition into the "three characteristics of existence"—suffering, impermanence, and the insubstantiality of all things—and, thereby, to achieve enlightenment and liberation from the suffering.

Unlike concentrative-absorptive meditation, mindfulness-insight meditation does not focus on an object. On the contrary, it is a meditation of completely open, nonselective attention. The meditator strives to be like a polished mirror, alertly witnessing whatever emerges in consciousness without reacting (e.g., pursuing, judging, clinging, resisting) in any way, allowing psychomental contents to come and go according to their own pace and rhythm. In the initial practice of mindfulness, of course, the meditator attempts to witness in this manner more by way of failure than success, falling prey repeatedly to inner dialogue, fantasy, fear, desire, torpor, and so forth. In noticing such lapses, however, the meditator regathers attention and returns to pure witnessing. It is because such pure witnessing is so difficult for beginners that Buddhism frequently recommends concentrative-absorptive meditation as a training practice to prepare for effective mindfulness-insight meditation. Once the meditator moves beyond initial concentration and achieves easily flowing focused attention—called *upacara samadhi* (access concentration) in Buddhism, corresponding to Patanjali's *dhyana*—the meditator is able to begin the practice of mindfulness-insight meditation in a strong and stable way.

In learning how to channel energy into a powerful, continuous current, one is able to sit with steady, alert mindfulness, as a pure witness of experience. This practice readies one for the awakening of insight—somewhat as, in Patanjali's concentrative-absorptive meditation, *dhyana* prepares one for *samadhi*. The awakening of insight is a breakthrough to a heightened awareness that brings with it acute mental intuition of the momentariness, "unsatisfactoriness," and insubstantiality of all psychomental contents (the three characteristics of existence). Initial awakening brings with it not only clear intuition of the three characteristics of existence but also, typically, the so-called *ten corruptions* or imperfections of insight: illumination, knowledge (inner sensory and extrasensory intuition), rapturous happiness, tranquillity, bliss, resolution, energy, anchored mindfulness, equanimity, and attachment (to awakened, energized, blissful experience). Infusions of numinous energy and waves of rapturous happiness are followed by feelings of being deeply anchored and profoundly at peace. Moments of clear mental insight into the three characteristics of existence are interrupted by episodes of inner sensory or extrasensory intuition. Experiences of bliss are followed by feelings of invincible resolution to devote oneself to the course of insight. Such extraordinary experiences as these are called corruptions or imperfections because they can lead to the belief that enlightenment or *nibbana* (Sanskrit: *nirvana*) has been achieved when in fact the meditator has only begun the path of awakened insight.

The meditator, therefore, needs to be disabused of the illusion that initial awakening is full enlightenment, and for this reason the period of initial awakening is typically followed by a period during which the meditator begins to see the merely passing and, therefore, unsatisfactory nature of even the extraordinary experiences of the awakened state. As this insight deepens, the meditator ceases delighting in such experiences and becomes revolted by them, seeing in them only disappointment and death. Working though this disillusionment, the meditator finally achieves a state of higher equanimity that is free of both desire and revulsion for awakened experiences. The achievement of such equanimity ushers in a period of numinously infused equilibrium and clarity during which all things are seen as utterly devoid of both substance and self. Such illumined equanimity eventually moves beyond all psychomental content, and the meditator enjoys states of plenipotent, illumined emptiness. These states represent the highest and most rarefied levels of conditioned existence. In achieving these states, the meditator is ready to pass from *samsara* (worldly existence subject to suffering) into *nibbana* (enlightened awareness free from suffering).

The Roman Catholic tradition of Christianity offers an account of contemplation that in many respects is similar to the Hindu-Yoga and Buddhist accounts just discussed. There is, however, a basic difference that should be stressed at the outset. The difference is this: The Catholic tradition conceives of contemplation not only as a practice whereby consciousness awakens to its highest source or nature but also as a practice that is essentially *relational* or *interpersonal* in character. In the Catholic tradition, contemplation is essentially *prayer;* it is a practice by which a person communicates with God, inviting God in the form of the Holy Spirit to enter the soul to perform redemptive work. Based especially on the testimony of St. Teresa of Avila, the Catholic tradition divides contemplative practice into three principal stages: (1) meditation or discursive prayer, (2) the prayer of recollection, and (3) infused contemplation.

Meditation or discursive prayer is properly described as discursive because it involves not only focusing on a devotional object or theme (e.g., figure, scriptural passage, image) but also inquiring about the meaning of the object or theme. Meditation thus conceived is similar to Patanjali's *dharana* in having a selective focus but differs from *dharana* in inviting rather than excluding arising thoughts. And it is similar to Buddhist mindfulness in being open to arising thoughts but differs from mindfulness in giving selective attention to a particular object or theme, in limiting openness, accordingly, to only those arising thoughts that are engendered by the selected object or theme, and in relating to these thoughts as an interested inquirer rather than only as a disinterested witness. Whereas *dharana* is the practice of selectively closed attention and mindfulness the practice of choicelessly open, disinterested attention, discursive prayer in the Catholic contemplative tradition is the practice of selectively open, inquiring attention. Because discursive prayer, like *dharana* and mindfulness, is a practice of steadfast alertness, it requires sustained effort and repeated restarts. The meditator must struggle against both distraction and drowsiness before sufficient energy is channeled to sustain the meditator's attention in an easy, effortless flow.

According to Teresa, as one matures contemplatively, one outgrows the need to focus on a specific object or theme and is able to meditate in a posture of alert supplicatory openness. This level of practice is what Teresa calls the prayer of *recollection* (see *Interior Castle,* Fourth Mansions, chapter 3 and *Way of Perfection,* chapters 28–29). Teresa describes the prayer of recollection in the following way:

> There is no need to pay any attention to this clamor [of the intellect], for doing so would make the will lose much of what it enjoys. But one should leave the intellect go and surrender oneself into the arms of love, for His Majesty will teach the soul what it must do at that point. (1980a, p. 331)

This posture of supplicatory openness is similar to advanced mindfulness practice in that it is choicelessly open to whatever may arise in and exit from consciousness. It differs from mindfulness, however, in its relational, invitational posture. The prayer of recollection is a state of gathered, quiet receptivity wherein the person in prayer invites infusion by the Holy Spirit. Similar to Patanjali's *dhyana* and advanced mindfulness, the prayer of recollection is, relatively speaking, effortless. Teresa makes this point by saying that the prayer of recollection is a transitional form of prayer "in which the natural and supernatural are joined" (1980a, p. 334). The prayer of recollection is a natural process to the extent that the person in prayer seeks voluntarily to enter the recollected state (later called *acquired* recollection); and the prayer of recollection is a supernatural process to the extent that the person in prayer is drawn into the recollected state by spiritual power (later called *infused* recollection). As in Patanjali's *dhyana* and advanced mindfulness, then, the meditator here becomes able to enter states of energic induction. The meditator no longer has to struggle to maintain alert meditative awareness and is energically sustained in the meditative state.

Recollection may eventually lead to infused contemplation proper. Here the person in prayer ceases being anchored in a state of gathered quiet and begins experiencing states of ecstasy, rapture, or transport. In the theological perspective of Christianity, such infused states indicate that the

Holy Spirit, which had been invited to enter the soul, now arrives and pneumatically inflates, intoxicates, and transforms the ego from within. The infused states that the person in prayer now experiences are highly energized numinous states rife with intense feelings, dramatic insights, inner sensations, and vivid images. Comparatively, such states resemble Patanjali's *savitarka samadhi* and *savichara samadhi* (i.e., absorptions alive with spontaneously emerging affective, imaginal, and mental-intuitive content) and Buddhaghosa's stage of initial awakened insight subject to the ten corruptions. A major difference, however, is, again, the relational character of the Christian experience, according to which contemplative infusion indicates not only an awakening to plenipotent numinous energy and powerfully charged psychoactive materials but also the beginning of an intimate relationship between the self and the Holy Spirit or Christ within. It is for this reason that, in the Roman Catholic tradition, the early stages of infused contemplation are described as a period of spiritual betrothal leading the way, ultimately, to the marriage of the soul with Christ.

Teresa is emphatic on the point that the period of dramatic infused states just described is an intermediate stage—the betrothal prior to the marriage—and that the culminating stage of the contemplative path is one in which raptures and other violent spiritual movements give way to a powerful inner quiet and lucidity. In the *Interior Castle* (1980a) she says:

> I am amazed as well to see that when the soul arrives here [the prayer of union] all raptures are taken away. Only once in a while are they experienced and then without those transports and that flight of spirit. They happen very rarely and almost never in public as they very often did before. (p. 442)

The disappearance of raptures is not the disappearance of awakened life; it is, rather, the stable integration ("marriage") of the soul with this life. As Teresa says, Christ now lives at the center of the soul as one's own innermost life.

Parallels with Patanjali and Buddhaghosa are again evident, although Teresa's relational perspective is again a major difference. For Patanjali, the less mature forms of *samadhi*, those with spontaneously emerging affective, imaginal, and mental-intuitive content, give way to more mature forms of *samadhi* that are increasingly stable, powerful, empty of content, and clear. And for Buddhaghosa, the extraordinary experiences associated with the ten corruptions of initial awakening eventually subside as the meditator achieves deeper insight, higher equanimity, and, finally, enlightenment. Patanjali, Buddhaghosa, and Teresa all agree that the path of awakened contemplation moves through stages of intense breakthrough and transformation before the transformative process stabilizes in higher states of power, radiance, and transparency. In arriving at these higher states, one is no longer captivated or inflated by numinous energy; one is no longer enthralled by inner sensory phenomena or epiphanies. One regains equilibrium on a higher, numinously infused and illumined plane. In achieving such higher equilibrium, according to Patanjali, Buddhaghosa, and Teresa, one is on the threshold of liberation, enlightenment, or union.

Implications

The foregoing cross-cultural survey of contemplative practices has, I suggest, the following implications for an understanding of transpersonal cognition: (1) transpersonal cognition presupposes an opening of consciousness to awakening nonegoic potentials of the deep psyche; (2) transpersonal cognition is not an exclusively cognitive affair, for the awakening of nonegoic potentials is an awakening not only of the autosymbolic imagination but also of plenipotent numinous energy and powerful inner sensations and feelings; (3) transpersonal cognition, supercharged with plenipotent energy, is an amplified or "illumined" cognition; (4) transpersonal cognition is initially unstable because the ego is at first unprepared for awakened nonegoic life; and (5) transpersonal cognition becomes progressively more stable as the ego adjusts to and is integrated with nonegoic life. I discuss each of these implications in turn, offering in each case a broadly psychoanalytic interpretation.

Transpersonal Cognition Presupposes an
Opening of Consciousness to Awakening Nonegoic Potentials

The accounts of Patanjali, Buddhaghosa, and St. Teresa of Avila suggest that transpersonal cognition presupposes an opening of consciousness to awakening nonegoic potentials. This opening of consciousness may occur spontaneously. For many contemplatives, however, it begins with a practice such as *dharana,* beginning mindfulness, or discursive prayer. These practices open consciousness because, as exercises requiring sustained attention, they work both to disengage the ego from its usual activities and to release the ego from all stances, including not only superficial postures but also embedded armors and even deep repressions. These practices are disciplined efforts both to "not do" (the ego is supposed to be unmovingly anchored if not also one-pointedly tethered to an object) and to "let go" (the ego is supposed to relinquish all stances so that it can be fully present as a pure witness). Actually, as we have learned, the ego in initial stages of *dharana,* mindfulness, or discursive prayer only *aims* at being unmovingly anchored and fully present while in fact it is subject to flights of distraction, defensive reactions, and deep psychodynamic constrictions (countercathexes, repressions). In aiming at being unmovingly anchored and fully present, however, the ego makes progress toward these goals. It gradually becomes more steadfast as a witness; it gradually overcomes resistances; it gradually dismantles or dissolves repressions.

As explained earlier, one reason the meditator makes progress in these ways is that the meditative process, sustained over time, accesses energy. This fact is not well understood, as Georg Feuerstein (1996) has observed:

> The inner continuum created through meditation is also highly energetic—a fact that is seldom appreciated by nonmeditators or even beginners on the meditative path. Indeed, meditation cannot deepen and give rise to ecstasy (*samadhi*) without being accompanied by an intense psychoenergetic charge. (p. 87)

The "inner continuum" to which Feuerstein refers is the steady current of energy that sustains evenly flowing attention (Patanjali's *dhyana*). Feuerstein's point is made in reference to the *dhyana* of classical yoga, but it applies to advanced mindfulness and to the prayer of recollection as well. All three of these practices presuppose a strong energy current that strengthens and stabilizes attention and, if there is a meditation object, cathects that object and in consequence draws attention to it. The emergence of *dhyana,* advanced mindfulness, or the prayer of recollection indicates not only that the ego has become more anchored and open but also that, in becoming more anchored and open, it has begun to tap nonegoic energy sources.

The continued practice of *dhyana,* advanced mindfulness, or the prayer of recollection leads to an awakening: *samadhi,* insight, or infused contemplation, respectively. Using terms introduced earlier, this awakening is a *re*awakening of nonegoic depth potentials, which now break through the vestiges of primal repression.[5] The ego's practice of anchored openness has at this point so loosened psychodynamic constrictions—including the deepest such constriction, primal repression—and so kindled nonegoic potentials that the latter spring to life with dramatic effects. The landscape of the meditative process is herewith radically altered, as we learned in the last section: The subject-object division collapses and an absorption alive with highly charged images, insights, and feelings ensues (Patanjali); strong, steady mindfulness gives way to initial awakened insight subject to the "ten corruptions" (Buddhaghosa); the prayer of recollection is brought to an end by raptures, transports, and inner perceptions caused by the influx of the Holy Spirit (St. Teresa of Avila).

Among the depth potentials that can awaken at this point, the one that is most important from a strictly cognitive point of view is the autosymbolic imagination, which, as explained earlier, is multimodal—perhaps primarily visual but not exclusively visual—in character. The person who experiences the awakening of this potential is witness to spontaneously forged images and, sometimes, to corresponding inner sensory experiences of auditory, olfactory, and even somatic and motoric sorts. These multimodal imaginal intuitions are communicative vehicles possessing potent symbolic significance. They can embody meanings associated with a meditation object, as in *savitarka* and *savichara samadhi;* or they can embody the meditator's deepest fears and highest hopes, as can happen in initial awakened insight and infused contemplation. Whatever specific form they take, however, these imaginal manifestations are highly condensed, creatively forged meanings that emerge unbidden and "out of the blue."

Transpersonal cognition is not an exclusively cognitive affair

The autosymbolic imagination is only one of the nonegoic depth potentials that can awaken in the breakthrough to *samadhi,* insight, or infused contemplation. Nonegoic life generally, which had been submerged by primal repression, awakens and rises into consciousness, including not only the multimodal imagination but also feeling, instinct, and, most importantly, plenipotent numinous energy. The meditator who is undergoing contemplative awakening may experience not only riveting imaginal formations but also powerful waves of affect, instinctual urges, and a sense of being in the midst of or being infused by an awesome energy. It is not only the autosymbolic imagination that springs to life here; nonegoic life awakens across multiple dimensions, pervasively transforming the character of the meditative-contemplative process.

Transpersonal cognition, supercharged with plenipotent energy, is an amplified or "illumined" cognition

The plenipotent energy enlivening awakened consciousness markedly raises the intensity level of awareness. Experience generally and cognitive experience in particular becomes highly energized, acute, abundant. Such supercharging of experience means not only that imaginal intuitions can be almost perceptual in intensity but also that mental intuitions and agentic operations, too, are enhanced or empowered, if not overpowered. The energy at work within consciousness is, to use an expression coined by Stanislav Grof (1975), a *nonspecific amplifier* of awareness. It is an energy that magnifies all contents of consciousness and empowers all activities of consciousness (amplifier) without being essentially tied to or expressive of any particular content or activity (nonspecific).

Awakened cognition is in this way illumined; it is fueled by "high octane" energy. The energy in question can be conceived in many ways, for example, psychogenically or metaphysically, immanently or transcendentally, dualistically (i.e., as an energy other than and opposed to libido) or integratively (i.e., as a higher expression of an energy that also expresses itself as libido). I have presented my own account of the status of this energy in other publications (1994, 1995, 1998a, 1998b) and will not pursue the matter here. The point here is that the energy in question functions as a nonspecific amplifier of awareness and, therefore, that transpersonal cognition, both agentically and intuitively, is a supercharged, illumined cognition.

Transpersonal cognition is initially unstable

Initial awakening is unstable. As we have seen, awakening consciousness is supercharged with plenipotent energy and rife with imaginal formations, affective upwellings, and even instinctual impulses. Awakening in its initial stages can for these reasons be turbulent, even frighteningly so. The ego may feel as though it is under siege, as it is in turn supercharged and overpowered, entranced and enthused, riveted and aroused, captivated and swept away. Initial *samadhi,* insight, and infused contemplation can be as unstable as *dhyana,* advanced mindfulness, and the prayer of recollection, respectively, are poisedly anchored.

Initial awakening is unstable because the ego is unprepared for the awakening of nonegoic life. Consciousness is at first overpowered by plenipotent energy and other resurgent nonegoic potentials. And cognitively, the ego's mental intuitions and formal operational thinking are disjoined from, and the ego is itself disconcerted by, the newly reemergent autosymbolic imagination. The representations forged by the autosymbolic process appear in consciousness unexpectedly; and as symbols of the derepressing unconscious, they communicate meanings that are often frightening and difficult to decipher. The ego participates in two disjoint types of cognition, one immanent to the ego, the other transcendent: the ego's own mentally intuitive, operational cognition on the one hand and the imaginal, enigmatic cognition of the deep psyche on the other.

Transpersonal cognition becomes progressively more stable as the ego adjusts to and is integrated with nonegoic life

The turbulence of initial awakening eventually subsides. It does so not because awakened potentials themselves subside but, rather, because the ego gradually adjusts to and is integrated with nonegoic life. According to Patanjali, the more volatile forms of *samadhi* give way to more stable forms.

According to Buddhaghosa, the intoxicating "ten corruptions" give way to states of higher equanimity and lucidity, leading ultimately to *nibbana.* And according to St. Teresa of Avila, the dramatic raptures and transports of the stage of spiritual betrothal subside as one approaches the spiritual marriage, the higher prayer of union with Christ. Authorities on contemplation from both East and West agree, then, that the turbulence of initial awakening gradually gives way to a higher stability and clarity in which awakened psychospiritual potentials are seamlessly integrated with consciousness. Once this higher integration is achieved, awakened psychospiritual potentials composedly empower and enrich consciousness without any longer overpowering or disorienting it.

This general process of stabilizing integration is evident in the development of transpersonal cognition, which evolves from the two disjoint types of cognition just described to an increasingly unified cognition integrating egoic and nonegoic spheres. An initial indication that progress is being made in this direction is that imaginal intuitions, which had presented themselves as mysterious communications from an unknown source, begin presenting themselves as responses to sustained meditative or reflective inquiry. Disciplined focusing on an object or theme, the ego learns, elicits imaginal intuitions embodying the object or theme in creative, heretofore unrecognized ways. The ego in this way becomes increasingly familiar with the creative process and finds that the creative process is increasingly responsive to conscious direction. The ego, of course, never acquires the same kind of control over the autosymbolic process that it has over its own functions and operations. As a nonegoic potential, the autosymbolic process is inherently beyond the ego's direct command; it always remains spontaneous to some degree. These facts notwithstanding, the ego *is* increasingly able to guide the autosymbolic process, the products of which, accordingly, gradually lose their strange, foreign character and begin being seen as symbolically embodied answers to the ego's own inquiries.

The autosymbolic process is in this way progressively integrated with the mental-intuitive, operational cognition of the personal stages of development. The network of abstract meanings and formal relationships established during personal stages works as a rich seedbed for the reawakened autosymbolic imagination, which, germinated in this way, fashions symbols embodying complex ideas and subtle possibilities. No longer disconnected from consciousness, the autosymbolic imagination is no longer the vehicle of the primitive primary process. Responsive to the conceptual framework developed and tested during personal stages, the autosymbolic imagination is now the vehicle of what psychoanalyst Silvano Arieti (1976) called the *tertiary process,* a process that integrates what *used to be* the primary and secondary processes, a process, therefore, that is at once creative and logical, concrete and universal, symbolic and theoretical.

Conclusion

Two points merit emphasis as we bring the discussion to a close: (1) Transpersonal cognition cannot be achieved by will alone; and (2) transpersonal cognition, although immensely powerful and creative, is likely, like all other human cognition, fallible and limited by personal and cultural factors.

The testimonies of Patanjali, Buddhaghosa, and St. Teresa of Avila establish quite clearly that transpersonal cognition—whether in the form of *samadhi*, awakened insight, or infused contemplation—emerges as part of a deep psychic transformation. Transpersonal cognition for this reason is as much something that "happens" or is "given" as it is something that can be achieved by steadfast effort. As Socrates put it, wisdom cannot be taught; we must awaken to it, and this awakening is not an isolated cognitive event but is, rather, a transformation of our whole being.

If wisdom cannot be taught, it can be *pursued*. And this, of course, is the purpose of disciplines like yogic concentration leading to absorption, Buddhist mindfulness leading to insight, and Christian prayer leading to contemplation. Disciplines like these are practices that, in simultaneously opening consciousness and kindling nonegoic potentials, create conditions conducive to awakening. Contemplative exercises, however, cannot force awakening. As in all matters spiritual, the will, having done its work, must wait upon grace. The practices described by Patanjali, Buddhaghosa, and St. Teresa of Avila are indeed "technologies of ecstasy" (Georg Feuerstein's, 1989 expression), but they are also practices by which the ego opens itself to being transformed by forces deriving from beyond the ego's own sphere.

Transpersonal cognition raises the following philosophical question: Is transpersonal cognition a means of accessing infallible knowledge of higher realities? It is important to ask this question because some recent authors writing on transpersonal cognition have advocated just such a rationalist-Platonic conception. Ken Wilber is the best-known exponent of this view. In distinguishing between Jungian archetypes (which, Wilber believes, are merely primitive vestiges of phylogenesis) and "true" Platonic Forms, Wilber (1995) says:

> In other words, the Jungian archetypes are *not* the transcendental archetypes or Forms found in Plato, or Hegel, or Shankara, or Asanga and Vasubandhu. These latter Forms—the true archetypes, the ideal Forms—are the creative patterns said to underlie all manifestation and give pattern to chaos and form to Kosmos. (p. 247)

Wilber (1986, pp. 123–124) believes that eternal ideal forms exist in a higher realm and are accessed by direct insight during the course of spiritual awakening. According to Wilber, these ideal forms are the Platonic

templates on the basis of which the phenomenal world was patterned during the course of cosmic involution, templates that we as individual know-
ers revisit during the course of our spiritual evolution back to the Absolute,
One, or Void.

In my opinion this rationalist-Platonic conception of transpersonal
cognition should be treated with suspicion. It is laden with epistemological and metaphysical commitments that are not only unnecessary but also
of the most extreme (essentialist, rationalist, idealist) sort. It is entirely
possible—and it seems to me much more likely—that transpersonal cognition, like all human cognition, is fallible and limited by personal and
cultural factors. Why, after all, do Catholic contemplatives have visionary
experiences of Christ and Christian saints, whereas Mahayana Buddhists
have visionary experiences of buddhas and bodhisattvas? Why is it that
even the highest mystical experience of undifferentiated illumination is
understood so differently in different traditions, for example, as coinci-
dence with an impersonal dynamic void by Mahayana Buddhists and as absorption in a godhead behind a personal god by Christian and other
theistic mystics?

The answer, I believe, is that visionary and mystical experiences—and
transpersonal cognitions generally—are an insufficient basis for drawing
traditional epistemological (rationalist or empiricist) and metaphysical
(idealist, materialist, or dualist) conclusions. It is possible that there is no
higher metaphysical realm that transpersonal cognition infallibly accesses
and that, on the contrary, this type of cognition is simply a capability we
have evolved to give vision—fallibly, and in culturally diverse ways—to our
developmental potentialities and possible historical destinies. This possibility, like Wilber's rationalist-Platonic view, cannot be established as fact; and
for this reason the epistemology and metaphysics of transpersonal cognition should, I believe, be left undecided or be put forward only as a matter
of faith or interpretation.

Notes

1. Tobin Hart, Peter L. Nelson, and Kaisa Puhakka read an earlier version
   of this paper and guided me through the revision process. I would like
   to thank them for their excellent advice on matters of both substance
   and style.
2. I use the term *mental* intuition rather than *intellectual* intuition because in
   the history of philosophy the latter term has acquired questionable rationalist and essentialist associations.
3. Cross-cultural and individual variations in the severity of primal repression should be acknowledged. Many have held that the West is more se-

verely dissociated than the East and that modern technological society is more deracinated than archaic indigenous societies. Others have held that, irrespective of cultural differences, some people (e.g., artists and psychics) remain significantly more in touch with the power, spontaneity, and creativity of the deep unconscious than others. Acknowledging these variations, it remains true, I suggest, that primal repression is a historically and culturally pervasive phenomenon. Not only Europeans but Asians, too, not only moderns but indigenous peoples, too, not only nonartists and nonpsychics but artists and psychics, too, have felt a need to reawaken, renew contact, or establish deeper connection with creative and spiritual resources that are normally inaccessible or hidden from view. This is a primary purpose of the meditative and ascetic practices of Asian traditions, of the shamanic practices and many of the tribal rituals of indigenous peoples, of the techniques for entering creative states employed by many artists, and of the seances and trance induction practices of many psychics.

4. Except in its Tantric versions, concentrative-absorptive meditation is rarely conceived in energetic terms. Neither is Buddhist mindfulness-insight meditation, to be discussed later. This is a shame, because both of these types of meditation are in essential respects energetic practices that, as such, can be properly understood only if the energetic dimension is taken into account. I shall be presenting an energetic account of both concentrative-absorptive meditation and mindfulness-insight meditation. The reader is alerted that, in doing so, I am adopting a somewhat novel perspective.

5. Again, there is no confusion of prepersonal and transpersonal levels here, no "pre/trans fallacy," as Wilber alleges. Nonegoic potentials, which had been repressed as pre, can reawaken as trans or as "on the way to trans," for they reawaken within a fundamentally different psychic context. The ego is now mature, and ego functions, therefore, can now enter into effective integration with nonegoic potentials. Ego functions can now give form, complexity, and reality testing to nonegoic potentials; and nonegoic potentials in turn can give body, energy, creativity, and Spirit to ego functions. This higher integration is a *transpersonal* integration.

References

Aranya, H. (1983). *Yoga philosophy of Patanjali*. Albany: State University of New York Press.
Arieti, S. (1967). *The intrapsychic self*. New York: Basic Books.
Arieti, S. (1976). *Creativity: The magic synthesis*. New York: Basic Books.

Arlin, P. (1975). Cognitive development in adulthood: A fifth stage? *Developmental Psychology, 11,* 602–606.

Arlin, P. (1977). Piagetian operations in problem finding. *Developmental Psychology, 13,* 297–298.

Arlin, P. (1984). Adolescent and adult thought: A structural interpretation. In M. L. Commons, F. A. Richards, & C. Armon (Eds.), *Beyond formal operations: Late adolescent and adult cognitive development* (pp. 258–271). New York: Praeger.

Arlin, P. (1989). Problem solving and problem finding in young artists and young scientists. In M. L. Commons, F. A. Richards, & C. Armon (Eds.), *Adult Development: Vol. 1. Comparisons and applications of developmental models* (pp. 197–216). New York: Praeger.

Baillargeon, R. (1987). Object permanence in 3- and 4-month-old infants. *Developmental Psychology, 23,* 655–664.

Basseches, M. (1980). Dialectical schemata: A framework for the empirical study of the development of dialectical thinking. *Human Development, 23,* 400–421.

Basseches, M. (1984a). *Dialectical thinking and adult development.* Norwood, NJ: Ablex.

Basseches, M. (1984b). Dialectical thinking as a metasystematic form of cognitive organization. In M. L. Commons, F. A. Richards, & C. Armon (Eds.), *Beyond formal operations: Late adolescent and adult cognitive development* (pp. 216–238). New York: Praeger.

Basseches, M. (1989). Dialectical thinking as an organized whole: Comments on Irwin and Kramer. In M. L. Commons, F. A. Richards, & C. Armon (Eds.), *Adult Development: Vol. 1. Comparisons and applications of developmental models* (pp. 161–178). New York: Praeger.

Bower, T. G. R. (1982). *Development in infancy* (2nd ed.). San Francisco: W. H. Freeman.

Buddhaghosa. (1975). *Visuddhimagga* (3rd ed.) (B. Nanamoli, Trans.). Kandy, Sri Lanka: Buddhist Publication Society.

Commons, M. L., Richards, F. A., & Armon, C. (Eds.). (1984). *Beyond formal operations: Late adolescent and adult cognitive development.* New York: Praeger.

Cowan, P. A. (1978). *Piaget with feeling: Cognitive, social, and emotional dimensions.* New York: Holt, Rinehart & Winston.

Diamond, A. (1993). Neurological insights into the meaning of object concept development. In M. H. Johnson (Ed.), *Brain development and cognition: A reader* (pp. 208–247). Oxford, UK: Blackwell.

Eliade, M. (1969). *Yoga: Immortality and freedom.* Princeton: Princeton University Press.

Feuerstein, G. (1989). *Yoga: The technology of ecstasy.* Los Angeles: Jeremy P. Tarcher.

Feuerstein, G. (1996). *The Shambhala guide to yoga.* Boston: Shambhala.

Fraiberg, S. (1969). Libidinal object constancy and mental representation. *The Psychoanalytic Study of the Child, 23,* 9–47.

Freud, S. (1959). Inhibitions, symptoms and anxiety. In *The standard edition of the complete psychological works of Sigmund Freud* (Vol. 20, pp. 87–156). London: Hogarth Press. (Original work published 1926)

Freud, S. (1964). New introductory lectures on psycho-analysis. In *The Standard edition of the complete psychological works of Sigmund Freud* (Vol. 22, pp. 3–182). London: Hogarth Press. (Original work published 1933)

Grof, S. (1975). *Realms of the human unconscious.* New York: Viking Press.

Kuhl, P. K., & Meltzoff, A. N. (1982). The bimodal perception of speech in infancy. *Science, 218,* 1138–1141.

Mandler, J. (1990). A new perspective on cognitive development in infancy. *American Scientist, 78,* 236–243.

Meltzoff, A. N. (1990). Towards a developmental cognitive science: The implications of cross-modal matching and imitation for the development of representation and memory in infancy. In A. Diamond (Ed.), *The development and neural bases of higher cognitive functions: Annals of the New York Academy of Sciences* (No. 608, pp. 1–31). New York: New York Academy of Sciences.

Meltzoff, A. N., & Borton, R. (1979). Intermodal matching by human neonates. *Nature, 282,* 403–404.

Meltzoff, A. N., & Moore, M. K. (1977). Imitation of facial and manual gestures by human neonates. *Science, 198,* 75–78.

Meltzoff, A. N., & Moore, M. K. (1983). Newborn infants imitate adult facial gestures. *Child Development, 54,* 702–709.

Meltzoff, A. N., & Moore, M. K. (1989). Imitation in newborn infants: Exploring the range of gestures imitated and the underlying mechanisms. *Developmental Psychology, 25,* 954–962.

Miller, M. E., & Cook-Greuter, S. R. (1994). *Transcendence and mature thought in adulthood: The further reaches of adult development.* Lanham, MD: Rowman & Littlefield.

Richards, F. A., & Commons, M. L. (1984). Systematic, metasystematic, and cross-paradigmatic reasoning: A case for stages of reasoning beyond formal operations. In M. L. Commons, F. A. Richards, & C. Armon (Eds.), *Beyond formal operations: Late adolescent and adult cognitive development.* New York: Praeger.

Riegel, K. (1973). Dialectical operations: The final period of cognitive development. *Human Development, 16,* 346–370.

Teresa of Avila, St. (1980a). The interior castle. In *The collected works of St. Teresa of Avila* (Vol. 2.) (K. Kavanaugh & O. Rodriguez, Trans.). Washington, DC: ICS Publications.

Teresa of Avila, St. (1980b). The way of perfection. In *The collected works of St. Teresa of Avila* (Vol. 2.) (K. Kavanaugh & O. Rodriguez, Trans.). Washington, DC: ICS Publications.

Washburn, M. (1994). *Transpersonal psychology in psychoanalytic perspective.* Albany: State University of New York Press.

Washburn, M. (1995). *The ego and the dynamic ground: A transpersonal theory of human development* (2nd ed.). Albany: State University of New York Press.

Washburn, M. (1996). The pre/trans fallacy reconsidered. *Revision, 19,* 2–10.

Washburn, M. (1998a). Psychic energy, libido, spirit: Three energies or one? *Personal Transformation, 31,* 62–67.

Washburn, M. (1998b). *Embodied spirituality in a sacred world.* Manuscript in preparation.

Wilber, K. (1980). The pre/trans fallacy. *Revision, 3,* 51–71.

Wilber, K. (1986). The spectrum of psychopathology. In K. Wilber, J. Engler, & D. P. Brown (Eds.), *Transformations of consciousness* (pp. 107–126). Boston: Shambhala.

Wilber, K. (1990). *Eye to eye: The quest for the new paradigm* (Expanded ed.). Boston: Shambhala. (First edition published in 1983)

Wilber, K. (1995). *Sex, ecology, spirituality: The spirit of evolution.* Boston: Shambhala.

Wilber, K. (1996). A more integral approach: A response to the *ReVision* authors. *ReVision, 19,* 10–34.

10

Transpersonal Knowledge

A Participatory Approach to Transpersonal Phenomena

JORGE N. FERRER

M y main intention in this chapter is to introduce a participatory approach to transpersonal phenomena as an alternative to the experiential approach that guides contemporary transpersonal studies.[1] In the
first part, I point out some of the main conceptual and practical limitations
of the modern understanding of transpersonal and spiritual phenomena in
terms of individual inner experiences. In the second part, I delineate a different framework within which to understand and live these phenomena,
the participatory approach, showing how it not only offers a way out of
these problems, but also situates transpersonal studies in greater alignment
with spiritual values and ways of life. Finally, I conclude with some suggestions about the relationship between the experiential and the participatory
approaches, and the implications of this participatory turn for the development of a more pluralistic transpersonal theory.

The Experiential Approach to Transpersonal Phenomena

Transpersonal theory conceptualizes transpersonal and spiritual phenomena in experiential terms.[2] In other words, transpersonal and spiritual phenomena are generally understood and defined as *intrasubjective experiences*
or *states of consciousness*.[3] The basic idea underlying this experiential approach is that individuals "have" transpersonal experiences, and then, during these states of expanded awareness, access sources of knowledge that
lie beyond their biographical histories and ordinary time-space limitations. Implicit in this view is the assumption that transpersonal experiences

provide individuals with transpersonal insights. In the experiential approach, that is, the experiential dimension of transpersonal phenomena is regarded as primary and results in the epistemic one. Transpersonal experiences, it is commonly believed, lead to transpersonal knowledge.

A couple of influential definitions will serve to illustrate the fundamental nature of the experiential approach. According to Grof (1988), "transpersonal experiences can be defined as experiential expansion or extension of consciousness beyond the usual boundaries of the body-ego and beyond the limitations of time and space" (p. 38). In a similar vein, Walsh and Vaughan (1993) define transpersonal phenomena as "experiences in which the sense of identity or self extends beyond (trans) the individual or personal to encompass wider aspects of humankind, life, psyche or cosmos" (p. 203).

Readers acquainted with the transpersonal literature will recognize that this experiential understanding has guided transpersonal studies since the early configuration of the field in the late 1960s. Actually, the past thirty years of transpersonal research have been primarily devoted to the description, classification, and interpretation—developmental, cognitive, phenomenological, systemic, evolutionary, ontological, metaphysical, and so on—of transpersonal experiences or states of consciousness (e.g., Grof, 1972, 1988, 1998; Hunt, 1995; Levin, 1988; Tart, 1971, 1977, 1983; Valle, 1995; Wilber, 1996b, 1996c). As should be obvious, this experiential approach continues to be the prevalent framework to understand transpersonal phenomena. Recently, for example, Walsh and Vaughan (1993) defined the transpersonal disciplines as "those disciplines that focus on the study of transpersonal experiences and related phenomena. These phenomena include the causes, effects and correlates of transpersonal experiences and development, as well as the disciplines and practices inspired by them" (p. 202). Likewise, Lajoie and Shapiro (1992), after surveying more than two hundred definitions of transpersonal psychology, conclude that this field "is concerned with the study of humanity's highest potential, and with the recognition, understanding, and realization of unitive, spiritual, and transcendent states of consciousness" (p. 91).

The Origins of the Experiential Approach

The origins of the experiential approach are manifold. To offer an exhaustive analysis of them here is not possible, so I will merely indicate the three interrelated sources I consider most significant: the historical, the philosophical, and the methodological.

1. Historically, the experiential approach is rooted in the modern conceptualization of spirituality in the West. According to Max Weber (1978) and Jürgen

Habermas (1984, 1987a, 1987b), one of the main features of modernity was the breaking down of the unified metaphysical-religious world views characteristic of the premodern era into three different domains or "worlds": The objective or natural world (realm of empirical science, approached by an instrumental-technical rationality), the intersubjective or social world (realm of politics and ethics, approached by a moral-pragmatic rationality), and the subjective or individual world (realm of arts, religion, and psychotherapy, approached by an aesthetic-expressive rationality). In this context, as Rothberg (1993) points out, all religious and spiritual phenomena were automatically relegated to the "subjective" world and invariably regarded as not meeting the standards of valid, "objective" knowledge characteristic of natural science (e.g., public nature of observation, repeatability, verifiability, etc.). Remember Whitehead (1926): "Religion is what the individual does with his own solitariness" (p. 26). In the modern West, then, spirituality has been primarily understood in terms of (1) individual inner experiences that are (2) epistemically empty, or not providing any form of valid knowledge.[4]

As I see it, the wide acceptance of the experiential approach in transpersonal studies suggests that, in spite of reclaiming the epistemic status of spiritual phenomena, transpersonal theorists have uncritically accepted the modern conception of spirituality as mere inner experience. Already at the dawn of the transpersonal orientation, we find extremely eloquent articulations of a vision of spirituality in terms of private, individual experiences. Consider, for example, Abraham Maslow's words on religion and peak-experiences: "What I have been saying is that the evidence from the peak-experiences permits us to talk about the essential, the intrinsic, the basic, the most fundamental religious or transcendent experience as a totally private and personal one which can hardly be shared" (1970, pp. 27–28). In this treatment of transpersonal and spiritual phenomena as individual inner experiences—and, consequently, of transpersonal knowledge as empirical—it becomes evident that transpersonal theory's emancipation from the "disenchanted world" of modernity—to paraphrase Max Weber—is still partial and, as I will argue, problematic and unsatisfactory.

2. *Philosophically, the experiential approach stems from the essentially humanistic origins of the transpersonal orientation.* Transpersonal studies were born at the very heart of the Western Humanist tradition, primarily concerned with the affirmation of the intrinsic value of individual human experience (Bullock, 1985; Davidson, 1994). It should not be surprising, therefore, that the emphasis on individual experience—on its potentials, its creative nature, its "peak" moments, and so on—emblematic of humanistic psychology was naturally incorporated into the root metaphors, philosophical assumptions, and research programs of the transpersonal disciplines.

As is well known, one of the direct humanistic sources of early transpersonal studies is Maslow's (1968, 1970) groundbreaking studies on peak-
experiences (i.e., the most fulfilling, joyous, and blissful moments in human
life). Crucial for the emergence of the transpersonal orientation was
Maslow's (1970) equation of the peak-experience with what he called the
"core-religious experience," that is, the essential, intrinsic, and fundamental
transcendent experience that he believed could be found at the heart of all
religious traditions.[5] It was this connection between psychological health and
religious experience that impelled Maslow to move beyond the mostly secular and existential concerns of humanistic psychology, and toward the articulation of a new psychology, a psychology that, in contrast to the humanistic
orientation, would be "transpersonal, transhuman, centered in the cosmos
rather than in human needs and interests, going beyond humanness, identity, self-actualization, and the like" (1968, pp. iii–iv). If one adds to the individualistic character of humanistic psychology and Maslow's account of
spirituality, the highly "experientialist" climate of the California of the late
1960s—the widespread experimentation with psychedelics, meditation, isolation tanks, and other technologies of consciousness alteration; the proliferation of experiential approaches to psychotherapy and self-growth, and so
on—the experiential nature of the emerging field of transpersonal psychology is not only comprehensible but also probably inevitable.

   3. *Methodologically, the experiential approach emerged as an epistemic strategy
to bolster the validity of transpersonal knowledge claims.* What I am suggesting
here is that one of the principal reasons for the turn to experience in
transpersonal studies was the attempt to appear "empirical," and therefore
"scientific," in the eyes of the wider academic and social communities.

   In my opinion, there are three main factors behind the quasi-obsessive
preoccupation of transpersonalists with establishing the empirical foundations of the field. First, the vast technological success and social prestige of
empirical science in the twentieth century. Second, the historical association between religion and dogmatism in the Western world. And third, the
modern marginalization of spirituality to the status of subjective experiences. Naturally, the combination of these factors made the empirical justification of transpersonal studies nearly imperative: If spirituality was
essentially a subjective experience, and if the only valid knowledge was the
empirical one, then the epistemic legitimacy of transpersonal studies had to
be defended in terms of a "science of human experience," an "inner empiricism," a "Taoist science," a "subjective epistemology," a "science of consciousness" or, more recently, a "science of spiritual experience." Although
these proposals in support of the empirical bases (meaning here anchored
in inner experience) of transpersonal and spiritual claims had different
emphases, they all had an unequivocally identical purpose: The legitimiza-

tion of transpersonal studies as empirical, and therefore epistemically valid, disciplines of knowledge.

Before concluding this section, I should clarify that my intention here has not been to criticize these early transpersonal developments. On the contrary, I believe that, at the time of the emergence of the transpersonal orientation, an experiential account of transpersonal phenomena was not only historically inevitable, but also methodologically crucial. That is, the legitimization of transpersonal studies in the intellectual climate of the late 1960s and 1970s (and even 1980s) *had* to be empirical. In a time when spirituality was confined to the merely private and individual, inner empiricism was not only a legitimate response, but also an adequate means to argue for the validity of spiritual knowledge. What I will argue, however, is that this experiential approach to transpersonal phenomena, although once indispensable and perhaps even salutary, has become today unnecessary and counterproductive.

The Fundamental Problems of the Experiential Approach

In this section, I want to present what I believe are several important limitations of the experiential approach. Conceptually, I argue that the experiential approach (1) perpetuates the modern restrictive understanding of spirituality as individual inner experience (*intrasubjective reductionism*); and (2) follows a Cartesian epistemology that is inconsistent with the nature of most transpersonal and spiritual phenomena (*subtle Cartesianism*). Practically, I suggest that this experiential account (1) fosters all types of "spiritual maladies" such as ego-inflation, self-absorption, and spiritual materialism (*spiritual narcissism*); and (2) hinders the integration of transpersonal phenomena into everyday life (*integrative arrestment*).

The Conceptual Betrayal. Once transpersonal phenomena are understood as individual inner experiences, transpersonal theory tends to fall into the two interrelated traps of intrasubjective reductionism and subtle Cartesianism. Let us have a closer look at these pitfalls.

Intrasubjective Reductionism. The emergence of transpersonal theory can be seen as an attempt to free spirituality from the constraints imposed upon it by the modern conception of the world. The transpersonal commitment to the cognitive import of spiritual experiences, for example, radically challenges the modern epistemic devaluation of spirituality. However, transpersonal theory's emancipation from the restrictions imposed by the structure of modernity is still an *incomplete project*. Essentially, the strategy followed by most transpersonal theorists to redeem spiritual knowledge has been the exaltation of the epistemic value of individual inner experiences. Nevertheless, it should be obvious that, in its focus on individual inner experiences, transpersonal theory perpetuates the modern marginalization of spirituality to the realm of the private and subjective. With these experiential premises, that is, transpersonal theory falls into what I call *intrasubjective reductionism* (i.e., *the reduction of spiritual and transpersonal phenomena to individual inner experiences*). As some authors have already observed (Rothberg, 1993; Wilber, 1995), however, this view represents a very one-sided and limiting understanding of spirituality. From a traditional perspective, for example, this experiential reduction is misleading because spiritual phenomena are seen as resulting from the participation in spheres of being and knowledge that transcend the merely human. Furthermore, as we will see, this experiential interpretation generates all sorts of problematic ramifications for how transpersonal and spiritual phenomena are lived. What is needed, I will argue, is to free transpersonal theory from these experiential prejudices—and thereby from its implicit commitment to modernity—and extend our vision of spirit to the entire cosmos.

Subtle Cartesianism. In short, *subtle Cartesianism is the understanding of spiritual and transpersonal phenomena according to a subject-object model of knowledge and cognition.* In this section, I want to suggest that although (1) it is widely recognized that this Cartesian framework is inappropriate in accounting for most transpersonal phenomena, (2) the experiential approach structures transpersonal phenomena in terms of a "subject" having experiences of different transpersonal or spiritual "objects."

Since its very beginnings, transpersonal theory has been explicitly anti- or post-Cartesian and searched for alternatives to objectivist and subjectivist accounts of transpersonal phenomena (Capra, 1982; Grof, 1985; Harman, 1988). As soon as it became evident, Cartesianism was an inadequate epistemology for transpersonal studies because transpersonal phenomena collapse the distinction between what had been traditionally regarded as objective and subjective. In transpersonal phenomena, it became strikingly obvious, *not only what is subjective can become objective, but also what is objective can become subjective.* On the one hand, "what is subjective can become objective" insofar as elements belonging to human subjectivity can become potential objects for the emerging transpersonal self. This subjective-objective fluidity has been noted, for example, in the dynamics of personal and transpersonal development, in which the self disidentifies from structures with which it was previously identified and can act upon them as objects of consciousness (Wilber, 1996b, 1997a), in mindfulness practices, in which certain subjective structures through which meditators experience themselves and the world can become objects for their consciousness (Nyanaponika, 1962), or in mystical phenomena such as *enthymesis,* in which the "empowered" imagination of the mystic is able to objectify the contents of his or her subjective space and thereby shape different spiritual landscapes (Hollenback, 1996).[6]

On the other hand, "what is objective can become subjective" because in transpersonal phenomenology what once were objects of knowledge can be incorporated, temporarily or permanently, into the very identity of the self. Intrapsychically, for example, archetypes that were first experienced as distinct from oneself can become, in transpersonal development, structures with which the self identifies (Wilber, 1996b). Extrapsychically, the self can also become identified with previous objects of the external world, as in nature mysticism, where the subjectivity of an individual can encompass aspects of the environment or even the entire natural world. As Grof's (1985, 1988) research has widely documented, human consciousness can become identified with a variety of biological, social, cultural, planetary, and cosmic phenomena. All these subjective-objective and objective-subjective transpositions, transpersonalists have rightly argued, rather than merely indicating the fluidity of these epistemic categories, strongly suggest that the Cartesian model of cognition is inadequate to account for transpersonal phenomena.

In spite of these apparent limitations, however, most transpersonal authors often conceptualize transpersonal knowledge according to a Cartesian model of discourse, for example, making objectivist claims (Levin, 1988).[7] Here I want to suggest that this subtle Cartesianism is largely rooted in the experiential understanding of transpersonal phenomena. The experiential approach is foundational for this self-betrayal because it structures transpersonal phenomena in terms of a "subject" having experiences of transpersonal "objects." The intentional structure connoted by the modern notion of "experience" linguistically manifests in the constitution of a grammatical subject (a "who") and grammatical object (a "what"). As a result, whenever we hear the word "experience," we immediately want to know "who" had "what" experience. In the context of transpersonal studies, then, the expression "transpersonal experience" automatically configures transpersonal phenomena in terms of an experiencing "subject" in relation to "objects" of experience. In other words, the "experiential talk" reifies both a Cartesian subject and a Cartesian object with respect to transpersonal and spiritual phenomena. On the one hand, it consolidates a subject of the experience with which the ego eagerly identifies itself. As we will see, this has pernicious consequences for how transpersonal phenomena are lived. On the other hand, it objectifies whatever transpersonal cognition is said to reveal, even in those cases in which what is disclosed is said to be "emptiness," "nothingness," or "pure consciousness."

To conclude this section, I would like to stress that these two problems can be seen as the result of two consecutive dissociative moves. First, *intrasubjective reductionism* isolates transpersonal and spiritual phenomena from the world and confines them into the limited realm of individual inner experience. Second, already in inner space, *subtle Cartesianism* creates a further division, this time between an experiencing "subject" and experienced "objects" of transpersonal cognition. With these two moves, the experiential approach not only betrays the transpersonal orientation, but also becomes vulnerable to all the anxieties and dilemmas of Cartesian modes of consciousness, such as the myths of subjectivism-objectivism, the aporias of absolutism-relativism, the riddles of mediation and construction, and, as we will see, the seductions of spiritual materialism.[8]

The Practical Betrayal. As Lakoff and Johnson (1980) explain, the way we conceptualize any phenomenon has a profound impact on how we live it. Here I want to suggest that the experiential approach has problematic implications for how transpersonal phenomena are engaged in everyday life. More precisely, I want to propose that the experiential approach breeds two potential pitfalls of the spiritual path: spiritual narcissism and integrative arrestment.

Spiritual Narcissism. There are many ways to understand spirituality. Different approaches emphasize diverse aspects of the spiritual life, the spiritual path, or one or another spiritual tradition. For our present purposes, I adopt the definition offered by Evans (1993) in his superb *Spirituality and Human Nature.* According to Evans, "spirituality consists primarily of a basic transformative process in which we uncover and let go of our narcissism so as to surrender into the Mystery out of which everything continually arises" (p. 4). Even though the means and goals of mystical paths are diverse, Evans explains, mystics tend to agree that any authentic spiritual transformation "involves a shedding of narcissism, self-centeredness, self-separation, self-preoccupation, and so on" (p. 158). In short, narcissism can be seen as diametrically opposed to spirituality.[9] The more we participate in spirit, the more we move naturally away from self-centered ways of being. And conversely, the more we preoccupy ourselves with self-gratification and self-grandiosity, the more we alienate ourselves from spirit.

By *spiritual narcissism* I understand a set of related distortions of the spiritual path, such as ego-inflation (the aggrandizement of the ego fueled by spiritual energies), self-absorption (the over-preoccupation with one's spiritual status and achievements), and spiritual materialism (the appropriation of spirituality to strengthen egoic ways of life). As I see it, the threat common to all these pitfalls is what I call *spiritual narcissism* (i.e., *the misuse of spiritual practices, energies, or experiences to bolster self-centered ways of being*). The main symptoms of spiritual narcissism are, among others, a fragile sense of empowerment and self-importance; a preoccupation with one's comparative spiritual status; a constant and repetitious chattering about one's spiritual experiences and achievements; a strong need for being positively reinforced and praised; a preoccupation with the sense of being special, chosen for some distinguished spiritual purpose, or preferred by spiritual teachers; an extreme idealization or demonization of spiritual teachers; serious difficulties in working with authority figures; and finally, an exaggerated susceptibility and defensiveness towards any sort of criticism.

There are two main reasons why the experiential approach nourishes, I believe, the different varieties of spiritual narcissism. First, its intrasubjective reductionism paves the way for the egoic appropriation of spiritual phenomena because it confines spirituality to the very realm where the ego believes itself sovereign and continuously struggles to dominate: the realm of inner experience. As Wilber (1996a) observes, an exclusive experiential understanding makes individuals prone to interpret spiritual insights "rather narcissistically as mere extensions of their Self" (p. 103). Second, its subtle Cartesianism effectively expedites the narcissistic appropriation of spiritual "objects" by a reified egoic "subject." Spiritual events in which I participate, that is, become *my* experiences. The association between Cartesianism and narcissism is also noted by Evans (1993). For this author, both subjectivism and objectivism are complementary epistemological stances of narcissistic modes of consciousness that preclude a genuine availability to others, and a real participation in the world and spiritual energies. While in subjectivism the world becomes *my* experience of the world, in objectivism, by contrast, I retreat to a position of a detached observer and the world appears as entirely outside me. However, Evans (1993) points out, "whether I include everything [subjectivism] or exclude everything [objectivism] I am like a god in my aloneness, my self-sufficiency, and my domination of the universe. In the one case, I dominate by devouring and assimilating into my experience. In the other case, I dominate by subjecting to my intellect and will" (p. 44).

Integrative Arrestment. The integration of transpersonal phenomena in everyday life is arguably one of the most urgent tasks of modern transpersonal psychology. A failure to adequately integrate spiritual openings, for example, is widely regarded as a potential source of psychotic disorders and spiritual pathologies (e.g., Grof & Grof, 1989; Wilber, 1986). In addition, while access to transpersonal states has become more widespread, their stabilization into enduring traits—a hallmark of genuine transpersonal development—continues to be a fundamental challenge for transpersonal psychologists. A basic issue here is that, as it has often been stressed in the religious literature, the goal of the spiritual quest is not "to have spiritual experiences," but to stabilize spiritual consciousness, live a spiritual life, and transform the world accordingly. And it cannot be repeated too often that, *regardless of the quantity, spiritual experiences do not "produce" a spiritual life.* A crucial task for transpersonal studies, then, is to develop both conceptual frameworks and practical injunctions that support the translation of transient spiritual states into the actual spiritual transformation of self and world.

In this regard, I believe that the experiential approach, rather than fostering this integration, raises several obstacles that crystallize in what I call *integrative arrestment.* By integrative arrestment I mean *the hindrance of the natural integrative process that translates spiritual realizations into everyday life toward the transformation of self, relationships, and world.*

There are at least two features of the experiential approach that contribute to this "sequestration" of the natural integrative power of spiritual phenomena. The first is the emphasis placed on individual inner experiences (intrasubjective reductionism), which comes usually accompanied by a disregard toward other elements of traditional spiritual paths, such as ethical commitments, community life, relationships with teachers, serious study of scriptures, and so forth (Rothberg, 1993). However, many of these non-experiential elements are traditionally regarded as essential to the integration of spiritual insights and the effective navigation of the spiritual journey. A correct understanding of spiritual doctrines, for example, is considered in most spiritual traditions a prerequisite for the practice of meditation and the trans-conceptual access to the ultimate.[10]

Spiritual systems offer an integrated understanding of the totality of reality and the role of humanity therein. The integrative power of spiritual realizations depends to a large extent on the meaning that such events possess in the larger scheme of things. Without such an integrated understanding, the serious difficulties of the modern Western self in integrating spiritual insights in everyday life should not be surprising. Divested from the cosmological meaning provided by spiritual traditions, these "experiences" not only often promote spiritual narcissism, but also tend to lose their natural transformative quality. Likewise, once spiritual openings are divorced from wider ethical and social contexts, their sacred and transformative quality substantially diminish. As a result, spiritual realizations become merely peak-experiences. From this viewpoint, peak-experiences may be seen, at their best, as *secularized spiritual phenomena,* and, at their worst, as temporary gratifications for an always hungry-for-depths Cartesian ego.

The second reason lies in the structuring of spiritual phenomena as "objects" experienced by a "subject" (subtle Cartesianism). One of the consequences of subtle Cartesianism is a conception of spiritual phenomena as transient experiential episodes that have a clear-cut beginning and end—in contrast, for example, to realizations or insights that, once learned, change the way one sees life and guide one's future actions in the world. This experiential understanding, then, precipitates the pitfall known popularly in spiritual circles as the "collection of experiences" (i.e., the search for a periodic access to spiritual "highs" outside the context of a genuine transformative process).

Taken together, these conceptual and practical limitations strongly suggest, I believe, that the experiential approach has become inadequate to meet the challenges that transpersonal studies face today. Therefore, I would like to make a plea to go beyond the experiential talk in transpersonal studies and explore alternative frameworks to understand and live spiritual phenomena.

The Participatory Approach to Transpersonal Phenomena

After the deconstruction carried out in the first part of this chapter, the more challenging task of reconstruction is called for. As I have suggested, the main objective of this task should be to develop a framework that is no longer limited by the inner and individualistic premises that dominate modern transpersonal studies. In short, I want to propose now that this reconstruction is possible, and that it needs to take the form of a *participatory turn,* (i.e., *a radical shift of emphasis from intrasubjective experience to participatory events in our understanding of transpersonal and spiritual phenomena*).

As we have seen, transpersonal phenomena dismantle the intentional structure inherent in the modern notion of experience. Both the Cartesian subject and the Cartesian object, as grammatical as well as experiential categories, are rendered implausible by the very nature of transpersonal phenomena. In the wake of the nonintentional nature of transpersonal phenomena, it becomes imperative to move beyond the notion of experience and reframe transpersonal phenomena in a way that does not connote intentionality.

But to take this alternative path leaves us in an even more perplexing predicament. If transpersonal and spiritual phenomena are not experiences, what in the world are they? Briefly, what I want to propose here is that transpersonal phenomena can be more adequately understood as *multilocal participatory events* (i.e., *emergences of transpersonal being that can occur not only in the locus of an individual but also in a relationship, a community, or a place*). In other words, I am suggesting here that what has been commonly called a transpersonal experience can be better conceived as the emergence of a *transpersonal participatory event.* The basic idea underlying the epistemic approach, then, is not that an expansion of individual consciousness allows access to transpersonal contents, but rather that *the emergence of a transpersonal event "forces" in the individual what has been called a transpersonal experience.* Thus understood, the ontological dimension of transpersonal phenomena is primary and results in the experiential one.

Transpersonal experiences do not lead to transpersonal knowledge, but rather transpersonal participatory events elicit in the individual what have been commonly called transpersonal experiences.[11]

I am not denying, of course, the existence of an individual inner dimension in transpersonal phenomena. On the contrary, the emergence of a transpersonal participatory event in the locus of an individual *demands* the participation of his or her inner consciousness. However, the participatory approach reframes this experiential dimension as *the participation of an individual consciousness in a transpersonal event.* What the participatory approach radically rejects is the anthropocentric, and ultimately egocentric, move to infer from this participation that transpersonal phenomena are essentially human experiences.

As virtually all mystical traditions maintain, spiritual phenomena are not to be understood merely in phenomenological terms, but rather as stemming from human participation in spheres of being and awareness that transcend the merely human. Listen, for example, to St. John of the Cross (1585/1979) concerning the union of the human soul with God:

> When God grants this supernatural favor to the soul, so great a union is caused that all the things of both *God and the soul become one in participant transformation,* and the soul appears to be God more than a soul. Indeed, *it is God by participation.* Yet truly, its being (even though transformed) is naturally as distinct from God as it was before, just as the window, although illumined by the ray, has being distinct from the ray's. (The Ascent of Mount Carmel, 2.5.7., pp. 117-118; my italics)

In other words, the participatory approach is reacting against *intrasubjective reductionism,* that is to say, the reduction of transpersonal and spiritual phenomena to the status of individual inner experiences.

Let us now have a closer look at this view of transpersonal phenomena as *multilocal participatory events.* The epistemic approach conceives transpersonal phenomena as (1) *events,* in contrast to intrasubjective experience, (2) *multilocal,* in that they can arise in different loci, such as an individual, a relationship, a community, or a place, and (3) *participatory,* in that they can engage the creative power and dynamism of all dimensions of human nature.

Transpersonal Phenomena as Events

The participatory approach regards transpersonal phenomena as *events,* rather than as experiences.[12] In order to clarify the contrast between experiences and events, I would like to draw an analogy with the *celebration of a party.* A party is a participatory celebration of life and of the other. A party is not anyone's property because it cannot be possessed. A party "occurs" whenever a certain combination of elements comes together, and the most we can do to facilitate it is to optimize these conditions. We can, for example, get mentally and emotionally ready for celebration, dress in a more festive, elegant, or colorful manner, invite open, interesting or like-minded people, arrange special and vivid decoration, cook succulent and nurturing food, or prepare games, rituals, or activities that promote self-expression, mutual participation, and openness to life energies. A party can also occur spontaneously, for example, out of the fortuitous encounter of several old friends in a café. An important point to notice is that both external and internal conditions seem to be important for participating in a party. As we know so well, if for some reason we feel detached or closed toward others or life energies, even the most festive environment will not be a party *for* us. Therefore, a party is neither "objective" nor "subjective," but rather a participatory phenomenon. A party is not a intrasubjective experience, but an event in which we can participate given the presence of certain external and internal conditions.

In drawing this analogy, I want to suggest that transpersonal phenomena are *like* a party in the sense that they are not individual inner experiences but participatory events; they are neither "objective" nor "subjective"; they cannot be possessed (they are not anyone's property); they can be optimized but never forced; and they can emerge spontaneously with the coming together of certain conditions.

The idea of transpersonal and spiritual phenomena as participatory events is consistent with Gadamer's (1990) notion of truth as an event of self-disclosure of Being. For Gadamer, truth should not be understood as correspondence with ahistorical facts or experiences, but as an ontological "happening" of Being in the locus of human historical existence. In Gadamer's words, "being is self-presentation and . . . all understanding is an event" (p. 484). Interestingly, in his discussion of Gadamer's notion of truth, Carpenter (1995) points out that, "As an event, truth is something one experiences. But this experience (in the sense of the German *Erfahrung*) cannot be understood as simply 'subjective' experience (*Erlebnis*), since all experience is a part of the historical context in which it occurs" (p. 195).[13]

Transpersonal Phenomena as Multilocal

In contrast to the individual focus of the experiential approach, the participatory approach recognizes that transpersonal phenomena are multilocal in that they can occur not only in an individual but also in a relationship, a community, or a place.

Space does not allow me to offer here an adequate explication of the multilocal nature of transpersonal events, so I will merely indicate that this notion finds extensive support in the world's spiritual literature. First, we are indebted to Martin Buber (1970) for having offered one of the most compelling expositions of a *relational* understanding of spirituality. In his shift from a mystical conception of spirituality—centered on individual inner experiences (*Erlebnis*)—to a dialogical one—geared to the intersubjective and the community (*Gemeinschaft*)—Buber (1970) proposes that the true place of spiritual realization is not the individual experience, but the community, the Between. In Buber's (1970) words: "Spirit is not in the I but between I and you, it is not like the blood that circulates you, but like the air in which you breath" (p. 89). Or as Mendes-Flohr (1989) puts it summarizing Buber's views: "The realm of the Between, that which establishes 'authentic' *Gemeinschaft*, is the locus of God's realization" (p. 115). And this community (*Gemeinschaft*), said Buber, "is an *event* that arises out of the Center between men" (quoted in Mendes-Flohr, 1989, p. 117; my italics). It is important to stress than Buber is not talking in metaphoric terms. For Buber, the realm of the Between or the interhuman (*das Zwischenmenschliche*) has an extramental, independent ontological status, and it is precisely this realm, not the one of individual inner experience, that is the locus of true spiritual realization.[14]

Second, *communal* spiritual events have also been frequently reported in the religious literature. This is the case in the Christian tradition, for example, with the descent of the Holy Spirit on the apostles at Pentecost or their communion with God at the Eucharist. As Johnston (1995) points out, "all through The Acts of the Apostles we find the Spirit descending on the group, communicating gifts and filling all with his presence" (p. 214). Communal spiritual events are also well known in other spiritual systems, as illustrated by the first phase of the Sinai revelation of God to the people of Israel,[15] the dance of the Whirling Dervishes in the Melveli Sufi order, or the ayahuasca ceremonies in certain native traditions.

Finally, there also exists a vast literature on *sacred places,* places identified by religious traditions as being particularly charged with spiritual power or presence (Eliade, 1959; Olsen, 1996; Swan, 1990, 1991). Every spiritual tradition has one or more sacred places whose special spiritual quality makes them privileged locations for ritualistic and religious practices such as, for instance, purification and healing, prayer and contemplation, vision quests and pilgrimages, or, more generally, spiritual renewal. Examples of these sacred places, by which even the modern self feels captivated, include Palenque, Mount Arafat, Delphi, Mecca, Mount Sinai, Lourdes, among many others. Although clothed in experiential language, the following passage by Swan (1988) is revealing of the nature of sacred places:

> If we find that many people, regardless of cultural heritage or prior awareness of the "power" of a place, go to that place and

have a transpersonal experience there, then perhaps we can begin to better understand why shamans revere the so-called places of power. (p. 22)

Recently, Halifax (1998) beautifully captured the essence of this expanded understanding of spirituality: "I hesitate calling myself spiritual," she tells us, "my sense is that the spiritual flows between beings, be they with humans or other beings" (p. 8).

Transpersonal Phenomena as Participatory

The most important feature of transpersonal events is that they are *participatory*. In this context, the term "participatory" has three different but equally important meanings. First, "participatory" alludes to the fact that, after the break with Cartesianism, transpersonal events — and the knowledge they usually convey — can no longer be objective, neutral, or merely cognitive. On the contrary, *transpersonal events engage human beings in a participatory, connected, and often passionate activity that can involve not only the opening of the mind, but also of the body, the heart, and the soul.* Although different transpersonal events may activate only certain dimensions of human nature, all dimensions can potentially come into play in the act of *participatory knowing*, from somatic transfiguration to the awakening of the heart, from erotic communion to visionary cocreation, and from contemplative knowing to moral insight, to mention only a few.[16]

Therefore, whenever I talk in the following pages about participatory *knowing*, this should not be understood as if I were talking exclusively of a mental, intellectual, or cognitive activity. Far from that. As used in this work, *participatory knowing refers to a multidimensional access to reality that includes not only the intellectual knowing of the mind, but also the emotional and emphatic knowing of the heart, the sensual and somatic knowing of the body, the visionary and intuitive knowing of the soul, as well as any other way of knowing available to human beings.*

Second, the term "participatory" also refers to the role that individual consciousness plays during transpersonal events. This relation is not one of possession, appropriation, or passive representation of knowledge, but of *communion* and *co-creative participation*.

Finally, "participatory" also refers to the fundamental ontological predicament of human beings in relation to spiritual energies and realities. *Human beings are* — whether they know it or not — *always participating in the self-disclosure of spirit by virtue of their very existence.* This participatory predicament is not only the ontological foundation of the other forms of participation, but also the epistemic anchor of spiritual knowledge claims and the moral source of human responsible action.

Since I am proposing to understand transpersonal phenomena in terms of participatory knowing rather than intrasubjective experiences, it may be important to clarify the conception of knowledge embraced by the participatory approach. Briefly, the participatory approach views transpersonal phenomena as participatory events that are presential, enactive, and transformative.

1. *Participatory knowing is presential.* Participatory knowing is knowing "by presence" or "by identity." In other words, in a transpersonal event, *knowing occurs by virtue of being.* To be sure, it may be tempting to explain this knowing by saying that "one knows X by virtue of being X." However, this account is misleading because it suggests a knowing "subject" and a known "object," the very epistemic categories that transpersonal events so drastically dismantle. Faced with the difficulties of adequately expressing presential knowledge, many mystics devised a new mode of discourse—the via negativa or *apophatic language*—which allowed them to convey the non-intentional nature of their realizations through a displacement of the grammatical object of their locutions (Sells, 1994). For my part, I am choosing at this point to depict presential knowing as "knowing by virtue of being." At any rate, what should be clear here is that participatory knowing is not geared to a Cartesian subject-object model of cognition. In contrast to traditional epistemologies, that is, participatory knowledge is not knowledge "of something by someone." Rather, participatory knowledge is lived as the emergence of an embodied presence pregnant with meaning that transforms both self and world. We could say, then, that *subject and object, knowing and being, epistemology and ontology, are brought together in the very act of participatory knowing.*

2. *Participatory knowing is enactive.* Following the groundbreaking work of Maturana and Varela (1987), and Varela, Thompson, and Rosch (1991), the participatory approach embraces an enactive paradigm of cognition. Participatory knowing, then, is not a mental representation of pregiven, independent objects, but an *enaction,* the "bringing forth" of a world or domain of distinctions cocreated by the different elements involved in the epistemic event.

The enactive nature of participatory knowing is crucial for its emancipatory power. Were the participatory approach to embrace a representational paradigm of cognition — according to which knowledge is the subjective inner representation of an independent objective reality—it would automatically relapse to the Cartesianism of the experiential approach and be burdened by many of its maladies. Contra Rorty (1979) and Habermas (1987a), however, not all epistemic discourse can be assimilated to foundationalist, objectivist, or representational frameworks. Participatory knowing is not afflicted by the problems of Cartesian modes of consciousness.

3. *Participatory knowing is transformative.* Participatory knowing is transforming at least in the following two senses. First, the participation in a transpersonal event brings forth the transformation of self and world. And second, a transformation of self is usually necessary to be able to participate in transpersonal knowing, and this knowing, in turn, draws forth the self through its transpermative process in order to make possible this participation.

The transformative quality of the human participation in transpersonal and spiritual phenomena has been emphasized by a number of contemporary consciousness researchers (e.g., Grof, 1985, 1988; Harman, 1994) and scholars of mysticism (e.g., Barnard, 1994, Staal, 1975): One needs to be willing to be personally transformed in order to access and fully understand most spiritual phenomena. The epistemological significance of such personal transformation cannot be emphasized enough, especially given that the positivist denial of such a requisite is clearly one of the main obstacles for the epistemic legitimation of transpersonal and spiritual claims in the modern West. In this vein, for example, Evans (1993) identifies as one of the main dogmas of skepticism concerning spiritual realities what he calls *impersonalism*, i.e., "the dogmatic rejection of any truth claim that requires personal transformation to be adequately understood and appraised" (p. 101).

The Emancipatory Value of the Participatory Approach

One the main advantages of this participatory account is that it radically undermines most of the shortcomings we identified in the experiential approach, such as intrasubjective reductionism, subtle Cartesianism, spiritual narcissism, and integrative arrestment. Let us briefly look at how the participatory approach can counteract these limitations.

Intrasubjective Reductionism. A multilocal conception of transpersonal phenomena is clearly inimical to the intrasubjective reductionism of the experiential approach. If transpersonal phenomena can occur not only in the individual but also in relationships, communities, and places, then their confinement to the realm of individual inner experience must be both inadequate and erroneous. As we have seen, modernity regarded spiritual phenomena as individual inner experiences without epistemic value. We have also seen how transpersonal theory, although reclaiming the epistemic status of spiritual phenomena, is still committed in several fundamental respects to the modern interpretation of spirituality as primarily private and individual. In affirming the multilocality of transpersonal events, the participatory approach gives the second, and perhaps final, step toward the emancipation of spirituality from this restrictive space. In maintaining that transpersonal events are multilocal, that is, the participatory approach frees Spirit from its inner and individualistic constraints, and extends its reach to the entire universe—from where, of course, it never actually departed.

Subtle Cartesianism. To view transpersonal phenomena as participatory events rather than as individual experiences eradicates subtle Cartesianism at its roots. As we have seen, events in which human beings participate are neither "of something" or "by someone," nor can they be understood as "objective" or "subjective." In addition, the presential and enactive nature of transpersonal knowing maintained by the participatory approach averts the structuration of transpersonal phenomena in terms of a "subject having experiences of transpersonal objects." To regard transpersonal phenomena as nonintentional events in which human beings can participate, then, effectively shortcircuits transpersonal theory's commitment to a Cartesian model of cognition.

Spiritual Narcissism. To draw transpersonal and spiritual phenomena out of the realm of inner experience is to pull them out of the realm where the ego believes itself sovereign and relentlessly struggles to dominate. And in doing so, I believe, the participatory approach thwarts to a large extent the illegitimate egoic appropriation of spirituality that we have called spiritual narcissism. Furthermore, the understanding of transpersonal phenomena as events undermines these distorted forms of spiritual participation insofar as, in contrast to experiences, events are not "something" that the ego can "have" or "take possession of." Since the most the ego can do is to *participate* in the event, the chances of egoic appropriation of spiritual energies are substantially diminished.

Integrative Arrestment. The integrative arrestment typical of the experiential approach is also undermined because, understood in terms of participatory knowing rather than transient experiences, transpersonal events can be lived as realizations that, once learned, transform how we see ourselves and guide our actions in the world. As Amis (1995) puts it in regard to spiritual knowledge (logos, gnosis) in esoteric Christianity, "This special kind of knowledge has the power to create this special kind of discrimination. Having the right knowledge, we become able to make the right choice" (p. 76). A series of compelling and evocative examples of the transforming power of spiritual insights in our times can be found in Ring's (1998) recent study on the existential consequences of near-death experiences (NDEs). What is more, as we will see in the next section, the participatory approach helps us reconnect the transpersonal enterprise with contemplative goals and values. In doing so, it offers a more adequate framework for understanding the nature of spirituality and for fostering the integration of transpersonal and spiritual events in everyday life.

In addition to these gains, the participatory approach releases transpersonal studies from the *dualism between experience and knowledge,* according to which transpersonal experiences lead to transpersonal knowledge. From this participatory viewpoint, this dualism is seen as not only unnecessary but also misleading and problematic. It is unnecessary because what has been called a transpersonal experience is now better understood as the participation of an individual consciousness in a transpersonal event (i.e., as how transpersonal events are lived from the standpoint of an individual consciousness). It is misleading because it suggests the centrality of human individual experience in transpersonal phenomena, overlooking both the multilocal nature of transpersonal events and the transhuman sources of spiritual creativity. And it is problematic because this dualism engenders the problems of mediation and construction, objectivism and subjectivism, and absolutism and relativism, intrinsic to any Cartesian-Kantian model of knowledge and cognition.

To conclude this section, I would like to raise and respond to a possible objection to the emancipatory value of the participatory approach. It may be argued that, although the participatory approach can free us, in theory, from Cartesianism, it cannot fulfill its promises in practice because the subject-object duality cannot be solved through any type of formal model or discourse, but can only be transcended in the territory of human life. This seems to be, for example, Wilber's (1997b) view on this matter, who points out that the subject-object dualism can only be overcome in postformal stages of consciousness development. I totally agree with the spirit of this remark: The value of non-Cartesian frameworks is close to nothing if they merely become new "theories" for the Cartesian ego. However, I should add that different metaphors and conceptual frameworks can either perpetuate Cartesian consciousness or promote its transcendence. For the reasons espoused above, I firmly believe that the participatory approach is a powerful tool for fostering such a transformation.

The Participatory Approach and the Spiritual Quest

Having shown how the participatory approach prunes many of the adverse ramifications of the modern experiential understanding of transpersonal phenomena, I want to suggest now that it is also more harmonious with the spiritual goals of the contemplative traditions. This point is extremely important because, in my opinion, transpersonal studies should not be dissociated from the spiritual enterprise, but rather be *in the service* of the spiritual transformation of self and world.

In brief, the participatory turn situates transpersonal studies in greater alignment with the spiritual enterprise because the aim of most contemplative traditions is not "to have experiences," but rather to realize and participate in special states of discernment.[17] These states of discernment are "special" in that they have a soteriological nature: Spiritual knowledge is knowledge that liberates. To be sure, the nature of this liberation may differ substantially among traditions. I should make clear here that I am not advancing a universalist thesis about the nature of spiritual knowledge. As I see it, there may be different ways in which human beings cocreate their participation in the Mystery and move away from self-centered ways of being. What I am merely saying is that most contemplative traditions are primarily concerned with the emergence of certain ontological-epistemic participatory events associated with such terms as "liberation," "salvation," or "enlightenment."[18]

This should not come as a surprise. After all, most contemplative traditions—especially those spawned in India—state the spiritual problem of humankind in essentially epistemological terms: Existential and spiritual alienation are ultimately rooted in ignorance (*avidya*), in misconceptions about the nature of self and reality that lead to craving, attachment, self-centeredness, and other unwholesome dispositions. Therefore, the attainment of final liberation (*moksa, nirvana*, etc.) does not result from meditative experiences per se, but from wisdom (*prajna*), from the direct knowledge of "things as they really are" (e.g., Hopkins, 1971; Potter, 1991).[19] The ultimate goal of most contemplative traditions, then, is not realized by entering any type of altered state, ecstasy, or trance, but by the overcoming of delusion and ignorance. In the words of Sankara, "Since the root cause of this transmigratory existence is ignorance, its destruction is desired. Knowledge of *Brahman* therefore is entered on. Final beatitude results from this knowledge" (*Upadesasahasri*, I: 5; in Mayeda, 1992, p. 103). Or, as Nasr (1989) puts it in relation to the goal of virtually all spiritual traditions, "The sapiential perspective envisages the role of knowledge as the means of deliverance and freedom, of what the Hindu calls *moksa*. To know is to be delivered" (p. 309).

The previous quotations may suggest a causal relationship between knowledge and liberation, a view of spiritual knowledge as *leading to* or *resulting in* liberation. However, according to most traditional accounts, it is inappropriate to talk in terms of causality between knowledge and liberation because, in the final analysis, there is no difference between them: Final liberation is not other than spiritual knowledge. Listen, again, to Sankara: "Liberation is not an effect—it is but the destruction of bondage (ignorance)" (*Brhadaranyaka Upanisad Sankara Bhasya*, 3.3.I; in Indich, 1980, p. 107). Or, as Hollenback (1996) writes in reference to *kaivalyam* (isolation), the ultimate goal of the Samkhya system and Patanjali's Yoga, "Isolation is not a mental state where the subject-object distinction has disappeared. Isolation is not a mental state because it is a *condition of naked insight* in which the soul [*purusa*] has utterly escaped bondage from prakrti and samsara" (p. 591; my italics).

I should stress here that this description of transpersonal and mystical events in terms of participatory knowing should not be understood as excluding the equally fundamental presence of *affective qualities*. On the contrary, as I suggested earlier, the participatory nature of *transpersonal knowing not only may entail an opening of the mind and the soul but also of the body and the heart.* In Christian mysticism, for example, knowledge of God, or the participation in the Divine Intellect, is invariably accompanied by a profound love toward God, the creation, and humanity (*agape, caritas*) (McGinn, 1996b). Similarly, in Mahayana Buddhism, the disclosure of wisdom (*prajna*) is inseparable from the development of compassion (*karuna*) (Williams, 1989). The same can be said of Sufism, where Ibn al-'Arabi's path of knowledge is beautifully balanced by Rumi's path of passionate love for the Divine (Chittick, 1983, 1989). These examples of the mutual interpenetration of love and knowledge in the spiritual journey could be multiplied endlessly.

An important point that follows from this analysis is that mystical ecstasies, trances, and absorptions are neither the final goal of the contemplative traditions nor should they be equated with final liberation. Actually, most traditions warn that these mystical states are not to be sought for their own sake, but are merely a psychospiritual preparation to participate in special states of discernment. Although an adequate justification of this claim would require a thorough exploration of different mystical texts that would move us away from our present focus, it may be helpful to offer at least several examples extracted from different traditions.

The trance of cessation (*nirodhasamapatti*), culmination of the four formless *jhanas* in Theravada Buddhism (Buddhaghosa, 1976; Griffiths, 1986), the state of absorption without support (*asamprajnata samadhi*) of the Yoga Sutras of Patanjali (Patanjali, 1977), or the state of transcendence of all duality (*nirvikalpa samadhi*) in Sankara's Advaita Vedanta (Mayeda, 1992), are neither synonymous nor should be confused with the achievement of final liberation in each of these traditions. Although these states are often regarded as important steps, it would be a serious mistake to confound them with final liberation as envisaged by these traditions: *Nirvana* in Theravada Buddhism, *kaivalyam* (isolation) in Samkhya-Yoga, or *moksa* in Sankara's Advaita Vedanta. And what is, according to these traditions, the nature of this final liberation? The nature of final liberation is essentially epistemic, that is, participation in spiritual states of insight. More precisely, *nirvana* is objectless discernment free from the mind constructing activities and defilements (lust, hatred, and delusion), that is, the double knowledge of the destruction of the fluxes (*asravaksayaj-nana*) and their absolute future nonarising (*ānutpadajnana*) (Cox, 1992; Harvey, 1995); *kaivalyam* (isolation) is the penetrating insight into the eternal self (*purusa*), which is independent from any kind of mental or material phenomena (*prakrti*) (Patanjali, 1977); and, finally, *moksa* is knowledge of Brahman (*Brahma-jnana*), or the direct recognition of the ultimate identity between one's innermost self (*Atman*) and the ultimate ground of the Universe (*Brahman*) (Mayeda, 1992). In other words, *nirvana*, *kaivalyam*, and *moksa* are not experiences but epistemic participatory events, emergences of liberating knowing.

The case of Zen Buddhism deserves particular attention, especially since its widely claimed experiential emphasis impacted so decisively on Western conceptions not only of Zen in particular but also of Eastern spirituality in general. Interestingly enough, historical analyses indicate that this experiential focus was not an original aspect of traditional Zen, but rather emerged at the turn of the twentieth century as a response to the modern Western critique of religion as dogmatic, irrational, and unscientific (Sharf, 1995a, 1995b). As Sharf (1995a) points out, "The Buddhist emphasis on 'inner experience' is in part a product of modern and often lay-oriented reform movements, most notably those associated with the *vipassana* revival in Southeast Asia, and those associated with contemporary Zen movements in Japan" (p. 246). This experiential turn is evident, for example, in the Japanese Kyoto school, especially in the writings of Nishida Kitaro, D. T. Suzuki, and Nishitani Keiji. These modernized movements became, in turn, the main vehicles of transmission of Buddhism to the West. In particular, D. T. Suzuki's popular accounts of *satori* as a "direct nondual experience," heart of all genuine spiritual traditions, substantially shaped not only the West's understanding of Zen Buddhism but also its overall approach to Eastern religions. Nevertheless, this experiential emphasis is absent in traditional Zen teachings, treatises, or practices. In this account, the following passage by historian of religions Sharf (1995a) deserves to be quoted at some length:

> The irony of this situation is that the key Japanese terms for "experience"—*keiken* and *taiken*—are rarely attested in premodern Japanese texts. Their contemporary currency dates to the early Meiji, when they were adopted to render Western philosophical terms for which there was no ready Japanese equivalent. One searches in vain for premodern Chinese or Japanese equivalent to the phenomenological notion of experience. Nor is it legitimate to interpret such technical Zen terms as *satori* (literally, to understand), or *kensho* (to

see one's original nature), as denoting some species of "unmediated experience" in the sense of Nishida's *junsui keiken*. (p. 249)[20]

But then, what is the original meaning of these terms for final liberation in Zen Buddhism? Sharf (1995a) offers us the answer:

> In traditional Chinese literature, such terms are used to denote *the full comprehension and appreciation of central Buddhist tenets such as emptiness, Buddha-nature, or dependent origination*. There are simply no *a priori* grounds for conceiving such *moments of insight* in phenomenological terms. Indeed, Chinese Buddhist commentators in general, and Ch'an exegetes in particular, tend to be antipathetic to any form of phenomenological reduction. (p. 249; my italics)

Before concluding, I should stress that I am not claiming that this account of liberation in terms of participatory knowing is paradigmatic for *every* mystic in *every* mystical tradition. Some mystics, like St. Teresa for example, frequently expressed their insights in intentional and experiential language, and it therefore will not be difficult to find passages in the religious literature that seemingly contradict my thesis. The mystical literature is so vast, rich, and diverse that one can probably find disconfirmation for any generalized statement about mysticism. What I do contend, in contrast, is that an understanding of spiritual liberation in terms of participatory knowing is more consistent with the dominant trends of most schools of Buddhism, Hinduism, Western esotericism, and also of many forms of Christian, Islamic, and Jewish mysticism, and probably shamanism as well.[21]

In any event, in the light of this prevalent identity of spiritual knowledge and liberation in most accounts, it is my belief that the participatory approach may help us not only to situate transpersonal studies in greater alignment with the spiritual quest but also to deepen our understanding of the nature of spirituality and the goals of the contemplative traditions. In this regard, the experientialist neglect of the centrality of participatory knowing in the spiritual quest makes the experiential approach a distorting and limiting framework for transpersonal studies.

Conclusion

Since its very origins, transpersonal theory conceived transpersonal and spiritual phenomena in terms of individual inner experiences. When one looks at the intellectual and cultural *Zeitgeist* of the California of the late 1960s, the tendency of the early transpersonalists to focus on individual experiences and to defend the empirical foundations of the field is certainly comprehensible. In this chapter, however, I have sought to show that this experiential approach, although once salutary and probably inevitable, is today both unnecessary and problematic. In particular, I have suggested that the experiential approach betrays on both conceptual and pragmatic grounds some of the central aims of the transpersonal orientation. Conceptually, the experiential approach falls into intrasubjective reductionism (the reduction of spirituality to the status of individual inner experiences) and subtle Cartesianism (the structuration of transpersonal and spiritual phenomena according to a subject-object model of cognition). Pragmatically, the experiential approach fosters spiritual narcissism (the egoic appropriation of spirituality at the service of a narcissistic motivation) and integrative arrestment (the "sequestration" of the natural integrative process of spiritual phenomena toward the transformation of self, relationships, and world). Some of the most insidious practical problems repeatedly reported by transpersonalists, then, may be to some degree systemic of an experiential understanding of spirituality.

As a radical antidote to these maladies, I have outlined an alternative framework for transpersonal studies that is no longer limited by these experiential and individualistic premises. According to this participatory approach, transpersonal phenomena are not individual inner experiences but participatory events (i.e., emergences of transpersonal being that can occur in the locus of a person, a relationship, a community, or a place). While affirming the existence of an individual consciousness that may participate in transpersonal events, the participatory approach challenges the egocentric move of inferring from this participation that transpersonal phenomena are fundamentally human inner experiences.

Basically, then, what I am proposing is a translation of the entire transpersonal project from an experiential framework, geared to a subject-object model of cognition, into a participatory framework that is free from rusty Cartesian moorings. This basic move enables us to emancipate transpersonal theory from many of its current conceptual and practical constraints. Some of the main direct consequences that follow from this conceptual revision are: (1) a more integral understanding of spirituality free from intrasubjective reductionism; (2) the dismantling of Cartesianism, and the dissolution of many of the dilemmas inherent to a subject-object model of cognition; (3) the undermining of spiritual narcissism and integrative arrestment; and (4) the realignment of transpersonal studies with the spiritual quest.

To avoid any possible misunderstanding of my position, I should say here that, although the problems of the experiential approach are legion, the participatory turn does not necessarily demand its abandonment, but rather its *limitation to certain dimensions or stages of transpersonal inquiry.* In other words, my critique of the experiential approach should not be taken as arguing for its repudiation and replacement. Rather, what I am suggesting is the need to move beyond a purely experiential interpretation of transpersonal and spiritual phenomena toward a participatory understanding grounded on liberating knowledge and practical wisdom.

On the one hand, I believe that experiential discourse can be legitimately used to refer to the individual inner *dimension* of spiritual and transpersonal phenomena. As pointed out earlier, the participatory approach does not deny or eradicate, of course, the experiential aspects of spirituality. The participatory approach simply reconceives this intrasubjective dimension in terms of the participation of an individual consciousness in transpersonal or spiritual events. The important point to realize, then, is that the experiential, although important, is only an aspect of spiritual events, and this recognition prevents the pitfall I have called *intrasubjective reductionism.* As most traditions tell us, spiritual events cannot be reduced to human experiences because they flow from dimensions of existence in which human beings can participate, *but* that transcend the merely human. With this in mind, it is safe to use, I believe, the experiential talk to refer to the individual inner dimension of transpersonal and spiritual phenomena.

On the other hand, it may be possible to regard the relationship between the experiential and participatory approaches in a developmental manner.[22] As transpersonal theorists Ken Wilber (1996b) and Michael Washburn (1995) point out, Cartesian consciousness may well be the necessary starting point of transpersonal inquiry (at least in the modern West, I would qualify). From this viewpoint, the descriptive value of the experiential approach—geared to a Cartesian model of cognition—may be limited to the first stages of the spiritual path, when the spiritual seeker undergoes temporary openings that are typically interpreted in Cartesian terms as transient personal experiences, being more prone to fall into spiritual narcissism and integrative arrestment. As the spiritual seeker deepens his or her understanding of these insights, as well as begins to embody and live them in the world, the limits of this experiential interpretation become evident and the participatory approach may start looking like a more adequate framework to understand transpersonal and spiritual phenomena. At this juncture, for example, individuals may tend to gradually feel that spirituality is not so much about having special experiences, but about cultivating emancipatory understandings that transform not only their inner being but also their relationships and even the world. The adequacy and validity of the experiential and participatory approaches, then, may be relative to different stages of spiritual development. In both cases, seen as limited to certain dimensions or stages of transpersonal inquiry, the experiential approach is not abandoned, but simply qualified, situated, and ultimately transcended by what I believe is a more adequate and fruitful understanding of transpersonal and spiritual phenomena.

Finally, although the metaphysical implications of the participatory approach cannot be unpacked here,[23] I would like to conclude this chapter by suggesting that, once we free ourselves from the Cartesian prejudices of the experiential approach and take seriously the participatory nature of transpersonal knowing, alternatives to the perennialism that predates transpersonal studies naturally emerge that allow us to look at the transpersonal project with fresh eyes. Eyes that discern that transpersonal studies do not need the perennial philosophy as its fundamental metaphysical framework. Eyes that appreciate and honor the multiplicity of ways in which the sense of the sacred can be not only conceptualized but also intentionally cultivated, embodied, and lived. Eyes that recognize, in short, that the sacred need not be univocally universal to be sacred.

Notes

I would like to thank Daniel Chapman, Brendan Collins, Steve Dinan, John Heron, Sean Kelly, Peter Nelson, Kenneth Ring, Larry Spiro, Richard Tarnas, Jenny Wade, and Michael Washburn for their helpful comments on earlier drafts of this chapter.

1. This chapter offers a very general and condensed account of both the experiential and the participatory approaches. For a more detailed exposition, see my *Revisioning Transpersonal Theory* (Ferrer, 1999b).
2. In the context of the experiential approach, the term "experiential" refers to the *individual inner* or *intrasubjective* character of the modern understanding of human experience. Notice, however, that the notion of experience can be used as the bearer of non-Cartesian and even transhuman semantic contents (like, for example, in the philosophies of James, Whitehead, or Nishida). These expanded meanings free the notion of experience from its modern intrasubjective constraints and are harmonious with the participatory approach to transpersonal phenomena introduced in this chapter.
3. In this chapter I will be referring to transpersonal, spiritual, and mystical phenomena somewhat interchangeably. Although the meaning of these terms sometimes overlaps, it is important not to lump them together. To be sure, since there is no consensus among scholars about how to define any of these three phenomena (e.g., Brainard, 1996; Dupré, 1987; Evans, 1993; Helminiak, 1996; Lajoie & Shapiro, 1992; Rothberg, 1996; Shapiro, 1994; Wilber, 1997a; Zinnbauer et al., 1997), the relationships among them largely depend on the semantic distinc-

tions with which one chooses to work. Rather than trying to offer a priori simple definitions of such complex phenomena as spirituality or mysticism—which today is both naive and preposterous—I will simply say here that, in my opinion, their relationship is more one of family-resemblance, rather than of identity, equivalence, or inclusion. For example, while certain phenomena can be regarded as both transpersonal and mystical (e.g., certain states of nonduality) all transpersonal phenomena are not mystical (e.g., a self-identification with botanical processes that may occur during a psychedelic session) nor are all mystical phenomena transpersonal (e.g., certain visions or locutions not involving an expansion of individual consciousness). This family resemblance-like relation operates, I believe, not only between transpersonal and mystical phenomena but also between mystical and spiritual phenomena, and between spiritual and transpersonal phenomena.

4. Contrary to popular belief, the notion of religious or spiritual "experience" is relatively recent. In Western religious studies, for example, the idea of religion as inner experience can be traced to Schleiermacher's *On Religion*, originally published in 1799, and whose explicit aim was to protect religious doctrines from the Enlightenment critique of metaphysics (Proudfoot, 1985). Likewise, in Buddhist studies, the focus on spiritual experiences stems in large part from the new Japanese Zen movements such as the Kyoto school (Nishida Kitaro, D. T. Suzuki, etc.) and the so-called *vipassana* revival of South Asia, both of which, deeply influenced by modern Western notions of religion, developed at the end of the nineteenth century as an attempt to ground Buddhism in a universal experience immune to emerging relativistic threats (Sharf, 1995a, 1995b). Similarly, the experiential emphasis in Hindu studies primarily derives from the works of nineteenth-century Neo-Hindu thinkers (e.g., Rammohan Roy, Debendranath Tagore, and especially Sarvepalli Radhakrishnan), who attempted to reconcile Hinduism and the empiricism of Western science (Halbfass, 1988). For a general critical analysis of the notion of experience in religious studies, see Sharf (1998).

5. In Maslow's views about the nature of peak-experiences, then, we find not only the seeds of the experiential approach but also the genesis of the general adhesion of transpersonal theory to a perennialist vision of spirituality; "To the extent that all mystical or peak-experiences are the same in their essence and have always been the same, all religions are the same in their essence and always have been the same" (1970, p. 20). Transpersonal theory, that is, was born in a perennialist world. For a critical evaluation of the relationship between transpersonal theory and the perennial philosophy, see Ferrer (1999a, 1999b).

6. Note that Hollenback (1996) is not proposing any type of solipsistic or projective psychologism in which mystics merely "create" their spiritual

universes by exerting the faculty of their empowered imagination. On the contrary, Hollenback believes that the empowered imagination can actually transcend the mystic's belief systems and become a source of novel revelations and creative spiritual insights.

7. Levin (1988) rightly argues that the pronouncement of objectivist claims betrays the transpersonal orientation because it assumes the very Cartesian epistemology from which transpersonal studies struggle to be free. The solution, for Levin, is that transpersonal claims should be articulated in an strictly phenomenological language (i.e., as statements referring exclusively to human experience). I believe that Levin (1988) is correct in his condemnation of objectivist language in transpersonal studies, and his paper is particularly helpful in showing how transpersonal phenomena render the structural opposition between subject and object suspect. However, as this essay should make obvious, to prescribe phenomenology as a remedy for transpersonal studies is to prescribe the illness for the cure.

8. As I argue elsewhere (Ferrer, 1999b), this experiential interpretation of spiritual phenomena is at the root of the riddles of mediation and construction that predate the modern study of mysticism (see, e.g., Forman, 1990, 1998; Gill, 1984; Jones, 1993; Katz, 1978, 1983; Perovich, 1985; Rothberg, 1989; Short, 1996). Having implicitly posited a subject-object model of cognition, that is, Kantian questions naturally arise about both the mediation between subject and object, and the construction of the objects of knowledge by the structures of subjectivity.

9. In this context, it is important to clearly distinguish between pathological or unnecessary narcissism and the "normal" narcissism that inevitably accompanies the aspirant throughout the spiritual path, and is said to be completely eradicated only in final realization (Almaas, 1996; Epstein, 1986; Wilber, 1986).

10. This is illustrated, for example, by the consideration of *lectio/meditatio* (meditative reading and repetition of texts) as giving fruit to *oratio* (prayer) and *contemplatio* (contemplation) in Christian monastic mysticism (McGinn, 1996a), or the need for *sravana* (listening) and *manana* (reflection) of *sruti* (revealed scripture) before *nididhyasana* (meditation) in Sankara's Advaita Vedanta (Rambachan, 1991). One of the most compelling articulations of the need for an adequate conceptual understanding as a prerequisite for accessing direct spiritual knowledge can be found in Klein's (1986) excellent study of the Gelukba order of Tibetan Buddhism.

11. In order to highlight the contrasts between the participatory and the experiential approaches, I am talking here of transpersonal events as they occur in the locus of the individual. However, it should be borne in mind that one of the fundamental features of the participatory ap-

proach is that transpersonal events are multilocal, that is, they can occur not only in an individual but also in a relationship, a community,
or a place.

12. Although to my knowledge the term "event" has never been applied in
a participatory manner to transpersonal or spiritual phenomena, it may
be necessary to mention two uses of this term in the modern literature
on mysticism. First, Forman (1990, 1993) proposes the locution "pure
consciousness event" to talk about a type of mystical experience "during
which the subject remains conscious (wakeful, alert—not sleeping or
unconscious) yet *devoid of all mental content*" (1993, p. 708; my italics).
For Forman, pure consciousness events are nonintentional experiences
devoid of mental content that can be found in virtually all mystical traditions. Second, Sells (1994) suggests that we talk about mysticism not
as experiences but as "meaning events." According to Sells, a mystical
"meaning event" is the semantic reenactment of mystical experiences,
that is, the meaning of the mystic's linguistic expressions. In his own
words, "In contrast to the realization as an instance of mystical union
that entails a complete psychological, epistemological, and ontological
transformation, the meaning event is a semantic occurrence" (p. 9). As
I see it, Sells's intention is primarily methodological. What he is suggesting is to bracket issues about what mystics encounter, experience, or
know and focus on the study of mystical modes of discourse, such as the
apophatic one. A similar suggestion has been recently made by Idel
(1996) in his plea to focus on "mystical expressions," rather than on
mystical experiences

Although neither Forman nor Sells talks about *participatory* events,
it is noteworthy that, facing the nonintentionality of some mystical
states, these authors chose to refer to them as events. The fundamental
difference between my approach and these proposals is that while Forman uses the term "event" to refer to an *experiential* state that is *epistemically void*, and Sells uses it to talk about *semantic* meaning of mystical
utterances, I am using it to refer to the *participatory* nature of transpersonal and most mystical phenomena.

13. For two lucid discussions about the often overlooked Gadamerian notion of "truth event," see DiCenso (1990) and Carpenter (1994). Interestingly, Carpenter's (1994) essay traces the roots of Gadamer's
notion of truth as an event to the Neoplatonic doctrine of emanation.
In another work, Carpenter (1995) applies this idea as a hermeneutic
tool to compare the nature of spiritual revelation in Bhartrhari and
Bonaventure. In total harmony with the idea of spiritual participatory
knowing here espoused, Carpenter (1995) concludes with the following words: "I would like to suggest that the striking similarities in
Bhartrhari's and Bonaventure's descriptions of the actual reception of

revelation, through which the individual moves from a naive experience of the world as given, as objective, *in se,* as *vikara,* to the disclosure of the world as relational, as *expressio,* as *anukara,* point to an experience of truth in this sense" (p. 198). And he adds: "In the actual *event* of revelation, there is no self-same 'object' 'out there' that remains beyond our purely subjective powers of knowing. Rather, revelation as an event can perhaps best be understood as the disclosure of a reality that is itself dynamic and relational" (p. 199).

14. For the relational nature of spirituality, see also Hershock's (1996) account of Ch'an enlightenment in terms of interpersonal intimacy, Achterberg and Rothberg's (1998) reflections on relationship as spiritual practice, and Wade's original research on sexuality and spiritual knowledge (in this volume).

15. Before the well-known second phase of the Sinai revelation, in which Moses became a mediator and received detailed spiritual teachings at the top of the Mountain of God, the Exodus relates a first phase in which God himself came down and revealed the Ten Commandments to the people of Israel in a communal fashion. As Holdrege (1996) points out in her rigorous study, *Veda and Torah,* "the Zohar thus represents the theophany at Mount Sinai as a collective experience, in which the mysteries contained in the Ten Words were apprehended by the people of Israel as a whole" (p. 323). Interestingly, Holdrege (1996) describes the Vedic and Sinai revelations as paradigmatic spiritual "events" to be reenacted by the Hindu and Jewish communities (pp. 334-339).

16. It is not my intention here to create an artificial dichotomy between Cartesian intrasubjective *experiences* and non-Cartesian participatory *knowing.* Since both experience and knowledge can be conceptualized in Cartesian and non-Cartesian ways, transpersonal participatory events could be equally understood in both experiential and epistemic terms. Therefore, it would also be valid to describe transpersonal and spiritual phenomena in terms of, for example, *participatory experiential events.*

17. Of course, some Western-influenced scholars have succumbed to the temptations of interpreting Eastern soteriological teachings in an empirical fashion, that is, as experientially originated and verifiable. In Advaita Vedanta, for example, this experientialist emphasis can be traced to Neoadvaitin thinkers such as Radhakrishnan (1923/1971), a Hindu educated in the West who had considerable impact upon many modern scholars like Smart (1964/1992), Paranjpe (1984, 1988), or Sharma (1993, 1995). For Radhakrishnan (1929/1957), "if philosophy of religion is to become scientific, it must become empirical and found itself on religious experience" (p. 84). As a number of historical commentators have pointed out, however, the projection of empiricist concerns

and foundations to the system of Vedanta is not consistent with the traditional teachings, whose emphasis was always placed on knowledge (*jnana*) and revelation (*sruti*) (Fort, 1996; Halbfass, 1988; Rambachan, 1991, 1994). Halbfass (1988) shows, for example, that in contrast to the cautious and skeptical attitude of classical Hinduism toward personal experience, Neo-Hinduism sees in experience both the quintessence and foundation of all religion. A parallel case has been made in relation to the traditional and modern interpretations of the Sankhya-Yoga school, and particularly to the textual tradition based on Patañjali's *Yogasutra* (Grinshpon, 1997).

The situation is analogous in Buddhist studies, where certain scholars such as Jayatilleke (1963) and his pupil Kalupahana (1975, 1986) have defended the position that Buddhist liberation is attained and confirmed by inner experiences gained during meditative practice. However, it is highly questionable that these empiricist interpretations can account for the nature of Buddhist doctrines, epistemologies, and liberation. In his analysis of Dharmakirti's theory of knowledge, for example, Hayes (1997) concludes that "the doctrine of radical empiricism may have its virtues, but it is clear that the virtue of being easily reconciled with classical Buddhist doctrine is not one of them. Each of the three classical formulations of the Buddha's awakening . . . involves the use of the intellect to arrive at a correct interpretation of the world of experience" (pp. 116–117). Although I cannot spell out here the arguments offered, the so-called "Buddhist empiricist thesis" has also been challenged and refuted on both conceptual and historical grounds in the works of Kalansuriya (1981, 1987), Hoffman (1982), Halbfass (1988), and Sharf (1995a, 1995b). In sum, what these and other analyses strongly suggest is that empiricist readings of Eastern spiritual endeavors are an apologetic response to the impact and prestige of Western's empirical science that has little or nothing to do with Hindu and Buddhist contemplative paths.

18. I am not suggesting, then, an identical or structurally equivalent goal for all contemplative traditions. As I have argued elsewhere (Ferrer, 1998a, 1999a, 1999b), the adhesion of transpersonal theory to a perennialist metaphysics may not only have been premature but also has problematic consequences for transpersonal hermeneutics, interreligious dialogue, and spiritual inquiry. For different articulations of a more pluralistic vision of spirituality and mysticism, see the works by Katz (1978, 1983), Vroom (1989), Griffiths (1991), Dean (1995), Heim (1995), and Irwin (1996). For an explanation of how the participatory approach addresses the diversity of mystical claims by embracing a position of *metaphysical pluralism*, see Ferrer (1999b).

19. From the perspective of the participatory approach, however, the expression "things as they really are" is seen as misguided insofar as it suggests an objectivist and universalist view of ultimate reality. What most mystical traditions offer, however, are not so much "descriptions" of a pregiven ultimate reality to be confirmed or falsified by experiential evidence, but "prescriptions" of ways of "being-*and*-the-world" to be intentionally cultivated and lived (Ferrer, 1998b). The descriptive claims of contemplative traditions primarily apply to the deluded or alienated ordinary human predicament, as well as to the various views of self and world disclosed throughout the unfolding of each soteriological path. But since there are many possible enactions of truer and more fully liberated self and world, it may be more accurate to talk about them as "things as they really *can* be" or even as "things as they really *should* be." While the former expression would remain more neutral, the latter would stress the all-important ethical dimension of the contemplative endeavor, for example, in terms of moral condemnation of egocentric understandings of reality and associated ways of life.

20. Note that these statements may not hold true for other Buddhist schools. As Gyatso (1999) recently showed, for example, Tibetan Buddhism does refer to meditative states through several lexemes (e.g., *myong-ba* and *nyams*) which seem to be synonymous to the English term "experience." Although Gyatso personally regards spiritual insights as "varieties of enlightened experiences" (p. 120), she tells us that, in Tibetan Buddhism, "when distinction between subject and object dissolves entirely, however, it is usually not labelled with any of the terms for experience discussed thus far but rather is cast as an enlightened realization, often termed *rotgs*" (pp. 119-120). And she adds: "*Nyams* [experience] in particular is, in fact, frequently contrasted with *rtogs* [realization], especially in the Mahamudra literature, where meditative experiences are sometimes said to precede, but in themselves to be bereft of realization" (p. 120).

21. The examples selected here derive exclusively from Eastern sources because these are the traditions that the proponents of the experiential approach usually rely on. Notice, however, that a parallel case can be made in the case of most Western traditions. For example, a classic account of Christian mysticism in terms of mystical knowing can be found in Maritain's (1932/1959) *magnum opus*, *The Degrees of Knowledge,* in which a hierarchy of forms and modes of knowledge (*sensible, praeterreal, transsensible)* leading to the ultimate goal of knowledge of God is presented. Likewise, in his highly acclaimed work, *The Foundations of Mysticism,* McGinn (1994) has recently criticized the modern tendency to describe mysticism in terms of inner experiences or altered states,

and found "the term 'presence' (of God) a more central and more useful category for grasping the unifying note in the varieties of Christian mysticism" (p. xvii). According to McGinn (1996b), even for the so-called "affective mystics" like Bernard of Clairvaux or John of the Cross, love of God included some form of intuitive knowing (*intelligentia amoris*). Likewise, the Islamic tradition has always emphasized sacred knowledge as both the core and goal of its mysticism and soteriology (Chittick, 1989). Experiences of self-annihilation (*fana'*) are not the salvific end in the Sufi path; the goal, in contrast, is to know God (*ma'rifa*), to be a perfect human being by being "with" God (Chittick, 1989). According to the Islamic mystic and philosopher Ha'iri Yazdi (1992), for example, "mysticism is a form of presence-knowledge . . . a form of human noetic consciousness in the sense that mystical moods and experiences are assertive and profoundly informative. Mysticism is characterized throughout by an orderly awareness of the world of reality. It puts something before us as the truth of this world" (p. 113). Finally, the attainment of metaphysical knowledge has also been the primary goal of the diverse traditions often amalgamated under the term "Western esoterism" such as Hermeticism, Gnosticism, Theosophy, and so on (Faivre, 1994; Faivre & Needleman, 1995). For a traditionalist account of the centrality of knowledge in most contemplative traditions, East and West, see Nasr (1989).

22. I am indebted to Steve Dinan (personal communication) for this interesting suggestion.

23. For an in-depth exploration of these implications, see Ferrer (1999b).

References

Achterberg, J., & Rothberg, D. (1998). Relationship as spiritual practice. In D. Rothberg, & S. Kelly (Eds.), *Ken Wilber in dialogue: Conversations with leading transpersonal thinkers* (pp. 261–274). Wheaton, IL: Quest.

Almaas, A. H. (1996). *The point of existence: Transformations of narcissism in self-realization.* Berkeley: Diamond Books.

Amis, R. (1995). *A different Christianity: Early Christian esotericism and modern thought.* Albany: State University of New York Press.

Barnard, G. W. (1994). Transformations and transformers: Spirituality and the academic study of mysticism. *Journal of Consciousness Studies, 1*(2), 256–260.

Brainard, F. S. (1996). Defining "mystical experience." *Journal of the American Academy of Religion, 64*(2), 359–393.

Buber, M. (1970). *I and Thou* (W. Kaufmann, Trans.). New York: Charles Scribner's Sons.

Buddhaghosa, B. (1976). *The path of purification* (Visuddhimagga) (Vols. 1–2) (B. Nyanamoli, Trans.). Berkeley: Shambhala.

Bullock, A. (1985). *The humanistic tradition in the west.* London: Thames & Hudson.

Capra, F. (1982). *The turning point.* New York: Simon & Schuster.

Carpenter, D. (1994). Emanation, incarnation, and the truth-event in Gadamer's Truth and Method. In B. R. Wachterhauser (Ed.), *Hermeneutics and Truth* (pp. 98–122). Evanston, IL: Northwestern University Press.

Carpenter, D. (1995). *Revelation, history, and the dialogue of religions: A study of Bhartrhari and Bonaventure.* Maryknoll, NY: Orbis Books.

Chittick, W. C. (1983). *The Sufi path of love: The spiritual teaching of Rumi.* Albany: State University of New York Press.

Chittick, W. C. (1989). *The Sufi path of knowledge: Ibn al'-Arabis metaphysics of imagination.* Albany: State University of New York Press.

Cox, C. (1992). Attainment through abandonment: The Sarvastivadin path of removing defilements. In R. E. Buswell, Jr., & R. M. Gimello (Eds.), *Studies in East Asian Buddhism: Vol. 7. Paths to liberation: The Marga and its transformations in Buddhist thought* (pp. 63–105). Honolulu: University of Hawaii Press.

Davidson, L. (1994). Philosophical foundations of humanistic psychology. In F. Wertz (Ed.), *The humanistic movement: Recovering the person in psychology* (pp. 24–44). Lake Worth, FL: Gardner Press.

Dean, T. (Ed.). (1995). *Religious pluralism and truth: Essays on cross-cultural philosophy of religion.* Albany: State University of New York Press.

DiCenso, J. (1990). *Hermeneutics and the disclosure of truth: A study in the work of Heidegger, Gadamer, and Ricoeur.* Charlottesville: University Press of Virginia.

Dupré, L. (1987). Mysticism. In M. Eliade (Ed.), *The encyclopedia of religion* (Vol. 10, pp. 245–261). New York: MacMillan Publishing Company.

Eliade, M. (1959). *The sacred and the profane.* New York: Harcourt Brace Jovanovich.

Epstein, M. (1986). Meditative transformations of narcissism. *The Journal of Transpersonal Psychology, 18*(2), 131–158.

Evans, D. (1993). *Spirituality and human nature.* Albany: State University of New York Press.

Faivre, A. (1994). *Access to western esoterism.* Albany: State University of New York Press.

Faivre, A., & Needleman, J. (Eds.). (1995). *World spirituality: An encyclopedic history of the religious quest: Vol. 21. Modern esoteric spirituality.* New York: Crossroad.

Ferrer, J. N. (1998a). Beyond absolutism and relativism in transpersonal evolutionary theory. *World Futures: Journal of General Evolution, 52,* 239–280.

Ferrer, J. N. (1998b). Speak now or forever hold your peace: A review essay of Ken Wilber's *The marriage of sense and soul: Integrating science and religion. The Journal of Transpersonal Psychology, 30*(1), 53–67.

Ferrer, J. N. (1999a). Teoría transpersonal y filosofía perenne: Una avaluación crítica. [Transpersonal theory and the perennial philosophy: A critical evaluation]. In M. Almendro (Ed.), *Psicología y conciencia* (pp. 72–92). Barcelona: Kairos.

Ferrer, J. N. (1999b). *Revisioning transpersonal theory: A participatory vision of human spirituality.* Manuscript in preparation.

Forman, R. K. C. (Ed.). (1990). *The problem of pure consciousness: Mysticism and philosophy.* New York: Oxford University Press.

Forman, R. K. C. (1993). Mystical knowledge: Knowledge by identity. *Journal of the American Academy of Religion, 61*(4), 705–738.

Forman, R. K. C. (Ed.). (1998). *The innate capacity: Mysticism, psychology, and philosophy.* New York: Oxford University Press.

Fort, A. O. (1996). [Review of the book *The philosophy of religion and advaita vedanta: A comparative study in religion and reason*]. *Journal of Religion, 76*(4), 664–665.

Gadamer, H. G. (1990). *Truth and method* (2nd Rev. ed.). New York: Crossroad.

Gill, J. H. (1984). Mysticism and mediation. *Faith & Philosophy, 1,* 111–121.

Griffiths, P. J. (1986). *On being mindless: Buddhist meditation and the mind-body problem.* La Salle, IL: Open Court.

Griffiths, P. J. (1991). *An apology for apologetics: A study in the logic of interreligious dialogue.* New York: Orbis Books.

Grinshpon, Y. (1997). Experience and observation in traditional and modern Patañjala yoga. In E. Franco, & K. Preisendanz (Eds.), *Poznan Studies in the Philosophy of the Sciences and the Humanities: Vol. 59. Beyond orientalism: The work of Wilhelm Halbfass and its impact on cross-cultural studies* (pp. 557–566). Amsterdam: Rodopi.

Grof, S. (1972). Varieties of transpersonal experiences: Observations from LSD psychotherapy. *The Journal of Transpersonal Psychology, 4*(1), 45–80.

Grof, S. (1985). *Beyond the brain: Birth, death, and transcendence in psychotherapy.* Albany: State University of New York Press.

Grof, S. (1988). *The adventure of self-discovery: Dimensions of consciousness and new perspectives in psychotherapy and inner exploration.* Albany: State University of New York Press.

Grof, S. (1998). *The cosmic game: Explorations of the frontiers of human consciousness.* Albany: State University of New York Press.

Grof, S., & Grof, C. (Eds.). (1989). *Spiritual emergency: When personal transformation becomes a crisis.* Los Angeles: Jeremy P. Tarcher.

Gyatso, J. (1999). Healing burns with fire: The facilitation of experience in Tibetan Buddhism. *Journal of the American Academy of Religion, 67*(1), 113–147.

Habermas, J. (1984). *The theory of communicative action (Vol. 1). Reason and the rationalization of society* (T. McCarthy, Trans.). Boston: Beacon Press.

Habermas. J. (1987a). *The philosophical discourse of modernity: Twelve lectures* (F. Lawrence, Trans.). Cambridge, MA: MIT Press.

Habermas, J. (1987b). *The theory of communicative action (Vol. 2). Lifeworld and system: A critique of functionalist reason* (T. McCarthy, Trans). Boston: Beacon Press.

Ha'iri Yazdi, M. (1992). *The principles of epistemology in Islamic philosophy: Knowledge by presence.* Albany: State University of New York Press.

Halbfass, W. (1988). *India and Europe: An essay in understanding.* Albany: State University of New York Press.

Halifax, J. (1998). *A Buddhist life in America: Simplicity in the complex.* New York: Paulist Press.

Harman, W. W. (1988). The transpersonal challenge to the scientific paradigm: The need for a restructuring of science. *ReVision, 11*(2), 13–21.

Harman, W. W. (1994). The scientific exploration of consciousness: Towards an adequate epistemology. *Journal of Consciousness Studies, 1*(4), 140–148.

Harvey, P. (1995). *The selfless mind: Personality, consciousness, and nirvana in early Buddhism.* Richmond, Surrey: Curzon Press.

Hayes, R. P. (1997). Whose experience validates what for dharmakirti? In P. Bilimoria, & J. N. Mohanty (Eds.), *Relativism, suffering and beyond: Essays in memory of Bimal K. Matilal* (pp. 105–118). Delhi, India: Oxford University Press.

Heim, S. M. (1995). *Salvations: Truth and difference in religion.* New York: Orbis Books.

Helminiak, D. A. (1996). *The human core of spirituality.* Albany: State University of New York Press.

Hershock, P. D. (1996). *Liberating intimacy: Enlightenment and social virtuosity in Ch'an Buddhism.* Albany: State University of New York Press.

Hoffman, F. J. (1982). The Buddhist empiricist thesis. *Religious Studies, 18,* 151–158.

Holdrege, B. A. (1996). *Veda and Torah: Transcending the textuality of scripture.* Albany: State University of New York Press.

Hollenback, J. B. (1996). *Mysticism: Experience, response, and empowerment.* University Park: Pennsylvania State University Press.

Hopkins, T. J. (1971). *The Hindu religious tradition.* New York: Harper & Row.

Hunt, H. T. (1995). *On the nature of consciousness. Cognitive, phenomenological, and transpersonal perspectives.* New Haven, CT: Yale University Press.

Idel, M. (1996). Universalization and integration: Two conceptions of mystical union in Jewish mysticism. In M. Idel, & B. McGinn (Eds.), *Mystical union in Judaism, Christianity, and Islam: An ecumenical dialogue* (pp. 27–57). New York: Continuum.

Indich, W. M. (1980). *Consciousness in Advaita Vedanta.* Columbia, MI: South Asia Books.

Irwin, L. (1996). *Visionary worlds: The making and unmaking of reality.* Albany: State University of New York Press.

Jayatilleke, K. N. (1963). *Early Buddhist theory of knowledge.* London: Allen & Unwin.

John of the Cross, St. (1979). The ascent to Mount Carmel. In the collected works of St. John of the Cross (pp. 65–292). (K. Kavanaugh, & O. Rodriquez, Trans.). Washington, D.C.: ICS Publications. (Original work published 1585)

Johnston, W. (1995). *Mystical theology: The science of love.* Maryknoll, NY: Orbis Books.

Jones, R. J. (1993). *Mysticism examined: Philosophical inquires into mysticism.* Albany: State University of New York Press.

Kalasuriya, A. D. P. (1981). On the notion of verification in Buddhism and in logical positivism. In N. Katz (Ed), *Buddhism and western philosophy* (pp. 287–305). Delhi, India: Stirling.

Kalasuriya, A. D. P. (1987). *A philosophical analysis of Buddhist notions.* Delhi, India: Sri Satguru Publications.

Kalupahana, D. J. (1975). *Causality: The central philosophy in Buddhism.* Honolulu: University of Hawaii Press.

Kalupahana, D. J. (1986). *Nagarjuna: The philosophy of the middle way.* Albany: State University of New York Press.

Katz, S. T. (Ed.). (1978) *Mysticism and philosophical analysis.* New York: Oxford University Press.

Katz, S. T. (Ed.). (1983). *Mysticism and religious traditions.* New York: Oxford University Press.

Klein, A. (1986). *Knowledge and liberation: Tibetan Buddhist epistemology in support of transformative religious experience.* Ithaca, NY: Snow Lion Publications.

Lajoie, D. H., & Shapiro, S. Y. (1992). Definitions of transpersonal psychology: The first twenty-three years. *The Journal of Transpersonal Psychology, 24*(1), 79–98.

Lakoff, G., & Johnson, M. (1980). *Metaphors we live by.* Chicago: University of Chicago Press.

Levin, D. M. (1988). Transpersonal phenomenology: The corporeal scheme. *Humanistic Psychologist, 18*(2), 282–313.

Maritain, J. (1959). *The degrees of knowledge* (G. B. Phelan, Trans) (4th ed.). New York: Scribner. (original work published 1932)

Maslow, A. H. (1968). *Towards a psychology of being.* (2nd ed.). New York: D. Van Nostrand.

Maslow, A. H. (1970). *Religion, values, and peak experiences.* New York: The Viking Press.

Maturana, H., & Varela, F. J. (1987). *The tree of knowledge: The biological roots of human understanding.* Boston: Shambhala.

Mayeda, S. (1992). (Ed.). *A thousand teachings: The upadesasahasri of Sankara* (S. Mayeda, Trans.). Albany: State University of New York Press.

McGinn, B. (1994). *The foundations of mysticism. The presence of God: A history of western Christian mysticism* (Vol. 1). New York: Crossroad.

McGinn, B. (1996a). *The growth of mysticism. The presence of God: A history of western Christian mysticism* (Vol. 2). New York: Crossroad.

McGinn, B. (1996b). Love, knowledge and *unio mystica* in the western Christian tradition. In M. Idel, & B. McGinn (Eds.), *Mystical union in Judaism, Christianity, and Islam: An ecumenical dialogue* (pp. 59–86). New York: Continuum.

Mendes-Flohr, P. (1989). *From mysticism to dialogue: Martin Buber's transformation of German social thought.* Detroit: Wayne State University Press.

Nasr, H. H. (1989). *Knowledge and the sacred.* Albany: State University of New York Press.

Nyanaponika Thera. (1962). *The heart of Buddhist meditation.* London: Rider.

Olsen, W. S. (1996). *The sacred place: Witnessing the holy in the physical world.* Salt Lake City: University of Utah Press.

Paranjpe, A. C. (1984). *Theoretical psychology: The meeting of east and west.* New York: Plenum Press.

Paranjpe, A. C. (1988). A personality theory according to Vedanta. In A. C. Paranjpe, D. Y. F. Ho, & R. W. Rieber (Eds.), *Asian contributions to psychology* (pp. 185–213). New York: Praeger.

Patañjali. (1977). *The yoga-system of Patañjali* (J. Haughton, Trans). Delhi, India: Motilal Banarsidass.

Perovich, A. N. Jr. (1985). Mysticism or mediation: A response to Gill. *Faith & Philosophy, 2,* 179–188.

Potter, K. H. (1991). *Presuppositions of India's philosophies.* Delhi, India: Motilal Banarsidass.

Proudfoot, W. (1985). *Religious experience.* Berkeley: University of California Press.

Radhakrishnan, S. (1971). *Indian philosophy* (Vol. 2). New York: Humanities Press. (original work published 1923)

Radhakrishnan, S. (1957). *An idealist view of life* (5th ed.). London: George Allen and Unwin. (original work published 1929)

Rambachan, A. (1991). *Accomplishing the accomplished: The vedas as a source of valid knowledge in Sankara.* Honolulu: University of Hawaii Press.

Rambachan, A. (1994). *The limits of scripture.* Honolulu: University of Hawaii Press.

Ring, K. (1998). *Lessons from the light: What we can learn from the near-death experience.* New York: Insight Books.

Rorty, R. (1979). *Philosophy and the mirror of nature.* Princeton, NJ: Princeton University Press.

Rothberg, D. (1989). Understanding mysticism: Transpersonal theory and the limits of contemporary epistemological frameworks. *ReVision, 12*(2), 5–21.

Rothberg, D. (1993). The crisis of modernity and the emergence of socially engaged spirituality. *ReVision, 15*(3), 105–114.

Rothberg, D. (1996). Toward an integral spirituality. *ReVision, 19*(2), 41–42.

Sells, M. A. (1994). *Mystical languages of unsaying.* Chicago: University of Chicago Press.

Shapiro, S. I. (1994). Religion, spirituality, and transpersonal psychology. *International Journal of Transpersonal Studies, 13*(1), 33–41.

Sharf, R. H. (1995a). Buddhist modernism and the rhetoric of meditative experience. *Numen, 42*(3), 228–283.

Sharf, R. H. (1995b). Sambokyodan: Zen and the way of the new religions. *Japanese Journal of Religious Studies, 22*(3–4), 417–458.

Sharf, R. H. (1998). Experience. In M. C. Taylor (Ed.), *Critical terms for religious studies* (pp. 94–116). Chicago: University of Chicago Press.

Sharma, A. (1993). *The experiential dimension of Advaita Vedanta.* Delhi, India: Motilal Banarsidass.

Sharma, A. (1995). *The philosophy of religion and Advaita Vedanta: A comparative study in religion and reason.* University Park: Pennsylvania State University Press.

Short, L. (1996). Mysticism, mediation, and the non-linguistic. *Journal of the American Academy of Religion, 63*(4), 659–675.

Smart, N. (1992). *Doctrine and argument in Indian philosophy* (2nd rev. ed.). New York: E. J. Brill. (original work published 1964)

Staal, F. (1975). *Exploring mysticism.* Berkeley: University of California Press.

Swan, J. A. (1988). Sacred places in nature and transpersonal experiences. *ReVision, 10*(3), 21–26.

Swan, J. A. (1990). *Sacred Places.* Santa Fe: Bear & Co.

Swan, J. A. (1991). *The power of place: Sacred ground in natural and human environments.* Wheaton, IL: Quest.

Tart, C. T. (1971). Scientific foundations for the study of altered states of consciousness. *The Journal of Transpersonal Psychology, 3*(2), 93–124.

Tart, C. T. (1977). Science, states of consciousness, and spiritual experiences: The need for state-specific sciences. In C. T. Tart (Ed.), *Transpersonal psychologies* (pp. 9–58). New York: Harper & Row.

Tart, C. T. (1983). *States of consciousness.* El Cerrito, CA: Psychological Processes Incorporated.

Valle, R. (1995). Towards a transpersonal-phenomenological psychology: On transcendent awareness, passion, and peace of mind. *Journal of East-West Psychology, 1*(1), 9–15.

Varela, F. J., Thompson, E., & Rosch, E. (1991). *The embodied mind: Cognitive science and human experience.* Cambridge, MA: MIT Press.

Vroom, H. M. (1989). *Religions and the truth: Philosophical reflections and perspectives.* Grand Rapids, MI: William B. Eerdmans Publishing Company.

Walsh, R., & Vaughan, F. (1993). On transpersonal definitions. *The Journal of Transpersonal Psychology, 25*(2), 199–207.

Washburn, M. (1995). *The ego and the dynamic ground: A transpersonal theory of human development* (2nd ed.). Albany: State University of New York Press.

Weber, M. (1978). *Economy and society* (R. Wittich, & C. Wittich, Eds.). Berkeley: University of California Press.

Whitehead, A. N. (1926). *Religion in the making.* New York: Macmillan.

Wilber, K. (1986). The spectrum of psychopathology. In K. Wilber, J. Engler, & D. Brown, *Transformations of consciousness: Conventional and contemplative perspectives on development* (pp. 107–126). Boston: Shambhala.

Wilber, K. (1995). *Sex, ecology and spirituality: The spirit of evolution.* Boston: Shambhala.

Wilber, K. (1996a). *A brief history of everything.* Berkeley: Shambhala.

Wilber, K. (1996b). *The atman project: A transpersonal view of human development* (2nd ed.). Wheaton, IL: Quest.

Wilber, K. (1996c). *Up from eden* (2nd ed.). Wheaton, IL: Quest.

Wilber, K. (1997a). *The eye of the spirit: An integral vision for a world gone slightly mad.* Berkeley: Shambhala.

Wilber, K. (1997b). An Integral Theory of Consciousness. *Journal of Consciousness Studies, 4*(1), 71–92.

Williams, P. (1989). *Mahayana Buddhism: The doctrinal foundations.* New York: Routledge.

Zinnbauer, B. J., Pargament, K. I., Cole, B., Rye, M. S., Butter, E. M., Belavich, T. G., Hipp, K. M., Scott, A. B., & Kadar, J. L. (1997). Religion and spirituality: Unfuzzying the fuzzy. *Journal for the Scientific Study of Religion, 36*(4), 549–564.

11

Deep Empathy

TOBIN HART

Most of us notice that when we pay attention and simply open ourselves to the person in front of us, we come closer to understanding their experience. This seems simple enough; although, for me at least, it can be easily forgotten when I become caught up in agendas and the hurry of daily activity. But when such an opening does occur, there are sometimes moments when understanding of the other deepens beyond what I can easily explain. I seem to experience the other's feelings directly in my own body or recognize patterns, histories, or meanings that do not appear to come from interpreting the words and gestures that we exchange. I remember this phenomenon happening spontaneously in my first psychotherapy internship, when I would experience an unusual connection with some clients. The moments seemed timeless; light in the room changed; background sounds retreated; and the boundaries between us seemed to collapse. I recall a sense of the client and myself being in a kind of luminous egg. Later, I experienced the deep connection as an exchange, like spiral waves flowing back and forth. Later still, I usually became less aware of the sensations and instead entered a more open awareness.

Beyond the exceptional depth that this knowing seemed to provide to the therapy, I came to rely on these connections as a kind of sustenance. At that time in my life, these were the moments when I felt most human, most intimate with the world, and I probably stayed working as a therapist for many years because this practice brought my heart and wisdom to the surface. When the office door closed, I could often depend on a shift in knowing. The focus, intention, and simple curiosity for what the encounter would bring helped to engender genuine meeting; and as Buber (1923/1958) suggests, "All real living is meeting" (p. 11). In retrospect, I see that even the bread and butter of empathic practice—active listening—functioned like some martial art or Zen practice that absorbed my attention and allowed the world of my internal chatter to dissipate, inviting an expansion of awareness.

Such experience is consistent with Tart's (1990) call for the development of "everyday" awareness practices that are appropriate to our non-monastic culture. In addition to the powerful benefit that this knowing provides to the therapeutic relationship, deep empathy may also serve as an opportunity for expanding the therapist's mindfulness or awareness (see Schuster, 1979). And once the therapist achieves a level of proficiency in a session, the next challenge may be to extend the practice outside the safe confines of therapy into meeting the world at large.

Empathy is almost universally considered central to psychotherapeutic practice; it has also been described as the base of moral development (Hoffman, 1990) and may even be the trait that makes us most human (Azar, 1997). However, the quality and content of empathy varies tremendously from one person and from one moment to the next. This variation grows largely from differences in how one knows the other, that is, differences in the specific activity of empathic knowing.

Empathy, while having many shades of meaning (see Bohart & Greenberg, 1997; Gladstein & Associates, 1987, for good summaries), is generally conceived of as understanding and "feeling into" another's world. The process of empathic knowing is most often assumed to be dependent on two complementary functions: affective sensitivity and cognitive perspective taking. The ability to listen for and have sensitivity to emotional material is common in this knowing, and as feeling capacity expands and skill at listening increases, the quality of empathy improves. In addition, taking another's perspective is conventionally understood as projecting oneself into the client's shoes by comparing one's own past experiences with the client's descriptions in order to infer what he or she might be experiencing. We also know, as this book provides argument and evidence for, the activity of knowing stretches beyond conventional conceptions. For example, many theorists have projected cognitive development beyond Piaget's formal operations (e.g., Commons, Richards, & Armon, 1984; Gebser, 1991; Wilber, 1995). There has also been a renewed appreciation for feeling capacity and the intertwining of affect and cognition (e.g., Goleman, 1995). If empathy is dependent on both affective and cognitive capacities, then it is reasonable to consider the implications for higher-order empathic potential. This chapter offers a sketch of this landscape, tracing the activity of knowing into deep empathy. While the discussion focuses primarily on the therapeutic encounter, implications for deep empathy extend into any meeting.

Empathic Foundations

Theories from object relations to transpersonal psychology presume that the newborn experiences the world in a pre-egoic fusion with the primary caregiver and the world in general. Hoffman (1990) refers to the capacity for empathic distress at this stage of development as *Global* and suggests that infants may "at times react as if what happened to the other happened to themselves" (p. 155). This capacity demonstrates primitive empathic distress but not empathic understanding in which one has both an experience and an awareness of the experience. Empathy involves both a perception of the other—empathic receptivity, sensitivity, awareness, listening with the "third ear," and so forth—and an understanding of that perception (and often, to be most useful in therapy, a communication of it back to the client). One may, for example, pick up a strong sensation from someone else but not recognize it as being the experience of the other person. On the other hand, one may have great interpretive capacity without much sensitivity and openness.

There may be a similar empathic fusion in adults who have unusually permeable boundaries and a symbiotic relational style (e.g., see Johnson, 1994). In conventional diagnostic formulations this fusion occurs with some regularity in borderline or dependent personality disorders. Symbiotic character styles may "know" the other by introjecting or swallowing whole the other's experience, without digesting the experience so as to understand or appreciate it as the other's, and then proceed to project their own experience onto the other.

As the self or ego differentiates, the child becomes aware of others as distinct from himself or herself and becomes capable of cognitive representation. As Hoffman (1990) describes, "the child may now begin to be aware that although he or she feels distressed it is not he or she but someone else who is in actual danger or pain" (p. 155). However, the *egocentric* or normal narcissistic nature of this knowing precludes the recognition of the other's internal states (Zann-Waxler, Radke-Yarrow, & King, 1979 provide some empirical evidence of this style).

As cognitive capacity develops so does the ability for role taking: "One becomes aware that other people's feelings may differ from one's own and are based on their own needs and interpretation of events" (Hoffman, 1990, p. 155). As one's own range of feeling capacity is differentiated, there grows capacity for empathy with increasingly subtle and diverse emotions. For example, a more nebulous sensitivity to another's pain, characteristic of more rudimentary empathy, may then be more precisely perceived as disappointment, longing, grief, and so forth. Hoffman (1990) describes such *empathy for another's feeling* as setting the stage for empathy regarding another's life condition in which the empathic individual combines immediate affective response with a general representation of the plight of the other outside the immediate context (e.g., an understanding of poverty or oppression). Here, the story of empathy in therapy really begins.

As just mentioned, most descriptions of empathy imply affective sensitivity and also sophisticated perspective taking, which formal operational cognition enables. One of Rogers's (1959) early descriptions captures the feel of this:

> The state of empathy, or being empathic, is to perceive the internal frame of reference of another with accuracy and with the emotional components and meanings which pertain thereto as if one were the person, but without ever losing the "as if" condition. . . . If this "as if" quality is lost, then the state is one of identification. (210–211)

Mahrer, Boulet, and Fairweather (1994) have referred to this style as *external* empathy, as the therapist recognizes but remains outside the experience of the other. Kohut (1984) suggests that empathy means to "think and feel oneself into the inner life of another person" (p. 82) through "vicarious introspection." As such, we know the other "because they are given to us in terms of the storehouse of images and memories that we have acquired through . . . our own introspection" (Kohut, 1980, p. 458). In describing this level of empathic knowing, Guntrip (1969) tells us that "Our understanding is an inference based on our knowledge of ourselves" (pp. 370–371). Therefore, I know the other through comparing what I understand of their experiences to my own (i.e., a logical inference and extrapolation). This requires a clear separate sense of self, against which I can compare my sense of the other's experience. This knowing is predicated on a split between self and other. The therapist attempts to be an objective observer who compares what he or she imagines that the client experiences to his or her own experience. Paradoxically, as Kohn (1990) points out, this type of empathic closeness is, in part, dependent on an ability to distance oneself from others in order to observe them "objectively." While this knowing seems safe and reasonable, its assumptions may limit empathic capacity. In addition, "there is real danger that one's cognitive and imaginative capacities will become so sophisticated that one has ceased sharing the experiences of real people" (p. 119).

Deep Empathy

At this point, a line is crossed toward a more direct knowing of the other that a postconventional epistemic process enables. The activity of knowing moves toward subject-object transcendence or a loosening of self-other boundaries. I have outlined several variations on the experience, although the distinctions between them are not necessarily sharp. In addition, the organization implies an increasing degree of refinement, but this is not to be taken as a purely linear or hierarchical progression.

As the distance between subject and object—between therapist and client—is reduced, there opens up the opportunity to know the client more directly. Therapists may attempt to put themselves "in the client's shoes," as Mahrer et al. (1994) have noted, or may experience *inclusion* into the life of the other (Heard, 1993). One does not achieve this experience via an observation of the other followed by a comparison of that individual's experience to one's own, as Guntrip described; instead one sees the world through the eyes of the client while retaining one's own identity. As Mahrer et al. (1994) write: "The therapist senses what it is like to be where the person is, yet always maintains [his or her] own individuality" (p. 189). It involves going back and forth between sensing what it is like to be in the patient's shoes and processing the material thereby disclosed (p. 189). While the separate self is maintained, the intent is to open to the other. Buber (1988) described this as "a bold swinging, demanding the most intense stirring of one's being into the life of the other" (p. 71). This is largely accomplished by a process of imagination and modeling, or mirroring the client in order to better experience the world through his or her eyes. It involves "imagining what the client is wishing, feeling, and perceiving so vividly and concretely that you experience the existence of the client as your own while remaining in your own existence" (Heard, 1995, p. 251).

A therapist may directly experience particular emotions, thoughts, and body sensations that seem to come from the client. One may, for example, feel the dissociated "fogging out" or the rage of the client in his or her own body, profoundly becoming participant-observer as the therapist attempts to walk with clients through their world space. The potential for distortion and the basic confusion regarding "what is mine and what is theirs" has significance throughout these stages, and one must constantly "check out" material with the client and "check in" with oneself. See Hart (1997b) for an elaboration of distortions and dangers.

In empathic inclusion it is easier to experience the unconditional positive regard, even love, that Rogers advocated so strongly. With deep empathy, however, love begins to emerge not as a result of an attitude of practice but as a consequence of knowing the other more directly. It may be experienced as an awakening of natural compassion (Dass & Gorman, 1996) or as an opening of the heart chakra described in tantric yogic tradition (see Nelson, 1994).

Rogers experienced this love or acceptance in moments of deep empathy with clients and understood the attitude of unconditional positive regard

as necessary for person-centered psychotherapy. He did not articulate as
clearly that this prizing emerged naturally as part of this deep empathic connection. This describes precisely the experience of moving from "I-It" to
"I-Thou" for Buber (1923/1958). The person-centered emphasis on unconditional positive regard in training therapists identifies an outcome or attitude, but this does not necessarily mean that one will have such an
experience. Aspiring therapists may achieve greater success if training focuses on the process of knowing itself, out of which the love or prizing may
grow organically and spontaneously.

Traditionally, a therapist's own reactions have been seen as needing to
be discarded or dominated so the therapist could view the other objectively.
However, the possibility for empathic understanding through *deep reactivity*
occurs when reactions are allowed to be experienced fully and understood,
at times, as representing a response that other individuals may have toward
the client or that the client may experience toward himself or herself. Therapists are often discouraged from being reactive to a client and encouraged
to maintain steady "objectivity." Of course, sometimes a therapist's reactions
serve as projections and do need to be sorted out or they will distort the empathic exchange. This whole process can be engaged in as a kind of awareness practice. Falling deeply into the scene, including experiencing our
reactivity to the client, can fuel the immediacy and richness of the encounter. A microcosm of the client's world may open up in this intersubjective space; and if the therapist is able to maintain some awareness, he or she
has the possibility of using his or her reactions as rich empathic information. Rogers (1980), who strongly objected to the more traditional understanding of counter-transference, describes the power of his own reactions:

> When I can relax and be close to the transcendental core of me,
> then I may behave in strange and impulsive ways in the relation-
> ship, ways in which I can not justify rationally, which have nothing
> to do with my rational thought processes. But these strange be-
> haviors turn out to be right, in some odd way. (p. 129)

Tansey and Burke (1989) elaborate Heinmann's (1950) view of the alternative epistemic process at work: "'the analyst's unconscious understands that of his patient' on a much deeper and more accurate level than
the analyst's conscious reasoning" (Tansey & Burke, 1989, p. 23). The term
projective identification has been used to describe this process, although the
meaning of this term varies tremendously, largely depending on what epistemic process is assumed to be at work (see e.g., Reik, 1948; Scharff, 1992;
Segal, 1964; Tansey & Burke, 1989). Scharff (1992) reports that in projective identification her impressions or fantasies may be "elicited by [the
other's] fantasies in unconscious communication" (p. 11). Segal (1964)

understands that "in projective identification, parts of the [client's] self and internal objects are split off and projected onto the external object [i.e., the therapist], which then becomes possessed by, controlled and identified with the projected parts" (p. 14). This "possession" characterizes just the quality of being carried along, or reacting in unexpected ways as Rogers describes herein.

This process can be understood through the concept of intersubjectivity as well as contemporary field theory. In such a view "patient and therapist together form a psychological system" (Trop & Stolorow, 1997, p. 279). The therapist has the ability to make use of information in this system by gaining awareness of his or her reactions. Achieving this requires not a distant observing stance but another form of participant-observation; the therapist enters the play rather than remaining in the background. Winnicott hints at this when he tells us that, "psychotherapy is done in the overlap of two play areas, that of the patient and that of the therapist. If the therapist cannot play he is not suitable for the work" (cited in Davis & Wallbridge, 1981, p. 65). Winnicott (1971) refers to the area where genuine encounter takes place as "potential space." Similar spacial metaphors include Heidegger's (1977) "clearing" and Buber's (1923/1958) "between." In this space the therapist makes particular note of his or her own reactions to the client and then must extrapolate understanding, as Scharff (1992) describes: "Metabolizing my own experience . . . I arrive at understanding" (p. 12). In order to do so Racker (1968) suggests that the therapist must "make himself [i.e., his own countertransference and subjectivity] the object of his continual observation" (p. 132). This requires "continuity and depth of his conscious contact with himself" (p. 131).

In many of his writings, Rogers describes empathy as a process of moving beyond a sense of self-separateness: "It means entering the private perceptual world of the other and being thoroughly at home in it. . . . It means temporarily living the other's life" (Rogers, 1980, p. 142). He moves from "as if" (an imaginative indirect knowing, a logical extrapolation) to actually entering the client's world—an act of alignment. In so doing the self no longer serves merely as an instrument for analysis and distant sensory observation, but becomes a direct participant in the other's world. As the therapist enters deeply into the client's world, he or she experiences becoming the other and forming one merged self. Watkins (1978) has described this as "co-feeling" or "co-understanding." The extent of the momentary collapse of the self, and the degree of participation rather than observation, depends largely on the therapist's ability to suspend his or her separate self. In Rogers's words, "you lay aside your self" (1980, p. 143). Whereas in the previous stages mentioned, the separate self serves as the reference point or reactor by which understanding of the other's experience is deduced, *alignment* can occur here because the other does not threaten the self as much. As ego defensiveness and fear decrease, one becomes free to experience the other more directly and spontaneously.

This experience is sometimes described as a "fusion" or "merging" or "melding" with the other, although distinguishing between pre-egoic (such as in Hoffman's description above) and trans-egoic fusion is important. Wilber (1995) refers to the blurring of these types of experiences as the pre/trans fallacy. Washburn (1995) suggests that the difference lies in mindless fusion (in the infant or regressed state) versus mindful (in the trans-egoic experience) fusion. The potential for distortion, such as narcissistic projection or a kind of invasiveness, in this type of empathy is significant (see Hart, 1997b).

In this kind of alignment, Mahrer (1993) suggests that "the therapist literally enters completely into being the person" (p. 33). "Instead of being empathic with the person, you are fully being the person. Instead of knowing the person's world, you are living it" (p. 34). You suspend your self-separateness and cross the threshold of subject-object dichotomy. In Mahrer's method, both therapist and client attend not to each other, but to a third center of attention: the patient's illness, problem, or life situation. "The therapist [allows] what the patient is saying to come in and through the therapist" (Mahrer et al., 1994, p. 193). In another technique, Sprinkle (1985) reports that he "mentally views the client and [him]self as one personality" (p. 207). "When I mentally pictured myself as the client to focus on his or her concerns, I learned that various thoughts and images came into my awareness" (p. 206). The therapist describes what he or she senses, feels, and thinks through the client's viewpoint.

It is important to note that deep empathy is not a particular technique but an activity of more direct knowing that involves a shift in being, consciousness, or awareness. One technique or another may help only to the extent that they engender such a shift in the activity of knowing.

For some therapists, deep empathic experience does not involve a state of fusion but a refined sympathetic resonance (see e.g., Larson, 1987; Rowan, 1986; Sprinkle, 1985). The phenomenon of sympathetic acoustical resonance parallels empathic resonance. With two violins located in the same room, a string plucked on one will vibrate the string tuned to the same frequency on the other and sound the same note. In a similar phenomenon, therapists may find themselves particularly sensitive to certain information in the other, such as specific emotions, and quickly resonate with and recognize these sensations in the client. Some therapists may be sensitive to feelings in general, others to a wide range of experiences (e.g., thoughts, perceptual style). Others become skillful at tuning into relevant material in a variety of forms. Not merely imagining, extrapolating, or interpreting cues, the epistemic process unfolds more directly. Subjectivity is suspended in order to attune with the other. Gestalt therapy recognizes this experience as using the self as "resonance chamber" (Polster & Polster, 1973, p. 18). Unlike the transient fusion in the experience of alignment, the phenomenology of *attunement* describes the experience of two selves connecting at a particular "frequency" of experience. Such models as field theory (e.g., Sheldrake, 1988; Smith & Smith, 1996) imply that we are connected through a variety of fields (e.g., electromagnetic, psychic). In such a reality it is not necessary to become the other or move into their "space," instead one interconnects through a kind of frequency attunement.

Husserl's (1929/1967) concept of intersubjectivity points to a general field or ground of subjectivity that also constitutes part of our individual subjectivity. He referred to the authentic meeting in that space as transcendental empathy. And as Rogers (1980) concluded, it represents not so much a state as it is a process. Deep empathy as authentic knowing is "not a state of consciousness but an activity of awareness that can integrate states of consciousness" (Puhakka, in this volume). The duality of self and not-self shifts in such direct knowing into an intersubjective experience—what Thich Nhat Hanh (1995) names as "interbeing," which refers to the fundamental connectedness of all things. As Rogers (1980) described, "it seems that my inner spirit has reached out and touched the inner spirit of the other. Our relationship transcends itself and becomes part of something larger" (p. 129).

Empathy, refined still further, involves neither objective observation, nor seeing the world through the client's eyes, nor reacting to, nor fusing with, nor attuning to; instead, the center of perception seems to occupy multiple perspectives simultaneously. One seems to become the field itself while maintaining awareness since one is less identified with the perspective from a single self or vantage point. Aurobindo says: "In order to see, you have to stop being in the middle of the picture" (in Nelson, 1994, p. 311). *Witnessing* is experienced with more emotional detachment, although it would be erroneous to confuse it with a distinct subject-object schism of more inferential or conventional empathy. As an example, Myss (1996) describes her experiences as having the quality of "impersonal daydreams" (p. 2). She suggests that "their impersonality, the nonfeeling sensation of the impressions is extremely significant" (p. 2) as an indicator of the epistemic process of receiving information.

Phenomenologically, information is often encountered as if it were coming from another source, perceived as outside or deep inside; this experience sounds similar to the phenomenon of inspiration (see Hart, in this volume). Some describe this process as the therapist's higher self tuning into the client's higher self. This may be invited by simply asking a question to oneself: "How can I be of help to this person; what should I be aware of?"

Developmentally, this knowing may correspond to experiences of Rowan's (1993) Surrendered Self and probably to the late Psychic and early Subtle stages of Wilber's (1995) developmental model, although I will not elaborate these here. As the therapist opens to this field of consciousness, other kinds of material become available (unexpected images, including possible archetypal themes, deep patterns, etc.) that may not be available to the client's immediate awareness. While one may be able to hypothesize origins and patterns in conventional empathy, in "witnessing," recognizing and appreciating multiple layers and patterns of experience intuitively and immediately becomes increasingly possible. For example, the strong imagery and body sensations so rich and available at previous levels may be recognized as constructed phenomena or consequences that have roots in fundamental beliefs or patterns of thought. The therapist becomes less likely to get carried away emotionally as the primary or exclusive emphasis shifts somewhat from feelings and thoughts to include the more subtle patterns that may underlie them.

As the gap between subject and object (or, self and other) is crossed and we become more available to the world at large, we may discover that our empathic meeting is not limited to the person sitting in front of us. For example, we may experience empathy for another at a distance, experience others not seemingly available to our senses, and experience openness to the world in general.

The evidence of nonlocal influence suggests that our direct connection with another is not confined to physical proximity. That special relationship we seem to have with our sibling or old friend and the synchronistic events such as shared dreams or telesomatic experiences (e.g., feeling your child's injury at a distance) provide anecdotal hints of nonlocal connection. From the fundamentals of quantum physics (e.g., Bell's theorem in which particles that have been in contact remain in communication even at a distance) to Sheldrake's field theory (1988) to shared dreams (e.g., Ullman & Krippner, 1989) to the effect of prayer on healing (Dossey, 1993), we find increasing support for the concept of nonlocal empathy. We can take this same principle out a bit farther and consider the experience of those who claim visitation by angels, hear voices of disembodied entities, and so forth. While validity claims and verification require a subtle science, this should not dissuade us from seeking evidence and understanding of these phenomena as some researchers have done (e.g., Alschuler, 1987; Liester, 1996; Nelson, 1990). Evidence suggests that such knowing may operate in a process very similar to deep empathy. Finally, we discover that the world—from a plant, to our pet, to the planet—may be available to direct knowing. Nature mystics have described their deep understanding and love for the natural world. This may emerge, for example, as a sensitivity to certain plants or to the earth as a whole. To name just one example from the scientific world, geneticist Barbara McClintock described moments of contact with corn plants when she talked about "a feeling for the organism," and an "openness to let it come to you" (cited in Keller, 1983, p. 198). The rise in the environmental movement in part results from this expanded awareness and empathy.

Degrees of Complexity

The content revealed through deep empathy may take shape in varying degrees of complexity including: a vague sense, manifest form (discrete impressions), underlying structure (a merged complex), pattern (a complex in dynamic flow within a context), symbols (a unified representation or theme), energy (or energetic forms), and meaning. Following an empathic feeling with one particular client gives these facets some color.

As I sit with a young woman a *vague sense* of discomfort comes into my feeling awareness. As we both stay with this, a *form* becomes clear; in this case the form is a feeling of anxiety and terror. In addition to feeling, empathy does not confine its sensory impressions to the five senses but may include subtle variations and combinations that reflect an expanded sensory sensitivity. It includes temperature, balance, movement, and directionality and perceptual combinations often take shape as a transient synesthetic event where shapes, colors, and feeling, or movement and sound, for example, merge into one another. One may experience initial sensations through a particular sense modality (e.g., kinesthetic) and then move to a more synesthetic impression in which one has a blended sensory perception.

Beyond sensory and feeling perceptions, thoughts may emerge as discrete words or more complex ideas. As one therapist described to me, "I sometimes 'hear' what the client is going to say before they say it, not just the general idea, but the exact phrase. At other times words, names, or ideas float in that seem to belong to the client." The *structure* of this specific feeling, thought, or image may come into awareness as a complex of feelings, sensations, and so forth. For example, the client's terror seems tied with feelings of inadequacy and existential responsibility; it draws the client's attention and provides a distorting center or anchor for her identity. The *pattern* of the feeling complex within various contexts (e.g., the historical replication of this terror in her life, a perceived karmic pattern, the origin and future potentiality or present consequence) may also become clear.

The pattern of one's "world space," or an overall conceptual schema may emerge. A therapist might experience directly (rather than as a logical deduction) not only discrete ideas but the pattern of the thinking and meaning-making. Or said another way, the perception is of how clients construct their mental world space. Their actions, beliefs, blocks, feelings, relationships, and so forth may make perfect sense given these mental patterns; in fact, they may be inevitable until the person modifies this superstructure. These structures are sometimes anchored by core beliefs (e.g., "I'm not good enough; I am unlovable") that have a tremendous density in the individual's mental space.

Symbolic representations of patterns and themes may emerge, such as the image of a frozen leaf that will shatter if it is touched but that will remain virtually dead if it is not moved from its situation. Symbolic impressions may often qualify as archetypal themes as well. These may also take the form of more abstract symbols of various sensory combinations—geometric shapes, movement, colors, and so forth, that may arise from some combination of symbol and *energetic* perception. There may be a symbolic or direct perception of the energetic experience of this feeling—in this case, the terror manifests as a dense imploding mass the size of a baseball that is lodged in the abdomen and that seems to serve as an energy sink, sucking the person's vitality into it. Or thoughts may be perceived as having an energetic physical reality. Finally, there may be some sense of the *meaning* presented for all this material, often in the form of a lesson to be learned or a pattern of thinking or action that is to be overcome. The client usually remains unaware of such meaning. This marks a distinction between empathizing with what resides in the immediate experience of the other (client-centered and existential therapies have focused on this) and shifting to a source of empathic understanding that may not be immediately available to the client's awareness.

Knowing and Being

As mentioned earlier, deep empathy is not a technique but a way of being. What follows names several qualities or dimensions that correspond with and seem to engender deep empathy.

In deep empathy there is a shift from the assimilating and categorizing of objects to a radical *accommodation* of the other (see Hart, 1997a). We move out of the steady mental processing of perceptions and thoughts, into meeting and receiving the other directly—a receptive mode as Deikman (1984, this volume) has named. Buber (1923/1958) tells us: "The relation to the Thou is direct. No system of ideas, no foreknowledge, and no fancy intervene between I and Thou" (p. 11). If we become preoccupied with thoughts of being an empathic therapist or trying to remember what the client said last time, we will distract ourselves from being fully present and making direct contact. This suggests that the degree to which we remain *present* to the other and to ourselves will impact the meeting. As we deeply and simply attend to the other, we may get absorbed in the meeting. Absorption has been identified with mystical and paranormal experience (see Nelson, 1990) because it permits a deep immersion in the field of experience. But while absorption enables rich experience, the information gained may not be easily used without *awareness*. An ability to maintain awareness (e.g., see Varela, Thompson, & Rosch, 1991) of our own processes, reactions, and those changes in the other enables us to be immersed in the meeting and witness it immediately in succession or even simultaneously. Perhaps the most familiar way to describe these aspects of being is to speak of the capacity and willingness to *listen*. Listening or paying attention permits empathy.

Deep empathy may involve both *reaching out* and *receiving in*. Husserl describes an "emotive and cognitive reaching out to the other in a self-transcending empathic understanding" (Kohak, 1984, p. 206). We may intend ourselves to make contact and this willfulness to risk may move us near the other; but the shift to receive the other, to experience our interconnection, feels more like a willingness than a willful intending or grasping. Receiving implies a temporary shift in cognitive style from mental processing or computing to receiving or allowing.

In deep empathy one opens the self to the other and transcends personal boundaries. Boundaries may be thought of as being more or less permeable or, as Hartmann (1984) has named, thick or thin. At the more permeable or thin end there is increased sensitivity that enables empathy as well as vulnerability. Some individuals find themselves particularly sensitive to the psychic distress of others, while some lie at the other end of the continuum and seem relatively impermeable, even impenetrable. Deeply empathic therapists have *permeable boundaries* and often are adept at regulating the degree of openness. And boundaries exist not only between ourselves and another person but also intrapsychically. Some rejected aspect of ourselves may form "an other," part of our shadow, until we empathize with, and eventually integrate it.

Like the mystical encounter, deep empathy is regularly described as including a feeling of *love* or appreciation, and of riveting *genuineness* or realness. The cohorts of deep empathy include love (sometimes described as communion), realness or authenticity, a sense of appreciation, and an unconditional, nonjudgmental acceptance. Again, this is the experience of moving from "It" to "Thou" for Buber. Simultaneously, mental processing and evaluating fades as we simply remain present and open. Personas may then recede, since they are created and maintained by mental processing.

So far these qualities have, for the most part, invited depth. However, if our epistemic style becomes deeply accommodative, it also becomes *flexible*.

A particular empathic focus may enable us to tune into particular dimensions of the other, such as strong feeling or bodily sensations. However, the most useful therapy often involves not only empathic depth but also flexibility or range. The therapist may attend not only to the content itself but to the form or style most relevant or understandable to the client. For example, insight into the origins of life scripts may help at one moment, deep feeling or pointing out a bodily sensation may help at another. This is not figuring out what is best for the client but allowing our deep connection with the client and our sustained and dynamic awareness to accommodate to the client's needs.

It becomes obvious that what the therapist perceives depends both on the client and on the therapist. That is, the therapist's subjectivity serves as a perceptual and interpretive filter, although the degree and style of filtering may vary greatly from one person to the next. Awareness and steady deconstructing and refining of the filtering system fine-tunes empathic capacities (not unlike what Nelson suggests regarding the opening into mystical experience as described in this volume). Perceptual and interpretive *discrimination* develops like any skill so long as the knowledge gained continues to inform the process of knowing itself.

Deep empathy emerges out of a natural *impulse toward deep contact*—to know and be known (Palmer, 1993). We see a dimension of the same impulse when we look at natural compassion (Dass & Gorman, 1985/1996), which may spill into social interest (Adler, 1929), critical consciousness (Friere, 1973), and prosocial behavior. Empathy emphasizes knowing where compassion implies an impulse toward mercy or service. Both spill from the same well of recognizing interconnection. And the "other" need not be a single person, but a group, a race, or nature as noted previously. The extent to which we are able to recognize and be moved by this impulse within us is reflected in our willingness for meeting.

Loosening up the *attachment* to and identification with the self enables genuine contact. It takes *courage* to risk exposing one's own being to the depth of another. Deep empathy can emerge because the other does not threaten the self as much, not that the self becomes invulnerable, but our attachment to it decreases.

Conclusion

I return to Buber's line that "all real living is meeting" and think of those times when I have been forced or been willing to meet the world on its own terms. These are the moments when life seems like it is actually being lived, rather than watched from the sidelines. This occurs when the other sneaks past the fortress of our categories and roles. It happens when we dive or are drawn into the other with clear eyes and ears, willing to be surprised by the pain, the love, and the mystery that may occupy the meeting. Such meeting necessitates the self being overwhelmed and forgotten, if only for a moment. And in that moment we transcend the confines of "therapist" and "client," "self" and "other."

All empathy is potentially transcendent in the sense that it takes us beyond ourselves, opening the possibility for uncovering and recreating ourselves with each meeting. As empathy stretches into the direct knowing of deep empathy the world falls onto our lap, or rather we tumble onto the world's lap. Beyond the benefits for the therapy, such meeting provides sustenance for the therapist in a profession noted for its burnout. As the practice of deep empathy is carried out into the streets of our daily activities, we have the chance to meet, to live, and to love the world as it is.

References

Adler, A. (1929). *The practice and theory of individual psychotherapy* (2nd ed.). London: Routledge and Kegan Paul.

Alschuler, A. S. (1987). Recognizing inner teachers: Inner voices throughout history. *Gnosis, 5,* 8–12.

Azar, B. (1997). Defining the trait that makes us most human. *APA Monitor, 28*(11), 1–15.

Bohart, A. C., and Greenberg, L. S. (1997). *Empathy reconsidered: New directions in psychotherapy.* Washington, DC: American Psychological Association.

Buber, M. (1958). *I and Thou* (R. G. Smith, Trans.). New York: Scribner's. (Original work published 1923)

Buber, M. (1988). *The knowledge of man: Selected essays* (M. S. Friedman & R. G. Smith, Trans.). Atlantic Highlands, NJ: Humanities Press.

Commons, M. L., Richards, F. A., & Armon, C. (Eds.). (1984). *Beyond formal operations: Late adolescent and adult cognitive development.* New York: Praeger.

Dass, R., & Gorman, P. (1996). *How can I help?* New York: Alfred A. Knopf. (Original work published 1985)

Davis, M., & Wallbridge, D. (1981). *Boundary and space: An introduction to the work of D. W. Winnicott.* New York: Brunner/Mazel Publishers.

Deikman, A. J. (1984). *The observing self: Mysticism and psychotherapy.* Boston: Beacon Press.

Dossey, L. (1993). *Healing words: The power of prayer and the practice of medicine.* New York: HarperCollins.

Freire, P. (1973). *Pedagogy of the oppressed.* New York: Continuum.

Gebser, J. (1991). *The ever-present origin.* Athens: Ohio University Press.

Gladstein, G., & Associates. (1987). *Empathy and counseling.* New York: Springer-Verlag.

Goleman, D. (1995). *Emotional intelligence.* New York: Bantam.

Guntrip, H. (1969). *Schizoid phenomena: Object relations and the self.* New York: International Universities Press.

Hanh, T. N. (1995). *The heart of understanding: Commentaries on the Prajna- paramita Heart Sutra.* Berkeley, CA: Parallax Press.

Hart, T. (1997a). From category to contact: Epistemology and the enliven- ing and deadening of spirit in education. *Journal of Humanistic Edu- cation and Development, 36*(1), 23–34.

Hart, T. (1997b). Transcendental empathy in the therapeutic encounter. *The Humanistic Psychologist, 25*(3), 245–270.

Hartmann, E. (1984). *The nightmare: The psychology and biology of terrifying dreams.* New York: Basic Books.

Heard, W. G. (1993). *The healing between.* San Francisco: Jossey-Bass.

Heard, W. G. (1995). The unconscious functions of the I-It and I-Thou realms. *The Humanistic Psychologist, 23*(2), 239–258.

Heidegger, M. (1977). *Basic writings* (D. F. Krell, Ed.). New York: Harper- Collins.

Heinmann, P. (1950). On countertransference. *International Journal of Psycho-Analysis, 31,* 81–84.

Hoffman, M. L. (1990). Empathy and justice motivation. *Motivation and Emotion, 14*(2), 151–172

Husserl, E. (1967). *The Paris lectures* (P. Koesternbaum, Trans.). The Hague, Netherlands: Martinus Nijhoff. (Lectures originally given 1929)

Johnson, S. M. (1994). *Character styles.* New York: W. W. Norton.

Keller, E. F. (1983). *A feeling for the organism: The life and work of Barbara Mc- Clintock.* New York: W. H. Freeman.

Kohak, E. (1984). *The embers and the stars: A philosophical inquiry into the moral sense of nature.* Chicago: University of Chicago Press.

Kohn, A. (1990). *The brighter side of human existence. Altruism and empathy in everyday life.* New York: Basic Books.

Kohut, H. (1980). Two Letters. In A. Goldberg (Ed.), *Advances in self psy- chology* (pp. 449–469). New York: International Universities Press.

Kohut, H. (1984). *How does analysis cure?* Chicago: University of Chicago Press.

Larson, V. A. (1987). An exploration of psychotherapeutic resonance. *Psy- chotherapy, 24*(3), 321–324.

Liester, M. B. (1996). Inner voices: Distinguishing transcendent and patholog- ical characteristics. *The Journal of Transpersonal Psychology, 28*(1), 1–26.

Mahrer, A. R. (1993). Transformational psychotherapy sessions. *Journal of Humanistic Psychology, 33*(2), 30–37.

Mahrer, A. R., Boulet, D. B., & Fairweather, D. R. (1994). Beyond empathy: Advances in the clinical theory and methods of empathy. *Clinical Psychology Review, 14,*183–198. Washington, DC: American Psychological Association.

Myss, C. (1996). *Anatomy of spirit: The seven stages of power and healing.* New York: Harmony Books.

Nelson, J. E. (1994). *Healing the split: Integrating spirit into our understanding of the mentally ill.* Albany: State University of New York Press.

Nelson, P. L. (1990). The technology of the preternatural: An empirically based model of transpersonal experiences. *The Journal of Transpersonal Psychology, 22*(1), 35–50.

Palmer, P. (1993). *To know as we are known: Education as a spiritual journey.* San Francisco: HarperCollins.

Polster, I., & Polster, M. (1973). *Gestalt therapy integrated.* New York: Vintage Books.

Racker, H. (1968). *Transference and countertransference.* New York: International Universities Press.

Reik, T. (1948). *Listening with the third ear.* New York: Farrar, Straus & Young.

Rogers, C. R. (1959). A theory of therapy, personality and interpersonal relationships as developed in the client-centered framework. In S. Koch (Ed.), *Psychology: A study of science: Vol. 3. Formulations of the person and the social context.* New York: McGraw-Hill.

Rogers, C. R. (1980). *A way of being.* Boston: Houghton Mifflin.

Rowan, J. (1986). Holistic listening. *Journal of Humanistic Psychology, 26*(1), 83–102.

Rowan, J. (1993). *The transpersonal: Psychotherapy and counseling.* New York: Routledge.

Scharff, J. S. (1992). *Projective and introjective identification and the therapists use of self.* Northville, NJ: Jason Aronson.

Schuster, R. (1979). Empathy and mindfulness. *Journal of Humanistic Psychology, 19*(1), 71–77.

Segal, H. (1964). *Introduction to the work of Melanie Klein.* New York: Basic Books.

Sheldrake, R. (1988). *The presence of the past: Morphic resonance and the habits of nature.* New York: Vintage Press.

Smith, N. L., & Smith, L. L. (1996). Field theory in science: Its role as a necessary and sufficient condition in psychology. *The Psychological Record, 46,* 3–19.

Sprinkle, L. (1985). Psychological resonance: A holographic model of counseling. *Journal of Counseling and Development, 64,* 206–208.

Tansey, M. J., & Burke, W. F. (1989). *Understanding countertransference: From projective identification to empathy.* Hillsdale, NJ: The Analytic Press.

Tart, C. (1990). Extending mindfulness to everyday life. *Journal of Humanistic Psychology, 30*(1), 81–106.

Trop, J. L., & Stolorow, R. D. (1997). Therapeutic empathy: An intersubjective perspective. In A. C. Bohart, & L. S. Greenberg (Eds.), *Empathy reconsidered: New directions in psychotherapy* (pp. 279–294). Washington, DC: American Psychological Association.

Ullman, M., & Krippner, S. (1989). *Dream telepathy: Experiments in nocturnal E.S.P.* (2nd ed.). Jefferson, NC: McFarland.

Varela, F., Thompson, E., & Rosch, E. (1991). *The embodied mind: Cognitive science and human experience.* Cambridge, MA: MIT Press.

Washburn, M. (1995). *The ego and the dynamic ground.* Albany: State University of New York Press.

Watkins, J. G. (1978). *The therapeutic self: Developing resonance—key to effective relationships.* New York: Human Science Press.

Wilber, K. (1995). *Sex, ecology, spirituality: The spirit of evolution.* Boston: Shambhala.

Winnicott, D. W. (1971). *Playing and reality.* New York: Routledge.

Zann-Waxler, C., Radke-Yarrow, M., & King, R. A. (1979). Childrearing and children's prosocial initiations toward victims of distress. *Child Development, 50,* 319–330.

12

The Love That Dares Not Speak Its Name

JENNY WADE

> They try to say what you are, spiritual or sexual?
> They wonder about Solomon and all his wives.
> In the body of the world, they say, there is a Soul and you
> are that.
> But we have ways within each other
> that will never be said by anyone.
> —Rumi (Barks, Moyne, Arberry, & Nicholson, 1995, p. 37)

I have lived in many places in my life, metaphorically and literally. Arriving at a new place, I am always intrigued to discover what question strangers ask most frequently after the usual courtesies have been exchanged. When I was young and moved to Texas, it was, "Where did you come from? How do you like it here?" and then, "Do you believe in evolution?" I have recently moved to California where the sequence is, "Where did you come from? How do you like it here? What is your spiritual practice?" This question was as disconcerting as the one about evolution, and I found myself far more reluctant to answer.

I soon learned that a proper response is a snappy word or two, like "Vajrayana Buddhism" or "Vipassana." "Spiritual practice" in California, at least among my new acquaintances, is presumed to be a contemplative discipline, usually Eastern, though it is very fashionable to be Sufi just now. Buddhist and yogic traditions, like the little black dress, never go out of style. Less correct but still acceptable are indigenous religions (e.g., shamanism, Wicca, various Native American paths, etc.).

But I had no ready answer. Treating spirituality as though it were a commodity appalls me, first of all. The glibness with which this question is asked renders spirituality little more than a canned classification, the latest in a recognizable series of such off-putting heuristics as "What's your astrological sign?" "What's your Myers-Briggs type?" and "What number are you on the enneagram?" As if this reduction were not enough, I also find myself recoiling because my spiritual life is both too sacred and too personal for casual discussion with the chance-met. My silence in conversation and in print up to now has been construed as benightedness, or worse, some kind of spiritual misrepresentation (Wilber, 1997).

The truth is, one significant part of my practice is far more than unfashionable. It is so outré that most of the perennial philosophies deny it; and though it is common enough to be frequently acknowledged in the contemporary literature, it is rarely discussed. In most spiritual circles, mine is the practice that dares not speak its name: unitive knowing through the experience of sexual love. Else my new California friends become too relieved, I do not mean Tantra. This knowing and this experience is quite different from what is found in that literature, though the gateway may be the same.

Historical Issues Concerning Sex and Spiritual Knowledge

The consensus concerning sexual spiritual paths has been, for the most part, one of increasing disrepute historically (e.g., Bonheim, 1997; Eisler, 1995; Feuerstein, 1989, 1992; Nelson & Longfellow, 1994; Roberts, 1992; Singer, 1983; Tannahill, 1980). In recent times, the sexual scandals concerning spiritual communities have become almost legendary, especially since many of them have been associated with traditions not normally known for venerating sexual expression. Tracing the relationship between sex and spirit to the present day is not feasible here, but three primary historical issues warrant mention as they still contribute to the marginalization of sexuality in many spiritual traditions. They are: (1) the separation of sex from spirituality, and the eventual repression of sexuality in major spiritual traditions over time, (2) debates over what constitutes legitimate or higher forms of spirituality, and (3) the inability to compare early sexual spiritual practices with contemporary ones.

First, spiritual attainment through sexual expression seems to have been on a long, steady decline over the course of human social evolution. Sex and spirituality appear to have been united in the earliest times, as attested by prehistoric finds, such as the Neolithic "Venus" or "Goddess" figurines (see, for example, Gimbutas, 1982; Stone, 1978, 1979), though the interpretation of these figures is debated (for a summary, see Tannahill, 1980). Some scholars (e.g., de Riencourt, 1974; Eisler, 1995; Stone, 1978, 1979) argue that the primacy of women's roles, fertility and sexuality, in general were stronger in "Great Mother" cultures than in successive, more patriarchal ones. In the earliest historical cultures, sex is often one of the first attributes associated with deity. Many of the first deities were divine hermaphrodites, such as T'ai Yuan of Chinese mythology (Campbell, 1991; Stone, 1978, 1979) and the Teutonic Ymir (Branston, 1980). In the ancient Indian tradition that gave rise to Hinduism, the original Divine Being was One, which split Itself into male and female parts, Shiva and Shakti, in order to love and be loved, to know and be known. The enduring importance of male and female principles in religion is still easily discernible in the yoni and lingam, yin and yang, and the mystical unions of Jesus and the church as the Bride of Christ, and of Shekinah and spiritual aspirants in the Kabbalah, to name only a few. Moreover, the language of sexual union has been used to describe mystical states for centuries.

> If anyone wonders how Jesus raised the dead,
> don't try to explain the miracle.
> Kiss me on the lips.
> *Like this. Like this.*
>
> —Rumi (Hamill, 1996, p. 78)

> Having wet me with love,
> why did you leave?
> You abandoned your unwavering consort,
> having ignited her lamp wick;
> she's like a pleasure boat
> set out to drift on an ocean of craving.
>
> —Mirabai (Hamill, 1996, p. 98)

> So high is my Lord's palace, my heart trembles to mount its stairs:
> yet I must not be shy, if I would enjoy His love.
> My heart must cleave to my Lover;
> I must withdraw my veil, and meet him with all my body.
>
> —Kabir (Tagore, 1991, p. 54)

Over time, however, the connection between sexuality and spirituality disintegrated until in many traditions it vanished altogether. Most religions began to regulate sex, regarding it as a spiritual distraction or hazard. Religious authorities increasingly regulated the free expression of sex, imposing rules on the number and sex of partners, the nature of their relationship to each other, their motivations for engaging in sex, the frequency of the act, the time of day when it could occur, the duration and positions assumed, and the type of climax permitted (e.g., Armstrong,

1993; de Riencourt, 1974; Eisler, 1995; Nelson & Longfellow, 1994; Pagels, 1988; Schacter-Shalomi, 1991; Tannahill, 1980; Waite, 1960). As spiritual growth became increasingly the purview of mental or psychological activity, the pleasure of sex changed from a celebration of divine forces to a distraction from the spiritual path.

Eastern religions, especially Buddhism, came to incorporate the denial of the body, often restricting sexuality (e.g., Feuerstein 1989, 1992; van Gulik, 1974; Tannahill, 1980). Aspirants were expected to be celibate, and spiritual masters no longer had any need or desire for sex (see, for example, the *Visuddhimagga*). Classic Sanskrit literature[1] regards sex as the greatest attachment or barrier to spiritual enlightenment. Tantra, a revolutionary spiritual and political movement deliberately breaking these taboos, Vajrayana Buddhism, a similarly revolutionary movement, and Taoism, an establishment religion that was to be ruthlessly repressed for many years were the exceptions. But even in these, sexual techniques aimed for greater and greater control of the body, especially of male orgasm, and the role of women gradually diminished to that of facilitator of the man's spiritual mastery.

In the West, sex reserved a place in religion, but it was never considered the way to salvation. Mystical Judaism probably retains more sexuality than mystical Christianity or Islam, but even in it sexuality is highly regulated as a potentially dangerous source of excessive enjoyment (Ariel, 1988; Hoffman, 1992; Pagels, 1981; Schacter-Shalomi, 1991; Tannahill, 1980). The Gnostic gospels (and similar sources, such as the Jewish Pseudepigrapha, the Christian Apocrypha, and the Dead Sea Scrolls), rejected for canon by early church authorities, contain much more sexual imagery and divine hermaphrodism than the authorized scriptures. Furthermore, Augustine's sexually repressive influence over what became Roman orthodoxy cast a lasting shadow over the Christian establishment in Western Europe (e.g., Pagels, 1981), though a mixing of spiritual and sexual imagery remains in the writings of many later Christian mystics (e.g., de Rougement, 1983). Mystical Islam likewise includes numerous references to a feminine principle and sexual metaphors for spiritual union (e.g., McDaniel, 1989). Nevertheless, spirituality and sexuality have long been seen as conflicting forces in mainstream Judaism, Christianity, and Islam (e.g., Armstrong, 1993; Eisler 1995; Nelson & Longfellow 1994; Pagels, 1988).

Feminists (e.g., Anderson & Hopkins, 1991; Anderson & Zinsser, 1988; Bonheim, 1997; Eisler, 1987, 1995; Roberts, 1992; Spretnak, 1991) point to the repression of incarnational spirituality, especially the spiritual power of women through sex, in virtually all traditions as they evolved, excepting only some indigenous religions. Extrapolating from the work of Eisler (1987, 1995) and Pagels (1981) and the history of Tantra and Taoism, it is possible to argue that sexuality as a spiritual practice has been repressed because of its accessibility to the population at large. Relative to the other paths, exoteric and esoteric alike, almost anyone can discover and cultivate this ability without the need for training, teachers, and authorities—reason enough for the establishment to marginalize spiritual sexuality. Feminists and other writers (e.g., de Riencourt, 1974; Feuerstein, 1989; Pagels, 1988; Tannahill, 1980) note that even traditions ideologically venerating women—such as the Kabbalah, certain gnostic sects, Tantra and Taoism—came to exclude women from full initiation and to treat them as a means of self-transformation for male initiates. Western and Buddhist traditions—and arguably any ascetic, celibate discipline—maintain the distance between body and spirit, or immanent and transcendent realities as modeled by these forms.

Second, many of the scholars just cited raise important questions about what we consider spirituality to be, in any case, especially given the ancient nature of sexual or incarnate spiritual traditions and their supercession by mystical and concomitant exoteric forms. Since the dawn of the "great religions" and "perennial philosophies" in Asia, spiritual attainment has generally assumed the guise of mysticism even when forced underground by the established exoteric religion. Goddess and indigenous religions as systems of incarnate spirituality are commonly not even called religions, but stigmatized as cults, myths, magic, and superstition in stark opposition to the "great religions" and "perennial philosophies" of their colonizers. (This latter designation seems a risible pretension considering that these earlier forms of spirituality were more ubiquitous and have persisted despite oppression into the present day.)

The difficulty of evaluating the nonordinary states of consciousness associated with advanced practice in both indigenous and perennial spiritual paths has been the subject of considerable debate (e.g., Washburn, 1988, 1998a, 1998b; Wilber, 1990, 1998). This debate is heuristically referred to in transpersonal psychology as the pre/trans issue, referring to the similarity between preegoic and transegoic states (roughly analogous to pre- and post-Piagetian Formal Operations types of subjective experience; see Wade, 1996). But the synonymy of mysticism in Western intellectual thought with advanced forms of spirituality has a long tradition, especially when compared to the status of indigenous religions. Mysticism is commonly understood to be the experience and then stabilization of increasingly subtle, complex, phenomenologically distinct, post-egoic states of consciousness, usually arising in a predictable progression through disciplined practice, culminating in the *unio mystica* or impersonal nonduality (cf., Goleman, 1988; Huxley, 1945; James, 1902/1985; Underhill, 1955; Wade, 1996; Wilber, 1977). However, the equating of mysticism, especially as handed down by the various male-dominated esoteric traditions, with spiritual mastery has been disputed by feminists (e.g., Anderson & Zinsser, 1988; Eisler, 1995; Wright, 1995, 1996) as egregiously hierarchical, androcentric, and oppressive. Theorists (e.g., see Ferrer, in this volume) have criticized the heuristic adoption of the perennial vision and its assumptions of hierarchy as absolute, especially in contemporary thought (see also Wade, 1996). Anthropologists (e.g., Kremer, 1996a, 1996b; Winkelman, 1990, 1993) point to the cultural bias and colonialism that champion these later Asian forms over the spirituality native to all other continents, as well as Eurasian indigenous belief systems. The elimination or marginalization of indigenous cultures through conquest and colonization over time raises many of the same questions regarding the relative value and meaning of historical succession in spiritual traditions as those addressed in other behavioral sciences: Is it progress?

Indigenous cultures surviving into this century[2] have traditionally been characterized as epistemologically pre-egoic, including their religions (cf. Lévy-Bruhl, 1910/1985; Werner, 1940/1980). The current debate is fueled by Wilber's adamantine and excoriating arguments (1986, 1995, 1998) distinguishing pre- and trans-personal spirituality using a historical context to determine the spiritual developmental levels of various cultures as demonstrated by the majority of their members. While acknowledging that the trans-egoic Great Goddess is distinct from the pre-egoic Great Mother in these cultures and that shamanic traditions were principally transpersonal (or at least that their highest practitioners were functioning at these levels),[3] he states that the average mode in these cultures was pre-egoic. According to Wilber, even the highest states attained by adepts in these practices fall short of the ultimate states possible in mysticism. Walsh, a supporter of Wilber's, in a contemporary study (Walsh, 1989a, 1989b, 1995) notes that shamanism can produce direct, intuitive, transcendental knowledge, similar to some advanced states attained through mystical practice, but he clearly does not consider these the equivalent of mysticism. The parity of spiritual attainments across cultures and over time is hotly debated (see, for instance, Ferrer, 1999; Rothberg & Kelly, 1998).

Third, even if these writers could agree about what constitutes spirituality, very little is known about the phenomenological or ideological link between sex and spirituality historically, so their arguments are not particularly helpful in learning about the spiritual attainments gained. The fact is, we can discuss sacred sexual traditions, but they are so old and obscure that the debate is theoretical from a phenomenological standpoint.

We have little or no idea what sacred sex felt like or meant to participants in the prehistoric Goddess religions and fertility cults. Even when some written records exist for later sexual mystery schools like the cults of

Isis, Pan, Dionysis, and Mithras, their arcane nature has been preserved. Were the rites merely symbolic acts whose agents tried magically to control their environment? Did they participate in an archetypal or morphogenetic field (Sheldrake, 1981)? Did initiates like the Mesopotamian priestesses who slept with men visiting the temples function as spiritual adepts, enjoying more transcendental sex than their paid, secular sisters, the prostitutes? Did their partners? To what extent were orgiastic rituals like the Mithraic gang-rape of boy initiates spiritually beneficial even in their own time and culture? Were altered states, pre- or transpersonal, involved? What spiritual insights came from these practices? It is impossible to tell from this distance what differences might have existed, if any, between "regular" sex and sacred sex outside the rituals, trappings, and status of the individuals involved. Obscurity also cloaks our understanding of the much later classic Tantric and Taoist texts whose symbolic language is extremely oblique (e.g., Tannahill, 1980; van Gulik, 1974). Their techniques are more or less clear, but the states and stages of spiritual attainment to be thus enjoyed are barely conveyed.

Yet the promise of spiritual realization from sexual practice has at least one compelling voice from ancient times, the *Epic of Gilgamesh*. First recorded about 3,000 years ago, probably from a much older oral source about an eponymous historical king of Uruk who lived about 2700 BCE, it contains a striking story of spiritual transformation via sacred sex. In it, Enkidu, a subhuman wildman, is transformed through sexual congress with Shamhat, a sex priestess from the temple. Furred with shaggy hair all over his body, Enkidu consorted with animals and behaved like one. He ate grass and fought for room at the watering hole. But when Shamhat made love to him, he changed to a higher form.

> She was not restrained, but took his energy.
> She spread out her robe and he lay upon her. . . .
> His lust groaned over her;
> for six days and seven nights, Enkidu stayed aroused,
> and had intercourse with the harlot
> until he was sated with her charms.
> But when he turned his attention to his animals . . .
> the wild animals distanced themselves from his body. . . .
> But then he drew himself up, for his understanding had
>   broadened. . . .
> The harlot said to Enkidu:
> "You are beautiful, Enkidu, you are become like a god."
> —(Kovacs, 1989, p. 9)

Knowing "in the Biblical Sense"

As a child, I was always fascinated by the King James Bible's use of the verb "to know" meaning to have carnal acquaintance or sexual intercourse with, as in "And Adam knew Eve his wife; and she conceived, and bore Cain . . ." (Genesis 4:1). When I became a student of Old English, however, I discovered that this late usage was a Hebraic adoption, although it has parallels in German and Latin. The Teutonic infinitive *cnáwan*, from which "to know" is derived, over time acquired the meanings of other Teutonic verbs, now obsolete, concerning special forms of knowledge, learning, perception, and identification, such as *cunnan* (cunning and to con) and *cænnan* (ken, kenning, and to ken) (Cassidy & Ringler, 1971; see also the *Oxford English Dictionary*) as well as the meanings of other etymologically-related roots, such as the Latin *gnoscere*. In today's English, "knowing" means both perceiving through the senses as well as recognizing or identifying by the mind. Thus it is not confined to the mental alone, nor does it contain the Cartesian split, which makes it a most suitable way of talking about the spiritual insights gained through sexual practice.

Current popular, quasi-academic, and scholarly titles attest to the interest Westerners now have in resolving the Cartesian split between intangible forms of agency and the body. One relatively small but growing portion of this literature seeks to reunite sexuality and spirituality, but it tells us comparatively little about the spiritual knowledge produced by these practices. In the first place, advocates of feminism and indigenous traditions have not produced maps of spiritual insight through sexual practice, despite their strong presence in the historical debates about sexuality and spirituality. Moreover, although a considerable literature has resurfaced from traditional sources, it has little to offer in terms of descriptions of the spiritual knowledge to be gained.

For some years now, Sanskrit and Taoist texts (e.g., the *Kama Sutra, Fang-nei-chi, I-shin-po*, etc.) have reappeared in updated, contemporary versions as Tantric and Taoist guides for sexual expression. Generally speaking, the spiritual underpinnings for these traditions arise from the belief that the ultimate Truth resides within the human body, and that consequently the body is the best medium for spiritual realization. These paths strive for a meditative process that will destroy the duality of sex, thereby identifying the practitioner with the Unitive Whole. Similar to many cosmologies, these traditions regard a kind of mystical hermaphrodite as the closest human likeness to Deity.

Traditional Taoist and Tantric texts stress the arousal and unification of both male and female principles in the practitioner's (usually male) body, which will effectuate the realization of nondual or mystical hermaphroditism, with or without an actual partner (e.g., Reid, 1989; Wang, 1986; see also Tannahill, 1980; van Gulik, 1974). This is typically accomplished through a meditative process based on the male's *coitus reservatus,* wherein the semen flows "backwards" into his own body, rather than into the woman's and "upwards" along the meridians associated with kundalini. Although some contemporary Taoist and Tantric sources address women's experience as well, these texts tend to dwell on technique and the control of physical and energetic forces rather than on the spiritual insights said to be the goal of the practice.

In fact, the bulk of the Tantric- and Taoist-inspired literature can be summed up as instructional manuals for meditation or sexual technique. Their phenomenological explications center on physiological or energetic dynamics, such as a "heart opening" or a "channeling" of energy through the partner's body into one's own, rather than a psychological or spiritual state. The occasional practitioner narrative appears in other sources, illustrating how these physical and energetic forces create a supraphenomenal experience that transcends normal spatial and psychological boundaries.

> I had a very powerful cervical orgasm. . . . There was an energy field . . . between us . . . communicated between the eyes . . . as though we recognized one another, not merely from the objective point of view, but as though we were one entity, or one field. There was no obstruction or delineation between us. My heart felt like it had burst open.—Ruth (Sokol, 1989, pp. 118–119)

> There was this etheric pleasure and awakening, this kind of etheric arousal, as well as actual hormonal, physical, fleshy arousal. . . . All of a sudden the cork was taken off the energy in me. And it started flowing out of me to Robert.—Sara (Sokol, 1989, pp. 124–125)

Incorporating male and female aspects for more spiritual sex is also important to contemporary writers with a Jungian orientation (e.g., de Rougement, 1983; Halligan & Shea, 1992; Haule, 1990; Jung, 1925/1993; Singer, 1983; Ulanov & Ulanov, 1994), but they eschew mechanical technique for contemplative, mindful approaches similar to Taoism.

> Sexual love, itself, may be experienced as a form of meditation. In this most intimate of relationships, it is possible to open oneself to the other, and to the wider context in which the two exist. . . . Each may approach the partner with the same openness and clarity as one would hope to find in quiet moments with the uncluttered mind, in silence. (Singer, 1983, p. 288)

Singer (1983) nevertheless does not otherwise treat the phenomenology of the sexual states, but instead goes on to give a detailed description of the meditational attitudes and states to cultivate in order to enter the act of lovemaking either with a partner or alone.

But what about the sexual experiences of ordinary subjects naive in the arts of energetic, bodily, and orgasmic control or meditative preparation? Sexual love provides us with a strong, inborn motivation to merge with something outside our encapsulated selves. It is potentially one of the most accessible paths to a realization of union beyond the limits of our mundane experience, so it should not be surprising to think that many ordinary people may have stumbled onto profoundly moving and transformative unitive experiences in the course of loving their partners. Indeed, the more general literature, such as the writings of D. H. Lawrence, suggests that ecstatic sex, though rare, can come to anyone. Furthermore, research not originally designed to investigate sex but transcendent experiences in general began to reveal how often the two are linked in naive populations (people with no experience in Taoist or Tantric techniques). Laski's (1961) classic research in secular and religious contexts showed that sexual love was a trigger for 43 percent of her subjects when asked to name experiences of "transcendent ecstasy" (p. 145). Maslow (1987) was initially shocked when his research of peak experiences derived not from theistic pursuits, but from some of the most physical:

> It was a very startling thing for me to hear a woman describing her feelings as she gave birth in the same words used by Bucke to describe cosmic consciousness or by Huxley to describe the mystic experience in all cultures and eras or by Ghiselin to describe the creative process or by Suzuki to describe the Zen satori experience. (p. 58)

Maslow (1987) went on to discuss the frequency with which his self-actualizing subjects mention sexual pleasure as a source of peak experience. Noting that self-actualizers have a healthy but not obsessive attitude toward sex, Maslow perceives their experience of orgasm to be not only similar to a mystical experience but also productive of some unspecified spiritual knowledge.

> There were the same feelings of limitless horizons opening up to the vision, the feeling of being simultaneously more powerful and also more helpless than one ever was before, the feeling of great ecstasy and wonder and awe, the loss of placing in time and space with, finally, *the conviction that something extremely important and valuable had happened, so that the subject is to some extent transformed* [italics added]. (Maslow, 1987, p. 164)

Laski (1961) also found that ecstasy has a transformative effect. In her research, sexual ecstasy, compared to ecstasies triggered by nature, religion, or art, were relatively high on scales of an increase in "loss of feelings of difference," "loss of self," and "feelings of renewal," but relatively low on increasing "feelings of knowledge."

More recent research on sex turns up the same small but apparently ubiquitous presence of transcendental sexuality in the general population, even when it is an unsought category of experience (e.g., Scantling & Browder, 1993). Sex researchers present stories of a profound transpersonal nature from people who follow no recognized body-oriented nor sexual traditions like shakti, kundalini, Tantra, or Tao. Their narratives also display the language of mysticism:

> When we make love, it's like I disappear. Athletes talk about being in the zone—this is like being in the zone for hours. It's not like I'm doing anything or making anything happen. In some religions they say it's the dance, not the dancer. This is like I'm being danced.—Alex (Maurer, 1994, p. 456)

> When we made love, I would experience my body dissolving, and there would just be flowers, thousands of flowers. Sometimes we seemed to be under the ocean, swimming like fishes. Everything would drop away except this consciousness of unfolding and melting and dissolving and flowing.—Hannah (Bonheim, 1997, p. 81)

> As the slave I get into a no-mind state, a Zen state. There's a quality of peace and serenity in giving it up to somebody who is willing and able to hold—the mystic "it". . . . Somebody wrote a book proposing that this condition is escaping from the self. That's not my experience. It's a *transcendence* of myself. I'm fully in touch with me, with all my parts, and I'm someplace else, too. That's why I say it's a spiritual path.—James (Maurer, 1994, p. 280)

It Was a Religious Experience

Because of the physiological changes occurring during sex, one could argue that any sexual experience—or at the very least, orgasm—comprises nonordinary states of consciousness that might be similar to those associated with spirituality. The physiology of sexual release can cause a momentary feeling of swooning and the loss of self, volition, time, and space. But people become so accustomed to this sensation as "ordinary" sex that it seems not to be confused with a strong spiritual dimension. In my own solicitation of narratives describing transcendent or spiritual sexual experiences, I have been struck by the certainty with which people aver that they have never had such an encounter, whatever they imagine it may be. Those who have had such an experience are equally sure. A great orgasm is not necessarily a religious experience in the sense used here, where the experient seems to enter a spiritual realm. If it were, far more people would be likely to say they have had transcendent sex. According to a man I will call Blake, losing himself in his partner, which is a common experience for him,

> has a tangible quality even in dissolving, a feeling of sensuality, a delicious feeling. It feels a particular sort of way, *that* way. This love you call transcendent doesn't partake of that. It has nothing to do with sensuality. It doesn't have to do with bodies. It has to do with something which is pure religious exaltation. It is the supreme experience that sex has afforded me.

So what makes a sexual encounter seem spiritual? The following conclusions come not only from the extant literature on Tantric practitioners and naive subjects but also from my own research to date of homosexual and heterosexual adults who self-identified as having had "mystical, transcendent, or spiritual experiences during sex with a partner." Two factors always appear in the narratives: first, the participation in an altered state that focuses on, or includes, the lover; and second, the felt experience of a cosmic force engaging one or both lovers in the context of relationship, especially their lovemaking. The subjective experience of the altered state and the felt sense of the numinous are rather idiosyncratic, but there are elements of commonality across all the narratives. The following description is from a letter I received from a Buddhist friend I will call Elaine. She succinctly captures the numinous qualities of the experience.

> The boundaries are completely dissolved and there is no longer any "you" or "I" but simply "THIS." Then the "THIS" becomes LOVE/COMPASSION *not only* for the other person . . . but something (or some *one*—if you're a theistic person) comes up from the depths so that there is only one word to describe it: YES! But this "yes" that comes from the deepest depths is a "yes" to the entire Universe, to a point where there is no longer a God out *there*, but rather one is dissolved into the GOD/NUMINOUS/UNIVERSE.

Tantric, Taoist, and kundalini practitioner records include high levels of physical arousal and sensory overload. Changes in the intensity or location of physical sensations after habituation seem to create a sense of supraphenomenal connection between the lovers' bodies perceived as having a spiritual basis.

My lover and I had been together in sexual encounter for more than an hour. Up to this time, I had experienced manifestations of kundalini such as spontaneous movements, a high humming sound in the throat, the rushes of energy up the spine, and visions of light and color. The energy that usually focuses in the genital area had spread to every cell of my body. . . . When I touched my lover's hand, I was that. (Sokol, 1989, p. 115)

The only sense of form . . . came from the movement. . . I felt myself to be radiance, tangible radiance and bliss. It was the two of us, and so my sense of what I was was completely inclusive of him. —Sara (Sokol, 1989, p. 125)

These sensations of energetic openings also occur spontaneously in naive couples, who usually interpret them as having a spiritual or, at least, supraphenomenal, basis. Since even "regular" sex often involves high levels of emotion, concentrated focus, sensory stimulation, and repetitive motions and sounds, it is not surprising to think that "amateurs" can achieve the same experiences as sexual "adepts." They may not know what to make of the unusual sensations they experience, as a discussion on sex as a spiritual emergency acknowledges (Bragdon, 1990). In one example Bragdon gives, a naive couple was surprised when their sexual experience went beyond genital sensation:

Suddenly, it seemed as if his heart became like a penis penetrating into my heart. My heart became like a vagina—opening to receive the new thrust of energy from my partner. Then, I felt my actual heart pulsate and throb as if in orgasm, followed by a tremendous release of energy. The only word for it is ecstasy. (pp. 144–145)

Nevertheless, the intensity of unusual physical sensations is of less interest than the psychological phenomena that make them seem spiritual to the lovers. Often these openings to nonordinary experience overcome the individual in the absence of any direct physical contact, but clearly within the context of sexual love. In these states, a merging with the beloved is often marked. For instance, Feuerstein reports a case in which after a night of lovemaking, a man and his lover lost their sense of being separate selves as each saw their "once separate and private emotions . . . appear on each other's faces" (1992, p. 40). His lover was simultaneously experiencing the same reversal, an experience that terrified both of them. A Tantric practitioner I spoke to said:

It's important to me to remain me, so my experience is with different levels of surrender so that I remain me at the same time I find that there's a new way of looking at me to get closer and closer to the Truth. The Truth is that different distinctions can be made. I feel my primary field goes all the way around a person and gets totally intermingled, and yet I can change my own identity without any significant degradation. An indication of how intimate this is is that if [my partner] has had a fair amount to drink, I will pick up that [chemistry] and become drunk, so I don't make love with people who are drunk or using drugs or in some chemically altered state.—Muntu

Loss of self boundaries in merging with the lover appears to be one of the most common characteristics of transpersonal sexual experience. People report the dissolution of the boundaries of their own bodies, being unaware of who was doing what to whom as they merge with their lovers (Bonheim, 1997; Maurer, 1994). The following stories come from people who do not practice Tantric or Taoist sex.

Making love with him puts me in an altered state, and on at least a couple of occasions, has put me beyond the world of duality entirely. At a minimum my boundaries collapse, the world of form disappears. Even afterwards when we are lying together it's a long time before I'm back within my skin. Whose leg is this? Whose genitals? Whose heartbeat? Where does my arm end and his chest begin? I have no sense of boundary between us.—Naia

After some of these cosmic moments, it's very hard and disorienting to disengage physically. I've had the experience that our cells had actually merged and interwoven so that coming apart can be very painful, a very deep sense of loss or amputation. It's true we've become one being here.—Roland

We would spend hours . . . pleasing each other. . . . It was a dance of entering into each other's soul and then out again, losing oneself, and then regaining oneself and then losing oneself again into the sensual experience.—Elaine

This loss of self can be so profound that some accomplished meditators say it matches and sometimes even exceeds states they have achieved through contemplative practice alone (Bonheim, 1997; Feuerstein, 1992; Sokol, 1989). According to Elaine, whose Buddhist meditation practice spans more than twenty years, "When experiencing the Other Person in this way . . . it was the *only* direct pathway to the Numinous. . . . It has to be the closest anyone can come to experiencing God."

As some of these narratives indicate, along with the dissolution of self boundaries, experiences out of body and outside the normal space/time constructions can also occur, similar to some of the "paranormal" experiences common to certain levels of meditation. Some lovers have visions or other "hallucinatory" experiences removed from the here-and-now of the bedchamber, transporting them to other worlds, reliving past lives with that lover, or filling their sensory field with blissful experiences. Common experiences involve a sense of being in outer space or underwater. Several people I interviewed said that the world became more vivid and that they perceived energetic patterns of light or understood the world at a microcosmic level. The following records illustrate the varieties of these types of experience.

> Then there are these wonderful possibilities, shooting through the sky together, suddenly flying, out in the stars. It's like going through galaxies or something, traveling at amazing speeds, and you're relaxed but it's very visual and physical. I've actually seen stars like galaxies rushing past and had a physical sense of my body rushing along.—Roland

> The area around me, the air seems to have texture as though it's fine grains suspended. Space itself seems to be about 10,000 grains per square inch in texture. It was sand colored, very light tan like sand. Everything looked perfectly all right, but the air appeared solid. Not really solid, but only in this inner psychic way, and there was a feeling of very strong well-being that is quite unusual.—Harold

> There was an amazing feeling of being, of opening up, and everything was *more*. I'm accessing more dimensions or more modes of thought than I do normally, and things are not as solid as concrete forms and shapes. It's almost like a biologist or physicist looking at subatomic particles or things under the electron microscope, the basic patterns of energy that the universe is made of. Forms of waves and rays and points and the interplay of expansion and contraction, progressions and experiences of densities.—Donna

> Colors, sounds, everything was lighter, brighter, clearer. My whole body seems less solid. I had visions of past-life experiences where I was in the body of another woman, feeling how it was to be his wife in other places and other times. The visions were usually where he was more restrictive, such as once when I was in a foreign country and was barren, and he'd beat me and rape me every day, and I

never did get pregnant. Now as he made love to me so beautifully, it helped heal the wounds of all those pasts.—Francine

Distortions of time are also common (Bonheim, 1997; Feuerstein, 1992; Maurer, 1994; Sokol, 1989), both the speeding up and slowing down of time or being in a place of timelessness.

Time doesn't seem to exist. Sometimes our lovemaking would last only a few minutes, but it felt like hours, and then the reverse would happen. It seemed as though only a few minutes had passed, and it was three hours. Time is totally unimportant. The experience brings you into the moment.—Francine

Time is like water here. When you're submerged in the experience, you lose your sense of it. Sometimes it's a pool, and you step in and out, and time is what you thought it was. At other times, it's rapids, and you don't know where you're going to come out. I never know what the clock time is going to be. Sometimes it feels like we've only been there a moment, but now it's dark outside. At other times, what seemed to go on forever was really over in a flash.—Gwen

For Tantric and Taoist initiates, accessing transcendent sex is a learned skill, often surrounded by preparatory rituals, and pursued using concentration and mindfulness techniques, but naive lovers are also aware that certain conditions assist their reaching a spiritual connection during sex.

What I want to do is surrender, not submit . . . not fight against the flow. This is the same. I want to be in that *condition.* I want to be in a state of meditation. . . . Making it deliberate is part of what makes it a spiritual path. . . . I am choosing over and over to be this way. —James (Maurer, 1994, pp. 275–78)

We did this by consciously bringing the World into bed with us: that is, we directed our energies through a total body-sense experience. We would spend hours . . . pleasing each other through simply gazing into each other's eyes; massaging each other's hands, feet; burning lavender oil for scent in the room; reciting poetry to each other.—Elaine

If we've had a period of intense closeness already or there's already a kind of opening, it is easier for me to get to that particular place than if we're tired or if we've quarreled, or if there's stuff to get through. . . . That sense of openness and connection creates a thinning of the veil that allows me to enter it more easily. I don't try to engineer it. I'm just grateful when it happens.—Blake

In some sense, the lovers do not feel in control of their experience, nor do they feel their partner is creating it, but that it originates outside themselves. This is true for initiates and naive experients alike. The sense of a cosmic force or presence outside the lovers and their activities seems to characterize spiritual sexuality. It takes a number of forms. One of Bonheim's subjects (1997) says her unending orgasmic state is more like an energy frequency she taps into that exists outside herself. She likens it to plugging into a circuit, while another speaks of her partner's disappearing to her ken altogether, having served as a conduit to take her to the light. Feuerstein (1992) interviewed someone who says, "I just 'fell' into the fullness that had arisen in and between us" (pp. 30–31). According to Naia:

> It's as if we exist at one level, and our love at another. There's our relationship, and what we call OneLove, because it subsumes us completely, and yet it's not us. Our relationship occurs in the ordinary world. I don't know if we created OneLove or it created us. When we quarrel, we can sometimes step back into it even in the middle of a horrible fight by really seeing or kissing each other. There we exist eternally outside of time and the vagaries of our relationship in a perfected love. In a way, how we are there has nothing to do with how we are in this world, and it is completely unaffected by it. It is more like our true natures, and the nature of our love. All we have to do is remember.

Haule (1990) calls this concept "the Third" to describe the autonomous field or force that seems to exist between the two lovers. Drawing on various sources, such as the writings of Meister Eckhart, Ibn al-Arabi's doctrine of angels, the Christian trinity, and Husserl's *Mitwelt,* Haule (1990) speaks of this third agency as arising from the mutuality of the lovers. The following stanza of Rumi's illustrates Haule's point.

> To watch and listen to these two
> is to understand how, as it's written,
> sometimes when two beings come together,
> Christ becomes visible.

> (Barks, 1987)

The Third is to some extent cocreated by the lovers' union but also impervious to deliberate manipulation by either of the partners and not reducible to them. This Third is frequently alluded to in spatial terms, as a special place or field (discernible in some of the earlier quotations), but it is also more theistically identified as an emanation of the Absolute.

There's more light than dark [when I make love with her]. So
what have we got here, angels or what? . . . I say to myself: There
are these two people, and they're an expression of God's love.
That's such a new thought to me that I don't even know what I
mean by it. So where is this coming from? . . . It's coming from
God, or grace, or somewhere. I can't even believe I'm saying this.
I used to be a Marxist!—Alex (Maurer, 1994, p. 459)

There is a unitive energy where the two truly become one. And
once in a while, you transcend even that, and you become one
with the universe. At times I have experienced that. It's like a great
light, but that doesn't exactly describe it, either. . . . That is just the
doorway you pass through into something beyond, something
transcendent.—Roseanne (Bonheim, 1997, pp. 40–41)

I just feel a surge of worshipfullness [*sic*] like I'm opening myself
up to God, or God is streaming through me in the act of sexual
union. Making love in this way is not just like praying to God, but
. . . a bottomless surrender to the infinite. . . . It's the most perfect feeling I can imagine. . . . Here there would be no barrier.
God is fully available to me. All I have to do is offer myself and
somehow through [her] I get to God.—Blake

The phenomenology of these transcendent sexual experiences reflects
what Kabbalists call "the breaking of the vessels" in which the dynamics of
the transcendent order are commingled with those of the material order.
These loosenings of spatial, temporal, and self boundaries, and the sense of
the numinous have obvious parallels in the transpersonal dimensions of
contemplative spiritual practices. They are less reflective of the visionary imagery associated with the nonordinary states of indigenous religions
(though visions obviously occur, as seen earlier). It is likely, however, that
the contextual cues and intentions of sexual activity may be sufficiently different to produce experiences that have certain distinctions or artifacts that
distinguish them from other altered states. Practitioners of both sexual and
meditative paths, such as Elaine earlier (cf., Bonheim, 1997; Feuerstein,
1992; Sokol, 1989) as well as naive sexual ecstatics, indicate that the states
gained through transcendent sex are the same kinds accessed by advanced
meditators.

I'm not thinking very much, where my experience is more meditative so that discursive thought drops away. A devotional quality
arises out of that meditative place in which my lover becomes the
most beautiful, precious, divine thing there is. It's not a rational or
intellectual experience, but apprehending what is. The quality of

gratefulness I have for this experience is what opens me. If I lose
that devotional and grateful quality, the experience is less. I become one with everything then. It's never confined to my lover
and me, though sometimes there's a focus, but about my oneness
with everything. My lover, the relationship, the sexual union [are]
a vehicle for that experience.—Donna

It's a combination of yearning, giving way to surrender, feeling a
tremendous joy, and it explodes in a way that doesn't even have
any content. I'm not comparing it with nirvana—you know how
they say you only recognize nirvana after you come back from
it—but it's a little like that. When I go in it, it's not a blank, but I
only feel the immensity of it after I come back. There's no sense
of union because that implies one thing merging with another.
But there's a predominance of transcendental feeling, not like
the sometimes rather bloodless descriptions one finds in Buddhism, but more as in the ecstatic traditions like Sufism and
Christian gnosticism.—Blake

I was suspended without the ego, yet somehow with an awareness
because I could remember it afterwards. It was as though I was inside a Vortex, where there was no sense of you/me/other. At the
same time, there was an almost overwhelming feeling of love *toward* the other person involved.—Elaine

There is considerable reason to think, however, that at least some of
the narratives speak of the nondual awareness associated with unitive
knowing. In these cases, the sense of being an observer or experient experiencing events dissolves into the "I AM THAT" of the highest states of
mysticism. After this happened to me the first time, I was forcibly reminded of Philip Kapleau's (1989) description of his own first experience
during his training over several years in a Zen monastery, "All at once the
roshi, the room . . . disappeared in a dazzling stream of illumination and
I felt myself bathed in a delicious unspeakable delight. . . . For a fleeting
eternity I was alone—I alone was. . . . Then the roshi swam into view"
(p. 239).
    For me, everything in the room was suddenly lost in a bright, white
light. Then suddenly everything appeared again as though the floodwaters
of the light were receding only with form. I can't even say things appeared
because that implies a separate vantage point. But there was really no separation between the things, the bed, the dresser, the window, my lover, me.
I was not separate from everything, though objects had the usual edges.
The "spaces" in-between were as alive and full as the "objects." We were all

not-same, not-different. There was only being. It was all part of me, and I was all of it, just the is-ness. There was simply nothing but me, and I was no more, no less—no more significant than all there was. Words fail me, but perhaps a better sense of it comes from other experients:

> All there was was energy that was somehow being generated be-
> tween the two of us, but I no longer had any perception of the two
> of us. It was just what was happening and I was that.—Sara (Sokol,
> 1989, p. 125)

> There was no me. . . . I remember looking over at the door to my
> apartment and thinking, "there is no difference between door
> jambs and smog." There is no difference between anything what-
> soever. . . . There is only apparent difference. . . . I felt as if I had
> just been born in that moment, or that I had been asleep all my life
> and had just awakened. . . . I was simply being what I AM, and what
> everyone else IS, in truth.—Trisha (Feuerstein, 1992, pp. 35–36)

In fact, using the comparative studies of Goleman (1988), Huxley (1945), and Underhill (1955) to delineate mystical experiences, we can eas-ily see that most of the previously cited records reflect all of the following characteristics of mystical states:

> Ecstatic unity suffused with bliss, love and joy characterized by
> no separation between subject and object, self and other, inner
> and outer.
> Transcendence of time and space, including plasticity of spatio-
> temporal boundaries, as well as their dissolution into timelessness
> and openness. Also the sensation that the self is simultaneously
> nowhere and everywhere.
> Paradoxicality in the unity of opposites without incompatibility;
> non-dualism.
> Sense of the numinous, including the oneness of all phenomena.
> Realness in the sense of being insightful beyond the kinds of
> truth available to discursive intellect. Having the sense of intrinsic
> authority.
> Ineffability.

We can use Walsh's dimensions (1995) for comparing the phenome-nology of different nonordinary mental states for a rough analysis. It is im-portant to qualify the effort by drawing attention first to the inferential nature of what we can learn from the few sexual narratives available; sec-ond, to the unsystematic way in which they have been collected; and third, to the potential for significant differences in the reported phenomenology by initiates and naive sexual ecstatics. Such an explication is therefore likely to be quite crude at this point, but Walsh's phenomenological dimensions can still assist in mapping states of sexual ecstasy.

Control refers to both the ability to enter and leave the altered state at will, and to the ability to control the content of the experience (Walsh, 1995). The degree to which sexual practitioners control their experience on either dimension seems partial, compared to shamanism and contemplative practices. Sexual initiates appear to have more control over the physiological and energetic components than naive practitioners. My research even indicates a certain reluctance on the part of many naive practitioners to force the control issue; they prefer an invitational and open approach. Also, a sexual practice performed alone would more likely permit greater levels of control than one involving a partner.

Awareness of environment changes in sexual experience. The objects of awareness can be internal, in which the outer world is largely lost, as in yogic practices, or external and internal, as in Buddhist mindfulness practices (Walsh, 1995). For some lovers, the partner becomes the object of concentration, but for others, awareness of the environment and even of the lover eventually falls away as they enter their own subjective world of bliss. In any case, the environment often seems restricted to the immediacy of the lovers' bodies rather than to the rest of the setting.

The *ability to communicate* with others during the experience exists in some contemplative and shamanic practices, but not in others. In sexual spiritual practices, communication of internal states may not occur for some, though the partner may sense that something extraordinary is going on. In other cases both lovers simultaneously enter into the same or similar states. This seems particularly true of Tantric partners who are deliberately manipulating their energy in mutually understood ways. Communication in these instances is seldom verbal. As Blake, a naive practitioner, says: "That openness of communication is odd in sex where there are often no words, but I feel I'm most in communication with [my lover] that way, communication both to [her] and through [her]."

Concentration seems to be both fluid, changing with changing circumstances, and fixed in the object of contemplation, depending on the circumstances. As lovemaking progresses, concentration seems to become increasingly fixed on one dimension of the experience. The bodies, their sensations, and activities seem to drop into the background of awareness (as in the case of altered states induced by sensory overload), even if a fairly active level of stimulation is maintained. The physiological and energetic sensations, and methods used to sustain them, become secondary to the states they are inducing. In fact, some persons I spoke to could not even recall whether they had had an orgasm.

In contrast to the very low levels of *arousal* associated with contemplative disciplines, physiological arousal in sexual practices is quite high, even if it is controlled by Tantric or Taoist methods. Walsh, in his comparison (1995) notes that shamanism, in which practitioners enter other psychic realms where they must perform duties and often contend with hostile entities, is also characterized by high levels of arousal physically and mentally. In a sexual practice, psychological and affective arousal is not associated with difficulty but with increasingly overwhelming sensations of physiological pleasure and bliss.

Affect is very positive, ranging from calm peacefulness to bliss to overwhelming ecstasy during the experience. The "afterglow" of these kinds of experiences may also be rather intense; some sexual practitioners remain in a blissful, open state ("no edges") for hours, days, or even weeks after the experience. Harold, like some other subjects, likened this feeling to having taken the drug MDMA ("Adam," "Ecstasy")—"A feeling of safeness, security and wellbeing . . . a beatific state."

The *sense of self* is not confined to the body, but seems merged with the object as in the case of some meditative practices, here usually the lover. Initial merging with the lover often seems to transmute to a sense of oneness with the greater environment or reality. Although this is a dualistic form of self because the observer still exists, it seems that some people actually enter a nondual state at least momentarily. The self does not seem to vanish so much as it becomes identified, in both dualistic and nondualist ways, with the Whole.

Walsh (1995) does not associate being *out of body* with advanced meditation, though he does observe the loss of body awareness ("enstasis"). A sense of being out of body exists in several records, and a certain diminishment of body awareness occurs for some lovers as the physical activities sustaining the state drop into the background while maintaining the foreground of psychological experience, which then dominates subjective awareness. For practitioners experiencing kundalini arousal, body sensations may be the dominant subjective experience.

Content changes dramatically. Discursive thought vanishes altogether. From the descriptions, most of these experients are aware of the "formless mental qualities and affects, such as intense happiness" that Walsh (1995) associates with the second and third *jhanas* of Buddhist practice (p. 47). It may also be that in some of the nondual states, unbounded impersonal consciousness is attained, but most describe it as qualitatively different from the Buddhist concepts, more like the ecstatic union of the Western esoteric traditions.

The Question of Spiritual Knowledge

Of course mystical states, whether realized through trance, absorption, or ecstatic sex, are not the final goal of any spiritual path. Knowledge of the ultimate nature of the self, reality, and their relationship is. But there are many stages of realization along the path to the ultimate knowledge to which mystical states are the stiles, and these realizations accrue as the practice deepens.

Although the insights occurring during ecstatic sex may have state-specific aspects and may also be fleeting, their memory transforms the practitioner's way of construing experience, even when the "afterglow" of the experience wears off. The knowledge obtained during sexual altered states need not be entirely state-dependent, any more than the memory, feeling tone, or insights of a dream are always lost upon awakening, though the experience of being in the dream is. In this way, sexually-induced altered states appear to have the same effect as altered states attained through other means, such as advanced spiritual practices. This kind of experiential knowledge, in which self, spatial, and temporal boundaries are breached, becomes integrated and contiguous with ordinary consciousness, permanently altering the way the world is understood, a transformation considered in developmental models to represent highly evolved ways of knowing that go beyond the personal (e.g., Wade, 1996).

According to Koplowitz (1984a, 1984b, 1990), post-egoic experients of altered states in which spatial, personal, and temporal boundaries are broken down recognize that they participate in the construction of reality, and that they are, therefore, not separate from it. They also begin to realize that although the world is still understood to be filled with permanent objects, whose existence does not depend on their being known, the boundaries separating them are open. That is, their forms are basic, but their meaning is constructed. Furthermore, experients come to understand that reality does not consist of states separated in time, but as a unity that includes the knower. Self-identification is no longer confined to the body, but with other selves (cf., Assagioli, 1965), in this case, especially the lover and reality. The transformative quality of the knowledge gained during transcendent sex is evident in the following.

> I suppose when I describe it, it will sound like a form of psychosis.
> . . . Of course, you know this is not a psychotic experience by its results; once time is no longer still . . . and normal life resumes, you are changed but in a good way; your other relationships are enhanced by the experience also because you have changed. Somehow a string of that love experience is woven throughout your other relationships, career, etc. [You gain] tolerance for others

who are not so knowing . . . and great compassion for them as well as others. Matter is viewed in a different way; it "feels" almost as though the world becomes (for a while at least) a prism and that you've seen the light piercing through, creating the rainbow colors. The light is sometimes named God (if you're from a theistic faith) and the rainbow colors represent matter. The impact of such an experience is immense. . . . I've gotten to a point that I can "become" a tree, a cloud, a lovely smell, in the same way in which I experienced lovemaking; they are no longer separate in my daily routine. Knowing on a *deep level* that . . . everything is dependent upon everything else; that there is nothing that exists *independent* of something else.—Elaine

I know now that [my lover] and I exist in that timeless, Absolute reality as much as we do in this bounded one of ordinary life. And not only we, but everyone and all things. Just as I can look at [my lover] and see through whatever is happening at the moment, however irritating, to his real Self, so I am more sensitive of the true natures of all I meet. It makes compassion, while still something I must practice, much more natural.—Naia

This is a way to know God, like you're practicing a form of epistemology when you're engaged in this type of sexual behavior. It doesn't give you specific knowledge; it's more like a reminder of what's there in going to the source. Knowledge sounds like knowledge *of* something or that you're apart from the knowledge, that it's outside yourself. It is not other, not God coming to me. I don't like to use the word God, but I don't know what word to use because it's an awareness of something vast beyond me. We are part of that, so it shows you what your true nature is.—Blake

In a postmodern critique of transpersonal theory, Ferrer (in this volume) suggests that in fact, transpersonal experiences, such as these sexual ones, are better understood not as experiences in which an expansion of individual consciousness permits access to transpersonal knowledge, but as the emergence of transpersonal knowledge in the locus of the individual that demands the participation of his or her consciousness. Thus the "experience" is no longer an individual, subjective event, but rather the participation of an individual consciousness in a transpersonal, epistemic event that is multilocal. In these sexual records, the multilocal nature of the transpersonal event—in, through, and with the lover as well as the self—is evident. This is Haule's (1990) Third, Naia's OneLove, the numinous field that enfolds and interpenetrates the lovers.

Ferrer's (in this volume) postmodern, participative approach to transpersonal theory also dissolves the dualism between experience and knowledge inherent in modern theories of transpersonal psychology. As he indicates, transpersonal events do not, by definition, occur in the absence of transpersonal knowledge. Whenever a person accesses transpersonal knowledge, that is, breaks through the self-identification of the biological and biographical history, linear time and bounded space, a transpersonal event has occurred. That is the necessary and sufficient condition for classifying an event as transpersonal. It is not the nonordinary dimensions of transpersonal "experiences" that define them as transpersonal, but the knowledge of the true nature of the self and reality that they convey. By eliminating the dualism inherent in earlier theories between transpersonal experience and knowledge, he has removed many of the category errors plaguing the validity of "subjective experiences" and opened up a way to consider the hermeneutics of transpersonalism without the hierarchical values associated with structural models that tend to discount certain kinds of experience.

Is Sex a Spiritual Practice?

Returning to the dilemma that induced me to write about sex as a spiritual path in the first place—my felt ambivalence about discussing any aspect of my spiritual life publicly, especially treating it as a label—I am faced once again with differences between my way of viewing spirituality and that of the present transpersonal community. These differences were brought into sharp focus by a book released as I was writing this chapter which takes the "California question" to its next step (Rothberg & Kelly, 1998). So that readers can immediately gauge the weight to accord each author's contribution, the book helpfully provides not only the names of their spiritual practices, but how many years they have devoted to these paths, even how many days each year are spent in spiritual pursuits. Giving dedication its due, is this kind of "my practice is bigger than yours" qualification useful in legitimating spiritual authority? Without wishing to sound sanctimonious, I incline toward the biblical injunctions, echoed in other traditions, that it is better to practice spirituality quietly, even in secret (Matthew 6:6), and that a practice should be judged by its fruits (Matthew 7:16, 20). I am not embarrassed about the nature of my practice, but it is not the practice that is important.

What constitutes a spiritual practice, its frequency, the degree of intentionality brought to it? No clear pattern yet emerges from my respondents, although most consider sex a spiritual path. Few approach it with the regularity of meditation. Some, but certainly not all, bring a deliberate reverence to the act or the partner. For some, but hardly all, it requires high levels of trust and love. For others, it was purely an act of grace that came out of nowhere and vanished again, and they have no idea how to recreate it, try as they might. Like a near-death experience for these people, it was a one-time miraculous transformation; they have not become like St. Paul or Ramana Maharshi, but they have never forgotten it.

Even for those who approach spiritual sex more intentionally, it seems not to be predictable; there is a large element of grace and mystery. Some of it is because of the introduction of another person into the experience, and some of it, to that mysterious Third created by the two. The more cultivated ways, such as Tantra, seem to produce records more linked to an ideology of physical states, lights, energetic states, and control. In contrast, the naive practitioners describe rich psychological transformations and altered states that sound mystical. The respondents who practice meditation not only compare these sexual experiences favorably with their contemplative states, but even resist bringing the same kind of intentionality to sex. According to Roland, a man whose spiritual practice includes meditation and other sacred relational experiences (sweat lodges),

> I don't know what's going to happen. I have no illusions that my partner and I are creating that. We're stepping into those other energy fields. Some of the native peoples call it the Great Mysterious, and I like that. . . . I don't have the same sense of control in sex [as in meditation], and that's part of the excitement of it. It's an exploration, and the most profound nature of it is in the relationship with my partner, how it's shifted, changed, solidified, expanded. The profundity is in the relational area, talking to my partner, and through my partner, talking to God.

The knowledge or fruits of these experiences is profound; former agnostics and skeptics in my sample have taken up spiritual inquiry and pursuits as a result of their sexual experiences. Some have changed careers and altered their life's direction because of their new-found gifts. As transpersonal psychology matures in a time when epistemological paradigms are shifting and when its major voices still incline to more familiar ways of thought, attempts to classify and position spiritual sexuality—if it is recognized at all—compared to the acknowledged traditions will undoubtedly be forthcoming. Perhaps any attempt to classify or deconstruct sexual spirituality is to revisit historical arguments that are, in the first place, epistemologically outdated in postmodern intellectual thought; in the second place, are too culturally bound and metaphysically questionable to be useful; and in the third place, are too reductionistic to capture the meaning of the experience without doing violence to it. Because of the private and isolated nature of transpersonal sex outside Taoist and Tantric communities, sexual spirituality has largely bypassed the structuralist forms popular in transpersonal psychology today, especially the authoritarian mechanisms associated with those forms (gurus, proscribed procedures, stages of cognitive and psychological deconstruction, etc.), keeping its accessibility for all and sundry.

I find this part of its appeal, even though by writing about it here, I am perhaps bringing some of that obscurity to an end. I write to honor and affirm what people have known in secret and to share the potential of this path with those who never dreamed it might be possible. The lovers' records speak for the beauty and knowledge spiritual sexuality can convey, surely not so different from the recognized practices. Spiritual sexuality is less hermetic, less cognitive, perhaps less deliberate and controlled than contemplative methods. It is more reliant on grace and openness than intent and regularity. The spiritual knowledge gained through sexuality can be powerful, transformative, and revelatory. Sexuality may not look like other spiritual paths, but it is a path that unites not only the mind but also the body and heart through the love of another human being with All That Is. In one informant's words:

> It gives you a glimpse of that, takes you so far beyond your body and your mental self that it shows you, this is what you are, this is where you are going, this is where you have always been.

Notes

1. Sanskrit handbooks on sex, such as the fabled *Kama Sutra,* are not, as many people think, guides for mystical sex for spiritual seekers, but practical handbooks for the average householder. Significantly, even ordinary householders in India are expected to abstain from sex by middle age, when carnality is considered unseemly (e.g., Kakar, 1994).
2. It should be noted that "pure" forms of shamanism and Goddess worship are virtually impossible to find (though more of the former than the latter still exist in the anthropological records). The shamanism referred to here is not those modern recreations seen in pop psychology and the New Age subculture. I am referring to anthropological records of indigenous cultures. Likewise, much of the popular conception of Goddess worship is as distorted as that of neo-shamanism (see, for instance, Gilmore, 1998a, 1998b). In either case, we do not know what really went on, though historical and anthropological records provide many indications that sexual activity, especially reproduction, was certainly central to Goddess traditions.

3. This distinction is often either overlooked or considered insufficient by
    his critics (see, for example, Rothberg & Kelly, 1998)

References

Anderson, B. S., & Zinsser, J. P. (1988). *A history of their own: Women in Europe
    from prehistory to the present* (Vol. 1). New York: Harper & Row.

Anderson, S. R., & Hopkins, P. (1991). *The feminine face of God: The unfolding
    of the sacred in women.* New York: Bantam.

Ariel, D. S. (1988). *The mystic quest: An introduction to Jewish mysticism.* New
    York: Schocken.

Armstrong, K. (1993). *A history of God: The 4,000-year quest of Judaism, Chris-
    tianity and Islam.* New York: Ballantine.

Assagioli, R. (1965). *Psychosynthesis: A collection of basic writings.* New York:
    Viking.

Barks, C. (1987). *Rumi: We are three.* Athens, GA: Maypop.

Barks, C., Moyne, J., Arberry, A. J., & Nicholson, R. (Eds. and Trans.).
    (1995). *The essential Rumi.* San Francisco: HarperSanFrancisco.

Bonheim, J. (1997). *Aphrodite's daughters: Women's sexual stories and the journey
    of the soul.* New York: Simon & Schuster.

Bragdon, E. (1990). *The call of spiritual emergency.* San Francisco: Harper &
    Row.

Branston, B. (1980). *Gods of the north.* London: Thames and Hudson.

Campbell, J. (1991). *Primitive mythology: The masks of God.* New York: Viking
    Penguin, Arkana.

Cassidy, F. G., & Ringler, R. N. (Eds.). (1971). *Bright's Old English grammar &
    reader* (3rd ed.). New York: Holt, Rinehart & Winston.

de Riencourt, A. (1974). *Sex and power in history.* New York: Dell.

de Rougement, D. (1983). *Love in the Western world* (Rev. ed.). (M. Belgion,
    Trans.). Princeton, NJ: Princeton University Press.

Eisler, R. T. (1987). *The chalice and the blade: Our history, our future.* San Fran-
    cisco: Harper & Row.

Eisler, R. T. (1995). *Sacred pleasure: Sex, myth and the politics of the body.* San
    Francisco: HarperSanFrancisco.

Ferrer, J. N. (1999). *Revisioning transpersonal theory: An epistemic approach to
    transpersonal and spiritual phenomena.* Manuscript submitted for
    publication.

Feuerstein, G. (1989). Introduction: Spiritual sexuality after the sexual rev-
    olution. In G. Feuerstein (Ed.), *Enlightened sexuality: Essays on body-
    positive spirituality* (pp. 1–11). Freedom, CA: Crossing.

Feuerstein, G. (1992). *Sacred sexuality.* Los Angeles: Tarcher.

Gilmore, L. (1998a). The whore and the Holy One: Contemporary sacred prostitution and transformative consciousness. *Anthropology of Consciousness, 9*(4), 1–14.

Gilmore, L. (1998b). *The whore and the Holy Woman: Ancient and contemporary myths of the sacred prostitute.* Unpublished master's thesis, California Institute of Integral Studies, San Francisco.

Gimbutas, M. (1982). *The goddesses and gods of old Europe.* Berkeley: University of California Press.

Goleman, D. (1988). *The meditative mind: The varieties of meditative experience.* Los Angeles: Tarcher.

Halligan, F. R., & Shea, J. J. (1992). Beginning the quest: Whither the divine fire? In F. R. Halligan & J. J. Shea (Eds.), *The fires of desire: Erotic energies and the spiritual quest* (pp. 11–26). New York: Crossroad.

Hamill, S. (Ed.). (1996). *The erotic spirit: An anthology of poems of sensuality, love, and longing.* Boston: Shambhala.

Haule, J. R. (1990). *Divine madness: Archetypes of romantic love.* Boston: Shambhala.

Hoffman, E. (1992). *The way of splendor: Jewish mysticism and modern psychology.* Northvale, NJ: Aronson.

Huxley, A. (1945). *The perennial philosophy.* New York: Harper.

James, W. (1985). *The varieties of religious experience.* Cambridge, MA: Harvard University Press. (Original work published 1902)

Jung, C. G. (1993). Marriage as a psychological relationship. In V. S. de Laszlo (Ed.), *The basic writings of C. G. Jung* (pp. 659–674). New York: Modern Library. Reprinted from R. F. C. Hull (Ed. and Trans.), *The collected works of Carl Jung, Vol. 17,* Bollingen Series XX. Princeton, NJ: Princeton University Press. (Original work published 1925)

Kakar, S. (1994). Ramakrishna and the mystical experience. *Annual of Psychoanalysis, 20,* 215–234.

Kapleau, P. (Ed.). (1989). *The three pillars of Zen* (Rev. ed.). Boston: Beacon.

Koplowitz, H. (1984a). *Post-logical thinking.* Paper presented at the Symposium on Thinking, Cambridge, MA.

Koplowitz, H. (1984b). A projection beyond Piaget's formal-operations stage. In M. L. Commons, F. A. Richards, & C. Armon (Eds.), *Beyond formal operations: Late adolescent and adult cognitive development* (pp. 272–296). New York: Praeger.

Koplowitz, H. (1990). Unitary consciousness and the highest development of mind: The relation between spiritual development and cognitive development. In M. L. Commons, C. Armon, L. Kohlberg, F. A. Richards, T. A. Grotzer, & J. D. Sinnott (Eds.), *Adult development: Vol.*

2. *Models and methods in the study of adolescent and adult thought* (pp. 105–112). New York: Praeger.

Kovacs, M. G. (Trans.). (1989). *The epic of Gilgamesh.* Stanford, CA: Stanford University Press.

Kremer, J. W. (1996a). Introduction: Indigenous science. *ReVision, 18*(3), 2–5.

Kremer, J. W. (1996b). The shadow of evolutionary thinking. *ReVision, 19*(1), 41–48.

Laski, M. (1961). *Ecstasy in secular and religious experiences.* Los Angeles: Tarcher.

Lévy-Bruhl, L. (1985). *How natives think* (L. A. Clare, Trans.). Princeton, NJ: Princeton University Press. (Original work published 1910)

Maslow, A. H. (1987). *Motivation and personality* (Rev. ed.). (R. Frager, J. Fadiman, C. McReynolds, & R. Cox, Eds.). New York: Harper & Row.

Maurer, H. (1994). *Sex: An oral history.* New York: Viking.

McDaniel, J. (1989). *The madness of the saints: Ecstatic religion in Bengal.* Chicago: University of Chicago Press.

Nelson, J. B., & Longfellow, S. P. (Eds.). (1994). *Sexuality and the sacred: Sources for theological reflection.* Louisville, KY: Westminster/John Knox.

Pagels, E. (1981). *The gnostic gospels.* New York: Vantage.

Pagels, E. (1988). *Adam, Eve, and the serpent.* New York: Random House.

Reid, D. P. (1989). *The Tao of health, sex and longevity: A modern practical guide to the ancient way.* New York: Fireside.

Roberts, N. (1992). *Whores in history: Prostitution in Western society.* London: Grafton.

Rothberg, D., & Kelly, S. (Eds.). (1998). *Ken Wilber in dialogue: Conversations with leading transpersonal thinkers.* Wheaton, IL: Quest.

Scantling, S. & Browder, S. (1993). *Ordinary women, extraordinary sex: Every woman's guide to pleasure and beyond.* New York: Dutton.

Schacter-Shalomi, Z. M. (1991). *Spiritual intimacy: A study of counseling in Hasidism.* Northvale, NJ: Jason Aronson.

Sheldrake, R. (1981). *A new science of life: The hypothesis of formative causation.* Los Angeles, CA: J. P. Tarcher.

Singer, J. (1983). *Energies of love: Sexuality re-visioned.* Garden City, NY: Anchor/Doubleday.

Sokol, D. (1989). Spiritual breakthroughs in sex. In G. Feuerstein (Ed.), *Enlightened sexuality: Essays on body-positive spirituality* (pp. 112–140). Freedom, CA: Crossing.

Spretnak, C. (1991). *States of grace: The recovery of meaning in the postmodern age.* San Francisco: Harper.

Stone, M. (1978). *When God was a woman.* New York: Harcourt Brace Jovanovich.

Stone, M. (1979). *Ancient mirrors of womanhood: A treasury of goddess and heroine lore from around the world.* Boston: Beacon.

Tagore, R. (Trans.). (1991). *Songs of Kabir.* York Beach, ME: Samuel Weiser.

Tannahill, R. (1980). *Sex in history.* New York: Stein & Day.

Ulanov, A., & Ulanov, B. (1994). *Transforming sexuality: The archetypal world of anima and animus.* Boston: Shambhala.

Underhill, E. (1955). *Mysticism: A study in the nature and development of man's spiritual consciousness.* New York: New American Library. (Original work published 1911)

van Gulik, R. H. (1974). *Sexual life in ancient China: A preliminary survey of Chinese sex and society from ca. 1500 B.C. till 1644 A.D.* Leiden, Netherlands: E. J. Brill.

Wade, J. (1996). *Changes of mind: A holonomic theory of the evolution of consciousness.* Albany: State University of New York Press.

Waite, A. E. (1960). *The holy Kabbalah: A study of the secret tradition in Israel as unfolded by sons of the doctrine for the benefit of the elect dispersed through the lands and ages of the greater exile.* New Hyde Park, NY: University Books.

Walsh, R. (1989a). Shamanism and early human technology: The technology of transcendence. *ReVision, 12*(1), 34–40.

Walsh, R. (1989b). The shamanic journey: Experiences, origins and analogues. *ReVision, 12*(2), 25–32.

Walsh, R. (1995). Phenomenological mapping: A method for describing and comparing states of consciousness. *The Journal of Transpersonal Psychology, 27*(1), 25–56.

Wang, S. T. (1986). *The Tao of sexology: The book of infinite wisdom.* San Francisco: Tao Publishing.

Washburn, M. (1988). *The ego and the dynamic ground: A transpersonal theory of human development.* Albany: State University of New York Press.

Washburn, M. (1998a). Linearity, theoretical economy, and the pre/trans fallacy. In D. Rothberg, & S. Kelly (Eds.), *Ken Wilber in dialogue: Conversations with leading transpersonal thinkers* (pp. 374–376). Wheaton, IL: Quest.

Washburn, M. (1998b). The pre/trans fallacy reconsidered. In D. Rothberg, & S. Kelly (Eds.), *Ken Wilber in dialogue: Conversations with leading transpersonal thinkers* (pp. 62–84). Wheaton, IL: Quest.

Werner, H. (1980). *Comparative psychology of mental development.* New York: International University Press. (Original work published 1940)

Wilber, K. (1977). *The spectrum of consciousness.* Wheaton, IL: Theosophical Publishing.

Wilber, K. (1986). *Up from Eden: A transpersonal view of human evolution*. Boulder: Shambhala.

Wilber, K. (1990). *Eye to eye: The quest for the new paradigm*. Boston: Shambhala.

Wilber, K. (1995). *Sex, ecology, spirituality: The spirit of evolution*. Boston: Shambhala.

Wilber, K. (1997). *The eye of spirit: An integral vision for a world gone slightly mad*. Boston: Shambhala.

Wilber, K. (1998). A more integral approach. In D. Rothberg, & S. Kelly (Eds.), *Ken Wilber in dialogue: Conversations with leading transpersonal thinkers* (pp. 306–369). Wheaton, IL: Quest.

Winkelman, M. (1990). The evolution of consciousness: An essay review of *Up from Eden. Anthropology of Consciousness, 1*(3/4), 24–31.

Winkelman, M. (1993). The evolution of consciousness? Transpersonal theories in light of cultural relativism. *Anthropology of Consciousness, 4*(3), 3–9.

Wright, P. A. (1995). Bringing women's voices to transpersonal theory. *ReVision, 17*(3), 3–10.

Wright, P. A. (1996). Gender issues in Ken Wilber's transpersonal theory. *ReVision, 18*(4), 25–37.

13

Service as a Way of Knowing

ARTHUR J. DEIKMAN

Service is usually seen as a moral issue, a matter of doing good, of being "spiritual" in an instrumental way. I suggest, however, that service is best understood as a matter of epistemology; it is itself a way of knowing and is one that goes beyond conventional empirical epistemologies. Service is a way of knowing our connection—at a deeper level—with a reality much larger than our object selves.

What we call "the spiritual" pertains to the connected aspects of reality; service enables us to experience that connectedness. The function of this connectedness or knowing is seldom appreciated; nevertheless, service is one of the most direct routes to the spiritual—a route often obstructed and confused by moral preaching, religious mythology, and everyday assumptions about the motivations and possibilities of human beings. To understand how this is so we need to consider instrumental and receptive functional modes of consciousness and also the way in which our intentionality determines the forms our consciousness takes. In this chapter, I discuss these two basic modes of consciousness, the role of intentionality, the survival self, the spiritual self, and the special function of service in allowing a shift from the exclusive experience of a separate self to a more balanced and connected self.

Instrumental Consciousness

Most of our lives are spent with a form of consciousness that enables us to act on the environment so that we will survive as biological organisms. This form or mode of consciousness develops to obtain food and defend against attack. In order to do so successfully, we need to learn to deal with the world *in its object aspects,* evoking a specific type of consciousness I call the instrumental mode.

The instrumental mode is the result of a developmental process. As the work of Gesell (1940), Erikson (1951), Piaget (1952) and Spitz (1965) demonstrated, the infant objectifies his or her world and uses the body as a template for learning. In one of Piaget's examples, a child is unable to solve the problem of opening a box with a lid, until he suddenly opens his own mouth, and then, immediately afterward, opens the box. In such ways the body becomes the means to organize and understand the world. Similarly, our early experiences with objects establish the structure of our thoughts. The most abstract and fundamental concepts ultimately are derived from the equation: object = body = self. The space, time, and causality with which we are familiar are the space, time, and causality that pertain to objects. That there are logics of reality beyond the instrumental or objective modes is indicated by the discoveries of modern physics, particularly the particle/wave duality of light, the evidence for nonlocality, and other paradoxes that have been proved true but that we cannot understand. The late physicist, Richard Feynman, commented:

> I think it is safe to say that no one understands quantum mechanics. Do not keep saying to yourself, if you can possibly avoid it, "But how can it be like that?" because you will "go down the drain" into a blind alley from which nobody has yet escaped. Nobody knows how it can be like that. (cited in Pagels, 1982, p. 113)

The limitations of instrumental, object-based consciousness can be experienced without the benefit of a degree in physics. Just try to imagine the universe coming to an end, spatially. I think you will find you cannot do so. Every object has a border and there is always space beyond any border you can visualize. Now try to imagine the universe not coming to an end. You can't do that either. Objects are never infinite. We cannot encompass the universe because it is not an object, and our thought processes, our very perceptual systems, have evolved to deal effectively with objects. Thus, we automatically perceive boundaries, discriminate between ourselves and others, and are wedded to linear time.

Other aspects of experience are affected also. Shapiro demonstrated that as children age, their responses to the Rorschach test change: The youngest groups responded primarily to the color and texture of the pictures, but those in the older groups paid progressively more attention to the shape and meaning of the figures (Shapiro, 1960).

Above all, we perceive the self as an object, separate, competing with others, dependent on others. That self—the survival self—is the one with which we are most familiar. Depending on what literature you are reading, it is called the ego, the Commanding Self, the drunken monkey, Small Mind, and so on. It is the organization of all the psychological structures that employ instrumental consciousness for its own benefit. This is the self that is busy acquiring, defending, controlling. All these functions are necessary, but they have their price: They set the agenda for the form of consciousness with which we experience the world and limit the information open to us.

We spend most of our lives in *instrumental consciousness,* serving the survival self. A summary of that mode's characteristic follows:

Example: Driving in heavy traffic
Intent: To act on the environment
Self:
　　Object-like, localized, separate from others
　　Sharp boundaries
　　Self-centered awareness
World:
　　Emphasis on objects, distinctions, and linear causality
Consciousness:
　　Focal attention
　　Sharp perceptual boundaries
　　Logical thought, reasoning
　　Formal dominates sensual
　　Past/future
Communication:
　　Language

This is the mode of consciousness we typically employ when driving a car in heavy traffic, or planning a business strategy, or maneuvering strategically at a social event. It's the one you are probably involved in as you read this chapter, checking for errors in logic, endeavoring to grasp my meaning, perhaps (if you are an author) waiting to see if I will reference something you've written. It's a good mode for that purpose.

Useful and necessary as this self may be, when it dominates consciousness it creates problems. It underlies the exploitation of others, it supports violence and war, all of which depend on separateness, on disconnection. Disregard for the natural environment is another consequence. From the point of view of instrumental consciousness, "When you see one redwood, you've seen them all." Furthermore, because it forms a barrier to experiencing the connectedness of reality, instrumental dominance leads to meaninglessness, "the mid-life crisis," alienation, fear of aging and death.

Thus, as infants and children we acquire concepts that later, as adults, we assume constitute the structure of reality. In the absence of alternative experience, these concepts are utterly convincing. But they are limited. The instrumental mode can raise the Big Questions: "Who am I? What am I? Why am I?", but it cannot hear the answers. A different mode of consciousness is needed, one responsive to reality in its connected aspects.

Receptive Consciousness

Suppose you've driven your car to the airport, have flown to another city and checked in to your hotel. You want to relax, to unwind, to be comforted. So, you fill the bathtub with steaming hot water, ease your body into it, and relax your muscles . . . Ahhhhh! How good that feels! Chances are you were able to shift out of the instrumental mode and into the receptive, that mode whose function is to receive the environment. In that mode, awareness of separateness diminishes, there is a sense of merging with the heat, the water, the surrounding environment. Boundaries relax; past and future drop away; the sensual takes over from verbal meanings and formal properties. Thinking becomes tangential, scattered, and slows down; boundaries blur. As boundaries soften, the sense of self becomes less distinct and less dominant, the object self subsides, relinquishing control. NOW, merging, and allowing are the dominant aspects of *receptive experience*. A summary of receptive mode characteristics follow:

Example: Soaking in a hot tub

Intent: To receive the environment

Self:
    Undifferentiated, nonlocalized, not distinct from environment
    Blurring or merging of boundaries
    World-centered awareness

World:
    Emphasis on process, merging, and simultaneity

Consciousness:
    Diffuse attention
    Blurred boundaries
    Alogical thought, intuition, fantasy

Sensual dominates formal
Now

Communication:
Music/art/poetry/dance

Intention

The critical dynamic that determines the form of consciousness is intention. The intention to act on the environment necessarily features control. In contrast, to take in the environment, to be nourished, requires *allowing* and a kind of merging. Just as the instrumental mode is associated with the understanding of objects, separation, and borders, the receptive mode gains access to knowledge of a different sort. In order to appreciate this, try an experiment. (A human partner is best, but a flower or a tree will do.) Look into your partner's face with the specific intent of making a model of it, a sculpture. Analyze the planes of the head, the spacing of the eyes, the balance of the shapes. Spend a few moments doing that. Then shift your intention to one of receiving, allowing. Relax your gaze, surrender to the experience, allow your partner's face to be whatever it may be. Stay open and receptive to what comes to you. The shift in intention is from controlling to allowing.

Most people notice a distinct difference in their perception of the other when they shift their intention in this manner. The instrumental experience is easier to describe, it lends itself to measurement, comparisons, analysis. The receptive experience is more difficult to talk about. Receptive perception evokes words like "mysterious," "deeper," "richer," "soul." Whether face or flower, the Other emerges as a presence, filling consciousness, saying, "Here I am!" Each mode reveals different aspects of your partner's reality.

Self

There is an additional dynamic shaping consciousness that is as important as intention: the degree of activation of the survival self. To get a taste of this, try the same experiment again. First look at your partner (or flower or tree) while maintaining a strong sense of your self. Then allow that sense of self to diminish, subside, and disappear. Notice the change in your experience of your partner. Again, I think you will find that as the sense of self diminishes and drops out, the experience becomes deeper, richer—your partner acquires the dimension of presence.

I had a vivid demonstration of this phenomenon while attending a seven-day Zen retreat. Part of the day was spent chanting. We held up stiff white sheets of paper covered with Japanese words printed starkly black. As the retreat progressed the words seemed to become more intense, more vivid. About the fourth day, I began to think that the letters didn't need me to be there, the chanting would continue and the words would go on marching across the page by themselves. The thought grew that the world did not need me to be here. In an internal dialog I urged myself, "Go on, disappear! Let yourself vanish from the world! Go! Jump!" And at one point I "jumped"; I made the leap to a world without "me". In some psychological sense that I cannot specify further, I gave up my existence in the world and let it exist without me. At that precise instant in which I allowed myself to disappear, the room and the others sitting there were suddenly transformed, becoming transfigured, archetypal, super real. Each student was a Buddha, awesome. At one point, a bell was rung and the sound rolled toward me like shimmering silver. I don't know how long the state lasted; I returned to my usual consciousness as we walked from the meditation hall. But afterward, I tried to understand what had happened, why my state changed so dramatically when my self "vanished." I now believe it was because the unusually profound deactivation of the survival self—its abdication of dominance—permitted a deeper experience of reality in its fundamental, holistic aspects.

The survival self of instrumental consciousness has distinct characteristics related to that mode. The emphasis is on boundaries, differences, form and distinctions. Consequently, the self is experienced as a discrete object, more isolated than not. And we suffer the consequences. After all, the goals of the survival self—acquisition, pleasure, and permanence—are doomed. Acquisition is defeated by death; sensual pleasure is defeated both by aging and by the invidious design of our central nervous system that adapts to most sensory stimuli—except that of pain.

This adaptation is an everyday experience. The initial ice cream cone may be thrilling, but if you want a repeat of the experience you will have to double the scoops and add sprinkles. The next serving had better be a banana split. And so on, until boredom or indigestion sets in. In contrast, a toothache never gets boring. Our response to money also demonstrates the problem. Lewis Lapham (1988) did an informal survey of his friends and acquaintances, asking them if they made enough money. All said no. When asked how much would be enough, they all named a figure double what they were currently earning, whatever that might be.

What is required for a healthy life is flexibility of consciousness. Most activities involve both modes to some degree and this ability to make use of the appropriate balance is essential to a healthy life. Flexibility is key.

When flexibility is absent we see pathological manifestations of the modes: obsessive-compulsive character disorder in the case of a rigid adherence to instrumental consciousness and hysterical character disorder in the case of overcommitment to the receptive, a fixation on impressionistic, diffuse consciousness (Shapiro, 1960).

Both modes are needed. Problems arise when one mode excludes or crowds out the other. In most of our spiritual experiences we are still conscious of the world's object qualities, but our perceptions take on additional qualities such that the experience is "deeper," "transcendent," "profound" by virtue of an increase in connectedness to and in the world. We feel gratitude for that widening, that larger sense of ourselves as part of a beautiful and awesome reality.

Especially in creative work, a balance of modes is critical. I think Yeats (1951) conveys the flavor of this when he writes of Michelangelo, "Like a spider upon the water, his mind moves upon silence" (p. 327). Most of us are limited by excessive instrumental dominance, but we do not realize this since our culture is strongly materialistic and our science is based totally on instrumental consciousness.

To the extent that instrumental consciousness rules experience, life can easily seem meaningless. Meaning arises from connection but instrumental consciousness features separation. This effects our experience of self. The self of instrumental consciousness is now described:

The Survival Self

Characteristics:
    Aim of self-preservation
    Self-focused
    Self as object distinct from environment
Positive Effects:
    Able to defend, acquire
    Able to achieve material goals
Negative Effects:
    Basis for traditional vices
    Dissatisfaction
    Access to conceptual meaning only
    Fear of death
Importance:
    Needed for individual survival

In contrast, experience of self when receptivity is high and the survival self subdued can be quite different. This other-centered consciousness produces a qualitative change in the experience of self. I will call that other-centered self the spiritual self since it exists in connection. Its characteristics and effects are now summarized:

The Spiritual Self

Characteristics:
    Aim of service, attunement
    Other-centered
    Self identified with larger life process, resonant with environment
Positive Effects:
    Satisfaction
    Basis for traditional virtues
    Experienced meaning
    Equanimity
Negative Effects:
    Tendency toward passivity
    Ineffective in defending, acquiring
Importance:
    May be needed for survival of the human species

Our scientific, materialistic society continuously reinforces the survival self, the object-like self of the instrumental mode. Once formed, the survival self activates the instrumental mode in its own behalf. Because of this, if we wish to experience the connectedness of reality it is necessary not only to shift our intention in the direction of allowing and taking in, we need also to lower the level of activation of the survival self. The overall situation can be expressed in an equation: $C = f[I + S]$. Consciousness is a function of intention and self.

It is particularly hard to lower one's invisible survival self aims, those that operate unconsciously and are reflected in our characteristic attitudes and assumptions. To do this generally requires help. For this we can turn initially to psychotherapy to decrease the intensity of intrapsychic threats (Deikman, 1982) and then to the spiritual traditions to deal with survival self aims that are hidden from our sight. The spiritual traditions assist in developing an ongoing attitude, an outlook, that facilitates the emergence of the spiritual self.

The Spiritual Traditions

The bimodal model of consciousness provides a way of understanding the spiritual traditions because the spiritual path is often described as learning to "forget the self." The self to be forgotten is the survival self that evokes a mode of consciousness featuring separation. To shift to an experience of reality in its connected aspects, receptivity must be combined with a decrease in control by the survival self. This is a straight-forward, functional matter. It has to do with an internal attitude, the guiding intent. I think that is what Thomas Merton (1968) was referring to in his book, *Zen and the Birds of Appetite* when he described meat-eating birds (the survival self) looking for carrion:

> Zen enriches no one. There is no body to be found. The birds may come and circle for a while in the place where it is thought to be. But they soon go elsewhere. When they are gone, the "nothing," the "no-body" that was there, suddenly appears. That is Zen. It was there all the time but the scavengers missed it, because it was not their kind of prey. (p. ix)

Outer behavior may be misleading. For example, acquisitiveness need not be directed at money alone. Imagine a very successful businessman who decides he is no longer interested in amassing wealth, because from what he has read the only true satisfaction comes from Enlightenment. So he joins a spiritual group. His new intention is faxed down to the computer center in his brain. There, an underling picks up the fax and runs to the boss. "He says he no longer wants money. Now he wants enlightenment. Shall we change the program?" "No" says the boss, "it's the same program: Acquisition."

In his case, and most others, the survival self is still running the show. After all, to use Abraham Maslow's wonderful phrase, "If all you know how to use is a hammer, you tend to treat everything you meet as if it were a nail." Being spiritual is no exception. What is needed for the perception of connectedness is for the survival self to become the servant, not the master. That is what "forget the self" means. The survival self is still needed to function in the world, but it must not be the boss if a different experience of reality is to be made possible. There is no cheating on this one. Sitting cross-legged, inhaling incense, wearing a saffron robe, and going vegetarian won't necessarily change the guiding intention. So what can be done to find freedom from self-centered motivations. How does the spiritual teacher help the student to "forget the self?" If we turn to the mystical literature we find that most traditions make use of meditation, teaching stories, and service.

Meditation can be viewed as enabling a person to identify with the observing self, the "I," and to separate that core self from the concerns and mental activity of the survival self (Deikman, 1982). This increases freedom from concepts and lessens the dominance of instrumental consciousness, especially as meditation is based on allowing rather than making something happen. Teaching stories can be viewed in the same way; they enable the student to recognize patterns of thought and behavior that would otherwise remain hidden, influencing the form of consciousness.

The functional approach to consciousness also can enable us to understand the emphasis on renunciation that can be found in most spiritual traditions. Renunciation is often misunderstood as giving up sensual pleasure, wealth, and power. When I first began doing research in the mystical experience I noted that the literature stressed both meditation and renunciation. Meditation was a lot more appealing than renunciation; I wasn't about to be an ascetic. So I began investigating meditation. Much later, Shunryu Suzuki-roshi, a Zen master, clarified the issue by explaining that renunciation was not giving up the things of this world but accepting that they go away (Suzuki, 1970). Such acceptance means an open hand, whereas the hand of the survival self is grasping, controlling.

We are now in a position to understand the vital function of service in providing access to the spiritual. You have undoubtedly heard the cynical argument that everything we do is selfish because even doing a good deed gives us pleasure. One expression of that idea view was provided by *Forbes* magazine in which the view of economists concerning charity was summarized: "People gain satisfaction from charitable giving. It makes them feel good, and they tend to consume more of this feeling as their incomes rise" (Seligman, 1998, p. 94).

There is some truth in that. Furthermore, a fantasy of a heavenly account book is often in operation, making good deeds a commercial operation—pay now, collect in Heaven. Perhaps that is why the Sufi saint, Rabia, prayed:

> Oh Lord:
> If I worship you from fear of Hell, cast me
> into Hell,
> If I worship you from desire for Paradise,
> deny me Paradise[1]

What she is countering in dramatic fashion is spiritual activity for gain, or from fear. Prayer, helping others, following a discipline, may all be performed on the basis of hidden vanity, greed, and fear, with the result that the survival self is enhanced, not diminished. Spiritual experience calls a marked decrease in self-concern. For this, service is ideal, permitting a "forgetting" of the self that markedly reduces survival self concerns.

However, the call to service usually arouses conflicted feelings, for helping others may feel like being good on command, showing that you are a good person because service is what good people do. People who spend their lives doing service are categorized as saints and saints are the most good of the good. So service is widely believed to be something you should do to show your spiritual side, your concern for other human beings.

This idea of service gets mixed with basic teachings learned by the child in the family setting: Do good and you will be rewarded; do bad and you will be punished. These childhood beliefs persist and suggest an omnipresent parent who is watching, keeping score (Deikman, 1990). Most of us do not admit to such notions, but I have found that almost everyone, including myself, has a background fantasy of some celestial entity that is watching, keeping track of what we do, keeping accounts for a final settling-up after we die. The idea of service seen in that context can easily result in a sense of obligation and nagging guilt, it can lead to resentment at the burden and resistance to action. For those who do act on the basis of reward and punishment—no matter how hidden the fantasy may be—there is the danger of self-inflation and self-righteousness on the one hand, disappointment and "burn-out" on the other. Perhaps most important of all, such expectations and reactions interfere with appropriate, creative action and render service useless for spiritual development. Fortunately, there is a way of acting that allows us to "forget the self." I call it serving-the-task.

Serving-the-Task

This type of service is not for any personal wish of our own, but to satisfy the needs of the task, to do *what is called for*. A carpenter may finish the underside of a chair because it feels right, is called for, even though the selling price will remain the same and the customer may not notice or care. I am aware that in writing this chapter, I have a mixture of personal motivations, concerns, and hopes, but I can also feel a sense of what is needed to accomplish the task. That guiding sense of what is needed is impersonal and may be resisted by my survival self, but it is there. It is not a compulsion but a recognition that tugs at me. When I surrender to it I get in touch with another dimension that is hard to describe and elusive to the grasp. This place, where I meet the task and merge with it, feels more important, more meaningful than personal desires. The surrender to the task can occur in any setting. Psychotherapists may recognize this as the "good hour" where everything flows and the therapist feels part of a subtle dance, one that carries as much as leads. Self-interest and self-concern subside and disappear as what-is-called-for takes over.

People who are truly serving the task experience something they cannot name, something that can answer the Big Questions. They do not ask, "What is the meaning of life?" because the question no longer arises. The answer is implicit in the experience of connection that service makes possible, the experience of a self enlarged by connection and freed from its object goals. This "enlightenment" is not a guru's gift; it arises as a consequence of the forgetting of the self that service makes possible. That is why it is said that if a person is ready for enlightenment it cannot be withheld; if they are not, it cannot be given.

You may wonder if an evil task can be served—such as following the orders of an Adolph Hitler—and still further spiritual development. The answer is No. Not only do motives of hatred and fear reinforce identity with the survival self, the task of harming another human being cannot be done in a state of psychological connection. Barriers must be raised, the Other must be established as different from oneself, inferior, bad—connection must be abolished. If you doubt this, experiment once again with a partner. Be receptive to his or her face, allow your experience of self to subside so that the other's presence extends to you. Now imagine you are going to stab your partner. Visualize it happening and notice the change in your experience as you carry it out. You will find that in order to do so, even in your imagination, you have to "step back" psychologically and separate yourself, breaking connection. Service must necessarily be generous, beneficial in intent, in order to open the gates of perception. The more the survival self can subside, can cease to dominate consciousness, the wider the gates can open.

Knowing by Being What is Known

Imagine that our awareness is a pond connected by a narrow outlet to the ocean. At the mouth of the outlet there is a standing wave—the survival self—that blocks the ocean currents from entering the pond. As the survival self subsides, more and more of the ocean currents can gain access to the pond that then begins to resonate with the ocean. The pond then "knows" the ocean by resonating with it, in part becoming it. Probably, it is this experience that underlies the statements of mystics such as the tenth-century Sufi, Hallaj, who declared, "I am God" and was executed for apostasy. He did not mean "I, Hallaj, am the object God of your imagination," but "I am at one with the Reality that transcends understanding." The perception of the ocean's currents may lead to the experience of serving the Truth or "serving the Will of God," a phrase often misused by those still serving the survival self.

Service is a way of knowing our connection. The experience of the ocean's currents provides a sense of purpose and a guide to action that can use the survival self to fulfill a larger task. This alignment with the currents is referred to by mystics as "choiceless choice." In this way, we best can balance the instrumental and receptive modes so as to preserve connection and yet be effective in the world.

The knowing that takes place is not easily communicated. You may be acquainted with someone who is very active helping others. If you praise such a person for what they are contributing they will likely reply, "I've received more than I've given." If you ask what it is they have received, they have difficulty saying. What they are experiencing is a kind of knowledge different from that to which they ordinarily have access. Rather than it being something they perceive, like a movie, or concepts, like a book, it is knowledge by being that which is known. Through service they are able to connect with the larger field and, to varying degrees, become it (see also "Knowledge by Identity" in Forman, 1999, pp. 109–127).

Here is the experience of a person who established an organization that cares for people suffering from AIDS. His life is focused on service. He was responding to my question "Why do you feel that you have received more than you have given?" He said he could only answer by referring to those times when he felt truly connected to the person he was serving:

> In the caregiving work itself, in the service work, itself, when I truly connected with the other person, what happened was something about healing the separation I felt in my own life and the separation I believe we are all born into. The connection with that person felt like a tremendous gift, a kind of union that I wanted more of in my life, not only in service encounters but in relationships outside the normal connection of personalities, outside of social norms, personal expectations. Something deeper was happening that I craved considerably; only aware of it when the need started to get filled, like a hungry person being weak but unaware of the source of the hunger and then food shows up—"This is it!"
>
> It all takes the form of my being the best person I could be, of my deepest humanity being expressed this way. "This is why I am here." Here is the answer to the question, "What am I here for? What is the purpose of my life?" Nothing else I do elicits the feeling of "Yeah, this is it!" more than service does—not creative work, not any other action in the world, not the completion of a project that I'm proud of. All that makes me feel good but nothing meets as deep a need in as profound a way as service work does. (C. Garfield, personal communication, 1998)

There is nothing exotic here, nothing hidden, nothing arcane. But the knowledge does have its own requirements. It is as if you came to a stream and wanted to drink. If you persisted in trying to grab the water—your usual approach—you would obtain nothing. If you want to drink you would have to cup your hands. It has nothing to do with piety; it has to do with the nature of water.

Advantages of the Functional Model

From a clinical point of view we can begin to understand the phenomena of mid-life crisis, meaninglessness, burn-out, and preoccupation with death as reflecting a weakness of connection to something larger than oneself. While these problems can reflect intrapersonal problems with intimacy and self-worth, we also need to evaluate the extent to which they may reflect self-absorption and isolation in that person's daily life, the extent to which he or she lacks activities that could connect and expand his or her identity. We may ask ourselves to what extent and how often does this person shift to other-centered consciousness?

This model featuring intention and self offers a means of evaluating spiritual groups and their leaders. Seekers can be tricked by the assertion, "The Teacher is enlightened and perceives things on a different plane. What he/she does has a spiritual significance that is beyond your comprehension. Therefore, you are not capable of judging the Teacher's actions." Whether or not the Teacher actually is fostering spiritual development can be assessed by listening carefully to what he or she says, noting whether or not the survival self is being stimulated or being subdued. If the Teacher emphasizes the promise of bliss or enlightenment, greed is being stimulated; if the seeker is defined as being special, vanity is encouraged; an emphasis on the harm seekers will suffer if they leave the group stimulates fear. Greed, vanity, and fear reinforce the operations of the survival self and the teacher who employs them is impeding—not helping—spiritual development. No matter what powers the Teacher might manifest, he or she is not a spiritual teacher, is not above criticism, and is not entitled to special prerogatives.

In addition to the considerations just described, it is important that we achieve an integration of the scientific worldview with our intuition of the spiritual. For myself, that has been a problem ever since I entered medical school. The reductionistic, materialistic ethos was totally incompatible with my own experience of the spiritual dimension. So, in the closet of my mind, I kept the spiritual domain in a shoebox on the top shelf. I would take it down for periodic inspection but couldn't help feeling that what it contained was not really real, not real the way my cadaver's brain was real. And yet, the shoebox contained the experiences most important to my life. When I was quiet, open, and receptive and looked into my wife's eyes the experience was mysterious and profound, different from our ordinary contact. I perceived something that carried beyond our location in time and space and conveyed the sense of a much larger, more important reality. What my scientific and psychoanalytic teachers offered as explanation for this I never found convincing. According to them, such perceptions should be regarded as a projection of unconscious wishes, memories, and primitive feeling states. In other words, it was something I imagined, something of internal origin that I misidentified. True, people do imagine and project, but these explanations seemed shallow, they did not fit the experience. I could not integrate this materialistic, positivistic world of science with the transcendent world labeled "spiritual."

Looking back over my research I can see that it has been a persistent effort to find a framework that could unite these domains in a nonmysterious manner. With the concept of different ways of knowing depending on intention and self, I think the integration can be accomplished in a straightforward way that is consonant with discoveries in developmental and motivational psychology, and with the world sketched for us by quantum physics, and with the spiritual traditions. Finally, the functional model of consciousness can help us understand service without interference from the myths of childhood and from religious dogma.

With serving-the-task as our motivational guide, we can spot the emergence of hidden self-interest and reestablish the task-oriented attitude that we need. This monitoring protects us from the distorted perspective introduced by self-centered consciousness, enabling our service to be more creative and effective and expanding our view of the world and of ourselves.

References

Deikman, A. J. (1982). *The observing self: Mysticism and psychotherapy.* Boston: Beacon Press.

Deikman, A. J. (1990). *The wrong way home: Uncovering the patterns of cult behavior in American society.* Boston: Beacon Press.

Erikson, E. (1951). *Childhood and society.* New York: Norton.

Forman, R. (1999). Mysticism, mind, consciousness. Albany: State University of New York Press.

Gesell, A. (1940). *The first year of life: A guide to the study of the pre-school child.* New York: Harper & Row.

Lapham, L. (1988). *Money and class in America: Notes and observations on our civil religion.* New York: Widenfeld & Nicolson.

Merton, T. (1968). *Zen and the birds of appetite.* New York: New Directions.

Pagels, H. (1982). *The cosmic code: Quantum physics as the language of nature.* New York: Simon & Schuster.

Piaget, J. (1952). *The origins of intelligence in children.* New York: International Universities Press.

Seligman, D. (1998, June 1). Is philanthropy irrational? *Forbes, 161*(11), 94–103.

Shapiro, D. (1960). A perceptual understanding of color response. In M. Richers-Ovisiankina (Ed.), *Rorschach psychology.* New York: Wiley.

Spitz, R. (1965). *The first year of life.* New York: International Universities Press.

Suzuki, S. (1970). *Zen mind, beginner's mind.* New York: Walker/Weatherhill.

Yeats, W. B. (1951). The long legged fly. *The collected poems of W. B. Yeats* (pp. 327–328). New York: The Macmillan Company.

About the Contributors

Tobin Hart, Ph.D., is an associate professor and member of the graduate faculty in the State University of West Georgia's humanistic/transpersonal oriented psychology department. He holds degrees from the University of Florida, St. Lawrence University, and a Ph.D. from the University of Massachusetts. His areas of research, publication, and teaching include consciousness studies, psychotherapy, revisioning education, and interdisciplinary combinations such as music and transpersonal psychology. A current research project explores the spiritual experiences of children. He is author of *From Information to Transformation: Education for the Evolution of Consciousness* (Peter Lang, 2000).

Peter L. Nelson, Ph.D., is a research consultant. He began his formal study of consciousness after graduating from both San Francisco State University with a degree in psychology in 1968 and the Haight-Ashbury in 1969. This interest led to participation in research in neuroscience in America, England, and Denmark. Finally realizing that the study of the brain may offer little to our understanding of consciousness, Dr. Nelson became a psychophenomenologist and went on to study people's religious and altered state experiences in Australia where he gained his Ph.D. degree at the University of Queensland. Since his conversion to the consciousness studies model he has worked as a research consultant, a psychology professor, an Australian Research Council Research Fellow, a Senior Research Officer at the Queensland Criminal Justice Commission, and as a social scientist doing end-user research for Texas Instruments. His published thoughts and research findings can be found in various international journals and electronic data bases.

Kaisa Puhakka, Ph.D., is professor and core faculty member at the Institute of Transpersonal Psychology, Palo Alto, California, where she teaches psychotherapy, transpersonal theory, and Buddhist thought and meditation.

She is editor of *The Journal of Transpersonal Psychology*. Puhakka holds M.A. degrees in philosophy and psychology, a Ph.D. in experimental psychology from University of Toledo, and a postdoctoral diploma in clinical psychology from Adelphi University. She has a book and some thirty articles published in the fields of comparative philosophy, phenomenology, and psychotherapy. She currently studies Rinzai Zen with Joshu Sasaki Roshi at Mt. Baldy, California.

Arthur J. Deikman, M. D., has done extensive work in the scientific study of meditation and the mystical experience. His thirty years of research in this area has resulted in numerous scientific papers and three books: *Personal Freedom* (Viking Penguin, 1976), *The Observing Self—Mysticism and Psychotherapy* (Beacon, 1982), and *The Wrong Way Home: Uncovering the Patterns of Cult Behavior in American Society* (Beacon, 1990). These works reflect a contemporary perspective on spirituality based on developmental, psychodynamic, and cognitive psychologies—informed by personal experience with the Zen Buddhist and Sufic traditions. Currently, Dr. Deikman is Clinical Professor of Psychiatry at the University of California, San Francisco, where he combines teaching, research, and private practice.

Jorge N. Ferrer, Ph.D., is a visiting professor at the California Institute of Integral Studies, San Francisco. Formerly a fellow of "La Caixa" Foundation, a research fellow of the Catalonian Council, and an ERASMUS scholar at the University of Wales (U.K.), he has taught at the Institute of Transpersonal Psychology, Palo Alto, California. He is the author of several articles and book chapters on transpersonal studies, and is currently completing a book, *Revisioning Transpersonal Theory*. Dr. Ferrer is member of the Planning Committee of the Buddhist Peace Fellowships's BASE (Buddhist Alliance for Social Engagement) and offers supportive counseling to marginalized Latino women at the center Arriba Juntos in the Mission district of San Francisco. His research interests include transpersonal psychology, spiritual inquiry, contemporary and socially engaged spirituality, comparative mysticism, epistemology and philosophy of science, and spiritual perspectives on sexuality and relationships.

Fred Hanna, Ph.D., is an associate professor in the Department of Counseling and Human Services at Johns Hopkins University in Baltimore. He has published many articles in professional journals on topics ranging from phenomenology and meditation to psychotherapy theory and practice. He also serves as a consultant to community agencies and schools regarding working with difficult clients. He has a book in progress for APA Press detailing a new model of psychotherapeutic change. He has studied and intensively practiced various forms of meditation for over thirty years.

Zia Inayat Khan is the grandson of Hazrat Inayat Khan, the musician-sage who first brought Sufism to the West. He has benefited from the tutelage of his father, Pir Vilayat Khan, in the inner school of Sufism. He received his B.A. in Persian literature from the London School of Oriental and African Studies and is currently a Ph.D. candidate in Islamic studies at Duke University. He is the editor of the forthcoming essay collection *A Pearl in Wine: Essays on the Life, Music and Sufism of Hazrat Inayat Khan* (Omega Publications, 2000).

Donald Rothberg, Ph.D., is on the faculty of the Saybrook Graduate School and Research Center in San Francisco and has taught philosophy at Kenyon College and the University of Kentucky. He is a coeditor of *ReVision*, and author of many articles on socially engaged spirituality (particularly socially engaged Buddhism), critical social theory, transpersonal studies, and epistemology and mysticism. He has served on the board of the Buddhist Peace Fellowship and has led groups, workshops, and training programs on spirituality, everyday life, social service, and social action. He is editor (with Sean Kelly) of *Ken Wilber in Dialogue: Conversations With Leading Transpersonal Thinkers* (Quest, 1998).

Jenny Wade, Ph.D., is a researcher and consultant in individual and organizational psychology, and is chair of the doctoral program at the Institute of Transpersonal Psychology. She is also a founding partner and principal of The Research Advantage Corporation. Her academic research interests focus on consciousness studies, especially unusual states of awareness at the extremes of the lifespan and developmental continuum. A published author and lecturer on a wide range of topics, she has written a new life span theory of consciousness placing developmental psychology in the post-Newtonian paradigm of the "new physics," *Changes of Mind: A Holonomic Theory of the Evolution of Consciousness* (SUNY Press, 1996). A graduate of Texas Christian University, Wade holds master's and doctoral degrees in human development from The Fielding Institute.

Michael Washburn, Ph.D., is professor of philosophy at Indiana University South Bend. He is the author of *Transpersonal Psychology in Psychoanalytic Perspective* (SUNY Press, 1994) and *The Ego and the Dynamic Ground* (2nd ed., SUNY Press, 1995). He has published articles in philosophy and psychology in many professional journals, including *ReVision, The Journal of Transpersonal Psychology, Journal of Humanistic Psychology, The Journal of the History of Philosophy*, and *The Journal of the American Academy of Psychoanalysis*. His writing explores the spiritual potentialities of human development from a psychoanalytic, depth-psychological perspective.

John Welwood, Ph.D., is a clinical psychologist and psychotherapist in San Francisco and associate editor of *The Journal of Transpersonal Psychology*.

His work, which focuses on psychological work in a spiritual context, seeks to integrate Eastern contemplative teachings with Western psychotherapeutic understanding. His books include *Awakening the Heart: East/West Approaches to Psychotherapy and the Healing Relationship* (Shambhala, 1983), *Journey of the Heart: The Path of Conscious Love* (HarperCollins, 1990), *Ordinary Magic: Everyday Life as Spiritual Path* (Shambhala, 1992), *Love and Awakening: Discovering the Sacred Path of Intimate Relationship* (HarperCollins, 1997), and *Toward a Psychology of Awakening: Buddhism, Psychotherapy, and the Path of Personal and Spiritual Transformation* (Shambhala, 2000).

Index

323

Breinigsville, PA USA
13 August 2010

243547BV00001B/70/A